D1264632

BEN W. HEINEMAN, JR.

THE
INSIDE
COUNSEL
REVOLUTION

RESOLVING THE
PARTNER-GUARDIAN
TENSION

Cover design by Kelly Book/ABA Design

The materials contained herein represent the opinions of the authors and/or the editors, and should not be construed to be the views or opinions of the law firms or companies with whom such persons are in partnership with, associated with, or employed by, nor of the American Bar Association or ABA Publishing unless adopted pursuant to the bylaws of the Association.

Nothing contained in this book is to be considered as the rendering of legal advice for specific cases, and readers are responsible for obtaining such advice from their own legal counsel. This book is intended for educational and informational purposes only.

Printed in the United States of America.

20 19 18 17 16   5 4 3 2 1

Library of Congress Cataloging-in-Publication Data

Names: Heineman, Ben W., author.
Title: The inside counsel revolution : resolving the partner-guardian tension /
    Ben W. Heineman, Jr.
Description: Chicago : American Bar Association, 2016. | Includes bibliographical references
    and index.
Identifiers: LCCN 2016005441 (print) | LCCN 2016005479 (ebook) | ISBN 9781634252799
    (hardcover : alk. paper) | ISBN 9781634252805 (ebook)
Subjects: LCSH: Corporate lawyers—United States.
Classification: LCC KF1425 .H45 2016 (print) | LCC KF1425 (ebook) | DDC 346.73/066—dc23
LC record available at http://lccn.loc.gov/2016005441

Discounts are available for books ordered in bulk. Special consideration is given to state bars, CLE programs, and other bar-related organizations. Inquire at Book Publishing, ABA Publishing, American Bar Association, 321 North Clark Street, Chicago, Illinois 60654-7598.

www.ShopABA.org

This book is for my wife, Cris Russell,
and for my sons, Zach and Matt.

Praise for Ben W. Heineman Jr. and *The Inside Counsel Revolution*

"Ben Heineman redefined the world of inside lawyers and corporate General Counsels. His book, *The Inside Counsel Revolution: Resolving the Partner-Guardian Tension,* provides a thoughtful and thought provoking analysis of the role General Counsels, and lawyers more generally, can and should play in business and society. Every lawyer working in or for a business should read this book. And every business leader who works with lawyers should read it. Ben's analysis will help them understand what to expect from their lawyers, as it also holds a mirror to what they should expect from themselves in handling the complex issues that define the modern corporate world."

—Frank Blake, former Chairman and CEO, Home Depot

"This powerful book explains how the inside counsel revolution has helped shape the role of responsible global companies and has transformed the legal profession. How should the corporation where you are general counsel deal with the use in China of the ultrasound equipment it manufactures to carry out sex-selection abortions aimed at favoring boys over girls? What's an in-house lawyer to do when her duty as guardian of the corporation conflicts with her role as the CEO's lawyer and partner? On these issues and everything else—from good citizenship, to managing the profit maximizing urges of outside law firms, to handling internal scandals, to managing risk, to dealing with laws and regulations that contradict each other once you cross a national border, to chiming in on appropriate executive compensation—Ben Heineman Jr. has provided the ultimate analysis of how corporations can, and should, function in a complex legal environment here and around the globe. More than that, he offers a fascinating set of examples of how it's done. Every board of directors should read this book—and make not just their lawyers but their executives, too, study it and take an oath to live it."

—Steven Brill, founder of *American Lawyer* magazine

"Ben Heineman is responsible for defining the modern Office of the General Counsel. This is a must read for all in-house attorneys—and for all outside lawyers who serve corporations."

—Michael J. Holston, Executive Vice President
and General Counsel, Merck & Co.

"This is a must-read for any director of a public company. Ben Heineman, legendary GE GC, makes a compelling case that the General Counsel is an essential partner for boards and business leaders on core issues of performance, integrity, and risk. The stories of right and wrong will stay with you for years."

—Shelly Lazarus, Chairman Emeritus, Ogilvy & Mather

"Major international corporations have become quasi-public institutions impacting the thousands, if not millions, who are either employed by them, use their output, or are impacted by their functioning, worldwide. Inside legal counseling of their management requires a vast combination of talents: law, obviously, and sensitivity to public policy, governmental concerns, and, most importantly, courage. Ben Heineman, the long-time leader of the inside counsel revolution, has that combination in abundance and brings to those attempting that counseling an aspirational model and to the general reader a fascinating glimpse of the tensions inherent in counseling the management of these unique institutions."

—Ira M. Millstein, Senior Partner, Weil, Gotshal & Manges

"Based on his pioneering work in creating the modern corporate law department, lawyer-statesman-teacher Ben Heineman ably sets out the core rules that must guide lawyers of skill and integrity as they advise businesses striving to achieve sustainable strong long-term performance. The challenges he faced and the lessons he learned provide an invaluable and practical vision for both inside lawyers and the external counsel who work with them."

—John F. Olson, Partner, Gibson, Dunn & Crutcher

"Ben Heineman puts forth a vision of the modern General Counsel that is both aspirational and profoundly practical. Refreshingly candid about the challenges facing global companies today, *The Inside Counsel Revolution* shows why Heineman's 'lawyer-statesman' General Counsel is an indispensable member of a winning leadership team. A must-read for CEOs and boards of companies seeking high performance with high integrity."

—Lynn Sharp Paine, John G. McLean Professor of Business Administration, Harvard Business School

"Ben Heineman, a renowned pioneer at GE, has written an extraordinary and definitive book on the role of the general counsel in companies today. It offers rich insights not only for those of us who serve in these positions, but for business people who must operate at the intersection of business, law, public policy, and corporate responsibility."

—Brad Smith, President and Chief Legal Officer, Microsoft Corporation

"No one understands better the critical role General Counsel play in assuring the success of global corporations than Ben Heineman, the former GC of GE. Expanding on his important and groundbreaking work and writing, Heineman's *The Inside Counsel Revolution* is deeply insightful—rich with detailed analysis and penetrating vignettes based on real-life crises. This is a must-read for anyone, not just lawyers, who wants a practical vision of how global corporations can thrive and avoid the reefs and shoals of today's treacherous legal environment."

—Larry D. Thompson, former Deputy Attorney General of the United States and former Senior Vice President and General Counsel, Pepsico

"Ben Heineman's extraordinary book, *The Inside Counsel Revolution,* is a must-read not only for inside corporate counsel at all levels, but also for all corporate officers in the C-Suite and senior outside counsel who regularly interact on major matters with the corporate team. Why? Two primary reasons: First, it is a richly textured and comprehensive chronicle of his remarkable first-hand experiences in high-level, real-world, and high-stakes settings. Second, it is chock full of wisdom, insightful analysis, and priceless advice for any lawyer sitting, or aspiring to sit, on the hot seat of the chief legal officer."

—E. Norman Veasey, former Chief Justice of the Delaware Supreme Court

"During and after his landmark tenure at GE, Ben Heineman became the leading voice articulating the highest aspirations for the general counsels that have followed in his footsteps. In this insightful and deeply practical book, he forcefully describes the tremendous potential that general counsels have to help their companies, the legal profession, and society as a whole achieve what he aptly refers to as 'high performance with high integrity.' His sustained and comprehensive analysis should be required reading for every academic, practitioner, and law student committed to making this ideal a reality."

—David B. Wilkins, Lester Kissel Professor of Law and Director, Center on the Legal Profession, Harvard Law School

CONTENTS

PART ONE

THE GENERAL COUNSEL AS PARTNER AND GUARDIAN

1

INTRODUCTION: THE INSIDE COUNSEL REVOLUTION

A. TRANSFORMATION

The core mission of the global corporation is the fusion of high performance with high integrity and sound risk management. The ideal of the modern general counsel is a lawyer-statesman who is an outstanding technical expert, a wise counselor, and an accountable leader and who plays a major role in assisting the corporation achieve that fundamental goal of global capitalism. For the lawyer-statesman, the first question is: "Is it legal?" But the ultimate question is: "Is it right?"

This book is about how the inside counsel revolution—which began in the late 1970s and has increased in scope and power ever since—is inextricably bound to the performance with integrity mission of the corporation. It sets out my deeply held prescriptive views about what it means for the General Counsel (GC) to be a lawyer-statesman, assessing all corporate action through the screens of performance, integrity, and risk. It focuses on enduring first principles the General Counsel should follow—now and in the future—in quest of what is "right." It describes how the General Counsel, working with the chief executive officer (CEO) and other senior executives, must forge an unbreakable

3

bond among performance, integrity, and risk on a set of foundational corporate issues: business strategy, culture, compliance, ethics, risk, governance, citizenship, and organization. In so doing, the General Counsel must help create the trust in the enterprise that is so vital to its sustainability and durability: trust among employees, shareholders, creditors, customers, partners, suppliers, regulators, media, nongovernmental organizations (NGOs), and the public. To help the corporation achieve its high performance, high integrity, and sound risk management mission, *the General Counsel must resolve the most basic problem confronting inside lawyers: being partner to the board of directors, the CEO, and business leaders but ultimately being guardian of the corporation.*

This *prescriptive* vision is attainable because General Counsel and inside law departments in top global corporations have become far more sophisticated, capable, and influential, transforming both business and law in two important *descriptive* ways I will also explore in this book.

First, *the role of the General Counsel inside the corporation* has significantly grown in importance.

- The General Counsel has now *often replaced the senior partner in the outside law firm as a primary counselor* for the CEO and the board of directors with very broad scope beyond law that includes ethics; reputation; governance; communications; public policy; enterprise risk; crisis management; and, ultimately, corporate citizenship.
- The General Counsel is now often a *core member of the top management team* and participates in discussion and debate—not just about defense, but also about offense; not just about law, but also about business; not just about risks, but also about opportunities; not just about public policy, but also about geopolitics.
- The General Counsel now often has a *broad organizational and leadership role beyond the legal department*—in such areas as tax, trade, environment, security, real estate, customer care, community relations, and public affairs. The GC can have operating responsibilities over diverse units that require broad managerial

skills and that, in many instances, make him the final decision maker in a corporation.

- The General Counsel is now often seen as having *importance and stature comparable to the Chief Financial Officer (CFO)* by directors, CEOs, and business leaders because the health of the corporation requires that it navigate complex and fast-changing law, regulation, litigation, public policy, politics, media, and interest group pressures across the globe.
- All these developments have now often combined *to increase dramatically the expertise, quality, breadth, and compensation* of the General Counsel and inside counsel, with a company's lawyers now being hired from the highest reaches of government, from leading law firms, and from a growing pool of highly talented inside counsel.

Second, *the role of General Counsel outside the corporation* has also significantly grown in importance with a related, dramatic shift in power from outside law firms to inside law departments over both matters and money.

- The General Counsel and inside lawyers, rather than just throwing issues over the transom to law firms, have taken on *day-to-day management and strategic direction of major matters* affecting the corporation—ranging from cross-border transactions to multi-front litigation to international enforcement investigations to consequential public policy debates to building a culture of integrity. This is so because corporate legal departments are increasingly staffed by outstanding specialists in all areas covered by private firms, including antitrust, litigation, tax, trade, mergers and acquisitions, labor and employment, intellectual property, and environmental law. Moreover, outstanding lawyers are now General Counsel of major divisions within companies, not just General Counsel of the whole company. These generalist and specialist inside lawyers—with skills and knowledge at least equal to their peers in law firms—lead mixed inside/outside teams in managing hard problems facing the corporation.

The days of information "asymmetry" when outside lawyers knew much more than inside lawyers are, for the most part, long gone in major corporations because sophisticated inside counsel today invariably know more about the corporation's business and know as much or more relevant law.

- The General Counsel and inside lawyers have also strongly *sought to reassert control over money*—over the corporation's expenditures on outside law firms. Inside lawyers have broken up monopolies or oligopolies that particular private firms had previously enjoyed with particular corporations. They have forced law firms to compete for business. They have focused on cost control through a variety of techniques, from front-end budgeting and negotiated fees to back-end audits and cost disallowance, from preferred provider relationships to "strategic partnerships." They brought important work inside the corporation by increasing inside legal staff, thus reducing the fees paid to outside law firms as a percentage of the corporation's total legal spend. Increasingly, they are using new technology and specialist vendors (e-discovery, specialized research, form drafting, contract lawyers) to reduce further the scope of traditional private law firms. *As many leading General Counsel are alums of major law firms, they can directly address the many techniques outside lawyers may improperly employ to pump up billing and revenues.*

- Finally, General Counsel and inside lawyers are increasingly advocates, points of contact, or negotiators with important public and private parties outside the corporation in both developed and developing economies. Because governments affect markets in all nations—along a spectrum from the state capitalism of former Communist states to the variety of "mixed economies" in traditional "liberal" democracies—the "business in society" issues in these diverse global economies pose serious risk and significant opportunity. Boards and business leaders now delegate major responsibility to the General Counsel to help the corporation reach its commercial and citizenship objectives across a minefield of policy, law, regulation, and public scrutiny. The General Counsel and inside lawyers increasingly have direct relationships with key actors in both the public and private sectors on matters ranging from major legislation to major deals.

In short, General Counsel have risen in power and status within the profession in the past 30+ years, becoming core members of top corporate management and dramatically changing the relationship between inside and outside lawyers. Said *The Economist* in 2012: "the power of in-house lawyers has grown hugely in the past 10 years. The chief legal officer (CLO) is now one of the mightiest figures in the C-Suite." A close observer of the legal profession recently stated: "The future and fortunes of most of the major business practice firms and their lawyers are now in the hands of corporate counsel . . . The status gap between inside and outside lawyers has largely been reversed." A preeminent scholar of the legal profession has noted the continuous growth of "the power and prestige of in-house lawyers," observing that: "In-house legal departments in the United States now also rival large law firms as a destination of choice for talented lawyers" and concluding that "[a]ll of this has profoundly restructured traditional mobility patterns and prestige hierarchies within the U.S. legal profession." And the authors of a book on the evolution of General Counsel have noted: "The story of the General Counsel role over the past fifty years has been one of increasing prominence, power and prestige."[1]

In light of this transformation, this book advances practical ideals about the mission of the global corporation and about the role of the General Counsel in helping to carry out that mission. It explores ideas that are potentially in tension: the pressures for high performance and the imperatives of high integrity, the GC both as lawyer-statesman and as subordinate to the CEO, the GC as partner to business leaders and as guardian of the corporation, and the importance of risk-taking and the necessity of risk management. In the analysis of key issues—compliance, ethics, risk, governance, citizenship, and organization—I hope to show that these potentially paradoxical ideas can co-exist and, indeed, can be complementary. The tensions—between performance and integrity, between the GC as leader and as subordinate, between partner and guardian, between risk-taking and risk management— can be resolved with the right approach and, ultimately, with the right culture. *I also deeply believe that the framework and ideas advanced here apply to small and medium-size companies, although the scope and degree of implementation may be less robust due to fewer resources.*

B. CREDIT WHERE CREDIT IS DUE

The book is, of course, based in important part on my 18 years at GE when I served under CEOs Jack Welch (Senior Vice President–General Counsel, 1987–2001) and Jeff Immelt (General Counsel until 2003; then Senior Vice President–Law and Public Affairs until my retirement in December 2005). As I traveled around the world, I gleaned ideas and practices from numerous exchanges with lawyers and business leaders in other global corporations. The book is also based on the many articles I wrote in the decade after retirement; on my presentations and discussions with lawyers and businesspeople at public and private conferences; and on my exchanges with students when teaching at law, business, and public policy schools, especially in a course co-taught at both Harvard and Yale Law Schools on "Lawyer as Leader: Challenges of the General Counsel."

But, although I am seen as *one* of the godfathers of the inside counsel movement, I want to be absolutely clear that the movement, in the modern era, began before I went to GE in September 1987. The initial inside lawyer counter-reaction to the dominance of large private law firms after World War II began in the late 1970s. It is symbolized by the founding of the American Corporate Counsel Association in 1982 (renamed the less U.S.-centric Association of Corporate Counsel in 2003). It is also reflected in a number of important articles and comments that reflected on the rumblings of revolution in the 1980s.[2] Importantly, in the nearly 30 years since my tenure at GE began, there has been an explosion of highly talented General Counsel and other highly talented inside lawyers at top American corporations—and increasingly at leading non-U.S. companies. This infusion of high-quality lawyers inside major companies has accelerated the changes in role, function, status, influence, and power of the lawyers corporations employ. So, I want to stress the obvious at the outset: I was just one of many creating the inside counsel revolution. And I want to salute my predecessors, my peers, and the succeeding waves of talented General Counsel across the globe for their salient importance and influence in shaping the fundamental shift in the inside counsel role.

But, the GE law department *was* important. That importance stemmed, directly and clearly, from other lawyers who came to GE Legal, not from me. It was due to them, not to me, that GE became one of the symbols of the inside counsel revolution. In the past, some corporations, seeking to enhance the legal function, had sought General Counsel from the outside—individuals who, like me, had experience in government and in private practice. One of the first and most notable in the modern era was Nick Katzenbach, who was hired by IBM after capping his Kennedy-Johnson years as U.S. Attorney General. What distinguished GE was not going outside for its General Counsel, but going outside for many of the GC's colleagues. In my first few years at GE, I replaced 30 of 33 direct or strong dotted line reports with leaders of the profession, drawn from government and private practice. They were equivalent in talent and experience to the top partners in private firms. My goal was straightforward: hire the best. These remarkable people filled key corporate specialty positions (e.g., head of tax, head of litigation, head of mergers and acquisitions, head of environmental health and safety). They also filled key General Counsel positions at our global business divisions (aircraft engines, power systems, medical systems, financial services), which were *each* the size of a *Fortune* 50 or *Fortune* 100 business. *Given the broad, almost Herculean, responsibilities of the General Counsel I outline here, I could hardly discharge them alone but was highly dependent on outstanding colleagues who had an incalculable role in realizing the promise of the inside counsel revolution.* The influx of such extraordinary legal talent into a corporation sounded a thunderclap across the profession and caused many lawyers in firms and in government to consider a position that had not been on their radar screen before: inside counsel.

The GE experience was thus not about the General Counsel, but about the many extraordinary lawyers who transformed GE Legal—not about an individual, but about the "inside partnership." Together, this multi-faceted and multi-talented GE team of lawyers experimented and innovated—helped shape the path of the inside counsel revolution.

Any influence I had was multiplied a hundred fold by the creativity, imagination, and excellence of my colleagues.[3] The GE experiment was totally dependent, as well, on the willingness of CEO Jack Welch and his successor, Jeff Immelt, to redefine the role of inside counsel, to hire from the outside, to drive the highest-quality lawyers across the top of the company—both at headquarters and in the operating divisions— and to pay market prices to acquire the best talent. Without the strong support—indeed, strong endorsement—of the CEOs for whom I worked, it would never have been possible to build an outstanding internal legal team that was an important exemplar of the inside counsel movement.

C. CAUSES: A SCHEMATIC VIEW

The inside counsel movement in the United States grew due to a series of interrelated and iterative causes, some of which have echoed across Europe and Asia (see pp. 450–454). First, as many have noted, the power and responsibility started to shift from large corporate law firms back to inside lawyers during the early 1980s. This was due, importantly, to outside firms' economic arrogance: charging ever-higher fees purportedly based on the number of hours worked and invoiced with a single line stating "for services rendered." The post–World War II era of economic globalization was beginning to take off, posing increasingly complex commercial problems in multiple jurisdictions. So, too, there was a litigation explosion in the United States. Increased global regulation as well as activism by nongovernmental organizations raised a host of ethical, legal, and policy questions for corporations. These forces increased the demand for inside lawyers who could work closely with business leaders in addressing that transnational complexity. More deals and more disputes required more attention of more business leaders, who began to discover that "making" expertise inside the organization, rather than "buying" legal services outside, could increase speed, quality, and productivity—and "all deliberate speed" of inside lawyers in a competitive business environment was seen as just as important as quality and productivity.

Second, as inside lawyers began to assert their power, the position of General Counsel, which had once seemed a backwater for lawyers who failed to make partner at major law firms, began, in the 1980s and 1990s, to attract many more premier lawyers from outside the company. Highly talented lawyers began to realize that the jobs as senior lawyers in a corporation had a number of advantages. General Counsel, and inside lawyers, are enmeshed in the fabric of the institution and positioned at the center of the action. They become clients and never have to worry about time sheets or billing, and, indeed, can control the substantive and economic relationship with outside counsel. Their work is diverse, covering a huge array of markets and products and geographies and extending far beyond the law. Inside counsel are part of an innovative inside legal partnership, which can be an authentic sharing and learning organization across businesses, specialties, and geographies. They can develop much closer relationships with business leaders, other staff, and operational peers than outside lawyers and can advise and execute on business as well as legal matters. They have substantial responsibility as leaders—and would be judged on results and not micromanaged. As leaders, they could prevent problems, rather than coming in as outside counsel to clean them up. Their career paths are enhanced because they could progress to higher legal jobs in the company, become lead lawyers in another company, or cross over to the business side and become business leaders. Finally, if they were willing to bet on themselves and on the company, their compensation—annual salary, annual bonus, deferred cash, deferred equity, and other company benefits—could equal the top of the law firm market or exceed it (often by significant amounts). The news across the profession about the value of inside counsel jobs and the hiring of outstanding lawyers as General Counsel made it possible to broaden the in-house talent upgrade and to hire outstanding lawyers from across the profession for many senior inside counsel positions, not just for the position of GC.

Third, as the inside counsel movement gained momentum in the 1980s and 1990s due to increased responsibility and new talent, more and more business leaders and boards of directors began to reassess the value that broad, creative inside lawyers could add to their company. This value stemmed, in essence, from lawyers being integrated into corporations and being able to act with knowledge and speed as partners in addressing commercial opportunities and risks and as guardians in protecting and enhancing the company's integrity. The result was that, as some business leaders supported new law department models, other corporations began to take note. They, too, started to hire the new breed of General Counsel who were outstanding practitioners and leaders. They, too, started to redefine the role of inside lawyers, both in the company and in controlling and coordinating outside law firms. Leaders of the legal profession became General Counsel, including former U.S. Attorneys General and Deputy Attorneys General, former Court of Appeals and District Court judges, former White House Counsels, former heads of regulatory agencies or elite units within those agencies, or the top partners in leading law firms. The status of inside counsel increased as a growing number of major corporations made such hires. In GE, after business leaders worked with the new breed of outstanding specialists and generalists, many realized that a step function increase in quality added markedly to their business teams. These operational leaders then supported the promotion of lead lawyers to the small universe of GE officers in a huge global company (inside counsel became 5 percent or more of the only 200 company vice presidents in an entity with more than 300,000 employees around the world).

Fourth, all the broad trends that had started the inside counsel movement in the late 1970s and early 1980s accelerated in the last decade of the 20th century and the first decade of the 21st. Faced with new global competition, corporations embarked on a never-ending pursuit of cost reductions and productivity increases. This included marked efforts to reduce outside legal fees and the overall legal spend by relying more on inside resources or non-law firm outside vendors. The day-to-day complexity of new technologies, new products, new global markets, and new competitors made ever-more important the day-to-day involvement of inside lawyers on business teams to achieve performance goals. The concept of simply manufacturing in the United States and exporting overseas became vastly more complicated, sophisticated, and nuanced. Global corporations often evolved into large, complex matrix organizations, with corporate functions from manufacturing to sales to marketing to finance under the control of distinct units in many nations. Such differentiation created the need not just for cross-functional integration, but also for uniform global standards on a host of issues from quality to compliance to security to ethics to values. Similarly, beyond dramatically changing business challenges, a host of trends increased companies' legal, ethical, reputational, country, and operational risks, which could best be mitigated by having inside lawyers working closely with other business and staff functions in company operations. These included endemic corruption in new markets, new employees in those markets with different values, complex global supply chains, and ever-present challenges of doing business in economies with deep government involvement in "markets." Moreover, regulatory trends continued to pose increasing challenges and risks, including, for example, treating accounting issues as legal violations; criminalizing aspects of regulatory enforcement; setting rules through enforcement rather than rule-making; an exponential increase in the size of criminal fines, civil penalties, and private settlements; and confronting multi-front wars as public and private parties investigated or sued corporations in multiple jurisdictions. All this was accompanied by striking increases in the sheer number and complexity of regulations in multiple jurisdictions, in the reach and voice of nongovernmental watchdog organizations, and in 24/7 "above-the-fold" or viral electronic media coverage of corporate misdeeds. Broadly speaking, all these trends combined to make "business in society" issues of vital interest to CEOs and boards of directors.

Finally, the raft of outsized scandals since the turn of the century underscored the need for boards of directors, CEOs, and senior business leaders—including, importantly, the General Counsel—to build strong integrity and risk disciplines into corporate business processes. These corporate failures began with Enron and WorldCom and were followed by a torrent of subsequent scandals, including HealthSouth billing fraud, Siemens and Wal-Mart bribery, BP's drilling rig explosion, the Toyota and GM product safety issues, and the plague of problems affecting the financial services industry (misdeeds relating to the mortgage market, money laundering, the Madoff hoax, disclosure failures, and collusion on LIBOR and currency). These front-page problems had a dramatic impact on companies: time and effort responding, executives fired (and indicted), huge expenses for internal forensic efforts, huge costs for external criminal and civil sanctions, and loss of reputation. But, the problems also affected stakeholders: market cap tanking, employees laid off, customer relations shredded, suppliers losing wounded corporate customers, creditors stuck with debt, and communities losing business and tax base. Importantly, the scandals also scarred the reputations of boards of directors and, notwithstanding director and officer insurance, even imposed personal financial loss on some directors in catastrophic matters like Enron and WorldCom. As a result, another boost was given to the trend toward hiring highly talented, highly sophisticated General Counsel with reputations for independence who could help prevent improprieties and who could credibly help respond to legislators, regulators, media, and NGOs when such improprieties occurred.

These reinforcing causes produced the inside counsel revolution in the United States. *That revolution was driven by the necessity of a changing business environment—and, if it endures as I think it will, that necessity will sustain it.* Right-minded companies needed broadgauged GCs. Today, the revolution is now reflected in the attention paid to the subject: special legal trade magazines covering the inside counsel "beat"; regular stories in the mainstream media; innumerable conferences pitched to inside lawyers (or to law firms trying to understand the strange new law department beast); and increasing attention to the role of General Counsel and corporate law departments in law reviews, in books, and in courses at law and business schools. It is also reflected in directional changes in the profession itself—for example, the growing number of lawyers working inside corporations; the exponential emergence of outside vendors selling a wide array of services to inside law departments; the decline in corporate spend on outside law firms for basic matters (although huge litigations, transactions, and bankruptcies will always boost outside firms); a whole new executive recruiting specialty devoted to finding and hiring lawyers for corporations; the growth of associations of inside counsel; and the increase in the number of General Counsel who are among the five most highly compensated executives listed in the proxy statement.[4]

A personal note about these developments, which I have described schematically. When Jack Welch offered me the job as GE's General Counsel in the spring of 1987, I was a Supreme Court and appellate litigator. I had never met him. I had not done one hour of work for GE. I knew not a single soul at the company. I said to Welch, "You know I am not a corporate lawyer." He laughed: "You'll figure it out." He wanted to transform the function and upgrade the talent both at headquarters and in the operating divisions. But, the simple fact was that, beyond those broad aspirations, neither he nor I had clear, preconceived ideas at the time of what needed to be done, what would happen in GE, or what the broad trends were that would transform the role of inside counsel in so many companies. Only through a glass darkly did I perceive the outlines of the revolution in which I was fortunate to play a part. Experience, not theory, was my great teacher.

D. THE PRESCRIPTIVE PERSPECTIVE

Although this book is about the General Counsel and inside lawyers, it is rooted in the framing prescriptive concept that the ultimate mission of corporations, especially global companies, should be the fusion of high performance with high integrity and sound risk management. I ask the reader not to move too quickly past that phrase—*high performance with high integrity and sound risk management*. It is elemental to a corporation's commercial success and to its standing in society. In my more than 30 years in big institutions, including almost 20 in one of the largest and most complex corporations in the world, I came to understand that the implications of that straightforward phrase were multi-faceted, complex, and, ultimately, profound.

High performance means strong, sustained economic growth through provision of superior goods and services, which in turn provide durable benefits for shareholders and other stakeholders upon whom the company's health depends. Such performance entails an essential balance between risk-taking (the creativity and innovation so essential to economic growth) and economic risk management (the financial, commercial, and operational disciplines so essential to the soundness and durability of business institutions). *In my view, it means a corporation-specific optimization of the legitimate interests of key stakeholders—shareholders, creditors, employees, customers, suppliers, and communities—over the short, medium, and long term to create value for all,* as I discuss in Chapter 8 on governance (pp. 275–315).

High integrity means robust adherence to the spirit and letter of *formal rules*, both legal and financial; voluntary adoption of binding *global ethical standards* that go beyond existing rules, including balanced approaches to public policy and political processes; and employee commitment to *core values* of honesty, candor, fairness, trustworthiness, and reliability. It involves understanding, and mitigating, other types of risk—beyond direct economic risk—that can cause a company catastrophic harm: legal, ethical, reputational, communications, public policy, and country/geopolitical. The core values of the company, as expressed through the core values of its employees, are essential to strong relationships inside and outside the company. These values, in turn, can only exist when the company adheres to the spirit and letter of the formal rules, when it adopts appropriate global ethical standards, and when it makes these precepts operational at all levels of the corporation.

The fusion of high performance with high integrity must, as noted, include sound management of economic and noneconomic risk. When I use the short-hand "performance with integrity" in what follows, the reader should understand that "with sound risk management" is always implied. But, high performance with high integrity and sound risk management is not just about risk mitigation. It is about creating affirmative benefits in the company, in the marketplace, and in the broader global society. Achieving high integrity obviously involves resources and cost. Sometimes, business leaders will face a trade-off between integrity and performance, between ethics and financials. But, the fusion of performance with integrity and sound risk management ultimately creates value in a wide variety of ways: attracting, motivating, and retaining superb talent; increasing productivity; enhancing customer loyalty; mitigating or eliminating far more expensive risks; increasing brand value; allowing premium pricing; creating operational efficiencies; and enhancing reputation with stakeholders both inside and outside the corporation.

Ultimately, I believe, high performance with high integrity and sound risk management creates fundamental trust among shareholders, creditors, employees, recruits, customers, suppliers, regulators, communities, the media, and the general public. This trust is essential to sustaining the corporate power and freedom that drives the economy—trust that has dramatically eroded over the past quarter century due to stark corporate scandals and stunning business failures. Over the past quarter century, many major corporations, especially transnational ones, have increasingly accepted this broad goal of high performance with high integrity. To be sure, each company might formulate those goals with different words. They may implement them with varying degrees of intensity, resources, and rigor. And, these broad goals do not, of course, command assent at the top of all major, global companies, either in word or deed, as reflected in the constant drumbeat of corporate scandal. But, directionally, I believe this is where global corporations are going—and must go.

In my last book, *High Performance with High Integrity* (Harvard Business Press, 2008), I addressed CEOs, who have the fundamental leadership responsibility for melding performance and integrity in a global corporation. I tried, in brief compass, to articulate a view of corporate purpose, explain why it was important, and describe how CEOs could implement it by following certain key principles and practices. In this book, I write primarily for inside lawyers, and those who work with them, to give my views on the critical role that they play as experts, counselors, and leaders in assisting the CEO, and the board of directors, to carry out this fundamental mission of global capitalism. It goes into more detail on how to attain a high performance with high integrity company through exposition of the GC's roles and responsibilities. It is a complementary, but quite different perspective. The book also articulates a capacious vision of lawyering—of the lawyer-statesman—which is far, far broader than what is taught in law school or tested on the bar exam. It is, in my judgment, a vision of the ultimate lawyers' role, as professionals and as citizens, that is suited to the complex, multi-faceted nature of the real problems that real lawyers in real institutions in real time face constantly.

As a lawyer-statesman who has a central role in setting the direction of the high performance with high integrity corporation regarding both opportunities and risks, the GC must navigate complex internal relationships (with business leaders, the board of directors, peer senior officers, the corporate bureaucracy, the legal organization) and challenging external ones (with diverse stakeholders, governments, NGOs, and media in nations and regions across the globe). The position of General Counsel, properly viewed, presents a rich, consequential opportunity to discharge and define what it means to be a great lawyer in the complex setting of the modern corporation—proactively assisting definition and implementation of growth strategies, helping or leading efforts to create an integrity culture, building systems and processes for compliance with law and ethics, addressing other types of economic and noneconomic risk, rebalancing relations with outside counsel, leading a global legal organization (and other corporate functions), solving complex problems across all those domains, and ultimately being both a partner and a guardian in helping define corporate citizenship for the enterprise.

Beyond speaking to current inside counsel in the United States at all levels of corporations, I especially hope this book will be of use to an emerging generation of General Counsels and inside lawyers, both here and across the globe, who seek to define a more central and proactive role inside their business. First and foremost, it is written for that next generation. I also hope that the book will provide an important perspective and framework for many other non-lawyers around the world who are deeply concerned about the role of the corporation in the world economy and the role of law and ethics in the corporation. Although I write from the perspective of a large, global company, *I believe that many of the ideas here are applicable to medium and small enterprises as well **if** the CEO and board of directors have a performance with integrity vision.* Some companies will have a BMW Series 7 approach; others, who are more resource constrained, will have a MINI Cooper approach. But the prescriptive issues must be faced no matter how large or small the company. Importantly, I hope that CEOs and boards of directors in enterprises of all shapes and sizes in all corners of the globe will engage with my detailed vision because, without their understanding and support, the practical ideal of the General Counsel as partner and guardian cannot be realized. I wish, too, that the perspectives offered here will interest others concerned with the rise and fall of corporations: lawyers in private law firms, regulators and media, and experts on business and society in academia and in think tanks.

I have a special hope that the framework will also have salience for General Counsel and other lawyers inside a wide variety of public, private, and nonprofit institutions, not just the publicly held global corporation. The independent expertise, judgment, and vision of the lawyer as expert, counselor, and leader should also obtain when inside lawyers work with Presidents, Cabinet Secretaries, Chairs of Congressional Committees, University Presidents, Foundation CEOs, or other leaders in public, private, and nonprofit institutions—and when they occupy comparable positions in nations all across the globe. Finally, at a time when economic issues threaten to obscure the ethical responsibilities of lawyers as professionals and as citizens, I put forward a contemporary vision of the lawyer-statesman ideal and the continuous quest for what is "right" in an attempt to refocus attention on core issues of "ethics" and "service" that have long motivated young people to pursue a life in the law. I try to demonstrate that these remain fundamental concerns even in complex, profit-seeking, global corporations.

The book's prescriptive perspective, ultimately, is in setting forth a *framework for identifying a set of sequential, interconnected, and first-order issues*, which I believe corporations—and General Counsels and inside lawyers—should address. This framework entails systems and processes to address those issues and, ultimately, to create the vital performance with integrity culture.

But I should also say what this book is not. First, it does not advance a particular political or economic ideology; it is not intended to be either "progressive" or "conservative." I raise a broad array of issues. I argue strongly for addressing those issues energetically, fairly, candidly, and systematically. I offer my point of view. But many of these issues are "open-textured" and may be answered in different ways by different corporations that identify and weigh "relevant" factors differently. Second, although I will weave into the discussion my direct personal experience on these issues—*and my mistakes*—this is not a memoir. It is instead a personal vision of the mission of the corporation and the role of the modern General Counsel. Nor does it advance the "GE approach," as I saw it. GE was unusual, if not *sui generis*, in terms of size, diversity, and global complexity. My observations, which I hope apply broadly to enterprises of all shapes and sizes, are based on research, writing, speaking, teaching, and conversations with many other leaders, not just my own GC experience (important though it was). And, there are certainly ideas offered here that I either had not thought of when I was at GE or, if did, failed to implement completely, if at all. Third, as I will emphasize later, the book does not argue that the General Counsel has a monopoly on shaping the normative positions a corporation takes. To the contrary, while the General Counsel, as lawyer and as citizen, should offer a strong, constructive perspective in high-level discussions and debates, he is a subordinate of the CEO and he operates in a complex web of shared authority with senior corporate staff and operational peers. He is an important voice on performance, integrity, and risk, with a vital, distinct point of view and strong proactive role. But he is one of a limited number of important voices. In corporations those voices also include a CFO-statesman, an HR-Leader-statesman, and a business leader-statesmen. The broad concerns this book addresses should command the attention—stimulate the views—of all the corporation's senior executives.

Although this book offers a prescriptive framework, it is built on a hard substratum of experience, trying to balance the ideal with the real, the aspirational with the actual. It seeks to discuss the obstacles that can moderate, alter, or defeat the core prescriptions of the General Counsel as lawyer-statesman and partner-guardian in the service of high performance with high integrity global companies. Such constraints include inherent pressures for corruption in capitalism, resource limits or cutbacks inside major corporations, business leader lack of vision, negative attitudes about lawyers and law, dysfunctional corporate culture, barriers in non-U.S. settings, and more limited resources inside medium and small enterprises. It is very possible that the ideals advanced in this book are achievable, but it is by no means certain. As I discuss at the end, the inside counsel revolution will not be rolled back, but its future growth—its breadth, depth, and rate of increase both in the United States and around the world—is an open question.

E. CORE CONCEPTS AND KEY ISSUES

In the rest of this book, I explore in more detail the role of the General Counsel and inside lawyers through the examination of three core concepts and through a critical assessment of eight core issues.

Building on the fundamental concept of high performance with high integrity, other core concepts are the bedrock of my prescriptive analysis. I hope to advance, in more detail, the *lawyer-statesman ideal* for addressing the "what is right" question in the context of a complex global business enterprise; explain how to resolve the *partner-guardian tension*—the ever-present conflict between helping the business leaders achieve performance goals, but also assuring that the corporation acts with integrity and manages risk; and illuminate the nature of a *performance with integrity culture*, which can withstand the unrelenting pressures, at the core of capitalism, for unethical, illegal, and ill-considered activities.

I then turn to the essential prescriptive approach on eight top-line issues, which are the core priorities of inside counsel: *compliance, ethics, risk and crisis management, governance, citizenship and public policy, the global legal organization, law firms and alternatives, and future possibilities and obstacles.* I do not, however, venture into the specifics of how particular legal domains should apply inside a corporation: for example, antitrust, litigation, mergers and acquisitions (M&A), taxes, trade, intellectual property (IP), labor and employment, environment, health, and safety. To do so would turn this into a multi-volume work.

There is *not* a separate chapter on *globalization* because that perspective is an essential aspect both of the core concepts and the key issues. I discuss the globalization dimension in different contexts throughout the book. Another major theme worth calling out here, but that is woven into all the chapters, is an *emphasis on function not form*. Most of the hard issues in corporations require an interdisciplinary, cross-functional approach. Breaking down the silos—or, to mix metaphors, making all the staff and business elephants dance together—is vital. And each corporation has its own culture and rhythms. The CEO must make sure that the right people are at the table on decisions and the right people work together on execution—and that the right checks and balances exist alongside the endless drive for productivity and efficiency. But debates about formal titles and organizational boxes—board chair v. lead director, centralized v. decentralized legal organization, reporting relationship of the Chief Compliance Officer—are far less important than addressing the substantive and procedural issues with the right mix of talent, the right level of attention, and the right balance of efficiency/speed and the checks/balances.

There is now an increasing amount of writing—from lengthy academic articles to short, law firm marketing blogs—on inside counsel and their issues. My goal here is not an encyclopedic and exhaustive literature review. Nor is it intended to be a "how to" manual on work-a-day issues. Rather, it is to present my own take on the prescriptive essence and key realities of being a General Counsel: top priority issues, first principles, hard decisions, and inevitable constraints. It is a prescriptive essence that has emerged from the past—from the inside counsel revolution that occurred over little more than a generation. It is a prescriptive essence that I believe will remain valid for a long time into the future, even in an era otherwise characterized by constant change.

It is, in some respects, my last will and testament on the role of General Counsel in the high performance with high integrity corporation— offering views accumulated over nearly three decades with the wish that they will have some benefit, however modest, for those who follow.

2

THE LAWYER-STATESMAN IDEAL

A. OVERVIEW: IS IT LEGAL? IS IT RIGHT?

In helping achieve the central corporate objectives of fusing high performance with high integrity, the General Counsel as lawyer-statesman must be deeply concerned not just about answering the first question—"is it legal"—but about helping answer the ultimate question: "is it right." In essence, this means *the General Counsel as lawyer-statesman must engage in robust debate on major corporate decisions of all shapes and sizes about what are the "ends" of that action, not just about "the means" for carrying it out; about "purpose" not just "process"; about consequences, not just acts. It means assessing those ends, purposes, and consequences rigorously, not just against performance criteria but through the screens of integrity (formal rules, ethics, and values) and risk (economic and noneconomic).* To advance such robust debate, the General Counsel and other inside lawyers must be able to introduce inside the corporation discussions about competing goals and values that are at the center of all hard decisions so that those decisions—whether by the directors, the CEO, senior business leaders, or the General Counsel herself—are as fully informed and fairly assessed as possible. The General Counsel is not unique: all senior officers of the corporation have this responsibility. And, like all senior officers, the General Counsel is subordinate to the CEO.

But, with training and experience in policy, law, ethics, and process and with independent expertise, breadth, judgment, and practical wisdom, the archetypical General Counsel is well positioned to introduce a dose of "constructive challenge" to such discussions. It is the perspective of the lawyer-statesman, *an old-fashioned term I use because I want to connote the General Counsel's search, in a practical, real-world setting, for what is the right action for a corporation embedded in a broader community*, because I want to signal that the General Counsel must operate effectively inside the corporation but with an external vision that helps define the role of business in society. Thus, I have chosen to use the phrase for its historical resonance but in a more modest sense than some Platonic guardian imbued with republican (small "r") ideals and supernatural character and wisdom. Instead, for me, the phrase connotes the practical act of asking, in a concrete, corporate setting, whether an action is "right" in light of its purposes and consequences from a broad array of perspectives, including commercial, prudential, legal, ethical, risk, and citizenship. *It is the deep commitment to the act of "asking" in an organization with shared powers—not the particulars of the answers (which will necessarily vary by institutional situation, mission, history, and culture)—that is my heart-felt, but in some respects modest, conception.* This role is, however, at the epicenter of the inside counsel revolution.

To do this, the General Counsel must have the character and independence to speak her mind on that basic issue of what is right. The GC must have the courage to stand up in contentious groups in high-pressure situations and to raise basic (sometimes obvious) questions others may be afraid to ask. She must have the capacity to see problems from different perspectives—drawing on outstanding legal skills but also having breadth of non-legal knowledge and vision in all aspects of business decision making, including commercial, financial, technological, ethical, societal, and political. She must be capable of analyzing and articulating a range of appropriate options involving different degrees of risk—commercial and other—before making a recommendation. She must have the self-confidence to help articulate a vision for the company and the backbone to resign if certain lines are crossed. And she must have the capacity to function, often simultaneously, in the three fundamental roles of a lawyer: technical expert, wise counselor, and accountable leader.

Put a slightly different way, the lawyer-statesman role inside the corporation involves not just dealing with past problems, but charting future courses; not just playing defense, but playing offense; not just providing legal advice, broadly defined, but being part of the business team and offering business advice. Even more broadly, it involves the wise counseling and leadership roles across a wide array of corporate issues that stem from broad experience, not just technical mastery; that require sound judgment based on knowledge of history, culture, human nature, and institutions, not just a sharp tactical sense; that flow from the ability to understand long-term implications, not just achieve short-term advantage; and that are founded on a deep concern for the public interest, not just the private good.

The General Counsel as lawyer-statesman is not a passive servant inside the corporation, doing what the "client"—the directors, CEO, and business leaders—tell her to do. Nor, however, is the General Counsel an aloof figure, acting alone. Instead, she is embedded in a complex organization where many have authority and voice. She must have the stature and standing to engage fully in debates about major decisions, even if, ultimately, the decision in a hierarchical enterprise is not made by her (although many will be) but by the board, the CEO, or other business leaders. It is within this web of both hierarchical and shared power that she must have the personal and organizational skills to find the difficult (at times treacherous) path between being both a partner to key businesspeople and guardian of the corporation in the service of the basic corporate mission: fusing high performance with high integrity and sound risk management. As a global General Counsel, with background in both private practice and government, recently said, the conception of the lawyer-statesman focusing ultimately on what is right "initially struck me as aspirational, unattainably so," but it "is actually a basic requirement for a senior in-house lawyer in a global, highly regulated corporation." And, as Ken Frazier, CEO of

Merck, said in a speech to the American Law Institute: "Sophisticated clients don't want 'pure' legal advice, they want workable solutions to their problems—problems that they understand to be situated at the intersection of law, business, technology, politics and moral judgment. Smart clients expect their lawyers to help them find these integrated solutions to their most vexing problems."[1]

B. HISTORICAL TRADITIONS

My vision and operative concepts of the General Counsel as lawyer-statesman stem primarily from my nearly 20 years of personal experience in the very specific context of a global corporation. But, two strands of American history inform my views on this contemporary role. For me, these historical traditions are *a call to engagement with big, broad, and important issues, not a set of particular substantive positions drawn from the past, because history is subject to myriad interpretations.* I hope that the reference to American usage will not be parochial but can also have meaning to lawyers outside the United States.

First, there is the classic 19th-century view of the lawyer-statesman: individuals who had law degrees and practiced law but who played a prominent role in the formation of the United States and in the national policy of a young nation. John Adams, Alexander Hamilton, Thomas Jefferson, James Madison, and John Marshall all had legal training, but it was not their activities as practicing lawyers in the private bar, but rather their prominence as great actors in the public sector that made them statesmen. These were men who gave seminal public service, articulated significant public ideas, exercised profound political authority, and expressed themselves in powerful writing about the nature of government. And this "statesman" ideal to advance the commonweal extended far beyond the Founders. As DeTocqueville famously said:

> In America, there are no nobles or literary men, and the people are apt to distrust the wealthy; lawyers, consequently, form the highest political class. . . . They are naturally called upon to occupy most of the public stations.

Thus, for these men, their "statesmanship" primarily occurred when they were active in the public sector. Even then, they should not be romanticized as disinterested actors for their "statesmanship" addressed profound issues, but also reflected sharply conflicting social, political, and economic interests—whether the mercantilist, manufacturing, strong government world view of Adams and Hamilton or the agrarian, slave-holding, weak government world of Jefferson and Madison. The early years of the republic witnessed historic statecraft and institution building. But it was also the dawn of political parties representing different interests and conceptions of the state—and was one of the most vitriolic and divisive periods in American political history. Adams and Hamilton, Jefferson and Madison were not just founding "fathers" united on some constitutional fundamentals, but also founding "brothers" beset by sharp rivalries through their "representation," not of private clients, but of competing political visions and of different private segments of society in acrimonious debate about the shape of the fledgling republic, debates that echo down to this day. DeTocqueville, too, clearly recognized the special interests that lawyers embodied and represented even as he characterized them as a natural aristocracy and noted their public-sector role.[2]

Although we today no longer use the phrase "lawyer-statesman" routinely; although we no longer accept that lawyers have a privileged position in national life; and although we quite frequently debate whether various aspects of law, lawyers, and the legal profession advance or retard the commonweal, the tradition of private lawyers providing important public service has been, and continues to be, an enduring feature of American life. In foreign affairs, for example, think of two Secretaries of State, Dean Acheson and James Baker. Indeed, the list of lawyers assuming important public-sector roles in the legislature, the executive branch, and the regulatory agencies at all levels of government during the 20th century is, quite literally, without limit. As was true at the founding, lawyers are active and influential in public life, representing a broad range of views. Leading lawyers are united in their desire to serve the public good, but, reflecting the genius of our pluralistic society, hardly uniform in their visions of what is the public good or of what is right.

A second strand of thought about the lawyer-statesman ideal was articulated more than a century ago by Louis Brandeis in a famous 1905 speech "The Opportunity in the Law." Brandeis noted that, in the second half of the 19th century, lawyers had increasingly become involved in the burgeoning financial and industrial enterprises, that their fundamental role was no longer trying cases but in *advising* leaders of commerce or even becoming business leaders themselves. Said Brandeis:

> [B]y far the greater part of the work done by lawyers is done not in court, but in advising men on important matters . . . [in] affairs industrial and financial. The magnitude and scope of these operations remove them almost wholly from the realm of 'petty trafficking' . . . *The questions which arise are more nearly questions of statesmanship.* The relations created call in many instances for the exercise of the highest diplomacy. *The magnitude, difficulty and importance of the problems involved are often as great as the matters of state with which lawyers were* formerly frequently associated . . . although the lawyer is not playing in affairs of state the part he once did, his influence is, or at all events may be, quite as important as it ever was in the United States, and it is simply a question of how that influence is to be exercised.[3] [Emphasis supplied.]

Brandeis recognized the dynamic growth in the power of private enterprise and the potential "lawyer-statesman" role that counsel could play inside those powerful agglomerations of wealth on matters of public importance. (He, of course, urged that corporations, to avoid "wild and intemperate" action from the public, support legislation of the Progressive Era relating, for example, to labor relations and working conditions.) He hoped that counselors inside corporations might help their enterprises resolve the clashes between the competing economic interests of the time, although he also recognized the need for lawyers outside corporations to represent the interests of the "people." He believed that inside counsel needed to bring independent judgment to their clients to mediate between private enterprise and public interests for the general benefit of society.

The General Counsel as lawyer-statesman draws from these two traditions of engagement. Obviously, it is risible to suggest that General Counsel can approach the iconic role of the great public statesman. But, the deep concern with the direction and strength of the polity that animated the classic 19th-century lawyer-statesmen—and the multitudes of lawyers since who were inspired by their legacy and have had prominent public-sector positions—should be of equally great concern to the corporation and the General Counsel. The fundamental economic, social, and political arrangements of society, and the social and economic well-being of its citizenry, have a profound impact on business's ability to be competitive, profitable, and durable. Similarly, Brandeis's observation about corporate counselors is also vital. Business has a profound impact on the fundamental political, social, and political arrangements of society. Appropriate corporate engagement with government is a vital aspect of the current GC role (see pp. 335–354). Great commercial enterprises have substantial power in the society. Their private-ordering decisions as well as their positions on public policy pose the challenge of independent judgment and statesmanship—understanding both private needs and public imperatives—for lawyers working inside corporations.

Indeed, as legal historian Robert Gordon has argued, these traditions merged in the middle of the 20th century:

> In the post World War II era, a group of lawyers and legal academics . . . theorized, from hints dropped by such Progressive lawyers as Brandeis and Adolf Berle . . . the role of the new corporate legal counselor as a "statesman-advisor." The counselor represents his client's interest "with an eye to securing not only the client's immediate benefit but his long-range social benefit." In negotiating and drafting contracts, collective bargaining agreements, or reorganization plans, the lawyer is a lawmaker of "private legislation" and "private constitutions," a "prophylactic avoider of troubles, as well as pilot through anticipated difficulties." The emphasis is on creative compliance with government regulators and labor unions, and on harmonious stable compromises with contract partners and the workforce. It is a vision

founded on a very particular model of corporate leadership as the ideal business client what we now call the "managerialist" model (Berle named the lawyer-executive Owen D. Young of General Electric as the exemplar of vanguard corporate leadership)—business leaders who had made their peace with the New Deal, accepted unions as the price of stability, and whose lawyers moved in and out of government.[4] [footnotes omitted]

These lawyers aimed, in the broad, to implement Young's famous statement about the role of corporations: business enterprises owed "the stockholders a fair rate of return but also bore an obligation to labor, to customers and lastly to the public" to whom he envisioned a responsibility to make sure that the corporation functioned "in the public interest as a great and good citizen should." These lawyers had outsized roles in the New Deal, World War II, and the post-war era in shaping the modern structures of the mixed economy and the international order and then serving corporations to navigate in the changed domestic and international world. They included people like Dean Acheson, Thurman Arnold, Abe Fortes, Thomas Corcoran, Lloyd Garrison, David Lilienthal, John McCloy, Paul Porter, James Rowe, and Simon Rifkind. We should not be dewy eyed: They, of course, had their ideological, personal, and monetary interests (like the lawyer-statesman of yore), but they also had a broad view of lawyers and law and helped shape the foundation of the world we still live in today (however much it is changing). I should note that, before becoming head of GE in 1922, Owen Young was the company's General Counsel for ten years.

But, commenting in the shadow of the Enron scandal in 2003, Gordon said the conception of the wise counselor/lawyer-statesman has been in decay since the 1970s. In his view, the causes include a more adversary relationship between the regulatory state and corporations, a move to "transactional" not "relational" connections between corporations and their outside firms due to competition, and increasing law firm focus on getting business and increasing profits per partner. Others would also identify increasingly narrow specialization of top lawyers. Wrote Gordon about the broad statesman-counselor role: "It is no longer recognized by most corporate lawyers as a norm . . . We cannot hope to revive the counselor's role as the profession's dominant role or self-conception or practical ways of life."[5]

But I believe that Gordon and many others who bemoan the state of the profession and the problems of being a lawyer-statesman, while identifying important changes in the legal profession, are overly simplistic. I am not so pessimistic. Of course, there are greedy and supine lawyers. And trends reflecting pressures to make profits and wealth the singular overarching purpose of corporations and law firms are real— and disturbing. The need for change is genuine. But I deeply believe there is a strong opportunity, in the right circumstances, for the General Counsel to exemplify the ideal in practice, to play an important role in the corporation and in society—just as many broad-minded lawyers continue to do today in private law firms and in periods of public service. Surely, a reference to the Dickensian epigram, which we all learned in high school, is appropriate—"it is the best of times, it is the worst of times"—because broad generalizations fail to capture the enormous diversity in law and lawyering. Even former Yale Law School Dean Anthony Kronman, author of a deeply pessimistic 1993 book lamenting the decline of his concept of lawyer-statesman in law firms, the judiciary, and law schools, observed more than 20 years ago, albeit with qualifications: "It is true that in recent years the position of in-house general counsel has become a more independent one . . . So there is reason to believe that, at the very top, in-house legal work now offers the opportunities for statesmanship that it traditionally did not."[6] Understanding how this potential can be realized begins with understanding in more detail the three fundamental roles the General Counsel and inside lawyers play.

C. OUTSTANDING EXPERT, WISE COUNSELOR, AND ACCOUNTABLE LEADER

Many have advanced a wide array of typologies to describe the role of General Counsel. The General Counsel role can be understood by her relationships with internal actors (the board, the CEO, staff leaders, business leaders, the GC's direct reports, the whole legal organization) and with external actors (shareholders, creditors, customers, corporate suppliers, law firms, regulators, other policy makers, trade associations, the media, communities). Or the General Counsel can be described by main functions: legal advisor, officer of the company, member of management, head of the legal department, and corporate agent dealing with third parties. Or the General Counsel position can be defined in terms of the various areas of the law affecting the corporation (from antitrust to tax to environment to labor and employment). Some have simply listed 19 different activities of a General Counsel with no organizing theme. But, in reality, the roles of the broadly capable General Counsel, who operates in a cross-functional, cross-company way, are as complex as a large corporation itself. They defy categorization in a simple descriptive typology. As the Association of Corporate Counsel has stated, the General Counsel wears "more hats than a hydra has heads."[7]

I believe that the best way to think about the *prescriptive role of the General Counsel* is to focus on the risks and opportunities of performance—of how to balance commercial risk-taking with commercial risk management—and the risks and opportunities of integrity (law, ethics, public policy, and employee values). In confronting those performance and integrity risks and opportunities, I have long believed that the General Counsel and inside lawyers have three fundamental roles:

- Outstanding expert.
- Wise counselor.
- Accountable leader.[8]

These roles are not discrete: the General Counsel and inside lawyers may, depending on the decision or action, be expert, counselor, and leader at the same time. The three roles involve both decisions and then implementation. And the roles apply to all the General Counsel's corporate relationships from the board of directors to the CEO to the field lawyer in Western China. Although stating the three roles is simple, fulfilling them is not. As Geoffrey Hazard noted more than 15 years ago, "[T]he role of corporate counsel is among the most complex and difficult of . . . functions performed by lawyers."[9]

First, lawyers are *technical experts* on law, policy, and legal risk. In this capacity, they help clients resolve fundamental legal issues due to their skill at legal analysis and their knowledge of the legal system and legal subject matter. This includes both solving legal problems and preventing them. It involves protecting value (defending the corporation in legal disputes or regulatory enforcement) and creating value (through, e.g., tax planning or licensing arrangements or creative contract or deal documents).

In simplest terms, the role of technical expert applies existing law to the particular facts in different settings: legislatures, the executive branch, regulatory agencies, the courts, negotiations with private counterparties, and private ordering inside the corporation itself. In their role as technical experts, lawyers, of course, perform a wide variety of legal tasks: from advising to negotiating to drafting to resolving disputes to advocating. As common, statutory, and constitutional law have become ever more detailed and fine-grained, and as global corporations must operate in different legal systems (think civil code or sharia law jurisdictions), this fundamental task of determining what is legal in complex contexts has fallen increasingly to specialists and sub-specialists in law's many substantive domains.

Thus, in the technical expert role, the questions asked and answered are (primarily) about what law is; how it is applied to a particular set of facts; how to prevent legal problems; whether various forms of corporate action are legal; and how existing legal mechanisms, rules, and traditional lawyerly functions may be used to achieve a variety of goals. When those questions are answered, then the lawyer as expert engages in action (as litigator, negotiator, tax planner, environmental protector, etc.). Advising about, and then helping to resolve, the strictly legal dimension of corporate problems requires traditional personal skills of fine lawyers—for example, analytic power, research ability, good judgment, personal connection to clients, capacity to communicate, ability to draft and negotiate, and skill at advocacy.

As technical experts, the GC and inside lawyers will seek to explain to business leaders the extraordinarily complex question of "what the law is" for a global company, as discussed in Chapter 5 on compliance (see pp. 131–182). But they also will seek to explain the legal hazards associated with that interpretation as applied to a particular course of action, given the inherent uncertainty and ambiguity of law—how law that exists or that evolves can affect the many different facets of corporate activity. A great deal of judgment may, of course, be involved in seeking to apply "existing" law to "particular" facts to solve present problems or to predict how existing law may be interpreted in the future in order to mitigate potential risks. The law may be ambiguous. Its real rationale may be hidden under doctrine. Different decision makers may have different histories and predilections or different ideological biases and unspoken "political" agendas. The "particular" facts are a narrative woven from many threads that require selection and concision and may require knowledge of scientific, technological, or social science underpinnings (express, implied, or unanalyzed). The law in one nation may, of course, be different in another. This application of "technical expertise," both legal and factual, is at the center of inside counsel's role—and increasingly difficult to carry out when the law is constantly evolving across highly specialized legal domains in many different jurisdictions.

In my conception of outstanding technical expert, however, *inside lawyers have an obligation to view law and regulation as binding judgments made by a society's duly authorized legal and political processes.* Global corporations must give deference to the law of the nation in which *they choose to operate, even if there is some discretion in determining what is the law of that society.* If a global corporation's ethical standards conflict with the law of a nation, then the corporation can stop doing business in that nation if it feels its ethics are more important than compliance with law, as I discuss later (see pp. 197–222). If a corporation does not feel the law is effective, equitable, or just, then another answer is to seek to change the public policy and law, also discussed later (see pp. 335–354).

But there are certain courses of action involving the supposed application of "legal expertise" that should be called out and **rejected** *by the General Counsel and by inside lawyers as completely inconsistent with high performance with high integrity, with the concept of the lawyer-statesman, and with the appropriate view of resolving the partner-guardian tension.*

- It is wholly inappropriate to ignore the law and hope the corporation can get away with it.
- It is wholly inappropriate to be Holmes's "bad man" and decide whether to follow the law based on a cost-benefit calculation: Do the benefits of disobedience outweigh the costs of being caught?
- It is wholly inappropriate as a technical expert to look solely at the "face of the documents" and render a hyper-technical judgment on legality and appropriateness that not only is outside the range of reasonable discretion, but also fails to ask hard questions about what the real purpose of the legal arrangements is and what likely, or even possible, consequences may result.

Although there may be corporate pressure on lawyers to avoid the force of law, these actions are, in my deeply held view, grossly antithetical to the proper conception of the inside counsel as technical expert. A person who assumes the role of inside counsel must accept the binding force of existing law even though that law, especially law around the globe, may be unwise or politically motivated. Leaving a country or seeking to change the law are acceptable courses of action in the face of a "bad" law. Ignoring it, weighing costs and benefits of noncompliance, or interpreting away its impact through noncredible hyper-technicalities are not.

The companion point is that when a corporate action crosses the line between black and white and is clearly illegal, then the General Counsel has a duty to stand up and say "no." This may not happen very often. Many issues will require legitimate interpretation and judgment about facts and law. But, in those instances when the only credible conclusion under the facts and the law is that the proposed or actual course of conduct is illegal, the GC must not mince words and must express that unequivocal view, in the strongest possible way, to business leaders, the CEO, or, if necessary, the board. "No" to price fixing. "No" to illegal pollution. "No" to false disclosures. Proposing options that *are* legal and that can accomplish some or all of the goals of the actual or proposed corporate action can make the delivery of a "just say no" message more effective. And such options may require the wisdom of a counselor, not just the expertise of a technical lawyer.

Second, lawyers are *wise counselors* moving beyond the "is it legal" question to ask: "Is it right?"

In the broad set of problems under the heading of "applying the existing law" just discussed, the lawyer may, of course, not just focus on technical legal options with different probabilities when, as is so often the case, the law, the facts, and the decision maker all present degrees of uncertainty. Rather, wise counseling—the provision of sound judgment to the client about the "right" course of action "under all the circumstances"—is often necessary. *This type of counseling, in essence, presents a broader array of choices for resolving the present problem than the narrower legal answers in the particular circumstances.* Such counseling can be complex and challenging because it involves widening the scope of the inquiry and assessing the broader context in which a decision or transaction is occurring. It can, for example, articulate a broader set of corporate goals than just "winning" the legal issue. Such "counseling under the circumstances" could lead to setting an ethical standard (disclosure in financial services) that goes beyond relief sought in a lawsuit; settling a case that might be won on the merits to avoid creating a public policy issue that could lead to adverse regulation; choosing not to press a legal advantage against a smaller party in an emerging market because it is not "right" for other business, ethical, or political reasons; or finding broader common ground with an opposing party in a narrow legal disagreement to advance a much broader, more constructive course of mutual conduct.

In making the decisions about "what is right" under the circumstances and whether resolution beyond the narrow legal issue is appropriate, the General Counsel can assess a range of issues: to understand if there is consensus or uncertainty in the knowledge relevant to the decision (science, technology, economics, psychology, etc.); to understand the nature of the institution making the decision; to discern the policy and personal preferences of the decision makers (not just their formal legal decisions); to weigh the interests and power of the opposing parties; to gauge the interest group and media impact; to place the issue in national debate; to assess the relative influence of those broader debates on the process of the decision; to evaluate the impact of different courses of action on relevant stakeholders; to consider the impact of the issue—and the different possible resolutions—on the corporation's reputation; and to take a longer view that places the issue in perspective.

In brief, the wise counselor goes beyond legal doctrine to develop—and help implement—alternative solutions to problems or issues in order to advance a broader concept of what is the "right" with respect to a specific, particular problem that arises initially as a legal matter. This wise counseling is one of the creative acts of the General Counsel and inside counsel.

Complicated as that type of counseling is, there is a related but broader conception. Under this second view of wise counseling, the corporation is making broader voluntary decisions about its future actions that arise not from a current legal problem, but from a view of the future trajectory of the corporation and of society's trends and expectations, from a broader view of "what ought to be." The ultimate question goes beyond what should be the "right" course of action under *both* current law and current circumstances. Instead, given the corporation's or stakeholders' broader interests and concerns, what is "right" in the sense of "what ought to be" law or policy or private norms in the future? Should a client seek to overturn a regulation or propose a new one? Should new public policy be advanced or opposed, including future legislative frameworks in vital areas like taxes, trade, energy, environment, and health care? Should the corporation take a broad set of ethical actions beyond what the formal law requires (banning all bribery, even when not technically prohibited by law or mandating labor standards for third-party suppliers in global sourcing)? What kind of internal whistleblowing or hotline system should be instituted so employees can fairly and effectively voice their concerns about possible undue risk or about possible violations of law and ethics? What is "corporate citizenship" for a particular multinational corporation? What kind of public reporting is appropriate for that concept of citizenship?

This kind of counseling about broader "what ought to be" questions is closely related to the first kind of "under the circumstances" counseling. But it often requires lawyers to consider a wider variety of factors. It can require even broader assessment of future trends—including such salient factors as institutional, political, economic, policy, reputational, ethical, geopolitical, risk, or media. Such counseling may require deeper understanding of other disciplines to describe complex institutional, social, or economic reality. Such counseling also may require creative and clear thinking about what should be the paramount goals of corporation (e.g., giving less weight to short-term profits and more weight to long-term investment or reputation), goals that may not be immediately apparent in a rush to decision. Such counseling requires development of broad options for corporate actions—sometimes "out of the box"—for discussion and debate at the top of the company and with the board of directors.

With respect to this second, broader type of "ought to" counseling, the General Counsel is helping the corporation decide what actions to take beyond what the current, formal rules (legal and financial) require. These issues of "organizational ethics" or "corporate global standards" or "public policy prescriptions" occur in four broad areas (as I discuss in detail in the chapters on "Ethics" and "Corporate Citizenship"):

- Responsibilities to the corporation itself, including its nonsalaried and salaried employees, who are high-priority stakeholders.
- Responsibilities to the people and organizations outside the corporation that it serves or affects—all other corporate stakeholders from shareholders and creditors to customers and suppliers.
- Responsibilities to the legal system and rule of law that are the foundation of sound political economy and healthy constitutional democracy, including such issues as access to justice and an independent judiciary.
- Responsibilities to secure other broad public goods and enhance sound private ordering in order to create a safe, fair, and just society in which individuals and institutions (including major corporations) can thrive over the long term.

The issue of what is "right," in the "ought to be" sense, may turn on "prudential" grounds—what is in the client's enlightened self-interest. Or, it may be some combination of prudential considerations and fundamental moral concepts such as loyalty, transparency, fiduciary duty, respect for individual dignity, or the proper balance between equity and efficiency. It will involve views of how the economy, society, and politics should operate—and for what purpose. It will surely involve finding some appropriate course between what is feasible and what is desirable. (See Chapter 6 on Ethics, pp. 183–227.)

But the "what is right" counseling may apply not just to issues of integrity, but to the "performance" side of the equation as well. General Counsel increasingly have a broad counseling role on what should be "corporate strategy" on commercial and financial issues as well as on integrity. CEOs and boards of directors are, increasingly, looking to their top lawyers to participate in debates and discussions about where the corporation should go on a broad array of business issues.

Regardless of whether engaging in "under the circumstances" or "what ought to be" counseling, the General Counsel, and other inside lawyers, need to draw on and engage with non-lawyers. People in different functions within the corporation (finance, human resources, compliance, risk, information technology [IT], technology, manufacturing, sales, marketing, research and development [R&D], etc.) will also have vital perspectives on what is the "wise" course. Similarly, people inside or outside the company with other core professional training—economics, finance, political science, sociology, anthropology, communications, physical or biological science, technology, etc.— may also bring different, critical perspectives to bear in counseling corporate leaders. The General Counsel and inside lawyers have a special responsibility and ability to ensure that important issues are raised systematically, analyzed thoroughly, considered carefully, and implemented properly in conjunction with other functions and experts.

Third, *lawyers are leaders* who have ultimate positions of responsibility and accountability. They do not just advise but decide. Although lawyers have assumed important leadership positions throughout our history, the paradigm of the "profession" is lawyer serving clients, not lawyers as leaders. But the inside counsel revolution has put the General Counsel squarely in that leadership role. As leader, a GC's ultimate decisions are often based on the broad factors similar to those considered by a wise counselor—institutional, political, economic, ethical, reputational, geopolitical, etc. The relevant decision factors go far beyond considerations relating solely to law as it exists or as it will evolve. As leaders, they have no choice but to ask "what is right," not just "what is legal." Moreover, the General Counsel position, and other senior legal positions, demand organizational capabilities—personnel, compensation, planning, budgeting, strategy, project management, continuous improvement—that are quintessential leadership and managerial, not uniquely legal, skills. As with other leaders in the corporation, the leadership of the General Counsel and other inside lawyers can take many forms: command and control, collegial, managerial, exemplary, charismatic, strategic. And General Counsel often have formal leadership and responsibility for other discrete units in the corporation beyond the legal department. In addition, they may be promoted to head business divisions in the corporation or, indeed, become CEOs of major companies.[10]

At GE, I was honored and privileged to face complex leadership challenges. I headed the law department, which, when I left, had more than 1,200 lawyers worldwide in more than 100 countries, in more than 10 major business units, and with activities encompassing the world economy from power to aerospace to communications to health care to financial services. I also had ultimate responsibility or co-responsibility (short of the CEO) for the company's environmental, tax, trade, public policy, and security and crisis management functions. These units each had sizable staffs, ranging from 100 to 1,500. I had more than 30 direct or strong dotted line reports. The inside and outside budgets of these units in aggregate were in billions of dollars. And, of course, the stakes on many of the issues for which these units were directly responsible totaled tens of billions of dollars.

If I wanted to go to school on the subject of lawyer as leader, there was no greater university than GE. And I was fortunate to have had prior leadership experience in huge organizations (as Executive Assistant to the Secretary and then Assistant Secretary for Planning and Evaluation at the Department of Health, Education, and Welfare and then the head of the Washington Office and member of the Executive Committee at the international law firm of SidleyAustin). The leadership challenges I faced at GE exist for General Counsel, and other inside legal leaders, at many great global companies—and at many great small and medium-sized companies operating in difficult and complex business environments, especially in the hot area of start-ups. Although I worked for two very demanding CEOs (Welch and Immelt) and for an outstanding board of directors, I was the final decision maker in GE on a broad array of issues for approximately 75 percent of my time. The CEOs didn't micromanage me. They just made it clear that if my results were consistently poor, they would fire me. I tried to follow the same approach with my 30-plus highly talented senior lawyers, who each led sizable organizations: delegate major (though not all) matters and judge them on results.

The concept of lawyer as leader is not limited to those inside lawyers who find themselves in formal leadership positions. Lawyers down in the organization often have to make the final calls on a variety of issues—either because time is short or because their direct business leader wants it. Such "having the gun" choices exhibit great variety: from approving important contract terms to setting up "private ordering" regimes that will govern the company's activities in areas where there is little or no relevant law to decisions about how to deal with opposing parties in litigation. Each of these situations, and many others like them, are an exercise of decision making—and leadership.

D. "COMPLEMENTARY" COMPETENCIES: BEYOND THE "CORE"

To discharge the lawyer-statesman's diverse roles of technical expert, wise counselor, and effective leader, General Counsel and other inside counsel in this era, even more than in the past, need broad knowledge and skills. This is so because, as I have indicated, wide counseling and leadership involve considerations far beyond technical legal knowledge and experience, perspectives that are hardly the unique province of those with a legal background.

The "core competencies" of traditional legal method and analysis derived from the appellate "case method" still occupy the curricular center at most law schools. They are still the foundation for all lawyers, including inside counsel: basic skills and knowledge relating to the legal system, issue spotting, legal concepts, close textual analysis, legal reasoning, and the importance and elusive nature of "facts." This type of critical thinking has served lawyers well over the years, has honed sharp analytic skills that are invaluable, if narrow. General Counsel and inside lawyers must, first and foremost, be outstanding practitioners of law. But, in this era, the appellate case method, while recognized for its value in teaching analytic thinking, is now widely recognized as seriously flawed in preparing lawyers for the far greater complexity of real problems in the real world.

In the context of inside lawyering, the question then is what other qualities of mind—modes of thinking—are necessary so inside counsel can be outstanding experts, counselors, and leaders in the ever-challenging and ever-changing context of a global corporation? The broad roles inside counsel have played in the past—and will increasingly play in the 21st century—require an even more expansive and systematic view of the competencies that are required to assume and discharge their complex and fast-evolving responsibilities. In my view, inside counsel who aspire to the lawyer-statesman ideal must acquire "complementary competencies" that will allow them to operate effectively across the broad sweep of functions they have within a corporation.

To underscore their importance, I offer here an exemplary (not exhaustive) discussion of important complementary competencies that are central to my conception of the roles of expert, counselor, and leader.[11] They are doubtless beyond the ken of a single person. Each General Counsel will need to evaluate whether she personally needs to develop such competencies, how the legal organization can provide education and training on this broader array of skills, and the degree to which they should be an important qualification in hiring direct reports and other senior lawyers in the corporation.

- Inside lawyers need to have a creative and constructive, not just a critical, cast of mind. Lawyers must be able to build solely, or in teams, an argument in a brief, a regulation, a complex piece of legislation, a compliance program, an ethical initiative, or a business plan that paints a persuasive vision about what "ought" to be as opposed to simply delineating what already "is." Inside lawyers must learn to *think analytically about the enduring ethical, reputational, and enlightened self-interest of their corporation*, not just about what is strictly legal or temporarily advantageous. So, too, they must continually and creatively explore ways in which *the corporation and the legal organization can innovate internally to better resolve performance, integrity, and risk issues.*

- In asking these "ought" questions, inside lawyers must base that inquiry on a *relentless, independent, and fair-minded empirical quest for a broad set of facts* that, to the greatest extent possible, reflect the complex reality of the world they would seek to influence or change—historic, cultural, and systemic—by drawing on a diverse set of empirical disciplines.

- In asking these "ought" questions, inside lawyers must also be able to articulate a set of *systematic and constructive options that expose and explore the value tensions inherent in most decisions.* In the context of business decision making, for example, when issues often come clothed in shades of gray, what are the alternatives for accomplishing a legitimate business goal with different degrees of legal, ethical, and reputational risk and with varying direct and indirect costs; for balancing risk-taking with risk management; for balancing the short term and the long term?

- In addition to exposing value tensions, inside lawyers must help *find and articulate clearly a fair balance, in the ultimate course taken, between legitimate competing values.* This may entail a balance between the business tensions just mentioned or, when the corporation is acting in the public sphere, explaining the balance the corporation is espousing between the values that underlie so much of American history, legal and otherwise—for example, between equity and efficiency; between freedom and equality, order and liberty, or individualism and community; or, most fundamentally in this context, between promoting private growth and protecting social goods and between private ordering and public regulation.

- In helping achieve a corporation's high performance, inside lawyers *must have business and financial literacy to understand business opportunity and risk.* Inside lawyers should be conversant—even fluent—in such subjects as accounting, finance, statistics, microeconomics, competitive strategy and marketing, business negotiations, company valuation, and supply chain economics.

- In making recommendations or decisions, inside lawyers must be able *to creatively assess all dimensions of enterprise risk (e.g., financial, operational, compliance, reputational, and geopolitical), but they must not be risk averse.* Making well-considered bets, with appropriate (but not illicit or outsized) risk, is vital to innovation and change in a corporation.

- Inside lawyers must have *the ability to get things done.* They must know how to translate decisions, rules, or norms into realities, particularly inside a complex corporate bureaucracy and outside the company in the hurly-burly world of politics, media, and power. Conception without execution is worthless. Inside lawyers must have skill at making things happen in a complex organization with competing hierarchies and different levels of authority. When addressing public issues in a democratic society, they must have skill at fusing policy and politics.

- Inside lawyers must not just be strong individual contributors, but have a *well-developed ability to work cooperatively and constructively in groups or on teams that are increasingly diverse and multidisciplinary.* Global corporations, especially, require people skilled not only in working on cross-functional teams (legal, finance, IT, marketing, sales, technology, etc.), but also on teams characterized by increasing variation across nationality, race, gender, cultural, and religious lines.

- Inside lawyers must not just be strong team members, but people who can *lead and build organizations*: create the vision, the values, the priorities, the strategies, the people, the systems, the processes, the checks and balances, the resources, and the motivation. Working on teams and leading them are interconnected. Much leadership today is not command and control of the troops but persuasion, motivation, and empowerment of people around a shared vision. Skills in institutional design are vital for inside lawyers working on fundamental issues of private ordering inside the corporation, but also when engaged in public policy in addressing questions of appropriate, effective, and efficient public-sector organizations.

- When working on teams or developing arguments or positions, inside lawyers must have *the ability to understand the validity, value, and limits of other disciplines and to work collaboratively with professionals from other fields.* Inside lawyers must have the aptitude and capacity to envision the relevance of other fields of study and then, through the expertise of others, mine these other spheres of knowledge to understand their strengths and the limitations inherent in their assumptions and their methods—and to separate what is established from what is hotly contested. Knowledge of emerging technology is an important aspect of this beyond-the-law learning. Scientific literacy—the ability to assess the validity of scientific arguments and to understand the degree of consensus or dispute on important issues—is also an essential skill.

- Inside lawyers today must have *global understanding, intuition, perspective, and respect with regard to the many different cultures across the world economy.* These "global brains" are essential if inside lawyers are, with other company leaders, going to address one of the most challenging issues facing business today: conducting business effectively but with integrity in emerging markets that have weak rule of law. This complementary competency has many dimensions, but one of the most important is an understanding of comparative political, governmental, and economic systems (including a sophisticated understanding of the increasingly fragmented and dysfunctional American political system). The challenges of operating global business across a range of economic systems from state capitalism in an autocracy to the mixed economies of a liberal democracy are daunting.

- Inside lawyers must, early in their careers, perform as outstanding specialists so that they truly understand and can achieve analytic rigor and excellence. But they must also *develop vision, breadth, and inclination to be outstanding generalist leaders later in life when involved in the decision-making process or making the final decision.* The quintessential quality of the great generalist is envisioning and understanding the multiple dimensions of issues—to define the problem or issue properly—and the ability to comprehensively integrate those dimensions into the decision. For example, a great business leader must balance risk-taking creativity with risk-management disciplines and must integrate the multiple internal disciplines—finance, human resources, law, engineering, marketing, sales, technology—with key outside perspectives—those of customers, investors, regulators, community. The General Counsel and inside lawyers must be active participants in that decision-making process. *They must be able to see issues from a broad perspective of the CEO, weighing all relevant factors.* And, ideally, they will have knowledge of different approaches to decision theory.

- Finally, with respect to all competencies, core and complementary, we need lawyers who can *communicate effectively and concisely in a wide variety of formats and venues.* Lawyers have always prided themselves on their ability to communicate. But as the range of problems they confront as experts, counselors, and leaders expands—and as the modes of communication multiply—lawyers must explicitly work on developing competency in the full range of mediums and disciplines required to inform, explain, and persuade effectively in today's information society.

One of the hallmarks of a great inside legal department is the ability to provide meaningful education and training to inside lawyers so that they develop these, and other, complementary competencies, either through special courses/assignments inside the corporation or through executive education at professional schools or through sophisticated online programs (see pp. 382–389). In a 2015 survey of Chief Legal Officers (CLOs), the Association of Corporate Counsel found that a high percentage of CLOs stressed the importance of professional development in non-legal skills for inside counsel, including business management and project management.[12]

E. ANALYSIS BEFORE RECOMMENDATION

When acting as a lawyer-statesman, the General Counsel must focus first on understanding the "facts" in the broadest possible way, using both core and complementary competencies, drawing on experts both inside and outside the corporation. One of the hardest tasks when acting as "technical expert" or "wise counselor" in business decision making is to build appropriate fact gathering, especially about societal impact, into business processes—whether the matter is a litigation, a deal, a new product, or a new geography. And a related task is to ensure, to the greatest extent possible, that the facts are independently derived and fairly presented. General Counsel and inside lawyers must continually fight a corporate tendency to rush to judgment based on biased or incomplete information, which flows up from business or staff functions. There is a broad continuum between decisions that, because of real-time pressures, really do need to be made "right now," and decisions that deserve a time out and a full development of their myriad, multi-faceted aspects, especially an understanding of the broader context and broader trends, through careful discussion among senior corporate leaders. So, too, General Counsel must fight the tendency to accept, without question, the views of "experts" or be bamboozled by the false precision of numbers, rather than trying to understand the assumptions upon which analysis is based and having the skill to cross-examine experts intensely to understand the strengths and weaknesses of their points of view or their numbers. Worshiping the false idol of numeracy is one of the greatest dangers in measurement-driven corporations.

When acting as the technical expert or wise counselor, the General Counsel's primary responsibility, in my view, is to help develop sophisticated analysis of the alternatives or options available to the CEO, in addition to finding the relevant facts. This analysis will invariably involve collaboration with other staff and operational leaders. Most difficult corporate decisions present themselves with significant degrees of uncertainty. They are invariably in a gray area with respect to business performance because they involve predictions about the future when the *pro formas* meet reality: how the technology will work, what customers will do, what the costs will be, and so on. But they are also likely to be in gray areas with respect to "business in society" issues, which are the special province of the General Counsel: What different ways are there to structure the action to lessen legal risk, to lessen reputational risk, to enhance the company's ethical posture, to avoid legislative or regulatory scrutiny that might lead to changes in public policy, or to appeal to important stakeholders from shareholders to employees to customers to suppliers? And they invariably involve trade-offs between worthy values (e.g., reducing cost v. ensuring quality, serving short-term needs v. advancing long-term goals).

Once there is an appropriate assessment of the complete factual context and an analysis of the options and trade-offs, then the CEO—or board or other senior business leader—will make the decision aided by a full discussion and debate of the analysis at hand. *I must repeat: At the end of the day, if an action under consideration is so clearly illegal or contrary to company policy that it is not defensible or so unethical that serious reputational harm is certain, then the General Counsel must oppose such a corporate decision. This "just say no" function is at the absolute center of the GC's responsibilities.* But in most instances, when the issues are in the "gray zone," the core task as technical expert and wise counselor is to give the CEO or the board of directors the best possible analysis of the choices at hand and their potential consequences.

The General Counsel should, of course, provide a personal recommendation with supporting reasons for a preferred option. Her voice should be heard on complex decisions that involve commercial, legal, ethical, reputational, public policy, risk, and citizenship issues. She should neither be afraid to state her view nor be bullied into taking a position when not ready. She must act with all deliberate speed—not gumming up the works, but not acting in haste. But, I must emphasize that *the first responsibility of the General Counsel as expert and counselor is an outstanding analytic process*—considering all relevant factors, properly weighting them, and delineating a range of options—when the decision should not be made by the General Counsel as leader, but instead by the CEO or others in the corporate hierarchy. *Only then can a strong, clearly supported recommendation combine appropriate deference to the authority of the decision makers with the personal wisdom and integrity of the General Counsel.*

Google's dilemma of whether to provide a search engine in China is a good example of a hard decision that, ultimately, the top leaders in the company needed to make—involving complex facts, ethical conflicts, "law" enforced by an autocracy, and global implications.[13] In 2007, after fitful attempts to introduce a Google search engine in China and after prolonged negotiations, Google agreed with the Chinese government to accept Chinese Internet censorship in exchange for a license to operate in China. If, for example, a person typed in "Tiananmen Square" in Los Angeles on the Google search engine (even on the Chinese language version), the iconic picture of a protesting student standing in front of a tank came up, followed by a description of the 1989 pro-democracy demonstrations. If that person did the same thing in Beijing, an innocuous picture of Tiananmen Square filled the screen, followed by bland content. Accepting such censorship from an autocratic regime was contrary to Google's general (if amorphous) motto of the time—"Don't Be Evil"—and contrary to its global ethical standards supporting an open Internet and free speech. In deciding to abide by the Chinese censorship system—to allow national Chinese law to trump its global standards—Google concluded in 2006 that allowing some information into China was better than not providing Google search at all. (It did inform users if content was being censored.) It also hoped that China's comprehensive Internet censorship—the Great Firewall—might erode over time and that censorship would become less intrusive. Obviously, given exploding Internet use in China, there were strong commercial motives as well.

But, in 2009, Google discovered that its servers had been hacked, its intellectual property stolen, and the accounts of dozens of human rights activists accessed by third parties. The unintended exposure of dissidents from hacking was different than a Yahoo! incident a few years earlier, which stemmed from a different Chinese licensing agreement that obligated Yahoo! to actively aid government inquiries. Under that agreement, Yahoo! was clearly complicit in the jailing of two dissidents. When this incident became public in the United States, Yahoo! was excoriated in the media, lambasted at a congressional hearing, and forced to quietly settle a suit with the family of one of the dissidents. Although different, the specter of dissidents being exposed in the Yahoo! event clearly was important background to the Google response to hacking, especially to Russian émigré Sergey Brin, a Google co-founder. So, too, the theft of intellectual property and access to confidential databases caused Google consternation. As a result of the cyber-attack, Google in 2010 reversed course and announced it was no longer going to accept Chinese censorship on its China search engine. Google was forced to close down Google search on the Chinese mainland. Google users were routed to Google Hong Kong, where the search engine has suffered from frequent outages, poor service, and severe censorship.

The General Counsel of the company, David Drummond, indicated in an online statement that Google was, in effect, closing down Google. cn because of increased censorship (contrary to initial hopes), because of the access by third parties to accounts of dissidents and other private parties, and because of IP security risks. Yet these risks were obviously present when Google received its license in 2007. And the risk that Google will be the target of cyber-attacks—with Gmail accounts disclosed and confidential information exposed—exists wherever Google operates given the global reach of sophisticated hackers. Moreover, Google does accept much more limited censorship (e.g., prohibitions on hate speech or on adverse depiction of religion or on illegal activities) in many countries across the globe, either voluntarily or when under legislative mandate or court order. In addition, Google search in China was struggling in 2010. Its market share was only a third of the main Chinese search engine, Baidu. (It has dropped dramatically since.) By leaving China, Google gave up on the possibility of providing more information to Chinese users than Baidu, however censored or otherwise limited. It also set its Chinese search employees adrift.

Thus, Google had to consider a variety of factors in China—legal, ethical, commercial, political, and personnel—and the implication of those factors for its operations all across the globe. It decided to compromise in 2007 and accept a censored search capacity in order to provide some information for people in China. It decided not to live with that compromise in 2010 and effectively shut down its China.cn search engine by refusing to censor, thus providing far less information to Chinese customers. Some would argue that 2007 was an improper compromise. Some would argue that 2010 was an improper retreat. The point here is the analysis of a variety of factors about accepting or rejecting Chinese censorship went far beyond law and posed a hard decision that ultimately the leaders of the company had to make. In 2007, Eric Schmidt and Larry Page outvoted Sergey Brin and decided to accept the compromise of entering China with a censored search engine. In 2010, Sergey Brin and Larry Page outvoted Erich Schmidt and rejected the compromise. The analysis of the law and of many other factors illuminated the choice but didn't dictate it. And other Internet services, like Microsoft's Bing search engine and LinkedIn's professional network, have chosen to stay in China, despite censorship. If the GC can help clearly expose the relevant factors and key trade-offs, and if there is no "right" answer, then the CEO or top business leaders must decide. (My personal view is that Google made the right choices both in 2007 to see if it could operate restricted search in China with the hope of change and then to stop China search in 2010 when the prospects for change in the near term worsened and potential harms became actual harms.)

F. ANALYSIS BEFORE ADVOCACY

Some might argue that the General Counsel and inside lawyers cannot be—or should not be—lawyer-statesman because the role of the lawyers is merely to be advocates, taking direction from executives and defending a "company" position. As such, they are amoral actors who simply argue for *any* position taken by business leaders. The in-house and law firm lawyers who worked for Enron are often cited as sad exemplars of blind, unquestioning defense of corporate actions that sacrificed the lawyers' independence on the altar of reflexive advocacy. Due to accounting fraud, among other things, Enron went bankrupt in December 2001, crashing to earth after flying too close to the sun as one of America's go-go energy and trading companies. The failings of the Enron lawyers include opinions approving sham transactions; opaque disclosure of those transactions to hide their purpose and effect; helping insiders secure inappropriate board waiver of conflict of interest rules; failing to disclose adequately compensation of senior officers obtained through improper self-dealing; and a pathetic noninvestigation of concerns raised to CEO Ken Lay by whistleblower Sherron Watkins.[14] The failures of the lawyers to ask hard questions or analyze the issues fairly is ascribed, in part, to their uncritical support of positions taken by forceful, if unethical, business leaders. Is such supine and uncritical advocacy inevitable? Of course not.

Although the role of the Enron lawyers was indefensible, it does not prove the point that independent judgment is not possible inside the corporation. Indeed, the charge really has the sequence backward. Advocacy does not preclude independent analysis. Independent analysis first, of the sort I urge here, dictates the type of advocacy.

Two cases from my experience illustrate the point.

In the first matter, GE personnel in Israel in the early 1990s were involved in a fraud against the U.S. government in the foreign military sales program. This program provided U.S. funds to Israel to buy U.S. military equipment (in this case, GE aircraft engines on U.S.-made jet fighters procured by the Israelis). Once we heard about the matter and conducted core fact-finding, it was obvious that GE employees had committed fraud and misappropriated U.S. government funds. The company undertook an extensive investigation, terminated or otherwise disciplined a score of employees, and implemented wide-ranging system reforms. It made the investigatory findings available to the Justice Department, the Securities and Exchange Commission (SEC), and congressional investigators before resolving the matter with criminal penalties, civil fines, and candid testimony about company failures before an aggressive House investigatory subcommittee.

In the second matter, by contrast, the company chose to fight a criminal price-fixing case the Antitrust Division of the Justice Department brought against GE's industrial diamond business (long since sold). Going to trial in a criminal case was a highly unusual step for a corporation, and management hated seeing GE's name above the fold in newspaper accounts of core antitrust violations. But here, after a thorough inquiry, the company believed that the government allegations were wrong. Fortunately, this decision was vindicated when the trial judge directed a verdict after the close of the government's case (failure to prove an element of the crime) and before the company had put on its defense.

In both instances, analysis dictated advocacy. This story is not aberrant but very typical of how General Counsel of the inside counsel revolution actually operate—or should operate. Not automatically or blindly defending the corporation, but, instead, focusing on the specific facts, undertaking in-depth analysis, and then making decisions/recommendations that are appropriate to the context. In one case, GE believed its integrity was protected by admitting fault, severely disciplining those responsible, and repairing broken systems. In the other, GE believed its integrity was advanced by going to trial in a case where criminal liability did not, in its considered judgment, exist.

G. **AN** IMPORTANT CONSCIENCE OF THE CORPORATION

Because the point is so important, it is worth emphasizing that the General Counsel as lawyer-statesman is, ultimately, **an** important conscience of the corporation when being technical expert and wise counselor to the board of directors, the CEO, and other business leaders. The General Counsel is a proactive voice in those settings—asking hard questions, helping to find accurate facts, providing independent analysis of issues, helping develop legitimate options, and making recommendations about the "right" course. She is not, to repeat, a subservient actor—simply following orders without independence of thought. She is, instead, an important actor in key discussions and debates in the endless drama of what a corporation should do to achieve high performance, to act with high integrity, and to manage risk soundly.

One leading General Counsel has argued General Counsel should not puff themselves up and argue that they are **the** conscience of the company. But he does not cite any prominent General Counsel who has said this. More importantly, after creating this straw man, he goes on to downplay the General Counsel's role in such debates, at times minimizing the GC function as being just an "honest broker," who merely summarizes disparate views. In tone, emphasis, and substance, this view is wrong in my view, as I argued strongly at the time.[15] No, the General Counsel is not **the** conscience of the company. That responsibility lies, in most cases, with the CEO or the board of directors. But, as lawyer-statesman, she has a prominent, *proactive* role in being **an** important conscience of the company in the innumerable settings where the final decision will be made by the CEO, the board, or some other senior leader. The GC introduces new issues and perspectives that should be included in decision making. And after presenting analysis and options, her voice should be heard directly and candidly about the proper course of action, *not muffled by some meek bureaucratic role in summarizing the views of others as a mere executive secretary.* She is not *the* voice, but she is more than one of many voices. She must be constantly mindful of her role as *an* important conscience of the company, concerned always about what is "right." (Of course, when the General Counsel is the ultimate leader—the last person making a decision for the company—then she does act as *the* conscience of the corporation, but even in those situations, the results are ultimately reviewed by the CEO and the board of directors.)

When acting as *an* important conscience of the company, the General Counsel and inside lawyers must address the most fundamental issue for inside counsel—the partner-guardian tension—to which I now turn.

3

PARTNER-GUARDIAN REALITIES

A. THE TENSION

The greatest challenge for General Counsel and other inside lawyers is to reconcile the dual—and at times contradictory—roles of being both a partner to the business leaders and a guardian of the corporation's integrity and reputation. Successfully resolving this tension is essential if a company is to attain the fundamental goal of fusing high performance with high integrity and if the General Counsel is to act as technical expert, wise counselor, and effective leader in realizing the broad lawyer-statesman ideal described in Chapter 2. *The inside counsel revolution is premised on resolution of the partner-guardian tension.*

General Counsel have failed as guardians. In the 21st century's first great wave of scandals, beginning with the collapse of Enron and WorldCom, the recurring question was: "Where were the lawyers?"—echoing a query from scandals past. In-house counsel were excluded from key decisions. They failed to ask probing questions about whether problematic actions were legal or appropriate. They passively rubber-stamped improper business decisions. But, compared with CFOs, they generally escaped formal sanctions. In a subsequent wave of investigations relating to options backdating, General Counsel were, once again, squarely in the middle of corporate improprieties—and in the line of fire. Formal investigations, indictments, settlements, pleas, and convictions of inside lawyers resulted. In notable cases, both the GC of Apple and the GC of Google were sanctioned by the SEC. Moreover, in another high-profile U.S. corporate scandal, the General Counsel on numerous occasions "touched" the use of "pretexting" to investigate leaks from the board of directors at Hewlett-Packard (obtaining phone records of directors through subterfuge and misrepresentations). But she was incurious about probing the legality of the pretexting practice and indifferent to its ethical propriety, even though the practice was fraudulent on its face. Insecure about her position, she was over-eager to please the board chair who was intent upon finding leakers. The GC was ultimately forced to invoke the Fifth Amendment at a congressional hearing and to resign, although, unlike another HP law department colleague, she avoided indictment.[1]

The Enron debacle, the backdating scandal, and the Hewlett-Packard "pretexting" case are just part of a parade of horribles where inside lawyers, in their eagerness to "partner" with business leaders, failed utterly in their responsibilities as guardians. Siemens, Wal-Mart, and GM are other examples (discussed later) in which General Counsel and inside lawyers, in their eagerness to appease business leaders, failed miserably as guardians with great damage to their corporations. And, there are a rising number of instances in which General Counsel and inside lawyers have been found culpable in criminal investigations, in SEC inquiries, in other enforcement actions, and in private civil actions because, in essence, they were supine in the face of business pressure or complicit in improper acts, failing, for example, to report problems up, to make adequate disclosure, or to act honestly in litigation.[2]

In the view of some commentators, exemplified by Professor John Coffee in his recent book, *Gatekeepers: The Professions and Corporate Governance,* General Counsel and other inside lawyers will inevitably fail. While well placed to play a broad guardian role, they simply lack "independence" because they are subject to "pressure and reprisals" from business leaders. Too often, Coffee contends, they also lack a strong reputation outside of the company to give them power to stand up to the CEO. To critics, the unceasing stream of major corporate scandals demonstrates that inside lawyers will inevitably be weak and compromised.[3]

By contrast, the New York City Bar Association's "Report of the Task Force on the Lawyer's Role in Corporate Governance," issued in November 2006, states that "the role of the general counsel of a public company is central to an effective system of corporate governance." (Disclosure: I was one of many people interviewed and cited by the Task Force.) The Task Force used corporate scandals, not to argue that General Counsel were always compromised, but rather to argue that these events demonstrated the need for strong internal disciplines and for a strong General Counsel to help integrate them into business operations. Similarly, the former Chief Justice of the Delaware Supreme Court, in a recent book, has argued powerfully for the General Counsel's essential role as a guardian of a corporation's integrity, endorsing the partner-guardian formulation I have long advanced. These are among the many voices maintaining that a strong guardian role for the General Counsel is both desirable and feasible.[4]

I do not believe that the choice for general counsel and inside lawyers is to go native as a yea-sayer for the business side and be legally or ethically compromised, or to be an inveterate naysayer excluded from key discussions and decisions and from other core corporate activity. Indeed, I think being both an effective partner of business leaders and respected guardian of the corporation is critical to the performance of each role. I deeply believe that this fusion is possible. But, for this to occur, very real obstacles must be overcome and certain key conditions inside the company must exist.

Building on my discussion of the practical lawyer-statesman ideal, I will, in this chapter, describe in more detail the affirmative fusion of the partner and guardian roles, discuss the key obstacles blocking integration of those roles, outline a number of different ways in which those obstacles can be overcome, and reserve for the end of the chapter a discussion of the most important obstacle/solution—the General Counsel's relationship with the CEO. This relationship is best understood when all other aspects of the analysis are on the table.

For purposes of this discussion, I posit that the General Counsel should be a direct report to the CEO, as is the normal case in the United States. But, in Europe and other parts of the world, that direct relationship may not exist, with the Chief Legal Officer reporting to the Chief Financial Officer or to some business leader under the CEO due to a cramped view of inside lawyers. I also believe that General Counsel should have a direct, unfettered relationship with the board of directors, as, again, is often the case in the United States.

B. THE FUSION

Acting effectively as a technical expert, wise counselor, and accountable leader and possessing broad knowledge and complementary competencies is the predicate for the General Counsel to function as a partner-guardian on both legal and business issues. In the optimal situation, the CEO and board of directors *explicitly authorize* the GC to act as both partner and guardian energetically and seamlessly to help create value, protect integrity, and manage risk. The CEO and board will seek a GC who can act on a broad array of issues of priority concern to the corporation. To effect the vital partner-guardian fusion, *the CEO and the board should ensure that the following conditions exist.*

- As partner-guardian, the General Counsel must have a *broad scope of responsibilities* to address the myriad business and society issues facing modern corporations. This means involvement, at the highest levels of the corporation, as expert, counselor, and leader in business, law, ethics, reputation, communications, risk, public policy, governance, and corporate citizenship.
- As partner-guardian, the General Counsel must have a *deep and broad understanding of the corporation's business activities in the context of the broader geopolitical environment* so that their role as expert, counselor, and leader occurs in the most sophisticated, multi-faceted context. The lawyers need to understand all aspects of a corporation's competitive and technological posture. As described by one thoughtful commentator, this business knowledge encompasses the five factors Michael Porter, noted Harvard

Business School professor, has said are essential to commercial success: "buyer power, supplier power, the current threat posed by current rivals, the availability of substitutes, and the threat of new entrants." The inside lawyers need to be financially literate on general issues of accounting. They need to be fluent in the company's own language of financial terms and acronyms used in every aspect of business from investor pitches to the "Management Discussion and Analysis" (MD&A) in the Annual Report to the company's method for analyzing deals to ways of evaluating resource allocation and capital expenditures. Increasingly, CEOs and boards of directors are seeking business knowledge and acumen in the corporation's General Counsel and its leading lawyers (indeed, among all lawyers). Simply stated, in addition to law, ethics, and public policy, corporations want their lawyers to be savvy about finance, technology, products, markets, geographies, competitors, and other major non-legal factors that affect business opportunities and risk.[5]

- As partner-guardian and as a senior officer of the corporation, the General Counsel should be *fully informed about high-level and high-priority issues facing the company both in the near term and in the longer term.* The General Counsel should be a regular attendee at the key business meetings that occur on a regular rhythm at the CEO level: annual strategic reviews of core business units; annual budget reviews; regular (often quarterly) updates with senior business leaders; and the frequent meetings of the top officials at corporate headquarters, often with the title "Executive Committee," to review top company priorities. He should also be involved in preparing the CEO's major presentations to analysts and investors. He should participate in top of the company decision meetings on all major issues, including vital "early warning" sessions, which systematically seek to anticipate a wide variety of risks and opportunities. And, he should (as is the normal practice in U.S. companies) attend all board and board committee meetings (perhaps with the exception of the management development and compensation committee). Attendance at all these core corporate meetings may not be possible given the General Counsel's own leadership responsibilities. But the CEO's standing invitation to those meetings should be immutable. Having a cross-business and cross-functional perspective is essential for the General Counsel. Such comprehensive access should also be mandated for other senior lawyers in the corporation at an appropriate level. For example, the General Counsel in a particular division should be involved in all the unit's regular strategy and budget reviews and in key decision meetings. The senior tax counsel should attend core meetings not just of senior company lawyers, but of senior company financial leaders. The senior M&A lawyer should attend the regular reviews of potential deals that the CEO convenes and, as possible, key business development meetings of the major business units.

- In *planning and decision meetings* with the CEO and top business leaders, *the General Counsel may function **both** as a lawyer and as a business person in being a partner.* As a lawyer, the GC is being a "partner" in finding effective, lawful ways to achieve legitimate corporate goals. In this legal capacity, the General Counsel has an important perspective on almost any major corporate strategy decision or any important operating decision: from acquisitions/dispositions to new products to new geographies to hard personnel decisions to major changes in company contracting to the host of legislative, regulatory, and litigation questions facing the company. In carrying out this fundamental task of giving legal advice, as I have emphasized, the General Counsel must argue, at a minimum, for following the letter of the law under a reasonable (not strained, narrow, or hyper-technical) reading of the relevant formal rules. *This legal role at decision meetings of insisting on following the law is the absolute core—which must never be compromised—of being General Counsel.*

- But, as a smart, informed generalist, the General Counsel can also be a "partner" by *bringing to the table other "wise counselor" perspectives—from "spirit of the law" and ethical and reputational issues to broader corporate strategy and business issues* (e.g., identification of risk, assessment of counter-party motives, helping define the key trade-offs in the deal terms of major transactions).

The GC must know when he is crossing over from being a lawyer proffering legal advice to a broader business counseling role, giving up the attorney-client privilege and making his comments subject to private discovery or government inquiry. And he must provide clear guidance and demarcate clear safeguards so that all inside lawyers can distinguish when they are serving as legal experts giving legal advice and when acting as business counselors providing broader strategic advice. At "decision meetings," all participants, except for the CEO, come with their unique perspectives (finance, HR, manufacturing, head of a business unit), but all, including the General Counsel, should try to advance discussion and debate by offering productive ideas as wise senior company leaders—beyond their expertise as heads of staff functions or business units. These broader perspectives help the CEO make a decision that integrates all relevant factors. In my experience, the CEO and other executives were very receptive to counsel participating in core business discussions, not just as "experts" but as "counselors," if the lawyers were knowledgeable about the broad business context and constructive about broad business issues.

- As partner-guardian, the General Counsel and inside lawyers obviously *play a vital role in implementing major strategic and operational objectives that create value and competitive advantage.* These include such issues as doing outstanding due diligence, negotiating the legal terms of key deals, simplifying contracts of general application, working on product development teams, reducing outside legal costs, and achieving public policy measures. Indeed, virtually every legal area in the corporation creates value and is vital to commercial performance. The tax function reduces the corporate tax rate to the legally appropriate minimum. The IP function protects and defends core technology assets. The labor and employment function participates as a full member of the team negotiating labor agreements. Antitrust counsel obtains clearance across multiple jurisdictions in large transnational deals. International counsel helps global operating units navigate the shoals of conflicting commercial laws in numerous countries. Litigation counsel defends the company (or settles cases) in high-profile matters—and may bring suits on the company's behalf. Environmental, health, and safety leaders can improve business processes by helping to introduce safety and quality that reduce costs and avoid expensive problems. This litany is virtually as long as each and every one of the company's value-creating activities. Moreover, there may be instances in which the General Counsel and inside counsel play a business role in implementation, such as acting as a business, not just legal, negotiator on major cross-border transactions or representing the company in meetings with customers or licensees or suppliers or governments on a broad range of company issues. There is little question that General Counsel and inside lawyers who "can get things done"—either in a legal or business capacity—to implement company performance goals in a legal and ethical way are able to develop great credibility with the board, the CEO, and other senior executives.

• The General Counsel as expert, counselor, and leader has *a vital job as guardian in devising and then implementing measures to protect the corporation's integrity and manage its risk. The guardian role is front and center in all the corporate settings previously described: strategy and budget meetings, decision meetings, and implementation efforts. But it also involves a host of specific tasks that must be integrated into business processes.* This GC guardian role encompasses such issues as compliance, ethics, risk, public policy, governance, and corporate citizenship, each of which I discuss in a subsequent chapter. It involves raising hard, uncomfortable issues. It involves, further, being a systems and process leader. The point here is that the General Counsel must have a lead role in addressing these issues on an ad hoc basis *but also* in ensuring that they are systematically addressed and solidly integrated into business processes that are owned by business leaders. Again, the trust built up by the General Counsel and inside lawyers as partners on performance decisions and on company execution give them great credibility in working with executives to address integrity issues and integrate them into business processes.

- In all these activities, the General Counsel as partner-guardian, along with the CEO and other senior officers, *needs to define the framework of appropriate internal governance and the proper approach to checks and balances in all aspects of corporate decision making and corporate action.* The values of speed and efficiency are important for corporations operating in a highly competitive world. But these values must co-exist beside the need to ask and answer important questions—to integrate checks and balances into corporate activities—and to find the right balance between creativity/innovation and risk assessment/risk mitigation. Addressing this issue head on is an important aspect of the partner-guardian role—working with the CEO and senior leaders to develop a system of checks and balances across multiple areas of corporate activity that are neither too confining nor too lax but are, in the context of the business and environment in which it operates, just right.

A leading commentator has summarized the partner-guardian fusion: "As a result of this dramatic shift, during the last quarter of the twentieth century, '[g]eneral counsel, not law firm partners [became] the 'statesmen' to chief executive officers (CEOs), confidently offering business as well as legal advice.'" [Brackets in original; footnotes omitted.][6]

C. THE OBSTACLES

But there are many potential obstacles inside corporations that might undercut a seamless partner-guardian fusion for the General Counsel and other inside lawyers. These obstacles can also apply to other senior staff leaders in Finance, HR, Compliance, and Risk who also have important guardian as well as partnering responsibilities.

- *Lack of understanding about law and policy among businesspeople.* Given possible limitations in their education and experience, business executives may understand neither how law works nor all the ways lawyers can create value and protect the corporation.

A lack of vision about the potential contribution of lawyers can bar adoption of a partner-guardian role.

- *Negative attitudes about lawyers at the top of the corporation.* The CEO and senior executives may hold many outdated, even antediluvian, negative clichés about lawyers. Lawyers are risk-averse. Lawyers are just a cost center. Lawyers are "Doctor No's" who are incapable of being constructive. Lawyers will never understand business. Lawyers, in short, are a barely necessary evil.

  Not surprisingly, if the senior business team has these negative attitudes or if bad lawyer behavior has created such attitudes, then many or all of the key elements of partner-guardian fusion may be hard to achieve for the General Counsel and other senior lawyers: narrow scope, limited information, no presence and role at key decision meetings, no involvement in key operational issues, no clout in seeking to advance the integrity of the company.

- *Negative attitudes about lawyers in middle management.* Even if top management has a positive view of the General Counsel and senior lawyers as partner-guardians, middle management may still have negative attitudes toward the inside lawyers working for them in their smaller profit-and-loss (P&L) centers in difficult environments all across the globe. These P&L leaders are often under harsh pressure to make their numbers. The combination of negative attitudes and unrelenting performance pressure can subject field lawyers to a very pinched, technical role divorced from the business and can lead to limited influence and impact. They may face overbearing and critical reactions in the field when they attempt to raise integrity issues or issues involving other types of risk. This problem is accentuated when lawyers are serving in remote places in foreign nations (e.g., rural Indonesia or India or China), with attenuated links to (or attention from) higher-level corporate or business unit leaders.

- *Negative group pressures in decision meetings.* Even if attitudes toward lawyers may be positive, the group dynamic in tense business meetings may shut lawyers down or frighten them into silence. CEOs are often impatient and want to make decisions, even big ones, swiftly. Other direct reports may routinely support the CEO for a combination of business or political reasons. In these situations, it can be very hard for the General Counsel (or other inside counsel) to raise fact questions, try to get more time for decision, raise broader considerations, or actually debate a group of senior executives aligned against the GC. (Only half-jokingly, I often urged GE lawyers periodically to watch the 1957 film, *Twelve Angry Men*, where a lone juror, played by Henry Fonda, resists group pressure to convict and ultimately sways the jury to acquit in a murder case.)

- *General group pressures of working inside a corporation.* There is a risk that lawyers' independence will be compromised by their conscious or unconscious socialization into the business organization, which may have a set of values more oriented toward performance than integrity. In particular, if companies are focused on short-term maximization of shareholder value, then lawyers may internalize this viewpoint at the expense of other nonfinancial or long-term performance, integrity, or risk perspectives. Obviously, it is highly desirable for inside counsel to be integrated into the business organization, but not at the price of compromising their independent point of view. This problem of a powerful group ethos can be a special problem in societies that value deference to authority.

- *Problems of working for a single client.* Unlike lawyers in private law firms who often work for many clients, the General Counsel works for a single client. Some argue that this fact, combined with pressures to conform, can lead to a pinched view of the world when seen through the lens of a single product or single industry. The single-client focus can thus impact the independence and broad view of "what is right" that is so necessary in a General Counsel.

- *Conflict between advising the CEO as business leader and advising the board as representatives of the company as a whole.* It is, of course, fundamental that the General Counsel represents the corporation, not the CEO or any particular individual the company employs. The board as a whole is viewed as representing the company, and when the General Counsel advises them in their collective capacity (not particular directors in their individual capacity), he is advising the company. Potential conflicts between the board and the CEO pose an obvious problem because the General Counsel works day-to-day with the CEO but owes ultimate responsibility to the company as embodied in the board of directors. For example, the CEO may zealously advocate an acquisition in an emerging market but not completely describe the legal and reputational risks the GC thinks the board should understand.

- *Lack of broad lawyer training/over-specialization.* Lawyers employed in corporations may not have had broad education and training in the different roles of expert, counselor, and leader or in the "complementary competencies" so essential to being an effective inside lawyer-statesman and partner-guardian. This lack of appropriate education and training can result from the continuing narrowness of most legal education and the continuing failure of law firms and corporations to understand the roles of contemporary lawyers and prepare them properly (e.g., for cross-functional, global, or management roles). It can also result from the pressures in the legal profession to specialize and thus to have only a narrow, very technical perspective on the world. Specialists, in particular, may not be skilled at asking a generalist's broader, more probing questions about business issues because their energy and experience has been spent mastering a narrow—extremely narrow?—domain.

- *Fear of being fired by CEO as an at-will employee.* In the United States, many General Counsel do not have employment contracts. They are hired by the CEO and report directly to him. They serve at will, like all other inside counsel. The fear of the "death sentence" reprisal—being irrationally or unfairly fired— is another potential obstacle to providing the necessary broad, wise, and independent advice in the fusion of the partner and guardian roles. This fear may also be a serious constraint on an important related trait: a willingness to question, challenge, or disagree with the CEO on critical issues of performance or integrity or risk. General Counsel cannot do their job if they operate under the constant fear of the CEO firing him *without* cause.

- *Fear of financial benefits loss; possible demotion or lack of promotion.* General Counsel earn a wide variety of financial benefits:

salary, bonus, stock options, restricted stock units, deferred compensation, and long-term incentive plans. They also have the expectation that these benefits will be constantly refreshed—and often increase—over time. Obviously, the A-bomb of being fired creates one type of fear, but there is the related fear of the tactical nukes: losing earned benefits that have not vested and losing the chance to earn additional benefits in the future. The amount of earned benefits can be in the millions or tens of millions of dollars, as can additional future benefits. Fear of losing these benefits is another potential restraint on the GC or inside counsel's willingness or ability to act as uninhibited partner-guardian. Getting cross-ways with the CEO can also lead to a GC demotion, either explicitly or implicitly—by having responsibilities diminished or access to key meetings limited. These harms of being fired, demoted, or denied financial benefits are also a risk for all other senior lawyers if their relationship sours with the CEO or with relevant executives.

- *Fear of injury to reputation.* A General Counsel who has a fight with the CEO also risks reputational damage with both internal and external constituencies to whom the CEO may speak. A reputational war with the CEO is a nightmare. The General Counsel may be constrained by the attorney-client privilege and, even if able to discuss failings of the CEO, the GC is likely to be diminished in a public wrestling match. Such fears of conflict with the CEO may cause inside counsel to speak softly and carry a small stick.

- *Potential conflict of interest about personal compensation.* In contrast to the inside lawyers' fear of being fired or having their benefits otherwise reduced is the risk that the lawyers will not provide their best judgment on issues because they want to increase their compensation. Whether it is salary increases, more stock options, increasing the value of the company stock, or a quest for other financial benefits, General Counsel and other inside lawyers may support business steps that skirt the law or are not "right" in order to stimulate questionable "performance" that increases their compensation at the expense of "integrity." Worse, such financial incentives may prompt them to engage directly in corrupt acts.

I have purposely painted a bleak picture of factors that can seriously undermine the General Counsel's ability to resolve the partner-guardian tension. All these obstacles to a constructive and seamless fusion of the partner-guardian roles can exist in complex organizations. In all human endeavors and relationships, the worst case is always possible—and a CEO–General Counsel engagement that starts out with sweetness and light can always turn sour and dark. There is, of course, no guarantee that a General Counsel and inside lawyers will successfully fuse the partner-guardian roles. No matter what we write or say in books, articles, company codes, employment commitments, corporate guidelines, CEO speeches, or job interviews, there is an inevitable contingency—or even tragedy—in human affairs.

But, given all the *external factors* that have led to the General Counsel's rise in stature, power, and prestige (see pp. 10–15), I believe that the "horribles" I have described here, while possible, are not likely to occur in most modern, major global corporations. Among other things, the striking increase in the importance of "business in society" issues demands a GC partner who can help navigate, as a corporate guardian, the shoals across the world of changing legislation, regulation, government investigations, enforcement, civil litigation, stakeholder demands, NGO critiques, and media attention. *Thus, the board of director, CEO, and business leader impetus for hiring a General Counsel who is a big player and for fusing the partner-guardian roles is driven by the realities of the marketplace and society, not just the power of a conceptual ideal.* In the rest of this chapter, I describe specific, additional *internal conditions* necessary to increase the chances that the partner-guardian tension can be resolved. But, if it cannot, the General Counsel must be prepared to resign and give up unvested financial benefits.

D. THE GENERAL COUNSEL'S CHARACTER, REPUTATION, AND IDENTITY

General Counsel success as a partner and guardian begins with certain key *character traits* beyond the core legal and complementary competencies that are fundamental to roles of technical expert, wise counselor, and effective leader. I could offer a laundry list of General Counsel "virtues" but, in my experience, four are vital.[7]

First, the General Counsel must have a strong sense of *independence*. This entails exercising and expressing judgments in the corporation's best interest independent of relations with the CEO, connections to other senior executives, or the General Counsel's own personal interests, especially financial interests. More affirmatively, it means an unbending insistence that the actions of the corporation comply with a fair interpretation of the law. It means an unyielding insistence on putting the "is it right" question front and center in all decisions and actions. It means an unflagging devotion to inculcating the corporate values of honesty, fairness, candor, trustworthiness, and reliability in all corporate employees.

Second, the General Counsel must have the *courage* to speak out, even in pressured situations and even when he may be a lone voice in a group of powerful people. Courage is often required when the General Counsel has to resist giving the quick, simplistic answer that executives often demand in fast-moving, complex situations. CEOs are often in a hurry. They may bridle at allowing time for needed legal analysis. They may not have the patience to listen to a nuanced presentation on the various risks involved and the various options available. Moreover, some of the toughest problems come in the form of crisis management, not stately, strategic decision making. The courage to stand in front of the tank is essential.

Third, however much they need to be independent and courageous, General Counsel must have *tact* in contributing their views and must act in a constructive manner that is firm but not offensive. General Counsel and other inside lawyers must live by the cliché of being able to disagree without being disagreeable. This is not easy when confronted by powerful executives who may be angry and aggressive, especially at those, like GCs, who do not readily kowtow. Effectively saying "no" or "wait" depends on place (in the meeting or afterward), form (offering other options is key), and style (when to duke it out or just make the point, without arguing it, and hope the CEO hears). Without question, knowing when, as well as how, to express independent perspectives and judgments is an invaluable trait.

Fourth, the General Counsel must also have *credibility and trust* so that his business superiors and peers believe that, although they may disagree, they appreciate that the General Counsel is trying to do the right thing for the corporation (and for them). This credibility, of course, comes from their experience with the GC, with the GC's effectiveness on both performance and integrity issues. A new GC, without a record, faces special difficulties if immediately faced with hard issues and a skeptical (hostile?) CEO and group of senior executives. Credibility and trust also stem from the skill to listen carefully and to communicate, both verbally and in writing, with clarity and conciseness: the ability to get to the essence of the matter, to pose issues in a crystalline way, to explain trade-offs succinctly, and to speak with confidence and authority (but not with arrogance). Most importantly, when more facts and analysis are truly needed before a decision, GCs need to engender CEO trust so that they can explain in a compelling, not overly complicated or academic, way why this is so, without being seen as just "bottle-necking" or "ass-covering."

In addition to these four character traits, the *professional reputation* of the General Counsel *outside* the company enhances his capacity to function as partner-guardian *inside* the corporation. A person who has occupied a position of prominence prior to corporate service brings such a reputation—a former Attorney General or Deputy Attorney General, a former federal appellate or district court judge, the counsel to the President or Vice President, a leading partner in a leading law firm. But an inside lawyer may also develop such a reputation by his prominence in bar activities, by being a national spokesperson on a particular issue (litigation, tax, trade, labor, and employment), by representing the company in major business association matters, by teaching or writing, or by *distinguished service as inside counsel in another company*. A strong professional reputation also helps the GC serve as a true "institutional intermediary" to external parties like investors or creditors or regulators and to vouch for the integrity of corporate representations and actions—a function that, in turn, can enhance the role of the General Counsel inside a properly led company. Such an institutional intermediary is acting as lawyer for the corporation, in the broadest sense, seeking to do what is right in the company's enlightened self-interest. This depends on a person being trusted by outsiders to give a balanced, honest view of facts or law or policy position, not a skewed one that, in the language of the street, was simply "bought." A sterling external reputation can thus be an important complement to the key traits of independence, courage, tact, and trust for a true partner-guardian role inside the corporation.

Finally, in addition to character and professional reputation, the General Counsel *needs to be explicit with his peers and his superiors about the core identity as partner-guardian* that he and other lawyers aspire to assume inside the corporation. The GC should not shy away from articulating his vision of such a role in the company. This starts with underscoring the corporation's goals of high performance with high integrity. It entails expressly discussing and implementing with senior executives the conditions of the authentic partner-guardian fusion set forth earlier, including scope of responsibilities, the integration in the business culture, having access to information, participating in business decisions, and helping a corporation in executing on its key objectives. The General Counsel must believe in this partner-guardian identity to his core and seek explicit consensus about it at the highest levels of the company.

A General Counsel may have the essential character, reputation, and identity I have just described. To function as a true partner-guardian, he must, in addition, forge working alliances with other main actors in the enterprise: the members of the legal department, senior corporate leaders, the board of directors, and, of course, the CEO.

E. PROTECTING OTHER INSIDE COUNSEL

The partner-guardian imperative applies to all the lawyers in the corporation, not just to the General Counsel. Whether hired from firms, recruited from government, or promoted from within, the company's lawyers—from lead specialists and division counsel to line lawyers across the globe—gain credibility for the legal function as a whole by being strong business partners. They also, of course, must serve as guardians in their direct dealings with peer business leaders at all levels of the enterprises, especially in the heat of battle.

To protect inside lawyers and to buttress their ability to function as partner-guardians for the company, not just for their particular business unit, the General Counsel must establish a living, breathing legal organization "protocol" under which division general counsel and other inside lawyers report their "concerns" about important commercial, legal, ethical, risk, and reputational issues directly up the line. In a decentralized legal organization, business lawyers work directly for business leaders. But even in a centralized legal organization where all lawyers technically report to the General Counsel, lawyers may be "embedded" in the line businesses and have strong relationships with the operating people in that business. Having direct, working relationships with business leaders is vital. But, regardless of whether they work in a decentralized or centralized legal organization, senior lawyers, reporting directly to the General Counsel (on either a direct line or dotted line basis), must also raise promptly with the GC any concern with major implications for a major division or for the company as a whole. The GC must also make clear that line lawyers should report to the General Counsel immediately if they are not receiving adequate attention in their business units. Formal governmental or ethical requirements to "report up" are important but narrower mandates. For example, the Sarbanes-Oxley Act requires certain inside lawyers (those representing the issuer before the Securities and Exchange Commission) to report threatened or actual material violations of relevant securities law or of fiduciary duties directly to the General Counsel. The Model Rules of Professional Conduct (adopted in many states) require, among other things, that inside lawyers refer an actual legal violation inside the corporation to "higher authority," including the General Counsel.[8] This is well and good.

But the protocol for "up-the-line reporting" in the legal organization, which I consider a best practice (and which we sought to institute at GE), is far broader. It involves "concerns," not just the likelihood of material violations under the securities law or actual violations under the Model Rules. The threshold for "reporting up" is thus much less strict; it should involve all lawyers across the globe, not just U.S. lawyers appearing and practicing before the SEC or operating under professional codes enacted by the states. And those concerns should not just be legal issues, but a broad array of issues that deserve analysis and discussion because they can significantly impact the health of the corporation in such areas as ethics or country risk or serious personnel issues. The reporting should be both to senior lawyers or the GC directly *and* to the company ombuds system (where broad concerns are formally docketed, staffed, followed, and closed out as discussed later). I periodically sent an e-mail to *all lawyers* in GE saying that, if they had an issue of concern and were not getting an appropriate response from their business unit, from the ombuds system, or from their senior lawyers, they should send an e-mail directly to me describing the problem. They should mark it "urgent." Or they should pick up the phone and call me directly. The purpose of this broad "reporting up" protocol was to make absolutely clear that inside counsel, while seeking to be partners to their business leaders, should also be a check on a variety of sensitive issues facing the company. In the four corners of the globe, often far away from the headquarters legal group, they also needed support to be guardians, sometimes lonely ones at that.

The General Counsel must earn the trust of the division General Counsel to make this reporting structure work (and the division counsel must earn the trust of the line lawyers). The GC must truly be available to senior inside counsel—to listen, to ask questions, to test ideas, to suggest possible actions, but *not* to assert immediate control over the matter, *not* to substitute his judgment, *not* to run to the CEO and burn the division counsel with the division leader. If, in the GC's judgment, the issue is significant and the company CEO should know immediately about a matter, then the GC should allow a very short period of time for the division business counsel and the business leader to bring it forward themselves to company headquarters and top company management. Failing that, the GC must go directly to the CEO. Such sensitive matters often must be managed jointly by "corporate" and "the business" because of the serious company-wide implications.

In return for that trust from the GC, division counsel and line lawyers must, in good faith, follow the protocol and report serious issues up to the GC. These attorneys cannot hoard sensitive information or overzealously guard their relationship with their business leaders. They should err on the side of disclosure under a broad "significant concern" standard. They cannot become "homers" or "go native." In my view, repeated failure of division counsel to discharge this broad (if judgmental) reporting obligation to the General Counsel is a firing offense (we never had to fire anyone for this at GE). An occasional if not constant failure is cause for a compensation hit (this did happen at GE).

Of course, the protocol for reporting up and down the legal organization is made possible not just by a shared ethos but by the power of the General Counsel over the promotion and compensation of both senior lawyers and line lawyers, whether direct reports or dotted line reports, whether in a centralized or decentralized law department, as I will discuss in detail in Chapter 10 on the legal organization (see pp. 374–380).

In sum, the General Counsel is ultimately responsible for reconciling the partner-guardian tension throughout the legal organization. In nearly 20 years of hiring senior lawyers at GE, a critical issue for me was whether they could work well with the business leaders as partners. But just as critical was the issue of whether I could also trust them to communicate honestly with me, and never forget that the good of the company—not the "good" of their business unit nor their business leader—was their ultimate concern as partner-guardians.

F. ALLIANCE WITH OTHER STAFF FUNCTIONS

The Finance, Human Resources, Compliance, and Risk functions inside corporations have partner-guardian responsibilities that are analogous to those of the Legal Department. They need the same involvement in the core activities of the corporation, and they face the same obstacles in attempting to fuse the partner and guardian roles. The heads of Finance, HR, Compliance, and Risk must be strong, independent actors in the web of shared corporate power and authority. They need similar character traits as I urge for the GC, a similar strength of reputation, and a similar strong sense of identity as both a partner and a guardian.

Legal, Finance, HR, Compliance, and Risk are essential elements of the company's nervous system. They connect, and signal to, all extremities of the corporate corpus. If they can act in alliance and support each other, the chances are greatly enhanced that these separate staff functions can overcome the obstacles to the partner-guardian fusion each faces alone. This is especially so when there is close cooperation between the General Counsel and the Chief Financial Officer. Recall that I have defined the first element of corporate integrity as adherence to the spirit and letter of formal rules legal *and* financial. The integrity of a company has as its foundation *both* the accuracy of its financials and its compliance with law. The fundamental compliance activity is heavily dependent on the GC and the CFO. Both must be deeply committed to performance, but in the right way. *Close collaboration and cooperation—and ideally close friendship—among these staff leaders is a critical aspect of real, effective corporate governance that has not received enough attention.* But there is always a risk that the occupants of these critical positions—Legal, Finance, Compliance, Risk, and HR—will be courtiers of the King, subservient to CEO whims.

It is hard to overstate the importance of these core staff leaders and the people all across their functions viewing their ultimate responsibilities within the same performance, integrity, and risk frame. They may, of course, not agree on specifics, but the deep commitment to broad corporate citizenship will have an incalculable effect on the framing of the myriad discrete issues that hurtle at corporate leadership at speeds from fast to warp. In my tenure at GE, I worked with two nationally recognized CFOs, Dennis Dammerman and Keith Sherin, and a superb head of HR, Bill Conaty. One of the most important, and memorable, parts of my GE career was our collegiality, our respect for each other, our commitment to a high-performance company that always sought high integrity (even if it didn't always achieve it), and the global cooperation of our respective staffs on a *vast array* of difficult problems.

G. THE BOARD OF DIRECTORS

In their oversight of the corporation, the board of directors must make clear both internally and externally that the fundamental mission of the corporation is the fusion of high performance with high integrity. Although many boards believe in the centrality of integrity, not enough articulate it forcefully and clearly. Opportunities to do so exist in the director-authored compensation section of the Proxy Statement, where integrity may often appear as an afterthought in the justifications for CEO pay. More importantly, in keeping with this mission, the directors need to make integrity an essential element of executive training and an explicit, fundamental specification when carrying out their most important job, choosing the CEO. As part of that specification, the board needs to clearly articulate, for the company and for external constituencies, that it seeks a CEO who believes in the partner-guardian vision for senior executives, especially the Chief Financial Officer, the General Counsel, and the head of Human Resources. Again, very few boards of directors actually do this, even though they may believe it. I will discuss the General Counsel's relation to these and other salient issues of corporate governance in Chapter 8, but here I want to emphasize the discrete aspects of the board relationship that bear directly on the General Counsel's ability to be both partner and guardian.[9]

First, the General Counsel should have constant and direct relationship with the board as a whole, with board committees (except perhaps compensation), and with individual directors. The General Counsel should be part of the board culture—attending board dinners, accompanying the board on business trips in the United States and abroad, and participating in board outings. The General Counsel should attend all board meetings and all board committee meetings, often as secretary to keep minutes. But, in addition to taking minutes and making formal presentations at the board or the committees, the General Counsel should speak out independently (if judiciously), either to clarify a matter or, at times, to express a view on a decision. The GC should not be a timorous underling. As part of the board culture, the General Counsel should develop relationships with individual directors and be available for one-on-one conversations to explain company activities when the director does not want to take CEO time. But the General Counsel should *never* be a member of the board in his corporation because of conflicts of interest (can't be both lawyer and client) and the incessant need to recuse himself from board deliberations.

Second, the board of directors should have oversight of both the hiring—and any firing—of the top staff officers, including the General Counsel. Although the CEO should, of course, formally hire the GC who should be a senior, direct report, the CEO should seek the advice and consent of the board on a small slate or on the favored candidate before an offer is extended. The board contact can be the lead/presiding director or members of the Audit, Risk, or Comp Committees. Ideally, the designated board member(s) would also interview the leading candidate for the General Counsel position. If the relevant board members have profound doubts about the CEO's GC choice, they should be able to prevent the hire. But otherwise, if the candidate is in the target area, they should defer to the CEO because of the intense CEO-GC relationship. This meaningful advisory role in the hiring process stems, of course, from the basic principle that the General Counsel's client is the corporation as embodied by the board of directors.

Similarly, the board of directors must clearly require that the CEO consult with the board before a General Counsel is fired or otherwise separated. This not only imposes a slight procedural delay so such an action is not taken in a fit of pique, but it also gives the board the opportunity to understand the circumstances and to ensure that the General Counsel is not being fired for attempting to be guardian or for generally speaking up on legitimate issues. Just the existence of this process provides some protection for the General Counsel from an intemperate firing decision (although how much will depend on how independent the board is from the CEO). But if the CEO really wants to get rid of the GC and is not complicit in some wrongdoing, then that separation will occur. This board role *in advance* of either hiring or firing the top staff officers, including the GC, should be explicitly raised by the board and understood by the CEO. It could also be reflected in the corporation's published governance principles or governance commentary.

Third, the General Counsel should report regularly to the board of directors or to one of the committees (Audit, Risk, Public Affairs) on key issues relating to performance with integrity and sound risk management. Subjects could include trends in the number of formal governmental enforcement actions (subpoenas/cases brought); detailed discussions of the most salient of those enforcement actions; trends, key issues, and results relating to matters reported into the company ombuds system; general litigation profile and trends; regular discussions of the cases with greatest risk (financial, reputational, precedential); the main take-aways or lessons learned from the annual business-by-business compliance reviews (in conjunction with the CFO and chief compliance officer); the results of compliance reviews by the external and internal auditors; and issues on the horizon that have emerged from the corporation's early warning systems. A striking example of what not to do apparently occurred when issues arose inside Wal-Mart about an extensive use of bribes in Mexico to expand its store locations. Despite discussions both in Mexico and in U.S. corporate headquarters among senior lawyer and senior business executives, the board of directors was not informed, according to news reports. The issue was sent back to Mexico for a quick and unceremonious burial. It only rose from the grave some years later when a whistleblower laid bare the seamy affair in a front page *New York Times* story. (See pp. 163–168.)

Fourth, the General Counsel should meet alone with the board as a whole or with the Audit or Risk Committee at least two times per year to discuss any issues of concern to the GC or to answer any questions from the directors. This procedure should be established by the board—just as the Audit Committee meets alone with the CFO, the head of the internal audit staff, and the external auditors. Making this private meeting a board initiative avoids—or at least mitigates— erosion of the critical trust that must exist between the CEO and the GC. Ad hoc meetings, especially if requested by the General Counsel, would be out of the ordinary and could be seen by the CEO as a potentially disabling act of disloyalty (although such meeting must be requested in extreme circumstances). The subjects of these regular, private meetings can include more detailed, "bark off" evaluations of the matters subject to periodic reporting to the board or entail communication of sensitive information that has been reported up through the legal channel.

As with the protocol I suggest for "reporting up" by inside lawyers to the General Counsel, the formal periodic reports on integrity and risk issues and these less structured but regular private meetings together constitute a more inclusive and appropriate method for General Counsel "reporting up" to the board than requirements imposed by law (i.e., Sarbanes-Oxley) or mandated by the Model Rules of Professional Conduct (i.e., Rule 1.13). Of course, the General Counsel should ensure that those narrower, more formal requirements are met—and evidence of certain potential or actual violations of law are reported to the board—but a much broader, much more regular relationship will give the board a far better feel for integrity issues that are on the horizon before they evolve into possible or actual violations, which must then be reported up under the law or the rules of professional conduct. The General Counsel would normally inform the CEO about the general topics of the private meetings with the board. But, this is a matter of courtesy, not an opportunity for CEO censorship. Hopefully, the CEO will already have knowledge of any integrity matters the GC discusses privately with the board, unless the CEO is involved in gamey activities or is failing to provide strong performance with integrity leadership. But there is no blinking the fact that these private board-GC meetings are a sensitive area in the CEO-GC relationship. That is why the board must insist that they occur.

Fifth, the Board should be involved in establishing the various components of the General Counsel's compensation. Several elements are vital to mitigate the risk that the General Counsel will be motivated to take improper actions in order to increase personal financial interests. All the elements of compensation—salary, equity grants, bonus, long-term incentives—should involve a clear component that rewards actions in support of corporate integrity. (For details, see pp. 280–307 and 363–370.) Much of the GC compensation should be spread out over time. Benefits like stock options, restricted stock units, deferred compensation, or long-term incentive grants that are awarded in Year 1 should not vest until future years so performance over time can be evaluated. And, like the compensation of all other senior leaders, the compensation of the General Counsel should be subject to the corporation's "compensation recovery" policies. If the General Counsel himself fails the integrity test in a significant way, the board can "hold-back" unvested benefits or "claw-back" vested benefits (see pp. 300–307).

The CEO and HR will design the compensation of the GC, CFO, and HR leader. But, especially with respect to these key staff leaders, the compensation committee or the whole board should review the structure of these packages carefully and explicitly approve appropriateness. Such an assessment may occur as a matter of course because many General Counsel and CFOs in major companies are now often in the "High Five"—the five most highly compensated employees—whose compensation must be disclosed in the Proxy Statement and who will thus be under careful board scrutiny. This approach to GC compensation should be a template for other senior lawyers in the company.

Sixth, the General Counsel must have the courage and judgment to recommend board retention of independent outside counsel when there are credible allegations of impropriety about the CEO or other very high-level executives who are peers of the GC. Even when the General Counsel has a strong reputation for probity, the appearance of a conflict of interest in having the Legal Department investigate the CEO or senior executives demands that the General Counsel advise the board on finding its own counsel to handle the inquiry. Unless the GC is personally implicated, board selection of independent outside counsel does not totally disqualify the General Counsel or the Legal Department. The GC and senior lawyers clearly can help the outside firm locate documentary and testimonial evidence. In light of the GC's knowledge of the corporation, he can review the findings of outside counsel to comment—but not edit—on issues that may have been missed or misinterpreted. He may give his advice on the ultimate disposition if asked by the board. But, he absolutely may not impede or interfere in any way with the process or substance of the independent inquiry by the board's outside counsel.

Use of outside counsel occurs regularly, of course, when a derivative suit alleging senior officer waste of corporate assets or other breach of fiduciary duty is filed. A special board committee is formed that hires its own special counsel. But the need for special board counsel can occur whenever there is an allegation from any credible source—including ones that come up through the company's ombuds system—that is both so significant and so factually specific about possible wrongdoing at the top of the corporation as to require additional investigation. Michael Holston, then Hewlett-Packard's General Counsel, acted in an exemplary fashion when Mark Hurd, HP CEO and a good friend, approached him with a letter to Hurd from plaintiff's counsel alleging Hurd sexually harassed a company contract employee. Holston immediately went to the board of directors, who hired special independent outside counsel. Holston told Hurd to get his own counsel. The directors eventually asked Hurd to leave as a result of the investigation. By contrast, Enron's use of its regular, highly compensated commercial law firm, Vinson, Elkins, to investigate allegations made by whistleblower Sharon Watkins to Enron CEO Ken Lay—and Hewlett-Packard's use of regular, highly compensated outside commercial law firm, Wilson, Sonsini, to help investigate HP board leaks—are examples of blatant conflicts of interest or very poor judgment on the part of the companies, their General Counsel, and the outside law firms.[10]

In addition to allegations against the CEO and senior officers, there are, of course, many instances where an independent assessment by outside counsel is needed to bolster the company's credibility with government officials. Typical examples are investigations or enforcement actions directed to major, widespread allegations of wrong-doing in the company that do not have direct involvement of the CEO or senior officers. The General Counsel should take the lead in identifying these situations and helping the CEO and the board either structure or oversee relationships with independent outside counsel retained either by the company or by the board itself (if the board concludes it needs separate counsel, in addition to both inside and outside counsel representing the company).

H. THE CEO

The right CEO is, of course, essential to successful resolution of the partner-guardian tension. Beyond having unquestioned personal integrity, the CEO must want to create a high performance with high integrity culture where most people want to do the right thing. But, *the CEO's explicit recognition and support of the dual partner-guardian role for the General Counsel and other top staff leaders—the Chief Financial Officer and the heads of HR, Compliance, and Risk—is a fundamental step in creating that culture.*

Such recognition can occur in a wide variety of ways. The CEO must hire people perceived both inside and outside the company as strong and independent to lead the key staff functions and to populate the senior ranks of those staffs. The CEO must make a demonstrable personal commitment to ensure that all the conditions necessary for fusion of the partner and guardian roles exist for the GC and other staff leaders—from a role with broad scope to information flow to involvement in decisions and to role in implementation. The CEO must encourage, not fear, a strong, independent relationship between the General Counsel and the board, its committees, and individual directors. The CEO must, at all meetings, even those occurring under high pressure, show respect for the General Counsel's point of view (even if the CEO doesn't agree) and not denigrate the GC. The CEO must give the General Counsel an important role at annual company-wide meetings of senior officers or general managers to talk about priority issues (geopolitics, law, ethics, public policy). Ultimately, the CEO must make clear to the company that the GC has a close professional relationship with the CEO—and has the CEO's trust and support—so that the General Counsel is viewed throughout the corporation as acting in the name of the CEO to carry out CEO objectives, policies, and vision.

Of course, a strong relationship of trust and respect must actually exist for the recognition and support of the partner-guardian to be authentic and credible. Without that relationship, the recognition is hollow—and will be seen as such inside the company. To achieve this, the CEO must believe deeply that the General Counsel and key inside lawyers are strongly motivated and highly effective in helping the CEO "win" inside the company and in the marketplace—helping the CEO to succeed by giving broad strategic advice and by assisting in implementing strategic goals. The CEO must believe deeply in the importance of the "wise counselor" role in providing the best possible analysis on hard problems and the best possible recommendation to aid the CEO (or the board) in making the best possible decisions on performance, integrity, and risk. Just as the General Counsel must understand business opportunities and risk, so the CEO must understand the opportunities and risks of law and ethics. The CEO must deeply believe in integrity, not just give lip service to that core idea but then undermine nominal commitment through winks and nods. So the CEO must, in his bones, want a General Counsel who is unafraid to speak his mind, with facts and care, but with self-confidence, force, and respect. The CEO must, in short, make clear to all that the CEO welcomes and wants the GC to be neither a "yea-sayer" nor "naysayer," but a strong, independent, and courageous voice to speak out about the GC's vision of the long-term, enlightened self-interest of the company—about what is "right."

The complex elements of chemistry and trust that must exist between the CEO and the General Counsel in support of the partner-guardian roles in a hard-charging global company are hard to describe and impossible to mandate. *The hard discussions of limitations and constraints in the present are made easier by business accomplishments in the past.* But successful resolution of the partner-guardian tension depends on that chemistry and trust, stemming from a shared vision about the fundamental mission of a performance with integrity corporation. My personal goal with the two CEOs I served—Jack Welch and Jeff Immelt—was to have a strong, respectful professional relationship built on their bedrock desire to have me honestly speak my mind on what I thought was in the broad interest of GE. Being a personal friend, while important, was secondary. I was very fortunate. Even when the discussions were intense or the stress was high, and despite their very different personal styles, they both wanted it straight. There is absolutely no question that any influence I had in GE was due to the general perception that I enjoyed the confidence and support of the CEO.

I. DEALING DIRECTLY WITH CEO RISK

Given the contingent nature of human affairs, the risks of working directly for a CEO always present a clear and present danger for the

General Counsel. To maximize their chances of being able to serve as a lawyer-statesman and a partner-guardian, General Counsel candidates must undertake serious due diligence not just about the CEO, but about the company. At the same time, to protect their personal integrity, General Counsel should never go to work for a CEO and a corporation unless they are prepared to resign and give up unvested financial benefits.

THE FRONT-END: DUE DILIGENCE

Although many aspects of the General Counsel's position have changed dramatically for the better in the past generation, one has not: GC job satisfaction is still largely dependent on the CEO. Being a General Counsel of a major global company is at least as fun, challenging, and intellectually rewarding as being a senior partner in a law firm (former partners turned GCs might say "more so"). But outside lawyers still have one advantage over GCs. They can fire the client much more easily than the GC can fire the CEO!

If the CEO-GC relationship is so obviously important, shouldn't GC candidates do careful due diligence on the CEO—and on the company itself—before accepting the job, especially at a time when corporations are beset on all sides by critics and when an integrity lapse can have catastrophic effects? The answer, of course, is yes. If few legal jobs are as good as being a GC in a good company with a good CEO, few jobs are worse than being trapped working for a CEO with questionable values in a company without a culture of integrity—of being ignored, being forced to do questionable acts, and being unable to escape without serious harm to reputation and pocketbook.

But how many GC candidates do systematic, in-depth diligence before signing up for a tour of corporate duty? I didn't. I flat-out flunked due diligence when Jack Welch offered me the job—and was lucky that it worked out. Such diligence certainly involves a detailed inquiry into the personality and values and integrity record of the CEO. But, it should also involve an examination of whether the CEO and the board of directors are committed to a lawful, ethical company—and how that commitment is carried out. This involves, in theory, an inquiry into the company's commitment to high performance with high integrity; into all the elements of the optimal partner-guardian fusion; and into the potential relationships with lawyers, senior officers, and the board. It can also involve an examination of how fundamental principles and practices relating to performance, integrity, and risk have worked on some of the key issues facing the corporation: emerging markets, government investigations, major pending litigation, acquisition diligence and integration, crisis management, public policy, and corporate citizenship.[11]

One obvious objection to detailed diligence is this: How can it be conducted in the company while the GC candidate is competing for the job? One obvious answer is that, on both sides of the interview table, there is both selling and assessing going on. Asking good, tough, sophisticated questions about the organization can help advance an applicant's candidacy because it reflects an understanding of how big corporations operate. Even more importantly, if offered the job, potential GCs can then ask for an opportunity to get a "better feel for the company" before accepting. They can get into more detail with key leaders in addition to the CEO (e.g., CFO, HR, Compliance and Risk leaders, selected business leaders, lead ombuds person, head of audit staff). It is also appropriate for the prospective GC to ask to speak to one or two members of the board (e.g., the head of the Audit or Risk Committees, although, as noted, the board itself should initiate such an interview as matter of course). The GC candidate can also run checks with people outside the corporation. There is also a significant amount of public material available that can inform the decision, including 10-Ks and 10-Qs, the annual, and quarterly SEC filings, which list some of the company's most important liabilities and cases, albeit in a summary, pro forma fashion. There is also something else that didn't exist when I started: Google (and other search engines). But, to state the obvious, this diligence must be undertaken with some delicacy.

When I was recruiting senior lawyers into GE, I would often say to the top candidates at the last interview that, while it was hard to know exactly where they were going to land, they should put on their star-spangled Evel Knievel suit, gun the motorcycle, and leap the chasm from practice or government to the corporation. Today, with business in society issues of far greater salience, with major integrity misses having calamitous impact, with corporate counsel in the gunsights of the regulators, and with the CEO relationship a crucial as ever, I might add to those being recruited as General Counsel: "But look—and look hard—before you leap."

THE BACK-END: RESIGNATION

Despite hopes of a happy marriage when the General Counsel starts work, the CEO can take umbrage at a wide variety of completely proper General Counsel acts (as opposed to poor GC performance) and the relationship can sour. For example,

- The General Counsel stands up to the CEO on important issues and disagrees in circumstances when the CEO is very committed to a position (and very emotional about it).
- The General Counsel "reports up" to the board of directors on a wide variety of risks or potential improprieties pursuant either to company policy and practice or to the requirements of SEC rules or to the strictures of the ABA's Model Rules of Professional Conduct. Given my broad view of the GC's additional, nonmandated "reporting up" responsibilities, such issues can go beyond serious risk of legal violations and include serious concerns about ethics or reputation or country/political risk.
- The GC can take a variety of actions in good faith that the CEO nonetheless judges harshly and that can impair the CEO-GC relationship because of stresses between the personalities or within the organization or in relations with outside institutions.

If these or similar events impair the CEO-GE relationship, the CEO has innumerable ways to undercut the General Counsel and make his life miserable due to the CEO's largely unfettered power at the top of the corporate hierarchy. When his role is reduced, or when his character is impugned, or when he sees serious company illegality or impropriety, the General Counsel must address the issues and not be passive. Broadly speaking, GC response to a difficult or intolerable situation can take place in three model scenarios (with real-world cases much more nuanced and complicated):

- *Good CEO and good board.* If the company has a good CEO and a good board, then the issues often involve disagreements and personal friction, but not impropriety. Decision making at the top of huge companies "ain't beanbag," as Mr. Dooley said about politics. But with a CEO who is committed to high performance with high integrity and with board support, the basic structure is in place for the General Counsel to work through tension by putting the issues on the table and perhaps using informal mediation by another senior staff officer or a leading member of the board until tough moments pass.
- *Bad CEO and good board.* The company has a CEO who is providing poor leadership on integrity issues or is implicated in bad acts. In this scenario, the General Counsel can report to the board on illegal, questionable, or negligent acts when direct recourse to the CEO himself is not possible or when it fails. The board can begin its own investigation with its own outside counsel. As this inquiry proceeds, the relationship between the bad CEO and GC is now probably beyond repair. The board can try to keep the GC in place until it decides on an appropriate disposition for the CEO. If this is not feasible or if the board decides the concern, while legitimate to raise, is not proven, the board can work out a separation agreement that seeks to protect the GC's reputation and financial interests. Or if the board determines that the CEO has committed the bad acts, then the CEO would go and the GC would remain. This occurred when Hewlett-Packard fired CEO Mark Hurd and retained General Counsel Michael Holstein, who had helped investigate Hurd.
- *Bad CEO and bad board.* The toughest case—and ultimate test of the General Counsel's character—is when both the CEO and the board ignore a General Counsel's concern about serious impropriety. If it involves certain types of threatened or actual violations of law (e.g., the company is about to commit perjury), then General Counsel is *permitted* to "report out" to regulators under a set of complex provisions in the securities laws and the Model Rules of Professional Conduct, which define an exception to the general rule of lawyer-client confidentiality.[12] But,

there may also be situations where the GC feels strongly that the company's actions are wrong but has no recourse to "reporting out," for example, when there is a serious ethical violation—like unsafe conditions in factories of third-party suppliers—or there is risk-taking that threatens serious harm to individuals or communities short of a legal violation. In either the "report out" or "no recourse" versions of this scenario, the General Counsel must resign if neither the CEO nor the board will address the serious illegality or impropriety. By taking a principled stand, the GC has impaired key relationships with "bad" actors. As important, his trust in the corporation's leaders has also been destroyed—and the leaders' view of the GC impaired. Remaining in the company is untenable, not least because the GC does not want to be implicated in improper behavior. But the GC's resignation will, in all likelihood, have severe consequences—from loss of significant financial benefits to loss of reputation when the CEO and the board criticize the GC. The obligation of confidentiality may prevent the General Counsel from fully explaining his actions. And his reputation may be sullied while the facts are sorted out by the authorities. It is possible that a separation agreement can be negotiated even with a bad CEO and a bad board. Or a wrongful discharge suit—or other action against the company—may be possible.[13] But, the General Counsel is clearly in a perilous situation. To retain his integrity, he has no choice but to leave. Resignation should never be threatened unless the GC is prepared to go through with it. But, when the circumstances warrant, the General Counsel, to protect his integrity, must resign.

When people consider becoming General Counsels, they should make detailed inquiries about the CEO and the company as I have suggested. But there are limits to what can be learned, and diligence at the point of hiring can hardly eliminate future risk. So, before accepting the job, General Counsel aspirants must also candidly and coldly consider the worst case. They must look hard in the mirror before saying "yes." They must be prepared to resign if neither the CEO nor the board will address properly serious bad acts on the part of the CEO or others in the corporation. They must anticipate defending their personal integrity, sacrificing substantial financial gains, and, perhaps, being bad-mouthed by the CEO and the board. They must consider the degree to which they may need to bring a wrongful discharge suit if separated for reporting up or out. The CEO-GC relationship should be one of trust, but it is inevitably one of power. The great advantage of coming to the General Counsel role from a position of prominence and with a high reputation in the profession and society is that this background may, to an extent, deter the CEO (and the Board) from undercutting the GC. This type of background also gives the General Counsel the advantage of not being dependent on the corporation, its only client. He will have the stature to find other ports of call of comparable importance, challenge, and remuneration after (if?) he has sailed out of the corporation and out of the storm.

But, I believe that an ever-increasing number of CEOs are acutely aware of the importance of fusing performance with integrity—and that an ever-increasing number of boards are exercising strong independent judgment on issues of integrity and risk, not just performance. In advancing the first two cases—good CEO/good board or bad CEO/good board—some might argue that I have defined the GC's problems with a CEO away. But I would argue that I have defined the problem. If we want performance with integrity companies, the place to begin—and to be most effective—is inside the company itself. Outside regulators can never be as potent—or as preventative—as internal governance on the front lines from the board of directors and CEO on down. General Counsels with experience, credibility, independence, guts, and reputation are key because, as even critics like John Coffee recognize, they are positioned to play a pivotal role as partners—and as guardians.

4

THE CULTURAL IMPERATIVE

A. PRIMACY

Without a powerful corporate culture, a company cannot fuse high performance with high integrity at all levels in all locations—from the gritty shop floor in Western China to the sleek headquarters tower in New York. Nor can the inside counsel revolution occur. Ultimately, the CEO must be fiercely dedicated to creating, leading, and maintaining a performance with integrity culture. The business executives at all levels of the corporation must have that commitment, intensity, and leadership. But, the General Counsel is a critical partner in the multiple, interrelated steps—the articulation of the aspirations and the implementation of the actions—so necessary to an authentic performance with integrity culture that binds together employees numbering in the tens of thousands or even hundreds of thousands. Without a strong culture, the efforts of the board, the CEO, the GC, and other senior executives will never catch up with the problems. As Lou Gerstner, former IBM CEO, said:

> Until I came to IBM, I probably would have told you that culture was just one of several elements in any organization's make-up and success—along with vision, strategy, marketing, financials

and the like . . . [But] I came to see, in my time at IBM, that culture isn't just one aspect of the game—it is the game.[1]

Culture may be simply defined: It is the shared principles (the values, the policies, and the attitudes) and the shared practices (the norms, systems, and processes) that influence how people feel, think, and behave, from the top of the corporation to the bottom, all across the globe.[2] But it is far harder to establish and sustain because it involves three never-ending complex and integrated activities.

First, the CEO—with the powerful support of the General Counsel, the CFO, the HR leader, and other senior executives—must *articulate in authentic terms the fundamental aspirations* of the corporation with respect to *performance* (outstanding products, meeting customer needs, ensuring growth, at good margins, in a competitive fashion, over a long time horizon, optimizing the interests of employees, shareholders, creditors, customers, suppliers, and other stakeholders), *integrity* (robust adherence to the spirit and letter of formal legal and financial rules; adoption of ethical standards that bind all employees; and employee embodiment of the core values of honesty, candor, fairness, trustworthiness, and reliability), and *the balance of disciplined risk-taking and sound risk management* in delivering performance with integrity.

The expression of these fundamental corporate principles or aspirations will take many written forms in all the basic documents of the corporation from the short to the long, from the summary to the detailed: for example, a code of conduct; a guide to the spirit and letter of core company policies; detailed guidelines for each policy area (e.g., antitrust, labor, and employment); the Annual Report; the Proxy Statement; a Citizenship Report; governance guidelines; and organic, accessible education and training materials. If just restated in rote form, the message becomes stale. If repeated in authentic, energized, and fresh form, the message helps create the culture.

Second, the CEO, with the powerful parallel efforts from the General Counsel and other senior executives, *must deliver the message of these aspirations directly through personal presentations to people inside and outside the corporation and indirectly through personal attitudes and actions.* Making the cultural aspirations and principles come alive through personal engagement is essential: at staff meetings, strategy sessions, decision meetings, budget reviews, and speeches to third parties. A cogent, consistent message delivered in person with authenticity and intensity is the essence of cultural leadership. So is personal behavior. Employees are exquisitely attuned to corporate hypocrisy, and when senior leaders' acts vary markedly from company values, the news spreads across the wired company in minutes. There needs to be a seamless consistency between leaders' personal attributes, their public and private statements, and their direct and indirect actions. High standards for employees demand high standards from senior leaders. No task of the General Counsel is more important than working with the CEO and other senior leaders on the forceful, continuous delivery of these core aspirations. And doing it herself. The mantra must be: "Do it, don't just delegate it. Live it, don't just preach it."

Third, the CEO, senior executives, and senior staff, including the General Counsel, *must develop and implement systems, processes, and practices—backed up with resources and driven by outstanding talent— that create an institutional infrastructure for integrating integrity principles into all performance aspects of the corporation.* The fundamental point is that the much-vaunted "tone at the top" is just eyewash, unless the CEO, the business leaders, General Counsel, and other staff leaders are committed to an institutional infrastructure with talented people, the right level of resources, key business disciplines, the metrics for ensuring required action, and corrective measures when steps are inadequate. Put another way, all the executive words, whether written down in core corporate documents or delivered with passion at employee meetings, mean very little without robust practices driven deep into business operations with real talent, real resources, and real consequences.

Combining core cultural ideas, authentic personal delivery, and an infrastructure made robust with talent and resources should, as a baseline, create a "negative" or "disciplinary" performance with integrity culture. Employees know about formal legal, financial, and ethical rules. They are concerned about violating them. They know if they are caught they will receive penalties—from pay cuts to demotion to termination. But, in the best companies, the integrity culture is largely "positive" or "incentive" driven. Affirmative values and norms are so widely shared—so credible—that people want to win the right way, want to perform with integrity. Peers model good behavior on the good behavior of peers. Such a culture is created as much (or more) with an appeal to aspirations, examples, authenticity, and incentives as it is with a resort to sanctions. The General Counsel should be intimately involved in these profound issues of "negative" and "positive" institutional design.

The shared principles and aspirations (values, policies, and attitudes) and the shared practices (norms, systems, and processes) must be uniform around the globe. The cliché "globalization through localization" means understanding commercial variation in order to develop appropriate products and appropriate marketing in distinct nations, provinces, or cities. But on the core values of the company and on the architecture of a robust, performance with integrity institutional infrastructure, the company must insist on a consistent message and a consistent approach worldwide. This must be so across varying business units, product lines, markets, and regions. There can be no geographic variation on these fundamentals. That would confuse people, appear hypocritical, and erode effectiveness. A company prohibition on bribery must be as strong in Beijing as it is in Boston or Brussels. Only a uniform and unyielding integrity culture everywhere in the world can defuse the integrity landmines that can blow up in the firm's face and that are not only buried at high levels, but can be found in all corners of the company. Again, helping shape this uniform global culture is one of the most consequential tasks of the General Counsel.

The ultimate goal of this effort should be keeping "bad acts" to an irreducible minimum through the blend of deterrence, aspirations, and incentives. The corporation is not going to repeal human nature. Individuals will commit illegal or unethical acts due to mistakes, negligence, recklessness, willful blindness, or intentional misdeeds. And, while the "stick" of the sanctions imposed by a disciplinary culture is an important deterrent, there are not enough internal cops on the corporate beat—and never will be. Nor can there ever be enough "rules" to cover all the risks facing a great global enterprise. The objective should be to make most employees, most of the time, sensitive to situations that *may* pose legal or ethical or reputational risk. And they should be trained to sense problems instinctively and to seek counsel on how to handle them, if they are not sure about a clear answer (no price fixing!). The hope is that this culture will prevent far too many people from doing far too many bad acts for far too long—prevent a major cultural breakdown—even though some sin in the city is inevitable.

B. THE PRESSURES THAT CORRUPT

One of the qualities of lawyers as great experts, counselors, and leaders is a gimlet-eyed view of reality. There are countless paeans to capitalism's virtues. But, in thinking about creating a performance with integrity culture, one must understand capitalism's vices. How can these be addressed?

The CEO, the General Counsel, and other senior executives must start from the proposition that there are pressures at the heart of capitalism that, if unaddressed and unconstrained, will cause corruption. Corporations set tough performance goals for divisions or product lines or regions: for example, net income, cash flow, return on equity, return on investment, economic value added, sales goals, product launch dates, stock price, and on and on. When retention, promotion, and compensation depend on meeting these or other "performance metrics," there is a significant temptation *and* opportunity to cut corners—to take illegal or unethical or otherwise improper steps—to "make the numbers." This temptation applies not just to individuals, but to corporate units or to the corporation itself. The "cutting corners to make the numbers" problem is as old as business.

The new global business environment exacerbates that ageless conundrum. For great global enterprises, more than half of revenues may come from sales outside the "home" nation, with a growing share from emerging markets. Those markets are characterized by endemic corruption, weak rule of law, and pervasive conflicts of interest. High-level officials in the public sector and high-level officers in the private sector often practice extortion as a way of business or governmental life. Winning major procurements or contracts may require use of shadowy "consultants" or "distributors" because the in-country counterparty will not deal directly with the employees of the corporation. Complex global supply chains pose a host of ethical issues. The temptation to make the numbers the wrong way in these tough global markets is a booster rocket to the historic pressures for corruption at the core of capitalism.

In making the case to the CEO and to other senior executives for the interrelated steps in creating a performance with integrity culture, the General Counsel can point to some of the most striking examples where corporations suffered grievous harm due to its absence. Here are thumbnail sketches of some prominent recent failures drawn from very different industries: automotive, heavy industrial, natural resources, financial services, and media. In these cases, the lead lawyers contributed to cultural failure and corporate breakdown. They were helpless, feckless, or complicit.

1. GENERAL MOTORS' IGNITION SWITCH[3]

In 2001, General Motors installed an ignition switch for the Chevy Cobalt that, it turned out, could accidently shut off the motor while the car was in motion. The car would then stall, disabling the airbags and impairing the steering and the brakes. As crashes occurred and injuries and deaths mounted, GM studied the problem. In 2006, an engineer secretly changed the switch design to address the problem in future cars. But, he did not change the part number or recommend a recall. Millions of previously sold cars remained on the road with the defective ignition switch. Finally, in the glare of national publicity, GM recalled the Cobalt and other GM models with the defective switch, but not until February 25, 2014. The ignition-related recall ultimately involved more than 2.6 million vehicles (and was followed by a record *26 million* total GM recalled vehicles in 2014). A subsequent GM compensation fund, directed by an independent attorney, Kenneth Feinberg, concluded at least 124 people had died in connection with the defective switch (at the time of the recall, GM put the number of deaths at 13) and more than 275 injury claims were valid. Expenditures to settle those and other cases exceeded $600 million following the recall (although other related cases remain outstanding).

To understand the failure to address the ignition defect, GM asked Anton Valukis, Jenner & Block partner and former U.S. Attorney, to answer a basic question: "How and why did it take so long for GM to recall the Cobalt?" His report, issued in May 2014, was a devastating indictment of the GM culture. In her remarks to employees on Valukas's findings, GM CEO Mary Barra said that the report is "brutally tough and deeply troubling," that the delay in the recall "represents a fundamental failure to meet the basic needs of . . . customers," and that there was "a pattern of incompetence and neglect." This pattern, she said, has two key components. First, "[r]epeatedly, individuals failed to disclose the critical pieces of information that would have fundamentally changed the lives of those impacted by a faulty ignition switch." Second, "numerous individuals did not accept responsibility to drive our organization to understand what was truly happening." There was a consistent "history of failures" to address ignition switch issues; "nobody took responsibility"; "there was no demonstrated sense of urgency, right to the end." According to Valukas, symbols of the complete cultural failure were the "GM Salute" (avoiding responsibility by crossing one's arms and pointing at someone else) and the "GM Nod" (nodding agreement to a proposed course of action but leaving the meeting with no intention of following through). This GM failure is especially striking when other systemic auto industry safety issues— the Ford Pinto gas tank explosions, the Ford Explorer/Bridgestone tire tread defects, and the Toyota stuck accelerator—had been major issues in the public eye in preceding years.

As a result of the report, 15 second-level individuals in the organization were fired, including the chief GM lawyer for safety, a lead lawyer for product liability litigation, and four other inside counsel. As a reflection of the broad cultural failure, the company also agreed to implement Valukas's 38 pages of detailed recommendations for systems reform in eight major areas. These reforms included such obvious steps as a product safety leader in the company to integrate all relevant processes quickly, an employee hotline, and a better process for elevating safety issues to senior management. As part of these broader changes, GM also adopted Valukas's recommendations for transforming the legal department. Again, these obvious reforms included improved identification of safety issues from technical reports and product liability suits, more frequent meetings to assess trends, and educating lawyers about their obligations to report problems up the line so that they are handled promptly and not ignored.

Although GM lawyers had a responsibility to defend the company in lawsuits, they had a higher duty in my judgment not to just do this reflexively but first to assess, with others in the GM organization, the risk to customers, an obligation the recommendations address.

But Valukas's report had a grave failing. After nearly 300 pages of analysis, it placed the blame on a broken bureaucratic culture. It failed to discuss, much less place, the responsibility for that broken culture where it belonged: on senior leadership; on the long line of CEOs, General Counsels, technology leaders, and product design and manufacturing leaders who should have created a healthy safety culture and robust safety processes that would have resolved the ignition defect problem long before 13 years had elapsed and significant loss of human life had occurred. Valukas's absurd defense of top executives in place at the time of the report was that they "didn't know" (he never looked at the role of senior executives in the past). But they should have known. And this includes the then–General Counsel who had been in his position from 2009 onward, a period when some of the most egregious failures to confront smoking guns about safety occurred. Ignorance is no defense for senior executives when this massive cultural failure is about the lives of people. And it is surely no defense for the General Counsel when the legal function is right at the core of the problem—with responsibility to determine if there is real liability due to design or manufacturing defects; to confront ethical issues about when the company should act to protect people, even though liability questions are not fully resolved; to push the organization to understand open technical issues; and to resolve them with all deliberate speed. CEO Barra refused to fire the General Counsel in May, after release of the Valukas report, despite many calls for his immediate resignation (including from me). But, following a drumbeat of criticism, he announced his retirement in October 2014, a symbol, like the "GM Salute," of the failed culture in one of America's most famous companies.

In September 2015, GM agreed with the Department of Justice (DoJ) to pay $900 million and to enter into a deferred prosecution agreement in order to settle criminal charges relating to concealing a deadly safety defect from U.S. regulators (the National Highway Traffic Safety Administration) and misleading consumers. The agreement imposes on GM an independent monitor to review and assess the automaker's safety policies, practices, and procedures. The DoJ will dismiss the criminal charges after three years if the automaker abides by the terms of the agreement. CEO Barra said, at the time of the settlement: "The mistakes that led to the ignition switch recall should never have happened."

2. SIEMENS BRIBERY[4]

During the past four decades, Siemens created about 2,000 bogus business consulting agreements to hide more than $1.4 billion in bribes to officials in 65 nations all across the globe. Using corporate slush funds and on- and off-book accounts, these bribes were used to win contracts for major Siemens product lines in health, power, telecommunications, and transportation. This came to an abrupt end in November 2006, when German officials conducted a dawn raid on Siemens offices and employees. Less than two years later, in December 2008, Siemens settled this towering bribery scandal in the United States and Germany with criminal pleas to U.S. Foreign Corrupt Practices Act (FCPA) charges of false books and records and failure of internal controls and to similar charges in Germany. It made an unprecedented payment of criminal penalties and civil fines to resolve the FCPA charges: $800 million to the DoJ and the SEC. It simultaneously paid another $528 million to German authorities. Eventually, Siemens paid approximately $2 billion in fines and penalties for these and other cases in other countries related to bribery during the relevant period.

According to charging and sentencing documents from the DoJ, Siemens exhibited every imaginable act of a failed global culture. There was no effective ethics training; no whistleblower outlet or protections; no effective restriction on use of "outside consultants" (a step rejected in 2000). Bribes were mischaracterized as legitimate consulting payments. The compliance and audit units were under-staffed and underfunded. Warnings from outside auditors and internal red flags were ignored. Some senior officers didn't follow up on a variety of warnings, and others were not disciplined when clearly complicit in wrong-doing. The Audit Committee of the board of directors was not given accurate information. Most importantly, senior management in Germany headquarters did not conduct serious reviews of business practices and, in fact, tacitly or explicitly promoted use of bribes by business units in far-flung regions. Said the DoJ in its Sentencing Memorandum: "there were knowing failures to implement, and circumvention of, internal controls up to the most senior echelons of management."

Beyond the payments for fines and penalties, the cost to Siemens was striking. The chairman of the supervisory board, who had recently been CEO, was forced to resign. His successor as CEO also left because the board would not renew his contract for the customary five years in the midst of a detailed internal investigation. Senior executives in charge of the major telecommunications, health care, transportation, and power divisions were terminated. So, too, the General Counsel and head of the audit and compliance functions were let go. Hundreds of employees across the globe were implicated—some were fired, and others received amnesty in exchange for full disclosure. Siemens paid almost $1 billion in forensic investigation costs to law firms and auditing firms. It had to take a $500 million charge for improperly deducting bribes as business expenses. In order to avoid debarment, it agreed with the World Bank to pay $100 million for anti-corruption projects with universities, think-tanks, and NGOs. A whole new senior executive team had to come in and right the ship while addressing the wrongs.

The new Siemens leadership spent enormous time and effort negotiating with the authorities and providing information during the government investigations (translated documents, the fruits of the forensic analysis, information collected on third parties). The new management team's first priority was to build a meaningful company integrity culture and to avoid debarment from government contracting. Steps included establishing an ombuds system; establishing central controls over bank accounts; constructing whole new systems of controllership, audit, and compliance; changing financial incentives; and introducing completely new education and training for global employees. The DoJ recognized the significant effort and allowed Siemens to plead to the most serious offenses through small subsidiaries and pay fines that were below the fines called for by the DoJ's own sentencing guidelines. It acknowledged the company provided "extraordinary cooperation in connection with past corporate conduct and has undertaken uncommonly sweeping remedial action in response to the discovery of prior misconduct." During the scandal, both the General Counsel and CFO were involved and failed to stop top management from condoning widespread wrong-doing. But the new General Counsel, working closely with the new CEO, had an important role both in negotiating with the governments around the world and in constructing a new culture in another old, well-known company that had gone far astray.

3. ENRON IMPLOSION[5]

Enron stands as one of the most vivid examples of a massive cultural failure because leaders were driven by greed and lacked an integrity compass. The absence of checks and balances—of vital systems and processes—led to a raft of improprieties. The board of directors waived the company's conflict of interest rules to allow the CFO, Andrew Fastow, to earn income not just from Enron but from special-purpose entities. These entities were back-stopped improperly with Enron stock. Enron borrowed money without properly recording it as debt and used the loan proceeds improperly as cash flow from operating activities. Its financial statements and other required disclosures obfuscated these actions, misleading shareholders, other stakeholders, and regulators.

All this was possible because every Enron function—from Legal to Finance to Risk to Operations—failed to ask hard questions and follow necessary institutional disciplines in making material decisions. Enron's lawyers, as noted, were totally supine in the face of business leader pressure. Their toothless opinions, opaque disclosures, blind support of conflict-of-interest waivers, and craven noninvestigation of serious whistleblower concerns were emblematic of a corporation that had bent and then broken under the pressures for corruption.

The result was one of the great collapses in American business history. In October 2001, Enron reported significant losses, including a $1.1 billion nonrecurring charge. Fastow was fired. And the SEC began an investigation. In November, Enron restated its earnings for the past five years and reported a loss of more than half a billion dollars. In December, the company declared bankruptcy. The stock, which had been $90 at the end of 2000, was $1 a share one year later. The debris flew everywhere. CEO Ken Lay, former COO (and briefly CEO) Richard Skilling, and former CFO Fastow were all indicted and convicted. Lay died before sentencing. Sixteen employees pled guilty. Twenty-thousand people were thrown out of work. Shareholders lost $80 billion in market cap. The directors were humiliated and forced to pay out of their own pockets to settle shareholder suits. Enron's outside auditor, Arthur Andersen, was found guilty of obstruction. Before that decision was overturned by the Supreme Court, the venerable accounting firm also collapsed.

Enron's code of conduct; its Finance, Risk, and Legal disciplines; and its board oversight were all a Potemkin village. There was no real aspiration of leaders to anything but their own enrichment. There was no effective infrastructure. The inside and outside lawyers should be pictured on a mocking "See No Evil, Hear No Evil, Speak No Evil" poster that hangs in the office of every inside counsel. The pressures for corrupt capitalism were unconstrained. The argument for a culture of performance with integrity is made with a bang by the implosion of Enron.

4. JPMORGAN'S MULTIPLE PROBLEMS[6]

JPMorgan Chase (JPM) reflects the challenges facing a huge global corporation with diverse lines of business—and illustrates the great costs when there is a striking failure to create a uniform integrity culture. From the beginning of the financial crisis in 2008 through mid-2015, the company has had to settle serious matters of depth and breadth, including the following:

- Improper disclosure relating to sale of mortgage-backed securities (settlements of $13 billion, $4.5 billion, and $300 million).

- Foreclosure abuses (settlements of about $6 billion and $2 billion).
- Money laundering (settlement of $1.7 billion).
- Failure of Madoff oversight (settlements of $1.7 billion and $350 billion).
- London "Whale" derivative improprieties (settlements of $920 million and $100 million).
- Improperly influencing LIBOR rates (settlement of $108 million).
- Improper currency manipulation through inter-bank collusion (settlements of $1 billion and $890 million).
- Energy market manipulation (settlement of $410 million).
- Failure to provide credit card customers promised products (settlement of about $400 million).

The headline $13 billion settlement of improper disclosure did involve, in important part, practices of other companies (Bear Stearns and Washington Mutual) that occurred prior to their acquisition by JPM. But JPM knew it was buying problems, paid fire-sale prices, had broad knowledge of questionable industry practices, and did not get a release of acquired claims. Moreover, that huge settlement also involved direct actions by JPM personnel. All the other settlements stemmed from actions of JPM employees and involved core, not esoteric, bad behavior: collusion, inadequate disclosure, money laundering, abusive behavior toward debtors, indifference to red flags of massive fraud. The disclosed cost in the five-plus years since 2010 of these matters is more than $25 billion, more than one year of JPM profits.

CEO Jamie Dimon and Steve Cutler, who was JPM General Counsel during this period (and former WilmerHale partner and former head of SEC's Enforcement Division), have reputations as high-quality people. But, as reflected in the broad array of serious and sizable problems, JPM's top management was unable to create a powerful culture and manage the pressures for corruption in a huge, far-flung global behemoth. Until recently, they and others in JPM had not right-sized the problem and effectively addressed the cultural failings, which led mid-level employees (and sometimes senior-level ones) to cut corners improperly in competitive, often global, businesses. Those failings are illustrated in particular by the London Whale trading fiasco, which led to $6 billion in losses and about a billion dollars in settlements. Although the "Whale" events occurred in 2012, four years after the financial meltdown, they eerily paralleled the causes of that crisis. The traders didn't understand the trades and doubled down when they went south. The Chief Investment Office that supervised them—and operated directly under Dimon—had inadequate reporting and risk controls and ignored red flags. So did the key controllership functions at the company level. Although Dimon originally said the matter was just a "tempest in a teapot," when the size of the losses emerged and the failures of the institutional infrastructure were revealed, Dimon himself concluded that "[t]hese were egregious mistakes. They were self-inflicted." And certainly the GC bears some responsibility as part of top management team concerned with compliance and risk.

More broadly, despite complaining, at times, about regulatory "piling on," Dimon has clearly acknowledged broader company failings and—with Cutler, a new compliance chief, and other senior executives—sought to remedy them. In letters to shareholders, Dimon acknowledged that addressing these issues was the company's number one priority. He hired more than 1,500 new risk employees and allocated several billion dollars to fixing the broken culture. He has said:

> *Adjusting to the new regulatory environment will require an enormous amount of time, effort and resources* . . . We have reprioritized our major projects and initiatives, deployed massive new resources and refocused critical management time on this effort. *We are ensuring that our systems, practices, controls, technology and, above all, culture meet the highest standards* . . . Eventually most of these new processes will be embedded permanently in how we conduct our business.[7] (Emphasis supplied.)

Yet, since Dimon wrote those words in his 2013 letter to shareholders, JPM and other banks have been caught up in yet another scandal—this one over illicit manipulation of foreign exchange trading, which led to major settlements late in 2014. And this for-ex failure sparked concerns from commentators and officials that the culture of huge financial institutions are inherently flawed because they are simply too big too manage, too big to create a powerful integrity culture with properly resourced and structured compliance and risk disciplines (see Chapters 5 and 7).

John Plender, long-time financial affairs columnist for the *Financial Times*, wrote in November 2014 that the foreign exchange scandal coming on the heels of the LIBOR rate rigging scandal showed that:

> The directors and top executives [of major banks] were in charge but not in control. Their response to earlier scandals had been hopelessly flabby . . . Meantime, traders left an incriminatory trail in the chat rooms. In effect, they are bonus-hungry hired guns who show no loyalty to their banks, customers or markets. They have . . . threatened the integrity of a systemically important market and undermined confidence in the wider financial system . . . Clearly the culture of the world's biggest banks is fundamentally rotten.

This view was echoed at the same time by William Dudley, president of the New York Federal Reserve Bank: The financial services industry is "not close to where it needs to be" in terms of culture and standards of behavior. He warned that banks risked being broken apart for failed cultures. Janet Yellen, the Fed's chairwoman, a few months later echoed Dudley's comments: "we expect firms to follow the law and operate in an ethical manner . . . Too often in recent years, bankers at large institutions have not done so, sometimes brazenly . . . there may be pervasive shortcomings in the values of large financial firms that might undermine their safety and soundness." And Lewis Kaden, former Vice Chair of Citigroup, noted

> a mounting concern about the institutional cultures and standards of conduct in the financial services industry—a concern rooted in the crisis, but clearly exacerbated by the succession of subsequent disclosures of fraud, collusion, and other unlawful conduct that have seemed to betray a pervasive breakdown in ethical standards, and have resulted in the imposition of fines,

penalties, and damage awards against the industry's largest banks and brokers in unprecedented amounts.

All these comments preceded a *second* round of civil and criminal settlements in May 2015 involving manipulation of foreign exchange markets ($5.6 billion), with criminal dispositions for four the parent companies (Citgroup, JPMorgan Chase, Barclays, and Royal Bank of Scotland), which agreed to plead guilty for conspiring to fix prices and rigging bids, raising even further questions about a recidivist culture in major financial services entities.[8]

5. NEWS OF THE WORLD: PHONE HACKING[9]

In Britain's highly competitive tabloid news business, the Sunday *News of the World* (NOW) stood out for its scoops based on seemingly confidential information. Following stories about Prince William's private conversations in 2005, NOW royal editor, Clive Goodman, and private investigator, Glenn Mulcaire, were investigated and charged with illegal phone hacking of royal voicemails. In 2007, they pled guilty and were sentenced to four and six months in jail, respectively. Andrew Coulson, editor of NOW, resigned the same day the guilty pleas were entered. Although police uncovered a trove of notes and phone numbers, no further official inquiries ensued. A "rigorous internal investigation" by NOW counsel concluded in March 2007 that Goodman acted alone and there was no systematic wrong-doing at the paper. NOW subsequently began, however, to settle phone-hacking suits quietly.

The lid blew off the cover-up in 2011 when News International, the UK parent of NOW and a subsidiary of Murdoch's global media company, News Corporation, publicly admitted numerous phone-hacking incidents and started to settle suits publicly. In June and July, other British newspapers alleged that NOW had hacked phones in highly sensitive situations: an abducted young girl subsequently found murdered, the families of soldiers killed in Iraq and Afghanistan, and the families of those killed or injured in the July 2005 terrorist bombing in London. In the furor that followed, advertisers pulled business from NOW. And on July 7, 2011, James Murdoch, Deputy for British Operations at News Corp, announced that NOW would cease publication.

Subsequent inquiries showed that phone hacking had been widespread for a decade, the 2007 investigation was a sham, and there had been an unchecked culture of illicit action (including questionable payments to the police) at NOW. Rupert and James Murdoch testified before a Parliamentary Committee later in July, and James acknowledged that News Corp and News International had failed completely in the 2007 investigation and had "wrongly maintained that these issues were confined to one reporter." In a full-page ad, Rupert said: "We are sorry for the serious wrongdoing that occurred. We are deeply sorry for the hurt suffered by the individuals affected. We regret not having acted faster to sort things out." But both statements were disingenuous. In an integrity culture, the leaders would have ordered a sweeping and effective independent internal investigation in 2007 *as soon as* one of their reporters had pled guilty to crime. The failure to do so was a classic case of ignoring the obvious on the part of both men. Such an inquiry, if it asked the most basic questions, would have disclosed how widespread the phone hacking was. But until forced out into the open by other reporting, the last thing the Murdochs apparently wanted to do was address the deeply entrenched culture of impropriety.

In addition to the shuttering of NOW, other damaging events followed the disclosures that NOW had engaged in widespread hacking of sensitive matters (murdered children, families of the war dead) for many years. Rebekah Brooks, a Rupert favorite, was forced to resign as head of News International (she had been editor of NOW during relevant periods). News Corp was forced to withdraw its offer to purchase the coveted UK television subscription broadcaster, BSkyB. James Murdoch was forced to leave his position overseeing News Corps' British media properties (*The Times* and *The Sun*). Les Hinton, who had been CEO of News International from 1999 to 2005, resigned as head of Dow Jones, a subsidiary of News Corp and publisher of *The Wall Street Journal*. A parliamentary investigating committee issued a report highly critical of the culture at NOW and its parent, News International. Andrew Coulson, former NOW editor and then advisor to Prime Minister David Cameron, was found guilty of a crime involving illegal interception of voicemails (Rebekah Brooks was acquitted). News Corp set up a blue ribbon internal Management

Standards Committee, which conducted further internal inquires and tried to resolve both public and private matters arising out of the hacking scandal.

The business pressures to increase scoops, circulation, and revenue—like business pressures in the other cases—twisted company culture to create a rogue organization. Until the scope of unlawful acts broke into the open in July 2011, the inside lawyers—joined by outside counsel in conducting the woefully inadequate investigation in 2007—simply helped sustain that culture by assuming a defensive, disingenuous crouch pursuant to the dictates of the business leaders.

These five cases in diverse industries (automotive, heavy industrial, natural resources, financial services, and media) are cautionary tales for boards, CEOs, GCs, and other senior executives in all corporations, but especially in large, complex global enterprises. And, as I was finishing this book in September 2015, Volkswagen admitted rigging intentionally up to 11 million diesel engines to defeat emissions standards on the road that those engines appeared to meet in testing. The failure was so blatant that the CEO of VW Group of America, not trying to avoid responsibility, said within days of the corporate admission: "It is clear our company betrayed the trust of you, our customers, our employees, our dealers and the public." Despite cultural failures of major corporations being in plain view, Volkswagen nonetheless engaged in striking, systemic, and improper behavior that would have severe adverse consequences across the world, including immediate CEO resignation, significant fines and penalties, and dramatic loss of reputation and trust.[10] Building a strong integrity culture begins with understanding how the fundamental pressures in a global economy on corporate officers, managers, and employees, if unconstrained, can lead to corruption and severe adverse consequences for the corporation. As Volkswagen shows . . . the beat goes on.

C. IMPOSING DISCIPLINE

When making presentations on performance with integrity to GE audiences, at professional conferences, and to law and business school students, I often begin by quoting GE CEOs. When addressing company executives, the CEOs would powerfully articulate core company values, pacing in the pit of the amphitheater and looking individuals directly in the eye:

- The company is built on trust—and high performance with high integrity is the foundation. That trust is of tremendous benefit.
- Each senior leader will be held personally accountable. It is your primary responsibility, through the right systems and processes, through creating the right culture.
- There will be *no* cutting of corners for commercial reasons—integrity must never be compromised to make the numbers.
- For those in this room—those to whom the rest of the company looks for guidance—one strike on first-order integrity issues and you're out. You can miss the numbers and survive. You cannot miss on integrity.

The company senior leaders took many lessons from these high-level meetings back to their businesses. But this key CEO message was always prologue and epilogue to the year's business narrative and was retold across the company (or, now, heard live by all employees via webcast). I used this story and this message across the company and across the world with all employees. It speaks about a fundamental company position in a way that gets people's attention. It is a message that applies to all corporations. It is, I think, a vital message all General Counsels can use.

It is also a message that iconic CEOs have delivered, using similar words, for years. In 1991, the leaders of Salomon Brothers Inc. resigned because the firm traded unlawfully in U.S. Treasury notes and because they had failed to act when confronted with that illegality. Warren Buffett became acting CEO of Salomon Brothers. At a 1991 congressional inquiry, he delivered a tough message to employees: "Lose money for the firm, and I will be understanding. Lose a shred of reputation for the firm, and I will be ruthless." Buffett has repeated virtually the same words for nearly 25 years in his annual memo to the senior managers of Berkshire Hathaway.[11]

When the rhetoric is then matched by tough but fair action, the signal sent across the company is received not just in the mind but in the viscera. *One aspect of the General Counsel's job that is not well understood: Every large corporation informally runs a huge internal justice system.* In terms of number of employees, GE had a larger "population" than the cities of Orlando or Buffalo during my years of service. Obviously, lots of personnel actions were resolved solely by HR and business leaders because they related primarily to business performance. But just as obviously, there was sin in the city, and so the meting out of punishment in this intra-company justice system was vital in underscoring the centrality of integrity, conveying the importance of fairness, and building the right culture. The legal organization, along with Finance, Audit, Compliance, and HR, developed facts and recommendations, but business leaders, up to and including the CEO, listened to the facts and the options and made the disciplinary decisions. Certain fundamental principles apply to these disciplinary determinations, principles the CEO must publicly embrace inside the company (so the staff isn't seen as unwelcome "cops"). But, the GC and CFO, in particular, play a key role in helping to give these principles operative force, not as "cops" but as wise counselors to the CEO in ensuring fairness and justice.

First, generals, not just the infantry, must receive discipline when they have acted outside company norms. This may seem elementary, but friendships exist across the top of any big institution, and peers may find it hard to sanction a person they have known for a long time. In decisions about how to discipline senior executives, the General Counsel can bring skill and knowledge about the severity of the offense and how it would be handled or seen outside the company. She can also work with the HR leader in assuring consistency across "like cases" inside the company, with higher standards of conduct often appropriate for higher-level officers. The General Counsel can also help present the "facts," the "standards," and company "precedents" to the board of directors. Ignoring executives' misdeeds or giving leaders a slap on the wrist has a toxic effect, corroding the respect of lower-level employees for the integrity message.

Second, acts of omission should be sanctioned, not just acts of commission. When an executive bribes to get business or retaliates against a whistleblower, those direct acts, of course, deserve discipline. Take the case of a senior GE business leader in Asia who was losing share and replaced his own sales force with third-party distributors who bribed to get orders. The leader failed to follow company due diligence on such distributors and, in fact, knew about the illicit practices of the new third-party sellers. He was terminated. But, when an executive fails to create a culture of integrity—a damning act of omission—so, too, should he be separated from the company. Take the case in which GE employees in a complex industrial business acquiesced in a customer's request to falsify sensitive data that, under the law, the customer had to send to regulators. Fortunately, this inaccurate data was not "safety critical" and no accidents occurred. But, before a company whistleblower surfaced the issue, the practice had gone on for far too long and involved far too many. The prolonged incident reflected the senior business leaders' indifference to integrity. Two individuals, who had headed this business over a period of years and who were officers of the company, were forced to leave. The principle was fundamental: Even though they had committed no offenses directly and even though they had been valuable company contributors, the senior officers were terminated because they failed to create a culture of integrity.

Third, when a first-order rule of an institution is violated, the person should be terminated without taking into consideration her past and future value to the corporation. There should be no balancing test. When Mark Hurd of HP lied about personal expense accounts to hide dinner meetings with a consultant, he violated a first-order rule of good corporations that financial data must be complete and accurate (even if the amounts are small and if other dynamics between Hurd and the HP board of directors were at play). Hurd was forced to resign, despite putting good HP financials up on the board. When a young bicultural, bilingual GE lawyer in Russia with a brilliant future used company funds on strip clubs and lied about it, he was summarily fired. His future value, which was great in a difficult business environment, wasn't taken into consideration. When a sophisticated and highly valuable senior international officer asks a young subordinate to have sex and she becomes distraught and reports the incident, he is summarily separated despite long service to the company and his role as a wise leader in global business. Or, in an analogous situation in a large organization (to put it mildly), Afghan Commander General Stanley McChrystal and his team gave unfettered access to a reporter. They then aired personal disputes relating to civilian authorities, made contemptuous comments about some of those authorities, and criticized the Pentagon policy-making apparatus and the Afghan policy itself. McChrystal was forced to resign. Despite a distinguished record and his critical importance in the Afghan theater, he had violated basic precepts of civilian control over the military and basic rules of the chain of command.

These cases illustrate the importance of sanctioning those offenders, at all levels of the organization, when first-order norms are violated. These rules—financial honesty, respect for subordinates, creating a culture of integrity, chain of command—are so central to the mission of the institution that when individuals cross those lines, they can just keep going out the door, regardless of their past, present, or future value to the organization. First-order corporate principles could not long endure if they can be trumped or compromised by other considerations in balancing tests. Hypocrisy kills. *This is a tough approach, but one that I believe is critical to an integrity culture.*

Such an approach is, of course, not self-executing. Each situation must be evaluated carefully to answer at least two vital questions. Did an improper action violate first-order standards? And what was the individual's intent? Because accurate financials are so central to the company's integrity and because leaders must drive this message home, Hewlett-Packard properly separated Mark Hurd, its CEO, for *knowingly* manipulating his expense accounts, even though the sums were small, indeed tiny compared to the positive HP numbers when he was CEO. At the other end of the spectrum, a person can obviously make a mistake (not a negligent or intentional act) in financial entries or in interpreting the law. The resulting sanction (if there is one) need not be the death penalty. But I want to be clear: If a first-order law or rule is violated due to negligence or some higher order of fault, the employee—from senior to junior—must go to create and maintain the right culture. A related point on the process is due. The General Counsel will need to decide whether counsel for the affected employee is allowed to submit a memorandum on facts, law, and standards as part of the disciplinary process. This is usually desirable if there is some ambiguity in the matter and can be decided case-by-case. These memoranda might prompt further investigation if employees' counsel raised new or convincing issues or might trigger further direct meetings between the lawyers to discuss the case. However, as General Counsel, I did not allow trial-type evidentiary hearings on internal disciplinary matters, which would be far too intrusive. If an employee wanted full due process, he could bring a wrongful discharge suit (although I hoped our fact-finding was accurate and our decision fully justified).

Fourth, a balancing test may, however, be appropriate in determining the exit package for an employee separated for fault in a first-order violation. The shape of that package will turn on the severity, duration, and impact of the problem and on the length and contribution of the separated employee. Both McChrystal and Hurd had constructive careers, sullied by acts of reasonably short duration and without major long-term impact on their institutions. As a result, they received most of the benefits they had earned. McChrystal was allowed to retire as a four star general. Hurd received a generous severance package of about $40 million (although he subsequently gave back a significant number of restricted stock units to settle a noncompete lawsuit brought by HP after he went to Oracle). Although Hurd's initial separation package may have been too rich, both he and McChrystal clearly deserved some severance for past accomplishments. But, in a case at the other end of the spectrum, an individual should receive little or nothing if she commits major fraud over a number of years that leads to major inquires, suits, restatements, and other damages to the corporation. Even in those cases, some relatively minor "financial consideration" for the terminated employee may be necessary in order to create a valid separation agreement that can have value for the corporation—requiring the employee to release all claims and to disclose all integrity issues to the company (so she doesn't raise them later). As I discuss later (see pp. 300–307), this determination about what is appropriate severance now takes place in the context of new laws and new company policies on "clawing-back" compensation.

Finally, the termination of senior executives provides extraordinary integrity teaching moments for the institution. They should be explained as clearly and forthrightly as possible. Hewlett-Packard did not meet that test. Investors and other stakeholders were surprised at Mark Hurd's sudden departure. But that understandable surprise was compounded by the company's confusing press release. It said that the investigation (by Covington and Burling) had not substantiated the contract employee's allegations of sexual harassment. It then only said the inquiry "did find violations of HP's standards of conduct." This vague statement about the resignation of a CEO—whom the market felt was highly successful—raised questions, rather than answering them. After the confusion sown by the press release, the General Counsel tried to clarify matters in a subsequent question-and-answer session with analysts by focusing on the expense account inaccuracies. But by failing to explain Hurd's leave-taking clearly in the official statement or in clear comments at the time of the release, the board of directors looked inept. From reading various materials relating to the matter, I surmise that, in addition to the expense account issues, Hurd basically lost the trust of the board during the month-long investigation into his relationship with the contract employee. The board could have initially (and generally) cited the expense account problems and conflicts in the investigatory process to note that they raised issues of integrity and trust. It would then have been more credible. By contrast, President Obama was quite clear when he accepted General McChrystal's resignation as the person responsible, under military mores, for his troops:

> the conduct represented in the recently published article does not meet the standard that should be set by a commanding general. That includes adherence to a strict code of conduct . . . That includes strict adherence to the military chain of command and respect for civilian control over that chain of command. And that's why, as Commander-in-Chief, I believe this decision is necessary to hold ourselves accountable to standards that are at the core of our democracy.

When GE terminated senior officers for failing to create a culture of integrity in the Israeli case (fraudulent expropriation of funds by a GE sales manager and an Israeli general) and in the complex industrial case (GE employees falsifying sensitive data at the request of the customer), the CEOs asked me to present these cases in some detail to the senior officers and managers at the annual strategy meetings. Transparency about discipline is important to the credibility of the company's commitment to integrity. I have spoken many times in my life in many venues. But I have never spoken to so rapt an audience. I was clearly delivering a message from the CEOs: "One bad apple will not blight your career. Individual employees can make mistakes or perform bad acts. But a cultural failure like the ones I am describing today and you are gone. You let your organization work on the dark side of customer satisfaction at your peril." These two cases—both involving improper behavior that went on too long and involved too many—were perhaps the most important decisions by the CEOs on integrity during my tenure at the company—and the most important communications on the subject to senior executives. They truly were teaching moments, just as the CEOs wished.

D. LETTING EMPLOYEES SPEAK— AND THEN LISTENING

If sanctions for individuals imprint an integrity culture through discipline, then giving employees voice to express concerns seeks to encode that culture through both potential discipline and through an appeal to aspiration and affirmation. Employees are encouraged to protect the corporation by reporting promptly to a neutral intake person any concerns relating to law, finance, risk, or reputation. Virtually every major corporation today has such outlets for employee concerns, whether they are called hotlines, whistleblower portals, or ombuds systems. *All are intended to counter another common vice in corporations—and all large institutions: a culture of silence where employees stand mute in the face of clear or likely wrongdoing.* Indeed, the cultural failures described earlier—and in virtually all corporate scandals—were due, in important part, to this culture of silence. They stemmed from the failure of people with knowledge or suspicions to come forward—or to have a place where they could come forward—and raise critical issues of concern.

Designing and giving real effect to channels for the expression of employee voice is another key task of the General Counsel and inside lawyers, working with other senior leaders. To defeat the deadly "culture of silence," certain elements of such a system are essential:

- The code of conduct and more detailed policy guides should encourage employees to report concerns. This message should be delivered across the company in every significant language. (At GE, the code of conduct and policy guide were distributed in more than 35 different languages.)
- A reporting of "concerns," not violations or probable cause of violations, is what is requested because employees cannot be expected to know the technicalities of the rules or policies. Rather, they should be asked to exercise common sense in reporting matters that bother them whether expressly covered in the policy guide or not. Over-inclusiveness in employee reporting is far better than under-inclusiveness. General Counsels need to assure business leaders and the board that a mere increase in reports shows confidence of employees in the system. That increase would only be a worrisome development if the jump in concerns reported was followed by confirmation of an increase in wrong-doing.
- Employees can report these concerns using their name or anonymously. And they can use any mode of communication: letter, e-mail, text, telephone, direct personal conversation. The concerns can be directed to a neutral ombuds staff person; to staff people in Legal, Finance or HR; or to their manager.
- All matters, wherever and however reported, are immediately put into the ombuds systems and tracked. Mechanisms should be established to report back to the employee on the status of their concern, including means that preserve an employee's anonymity.
- The company ombudsperson and her subordinate ombuds people are neutral and independent (although they may technically

report to the legal and finance functions). Their fundamental job is to receive concerns, assess the issue raised, and refer to the appropriate staff for inquiry (e.g., both legal and financial staffs for allegations of accounting fraud). A key personal attribute of people in this position is that they have the trust of employees.

- The ombuds staff keeps comprehensive records on the types of concerns, the units from which they came, the status of the inquiry, the time to completion, and the nature of the disposition.
- These records—and the trends they illustrate—must be shared regularly with the CEO, senior staff leaders, and senior business leaders. Importantly, the Audit Committee or the board itself sees these records either quarterly or twice a year.

Within such a system, there are four principles that must be rigorously followed: (1) Employees have a duty to report concerns. They can be sanctioned (up to and including termination) for failure to report a red flag of consequence. More than 15 employees were fired, each time, for failure to report in the major GE Israeli and industrial cases. (2) Retaliation against employees who report concerns—from verbal harassment to job actions to pay reductions—is a prima facie firing offense. (3) The Legal, Finance, Compliance, and HR staffs who investigate these issues must do so without fear or favor: following the facts wherever they lead—up, down, or sideways. If the matter genuinely involves concerns about senior executives, retention of independent outside counsel of high reputation is necessary, after consultation with the CEO and/or the board of directors (see pp. 80–81). (4) The company-wide and business-wide trend reports must be used by the board, CEO, and senior executives to identify problems and craft remedies as necessary (e.g., addressing a sharp increase in reports about possible bribery in Brazil). Under Sarbanes-Oxley, the Audit Committee of the board of directors also must establish its own hotline where employees can report concerns directly relating to accounting, internal accounting controls, or auditing matters.[12]

Perhaps the most famous whistleblower is Enron's Sherron Watkins. Ironically, the deep issue was not Enron's woeful response to her concerns, but Enron's even more woeful failure to have any meaningful ombuds system in place in prior years. In August 2011, Watkins met privately with Ken Lay, Enron CEO, after writing him a letter that set out the need for a restatement in light of Enron's business and accounting failures. Lay said the matter should be reviewed, but then sent it to Enron's outside law firm, Vinson & Elkins, with instructions not to examine the accounting issues that were at the core of Watkins's concerns. (She had warned that the company was about "to implode in a wave of accounting scandals.") The General Counsel, a former V&E partner, passively accepted the CEO's approach. He and Lay also rejected her request for an examination by independent lawyers and independent accountants. The V&E "inquiry" was superficial. The V&E "report," issued in an October 15 letter to the Enron GC, will have its own room in the corporate scandal Hall of Shame. It concluded that no further inquiry by independent lawyers or accountants was warranted. But, in the next paragraph, it speaks of concerns about "bad cosmetics," coupled with "poor performance," creating a "serious risk of adverse publicity and litigation." Within six weeks, Enron declared bankruptcy. The great irony of the Watkins letter is that it came far too late. Her issues could not be remedied without tanking the company. Thus, the real failure of Enron was not just the shameful treatment of Watkins's concerns. It was the absence for the years that preceded them of any avenue for any employee to express candidly to an independent office or to have explored fairly any of the myriad problems that sunk Enron.[13]

In addition to a serious ombuds system, an annual "bottoms up" review of employees is another important way to give employees voice on integrity issues. The process starts literally at the bottom of each business—on the shop floor of a factory in Indiana or Indonesia. Legal, compliance, risk, or finance staff meet with employees, either singly or in groups, and ask about any issues they see in the way business is conducted in the unit. These questions go to general systems or process issues. If the employees have more concrete concerns, those should also go into the ombuds system. This review then builds up through countries and regions, giving employees at all levels of the business unit an opportunity to express their views. It ends in a report on results for the global business division as a whole that prioritizes which policies, risks, systems, and processes have drawn the most questions or comments, often leading to recommendations for improvements.

Moreover, as noted in the partner-guardian discussion, the unconstrained voices from the staffs—legal, compliance, finance, and HR—must be heard through the special, unfettered channels in each function. The General Counsel, for example, should insist that staff lawyers at all levels of the legal organization report directly and immediately to her about "serious" issues with possible company-wide implications even when they are lodged in the ombuds system or raised in the annual "bottoms up" review. The GC should then exercise her judgment about whether the matter deserves special, higher-level attention or whether it should just stay in channels for the moment.

Finally, in addition to the channels previously described, corporations should pulse employee attitudes through regular survey techniques. As part of a periodic poll of employee attitudes, corporations can include scalable (1–5) questions about whether leaders cut corners to make the numbers, whether the unit has a culture of integrity, or whether they can raise concerns without fear of retaliation. The answers to these broad questions can indicate business units or geographies where there are issues requiring further inquiry. Alternatively, there are now sophisticated survey techniques that can ask employees, first, whether they believe a particular element of a code of conduct should be part of their business (e.g., no bribery) and, second, whether that element in fact exists in the business unit. This provides a more detailed road map to employee attitudes and to employee identified problems.[14] And, of course, focus groups under the direction of independent third parties can also uncover important employee perspectives and concerns about corporate culture.

A number of government programs provide "bounties" to internal whistleblowers who surface company problems in court claims (e.g., False Claims Act cases seeking compensation for exposing corporate fraud in government contracting) or in submissions to regulatory agencies (e.g., the Internal Revenue Service [IRS] or SEC). These legally mandated bounty provisions typically do not require whistleblowers to "exhaust internal company remedies" before bringing a claim to outside authorities. When Congress was considering a provision in

Dodd-Frank to reward whistleblowers who brought claims to the SEC, some members of the corporate community lobbied unsuccessfully for an "internal exhaustion" provision; an employee had to go first to the company's reporting system before going to the government. This effort was rebuffed, but the SEC's final rule did provide some incentives for a whistleblower to go to company ombuds programs first (e.g., the SEC will consider a bigger award if this happens). The question raised by these government programs is whether providing a bounty and not requiring exhaustion will undercut a corporation's attempts to give employees voice. One answer is that not all corporate hotline programs work, and these government programs provide an important outlet in such instances.[15]

But the more complete answer is that companies should create a performance with integrity culture and provide the best possible systems for ensuring employee voice. In such circumstances, I believe a high proportion of employees will use that program even without a bounty. Companies encourage internal reporting by a combination of sticks and carrots. I believe that reporting concerns is a basic duty of every employee and that employees should be sanctioned for a failure to report in instances where a serious possibility of wrongdoing was apparent. Because it is a fundamental employee duty, I thus do not believe that employees should automatically get a bounty for such reports. But, selective and visible recognition in special and important cases is justified, using sound executive discretion in deciding when appropriate. This can occur as a one-off event in a unit or business or can be part of the annual bonus in a compensation system that properly focuses on paying for performance *with integrity* (see pp. 280–307). In a company with a strong integrity culture, employees will often use the system because they support the company, because it is easier to access under very broad standards than the government programs (one need only report a "concern" in a variety of ways), and because they trust the system to investigate concerns fairly and thoroughly. If they instead choose to go into a government program and then prove their case, so be it. Wrongdoing will have been remedied. The existence of government bounty programs should provide an incentive for companies to do a better job of creating an integrity culture and providing employees with real voice.

In the early 1990s, not long after I became General Counsel, I went to see Jack Welch about starting an ombuds program. He was skeptical because GE was still in the midst of major restructuring: "people will just use the system to complain and moan." I responded with a quote from Lyndon Johnson: "Better to have them inside the tent pissing out, then outside the tent pissing in." We discussed the issue several times. After the last discussion, I said: "Ok?" He didn't say "yes," but he didn't say "no." I left the room taking his nonanswer as a "yes" but still with doubts. At that time, plaintiffs' lawyers were finding employees to bring False Claims Act suits in our Defense business, alleging contracting fraud. After we instituted the ombuds system, the number of False Claims suits against the company dropped to almost nothing.

My personal take, confirmed in many conversations with other General Counsel, is that giving genuine voice to employees throughout the company and treating their concerns with respect and professionalism is an unquestioned foundation stone of a self-cleansing integrity culture. This culture candidly surfaces what is wrong and candidly discusses what is right. It doesn't just detect. It also deters. An unethical business leader has to think twice before asking in a quarterly closing meeting that the business use improper accounting to make the numbers. Anyone around the table can lodge a concern in the ombuds system that will make her the subject of an inquiry. With a credible, professional program, these channels for employee voice are rarely misused and do not create a climate of fear and back-biting. Reporting employees know that their legitimate concerns will be handled independently, reviewed professionally, and decided fairly based on facts, not internal politics. They also know that cheap shots don't work.

E. AN INTEGRITY "LEARNING CULTURE"

Corporations often extol their "learning culture." Employees join a company to receive education in subjects that can advance their careers—finance, HR, marketing, sales, engineering, manufacturing, and technology. Another salient challenge for the General Counsel is to help make education and training on integrity as important and effective as training on other business subjects in a global company. Significant challenges exist because many business-oriented employees—especially those from emerging markets—are not naturally drawn to business and society issues they can find irrelevant, sterile, and boring. Integrity education and training is of signal importance for employees of acquired companies, especially those operating in emerging markets.

As a complement to the broad corporate aspirations senior leaders articulate, education and training on formal rules, ethical standards, and core values at a more granular level has three underlying purposes. It must create awareness, knowledge, and commitment so that employees at all levels of the company (1) understand their obligations; (2) do things right by acting on those duties; and (3) do the right thing by exemplifying honesty, candor, fairness, reliability, and trustworthiness. Working with other inside leaders and with outside learning experts, the General Counsel must counter directly the long-standing rationalizations that employees use for illicit or unethical conduct, especially in emerging markets: "It is the custom here; it is not really improper; no one will know; the company condones it; there won't be consequences." To counter these shop-worn rationalizations, powerful education and training programs must focus not just on the formal legal and financial rules that are the basis of "compliance," but also on the voluntary choices the corporation and its employees must make to act ethically *and* to live the essential integrity values. Rules, ethics, values—all must be communicated in a powerful way.

The corporate ethos on the contours of integrity ranges from the elemental (the code of conduct) to the fundamental (the basic policy guide) to the complex (e.g., detailed guidelines on how to reduce corruption risks when using third parties in major procurements in emerging markets). After years working on the design of such communications, I believe that they must not only discuss "what to do" but also "why to do it." Why do employees have not just an opportunity, but also a duty, to report concerns into the ombuds system? Why is bribery wrong as a matter of company ethics, not just as a violation of law? Why does the company have conflict of interest policies—or policies against excessive gifts and entertainment. Brute, rote rules are attention killers. People don't want just commands; they need explanation and understanding of real-world situations. They need to understand, in very human terms, the reasons for a prescription ("Why is it important?") and its adoption ("Why is it important in context to this global company?"). They need to be treated with respect and not just told what to do.

To illuminate the "why" not just the "what" from simulated or real cases should be the core of any curriculum. It is not necessary to be an expert in education to know that presenting real problems in actual settings can engage the heart and the mind, the feelings, and the intellect. This is especially so for active people in business. Putting them into tough situations that they may actually face—you are trying to run a cash-based business in Romania where money laundering is rife—forces them to confront competing concerns, to play different roles, to assess different approaches to the problem. The inside lawyers can create simple hypothetical cases. Or the inside lawyers can also put prurient interest to work in a good cause by using real company problems. They can modify the facts slightly to protect identities, lay bare the root causes, explain discipline, and describe system remedies. And, of course, more complex ethical cases may be obtained from a variety of professional schools and consultancies. Although it is resource intensive, Socratic teaching in person, especially in less-developed nations, is the most potent way to connect with people, to answer questions that may arise, and to let them reach the conclusion about why the precept is important in the company. This may be an instance where the General Counsel has to ask the inside lawyers to work 125 percent of their time—to make an extra effort to connect personally with employees through education and training delivered in person.

Education and training is also a complex, continuous process that, for individual employees, proceeds in distinct but interconnected phases. In addition to core integrity training given to every employee, many jobs in the company need to be "risk assessed." What particular subjects does a person in this position need to understand? A salesperson in Western China needs special courses on, for example, anti-bribery, proper use of third parties, appropriate disposition of a competitor's information, or acceptable gifts to customers. Training modules on such subjects must be developed, if they don't exist. They must be tailored to China. As individuals move from job to job, they must receive the "risk-assessed" education and training appropriate for that position—immediately through online courses and then with a "live" teacher whenever possible: one module for plant managers of chemical operations with complex environmental responsibilities; another module for a finance person in a tough market like Russia or Nigeria facing money laundering or currency issues. The training should include a testing component on retention: after training, what is learned and what needs to be reviewed immediately? Such testing should occur at regular intervals thereafter—to see if further retraining is necessary. Lack of retention makes the training exercise pointless, especially on integrity issues.

In promoting a uniform global integrity culture, education and training must candidly address local practices that are in conflict with the company's norms. In foreign markets, the great proportion of company employees may be local nationals who either have had no training at all or have worked for companies with different standards. Education and training is most effective when it does not heap scorn on local practices (and, by implication, the employees' family, friends, and former colleagues), even if those practices are antithetical to a multinational's global standards. Instead, talk positively about company standards: "You are choosing to join our community. We ask that, in doing so, you adopt our standards. These standards may be different than those you followed before. But they are vital to being a member of our community." In Asia, of course, we constantly had to explain why awarding business to family members or "greasing" a deal, although locally acceptable, was not allowed under our global ethics. Similarly, in Europe, our ombuds system of reporting concerns about fellow employees ran up against a tragic history of collaboration with the secret police (the Gestapo or the Stasi). We had to explain that the purpose of our system was not to carry out political vendettas and support a police state, but rather to promote an open company that believed in integrity and could admit fault. More important than our words was the practice of hiring as ombudsmen highly respected local employees who had lived through some of the horrors in those communities. Understanding these cultural differences and firmly but sensitively addressing them takes the legal organization (and other staff functions) into very challenging spheres of culture and history.

Finally, education and training on integrity is given a huge boost in effectiveness when it is not a separate, stand-alone event, but rather is combined with business training led by middle-level executives. When the sales team meets, the legal, compliance, and sales leaders should build modules into business sessions on proper pricing practices or gift and entertainment limits. Or when plant managers meet, the environmental, health, and safety staffs should integrate environmental requirements into presentations on operational excellence. Or when mid-level managers in tough global environments meet with their country or regional teams, they should integrate the pressing problem of integrity in those markets into the business program. The General Counsel and senior inside lawyers must forge these kinds of relationships with their peers on important cross-functional dimensions of integrity education and training. A special focus should be the training of mid-level managers and then helping those managers deliver the proper performance with integrity education and training to business teams on the ground.

F. FINANCIAL REWARDS

Working with the compensation committee of the board of directors, the CEO, the General Counsel, and the head of HR need to help design a corporate approach to compensation that does not just address the elusive goal of "pay for *real* performance." Instead, a corporation with the right culture must have a system that "pays for performance *with integrity.*" I deeply believe that integrity measures can be defined and rewarded in the day-to-day actions of business leaders as well as the rank-and-file employee: explicit goals and objectives, hard numbers about the incidence of problems occurring or of problems solved, employee surveys, internal or external audit results, and forced ranking of a corporation's business units on key metrics (e.g., environmental exceedances).

Integrity must be a meaningful component of basic compensation processes in global corporations. It should be an explicit baseline behavior addressed in salary determinations. It should be an important consideration in both annual incentive compensation (bonus) and in awards of multiyear deferred cash or equity grants. In addition, as part of a performance with integrity culture, the General Counsel should be part of a team that designs clear "compensation recovery" policies that allow a corporation to "hold back" or "take back" unvested or vested benefits when an executive or employee engages in serious improper acts. Such design includes important questions about triggering events, nature of evidence, employee due process, and precise methods of compensation recovery. In Chapter 8 on governance (pp. 275–315), I discuss in more detail the design of affirmative pay for integrity and negative compensation recovery approaches for improprieties. But it is important here to note that making integrity an important, explicit element of compensation addresses the corporate truism that "you get what you pay for" in building the right culture. Compensation for performance with integrity is yet another subject of institutional design where the General Counsel plays an important role.

In addition, the CEO and staff/business leaders should give special awards in public settings to worthy employees for extraordinary integrity actions (e.g., finding ways to avoid third-party consultants when seeking major procurements in emerging markets). The General Counsel may need to make this case to the CEO and to her peers. At signature corporate, staff, or business meetings, recognizing special-integrity initiatives and efforts—just as special efforts in other corporate domains like sales or technology are recognized—sends a powerful leadership signal to employees that integrity is integrated into the life of the corporation.

G. ASSESSING CULTURE

Because a performance with integrity culture is so important, corporations should annually assess its strength. Corporations are perpetually and properly establishing baselines and assessing all sorts of vital performance dimensions. The General Counsel, again working with the board and company leaders, should design a method for addressing the basic question of whether the company has an integrity culture and how strong it is. This will obviously involve the assessment, weighting, aggregation, and integration of multiple factors: attitudes of leaders; attitudes of employees; perceptions of the company by various stakeholders; plus a variety of objective trend indicators such as pending government actions, customer complaints, activity in the ombuds system, results of "bottoms up" reviews, disputes brought against the company, types of audit issues raised by internal and external auditors, periodic evaluations by third parties expert in both integrity issues and cultural issues.

The General Counsel, in short, should engage with Finance, Compliance, Risk, and HR in designing methods to answer the basic questions for the corporation: How should we define a performance with integrity culture? How strong is it? What can we do to improve it? In light of the spate of scandals, for example, banks now are "paying tens of millions of dollars to consultants to help them measure and enforce culture . . ."[16] Because culture—the way people feel, think, and behave—is so basic to a durable corporation that inspires trust among all stakeholders, it is hard to imagine a more important, if difficult, task for a person who would aspire to be a partner-guardian in a large, complex global corporation.

* * * *

The issues for the General Counsel and inside lawyers addressed in this chapter—employee discipline, employee voice, education and training, compensation—are building blocks for a powerful performance with integrity culture. Creating the performance with integrity culture involves attention at all phases of the employee life cycle: recruiting and hiring at the beginning but extending to training, compensating, promoting, and disciplining throughout an employee's career. But, so too, the systems, processes, and practices that create the institutional infrastructure for that culture must be integrated into business operations across all performance aspects of the corporation. In succeeding chapters, I address this broad set of integration issues from the General Counsel's perspective in the essential areas of compliance, ethics, risk, public policy, governance, citizenship, and the legal organization itself.

PART TWO

KEY ISSUES

5

COMPLIANCE AND LEGAL HAZARD: THE ESSENCE

Driven by major scandals, there has been a dramatic increase in regulation, enforcement, and sanctions in the past 25 years. This, in turn, has led to a vast outpouring of writing on compliance and legal risk. Having lived through these changes, I try in this chapter to state the prescriptive essence of ensuring compliance and mitigating legal hazard. Without question, *the most basic job of the General Counsel is to determine what is the law and to help shape messages, systems, and processes so that the corporation adheres to law and avoids legal hazard all across the globe. This is a cornerstone of the inside counsel revolution. Compliance avoids harm to the corporation, but it also creates value inside the corporation, in the marketplace, and in broader society by underscoring the corporation's commitment to integrity and differentiating it from less scrupulous rivals.*

Several introductory comments: First, I focus on formal legal and financial rules promulgated by authorities outside the corporation in this chapter. In Chapter 6, I discuss binding ethical precepts beyond what those formal rules require, which the corporation voluntarily adopts. The systems and processes for ensuring corporate adherence both to formal legal rules and to binding company ethical standards are congruent, and law and ethics are often lumped together with respect to this "implementation." But, they are quite different in their origins: Formal rules are imposed externally, and ethical standards are adopted internally. So, this chapter focuses on the complexities of determining law imposed from the outside, and the next focuses on the derivation and adoption of ethical standards on the inside. Second, compliance with the formal rules also means addressing the problem of "legal risk" or "legal hazard" because there is uncertainty both about "what is the law?" and "what will be the law?"—and uncertainty about how different authorities in different nations will interpret and enforce that law or how private litigants may seek to use the law in actions against the corporation. A good compliance approach will both ensure compliance with existing law and anticipate and address emerging legal risks. Other types of risk (ethical, economic, geopolitical) are addressed in the separate ethics and risk chapters (Chapters 6 and 7, respectively). Third, compliance also includes adherence to financial, not just legal, rules. Compliance with financial rules are the special province of the Controllership, Audit, and Risk arms of the Finance function. Moreover, as financial and accounting issues are increasingly the source of enforcement, Legal and Finance need to work together not just on lawful financial disclosure but also on substantive, "gray-area" finance decisions that have legal dimensions and legal risk. I focus on legal rules in this chapter, but I want to emphasize at the outset the importance of compliance with financial rules and the importance of Finance function leadership in corporate compliance. Fourth, when writing about "compliance" with law, there is great focus today, appropriately, on compliance with anti-bribery laws, especially the Foreign Corrupt Practices Act. But, properly understood, compliance, of course, covers a huge range of legal subjects, from labor to environment, from taxes to trade. A point I turn to now.

A. COMPLEXITY

The General Counsel in a great global company must view compliance as a striking management challenge. In the business literature, *"management" is defined as the ability to handle complexity* through disciplines: planning, goal setting, organizing, staffing, budgeting, and auditing. A thumbnail description of the complexity of compliance and legal hazard would include the following basic points.

Every single corporate process from beginning to end is cross-cut by legal rules, which constrain business practices. This truly means every single one: finance, human resources, sales, marketing, pricing, engineering, manufacturing, research and development, importing, exporting, sourcing, technology development, product development, product surveillance, customer relations, etc.

At just the federal level, in the United States alone, the number and types of legal restraints on business are almost incalculable. Inside lawyers need to explicate for business leaders that public law addresses broad but discrete topics: promoting economic growth and competition, protecting workers, protecting consumers, and protecting other social goods.[1] When one starts to disaggregate those broad public law goals, myriad specific bodies of law are laid bare: for example, antitrust, tax, trade, IP protections, labor and employment, corporate governance, disclosure, environmental protection, consumer protection, civil rights, campaign finance and, quite literally, on and on.

This complexity, which cuts across all business processes, has an exponential dimension when the General Counsel must consider all the state and local laws that cover the same corporate processes and the same broad public law concerns. Although federal preemption may exist in some cases, there is often concurrent jurisdiction, which means corporations will have to follow federal, state, and local rules— which are not uniform or consistent. And, of course, there are myriad stand-alone state and local laws. In addition, laws often do not sunset, so the accretion of new laws at all levels of government on top of old, often-not-used-but-still-valid laws is yet another layer of complexity. The old chestnut oft-cited by "too much law" commentators—that is, the number of pages in the *Code of Federal Regulations*—still gets anyone's attention: 175,496 in 2013.[2] To this complexity, one must add, of course, private rights of action created either by public law or by common law.

The General Counsel must then take the multi-tiered complexity of the United States and multiply it more than 100 times because a global company may do business in that many different nations (or more).

Each nation will, of course, have an equally broad panoply of laws with equally broad public goals—promoting growth and competition, protecting workers, protecting consumers, protecting other broad social goods—and a similar armament of specific and very detailed laws and regulations to achieve those ends. So, too, each nation may well have regional and local strictures that exist alongside laws of broad national application: local and national laws in China; Pan-European, member-state, and local law in the huge market of the European Union; and, again, on and on . . . with a variety of entities or persons, both public and private, who may seek legal redress against the corporation.

In a global economy, legal systems may also vary—from common law nations to those with civil law regimes to those with Islamic law—with quite different history and culture. This entails not just "on the face of it" differences on substantive legal provisions, but also on the "process that is due." Just the differences between the two great developed world trans-Atlantic trading blocs—the United States and the European Union (EU)—are both striking and significant on a variety of issues such as principle-based regulation (EU) v. rules-based regulation (U.S.).[3]

The law in these other nations—especially in emerging markets—may not exist in a coherent form: laws, regulations, and decisions under them may simply not be published. To obtain records is to overcome major obstacles—and it may not be possible. The fundamental issue of when national law has primacy over local law may be murky. So may the effect of "precedent." So, just determining what the law is—and will be—presents a significant challenge, or worse, in many nations.

This welter of laws may not be consistent or, indeed, may be in conflict. Data privacy rules in the EU may be more restrictive than data privacy rules in the United States (introducing great complexity in a transnational company's need to create a global HR database on all its employees). Complying with anti-bribery laws by sharing information among companies on corrupt foreign agents or improving supply chain performance by jointly identifying poorly performing third parties may run afoul of competition law prohibitions. Exploitation of legally granted patent monopolies may run afoul of antitrust laws. Indeed, in many areas of commercial law, there are conflicting standards. In the

United States and Europe, for example, manufacturing standards for medical equipment or environmental standards for automobiles are different. These conflicts are the reason we have trade talks not just on tariffs, but on "non-tariff" (i.e., regulatory) barriers. *It is why the problems of harmonization, or at least convergence, of commercial law in the nations of a globalized economy is one of the great projects facing corporate counsel for the next half century.*

To all this, we must add the conundrum of the enforcement policies and practices of even more numerous—and often unaccountable—prosecutorial and regulatory authorities. That enforcement may be episodic, erratic, and corrupt—a problem in all jurisdictions, but especially so in emerging markets. It may also be driven by anti-business or anti-American attitudes.

Finally, there is the "intensely" political nature of law, which, ultimately, is about exercising the power of the state. Every public actor in making, interpreting, and enforcing "law"—legislators, regulators, prosecutors, judges—has an "ideological" or "psychological" bias (nice word: orientation) and is influenced by the "politics" of their circumstance (from the politics of their own institutions to the struggle for power in the broader polity). The only question is the degree of those influences. But it is a factor everywhere.

These summary points underscore the dramatic problems of complexity, ambiguity, uncertainty, inconsistency, incoherence, and undue influence the General Counsel faces in determining "what is the law?" and "what will be the law?"—problems that apply to all phases of all company operations and processes, especially in a global corporation.

B. REGULATORY TRENDS

The planets of legal rules and regimes are not in stable orbit. The vast global galaxy of law and regulation is in constant flux. And recent regulatory trends only exacerbate the significance, the complexity, and the difficulty of compliance.[4]

There has been re-regulation in the United States, with major changes in laws relating, for example, to financial services (Dodd-Frank), health care (the Affordable Care Act), and the environment

(EPA regulations regulating carbon dioxide). Moreover, there are many new areas of regulatory emphasis such as the "legalization" of accounting issues that were once subjects for the SEC's chief accountant but are now forensic issues for the Enforcement Division. Or, to take another example, many nations (China) or regional authorities (EU) have adopted and begun vigorously to enforce competition law regimes that are different from the U.S. approach so that "clearing a deal" may now mean clearing multiple regional or national ("nationalistic") hurdles.

As a result of re-regulation, the budget authorizations and headcount at regulatory agencies is growing. For example, the SEC budget grew from $297 million in 1995 to nearly $1.6 billion in 2013, an increase of more than 400 percent. And the pace of government investigations and enforcement actions in the United States (federal and state) has accelerated in recent years, including investigations by U.S. authorities of corporate action in emerging markets.

Across the globe, governments at an increasing rate are also enacting new laws and regulations to address a wide array of issues affecting business, often following the lead of the United States and the EU in terms of subjects addressed, if not in the precise structure or content of the rules. In China, for example, there has been a huge outpouring of "law" in the past 15 years, even though rule by the Party, rather than rule of law, controls. This is matched by increased enforcement, sometimes for regulatory purposes and sometimes as a geopolitical weapon. Despite rampant corruption, Chinese enforcers are going after multinational companies and exacting significant penalties in such areas as anti-bribery and antitrust, in part to promote "national champions" over international competitors.

The pace of criminal actions against corporations is also accelerating. There were more than 2,000 criminal guilty pleas or verdicts entered against corporations in the United States from 2001 to 2012. Two hundred and fifty of these cases involved "large public corporations" like AIG, BP, Google, HealthSouth, JPMorgan Chase, KPMG, Merrill Lynch, and Pfizer, according to Brandon Garrett, professor at the University of Virginia Law School. And an outdated study from 20 years ago noted that as many as 300,000 regulatory statutes carry criminal penalties, a number that is surely larger today. In addition, there has been a marked growth in non-prosecution or deferred prosecution agreements (NPAs; DPAs) in lieu of formal criminal dispositions: a total of 255 in the 2001–2012 period. These NPAs or DPAs customarily involve corporate agreement to a government-appointed monitor. That monitor assumes significant control over the corporation's compliance program, culture, and other internal processes for a two- or three-year period, often without any judicial supervision.

The size of the sanctions against companies has dramatically increased since the turn of the century. In 2014, global antitrust authorities exacted $5.3 billion in fines from cartels for anticompetitive behavior, an increase of more than 30 percent from the prior year. From 2010 to 2014, the top 16 financial service institutions paid about $300 billion (!) in penalties, fines, private settlements, and forensic costs for such misdeeds as rate rigging, sanctions busting, money laundering, and loan fraud/defective disclosure. Mortgage-related misdeeds alone led to about $40 billion in penalties. In that 2010–2014 time period, Bank of America paid more than $60 billion in total legal costs and JPMorgan Chase more than $25 billion for a series of cases. In a single matter, BNP Paribas paid $9 billion for ignoring U.S. sanctions on Sudan and Iran. The "numbers are getting bigger and bigger . . . astonishing," said a law professor at the London School of Economics who analyzed the issue.

This increase in the size of sanctions has occurred outside of financial services, too. The average cost of a resolution under the Foreign Corrupt Practices Act rose from $7.2 million in 2005 to $157 million in 2014. The top 10 FCPA resolutions have all occurred since December 2008 and ranged from approximately $200 million (Daimler) to $800 million (Siemens). In the middle of 2015, BP costs topped $50 billion for the *Deepwater Horizon* explosion in the Gulf of Mexico to resolve government criminal and civil cases and private death, injury, and economic claims, with some issues still unresolved. Moreover, the size of whistleblower awards under government programs authorized by Dodd-Frank or the False Claims Act are "increasing in value at a dizzying rate," although these awards are relatively small ($30–$100 million) compared to overall corporate exposure in the big cases.

Under public pressure to hold executives—not just corporations—accountable, there has also been an increase in governmental actions—both civil and criminal—against individual corporate employees and officers. The DoJ has charged more than 4,000 people for mortgage fraud and 46,000 for white-collar crime since 2009. There is a debate about whether these prosecutions reach high enough up in corporations. But, government officials have clearly stated that corporate individuals, including high-ranking officers, are in the civil and criminal gunsights. Companies will not be given credit for cooperating in investigations unless they finger individual executives and other employees; criminal prosecutors and civil enforcers should be focusing from the outset on individuals, not just corporations; and enforcers should pay closer attention to the possibility of civil actions against corporate executives even if the elements of a crime cannot be proven. Indeed, in the last 15 years, General Counsel, inside lawyers, and compliance officers have "been swept up in criminal investigations, civil suits and SEC professional responsibility proceedings," with some going to jail.

These factors combine to subject corporations to expensive, multi-front wars when there are prominent allegations of wrong-doing and when parties investigating or suing the company compete for money, publicity, and broader political advantage. A pattern of bribery can lead to enforcement actions by different but cooperating governments all across the globe, to shareholder and derivative suits, to debarment actions by national or international agencies, and to formal inquiries by legislative committees. In the Gulf spill, BP faced a bewildering array of actions from federal, state, and local governments under a plethora of environmental and tort laws, which were compounded by an outpouring of private damage actions as well as the need to respond to numerous congressional and other investigations seeking to explicate causes and lessons learned. When there is a major compliance problem in one nation, boards of directors often feel compelled to order a global investigation to see if the impropriety is part of a larger international pattern. For example, after bribery problems surfaced, Siemens, Wal-Mart, Avon, and Daimler, to give just a few examples, all undertook expensive, in-depth reviews of practices across countries and (as appropriate) across product lines.

As a result of these developments, the forensic costs alone associated with compliance controversies have also mushroomed. Siemens spent nearly $1 billion on its bribery scandal; Avon spent nearly $300 million on its corruption case; Wal-Mart has spent nearly $600 million on its internal inquiry—and as of this writing isn't finished. And, of course, the legal and accounting costs in the raft of financial services cases since 2008 total in the tens of billions. These direct forensic costs *plus* the actual costs of fines and penalties and the provisions for legal reserves have dramatically cut into corporate profitability. And, in the Internet age, there are the additional customer, community, and public relations costs of trying to repair corporate reputation when adverse events go viral across a whole new panoply of communications platforms.

Underlying all these trends in the substantive law are changes in governance laws—through regulation (e.g., Sentencing Guidelines), case law (e.g., *Caremark* and *Ritter*), legislation (e.g., Sarbanes-Oxley/ Dodd-Frank), or heightened supervision (e.g., Comptroller of the Currency)—which impose on boards of directors and CEOs more explicit responsibilities for designing and implementing compliance programs and mitigating legal risk. We also live in an era where every injury has a remedy. Mistakes invariably are characterized as negligence or worse. Neither private parties nor government are inclined to accept the risk that "bad things happen" but, instead, seek new rights of action or resurrect old ones (e.g., Elliot Spitzer's use of a dormant state law—the Martin Act—in his actions against the financial services industry). If God is dead, there are no Acts of God, only Acts of Man— which in our litigious age must always have a legal remedy.

The daunting complexity and the dramatic trends are the reason that *issues of legal compliance and regulatory enforcement are at or near the top of most lists of future priorities for boards of directors, CEOs, and General Counsels.* Especially vexatious are issues in foreign jurisdictions, where the knowledge of inside counsel in newly globalizing corporations is often limited.

C. DETERMINING WHAT IS THE LAW

A corporate program aimed at complying with law must first determine, of course, "what is" the applicable law. *Writers about compliance often glide over this most fundamental question.* The General Counsel and the lead lawyers with responsibility for specific legal areas must evaluate and articulate what formal legal and regulatory rules around the globe apply to corporate operations and processes. Similarly, the Chief Financial Officer and financial experts, perhaps in conjunction with lawyers, must also determine what formal financial rules apply to ensure the accuracy and integrity of the company's numbers and their required disclosure (e.g., must address a host of accounting improprieties in areas like special-purpose entities or revenue recognition or "cookie jar" reserves). It is in this bedrock compliance function that the General Counsel and inside lawyers play their core role as technical experts. Formal rules—whether legal or financial—have meaning in the context of facts. So, the General Counsel and the CFO must determine what "key facts" must be part of the statement to the corporation about "what is the law" or "what are the formal financial rules." For competition law, how are markets defined, or when is there improper division of markets, or what constitutes illicit signaling? And, of course, there is the challenge of articulating to employees—who are not law students—that as certain key facts vary so may the nature and application of a rule and so may the need to seek guidance. Moreover, in addition to laws mandated by public authorities, corporations are also bound to follow rules created under contract and tort regimes. But, even when the contract specifies that a law of a particular jurisdiction applies, there can, of course, still be significant uncertainty about the meaning of contract provisions.

Given the dynamic complexity of law as it evolves around the world, the General Counsel and inside lawyers have to make important judgments that involve not just superb technical lawyering, but also wise counseling in answering this deceptively simple question about what is the law. *Let me first reiterate what I have said about the gross impropriety of inside counsel taking certain positions in a high performance with high integrity company.* The General Counsel and the inside lawyers must **never** (1) ignore the law and hope the company won't be caught;

(2) act as Holmes's bad man and try to assess whether the benefits of noncompliance outweigh the costs of being caught; or (3) try to interpret away the law's purpose and effect through strained, hyper-technical readings that are obfuscatory and not in the range of cred-ibility if viewed by an independent third party.

But, for all the reasons noted, the important, legitimate judgments are not easy to make or to articulate to businesspeople. They require sophistication—a paradoxical combination of nuance and clarity. For example, if faced with a "rule" that is "gray"—where the legal answer is not certain—where on the spectrum of "reasonable discretion" should the General Counsel and the inside lawyers decide what interpretation should apply to the company either to comply with the law or to avoid possible problems of interpretation by regulators or judges? For exam-ple, what kinds of disclosure are proper under certain financial ser-vices laws relating to consumers—where should the company be on the "legitimate" spectrum of as little as possible for commercial reasons or more than may be required for preventive or ethical reasons? Consider again the range of corporate processes and operations and the huge variety of regulations, with "gray-zone" uncertainties, that intersect these business operations. Determining a reasonable "interpretation of law" is a significant task across this vast range of issues, requiring specialized knowledge either from inside or outside experts. But that interpretation may also require a business judgment about how much legal risk (assuming the choices are "credible" and "legitimate") the company wishes to take. Frontier issues in business frequently put the lawyers on frontier areas of interpretation, where "black letter" law does not provide a complete answer. Thus, these decisions in a state of uncertainty or complexity turn on yet another recurring question: How much "legitimate" legal risk does a corporation wish to take?

A second major question is deciding between pluralism or unifor-mity when the type of law in question has different interpretations in multiple jurisdictions. Should the corporation try to have an inter-pretation that is "reasonable" in each jurisdiction because the laws are so different (e.g., different privacy standards in the United States and the EU), even though that will involve significant administrative complexity? Or should the corporation decide on a uniform, global, legal interpretation that is at the "most compliant" end of the international spectrum and thus allows for administrative simplicity but may also lead to "overregulation" in less severe jurisdictions? For example, although the child labor laws in various nations set different ages for when children may not work (i.e., from 13 to 16), the General Counsel, in consultation with business leaders, may decide that a single age mandated in the most restrictive jurisdiction should apply across the globe both in its own facilities and in labor standards applied to third-party suppliers. In other words, the company will simply not hire anyone under the age of 16 even though, in some nations, a younger age is permissible under child labor laws. Should a company, to take another example, adopt stringent environmental standards drawn from an advanced jurisdiction when building a manufacturing facility in an emerging market nation, rather than the law of the host nation, which may be more lax? A third major, related question is whether the company should adopt the "spirit" of the law—that is, should the company look at the underlying purpose and fashion a voluntary prescription for the company that advances that purpose but is not "required" by law? This question about following the "spirit" of the law is addressed in Chapter 6 on ethics.

This discussion only opens the door on the law's complexity, ambiguity, uncertainty, inconsistency, and incoherence. But one thing is for sure: The General Counsel and other lawyers in a global corporation have a challenging threshold task in determining "what is the law" with which the corporation must comply and expressing it in ways that are understandable to businesspeople operating across widely diverse corporate functions and even more diverse geographies.

D. THE CEO AS CHIEF COMPLIANCE OFFICER

Important as determining what is law, the essence of compliance, as I noted at the outset of this chapter, is *management of complexity* through very disciplined systems and processes. Simply stated, compliance involves ensuring across an organizationally diffuse and fragmented global corporation that such systems and processes prevent compliance misses, detect those that do occur as soon as possible, and respond quickly and effectively. For all the volumes on compliance, it really comes down to three words: *prevent, detect,* and *respond*—and it is toward these objectives that classic management disciplines of planning, goal setting, organizing, staffing, budgeting, and auditing must be directed. But, those goals are only accomplished when compliance issues are integrated into business process, when a compliance infrastructure is built into business operations that have a performance with integrity culture.

This is why I believe that the CEO must also be the company's Chief Compliance Officer (CCO), in a leadership, if not day-to-day, sense. There is much debate in compliance about the respective roles and reporting relationships of the General Counsel, the Chief Financial Officer, the Chief Compliance Officer, the head of internal audit, the ombudsperson, the Chief Risk Officer, and the head of the HR function. But whatever the organizational formalities, there is no doubt that these staff officers, who are jointly responsible for compliance, must ensure that the program is carried out with intensity and integrity and independence.

But, there also can be no debate that if the CEO does not view compliance as one of his core jobs, then all the efforts of corporate staff are not worth much. Adoption of such a leadership role by the CEO means that he, in turn, makes business leaders directly and primarily responsible and accountable for integrating integrity into all their business processes—and together they must drive this ethos of responsibility and accountability down into the company so that the critical, middle management leaders of P&L segments in far-flung corners of the world know that it is at the core of their job, too. And accountability is key: Senior executives and middle managers must know that the failure to create an integrity culture is a firing offense, as I noted earlier ("one strike on integrity and you're out"). Moreover, as I have also noted, the business leaders must live compliance: Speak about it personally and publicly; emphasize integrity as the foundation of the company; lead compliance reviews; and, in their own personal behavior, exemplify core integrity values.

The General Counsel, and other key staff officers, must thus work with the CEO and business leaders all across the company to ensure that *those business leaders have management "ownership" of the systems, processes, and resource allocation so essential to an effective integrity infrastructure that is embedded in business operations.* Plant managers must have the lead on environmental, health, and safety in their facilities. Sourcing leaders must ensure that their third-party vendors follow local law. At a higher level, heads of major divisions must have a comprehensive view of what is needed to follow the law and reduce legal risk—and then be effective building those systems and processes into the business, resourcing them, and ensuring implementation. That is addressing complexity. That is called *management*—by systematically applying disciplines to the different elements and operational details of prevention, detection, and response. I continue to be surprised at how legal, finance, or compliance experts puff about the staff roles in compliance when writing about compliance outside the corporation without acknowledging the centrality of business people. *The reality is that business leaders must lead on compliance*—with the assistance of the staffs.

At the same time, the CEO and business leaders, however, have to embrace a paradox. Yes, compliance fundamentals must be built into business processes—and this is especially so for effective prevention. Yes, the business leaders must make this a genuine, operational priority. But, the CEO and business leaders also have to embrace the critical importance of the staffs—legal, finance, compliance, and risk at both corporate and operating levels—who must have an independent role in the design, implementation, and monitoring of those prevent-detect-respond systems and processes. *The CEO and the business leaders must, in sum, unequivocally support the paradox that compliance is a fundamental business operation but also a subject requiring independent staff involvement and review.*

E. PREVENT, DETECT, AND RESPOND

I argued in Chapter 4 that fair discipline, employee voice, education/ training, and financial rewards for integrity are fundamental to a high performance with high integrity company. They are, of course, also core aspects of the compliance verities of prevent, detect, and respond.

Here are other aspects of these three fundamental compliance tasks I consider essential.

1. PREVENTION

The key to prevention is risk assessment and risk abatement. These tasks are based on process mapping *all* basic business functions against the legal (and financial) rules that impose limitations. Again, this means *all functions*: from finance to sales to marketing to manufacturing to technology development to sourcing. What are the sensitive legal points in the complex process of sales where applicable laws apply—for example, prohibitions against bribery, competition law strictures, rules against false product claims, and required disclosures to customers? That *process mapping and risk assessment* in each basic business function is the first step in making compliance operational. Within *each* function (sales, marketing, manufacturing, etc.), there must, however, be a threshold assessment of priorities: Which elements in that operation pose the greatest risks and deserve the most careful and detailed attention? Given the inherent difficulty of the process and a finite amount of resources, decisions must be made, for example, about which aspect of the sales process requires the most careful process mapping to determine points of risk.

The headquarters Legal, Finance, HR, Compliance, and Risk staffs must coordinate their efforts with the business leaders, their staffs, and their operational personnel to do the analysis—both prioritizing risky elements of the various business operations and then mapping in detail the relevant process within the discrete operations to understand where problems are most likely to occur and where risk abatement should take place. This must occur in each market in each business. With the insight and involvement of the business leaders, the inside lawyers, compliance staff, and other relevant business actors must not only evaluate the risks inherent in the process, but also the risk presented by other internal and external factors specific to the line of business in a particular geography. How corrupt is the country in general? What are the risks in the particular industry? How much of the commercial activity conducted in the market involves particular requests by competitors, either for contracts or approvals, to government officials or others who may want an improper quid pro quo?

Once this type of process mapping and contextual risk assessment has taken place in discrete company operations, then it is necessary to make another assessment of comparative risk across the universe of issues facing the corporation in particular geographies. What are the highest risks facing the company as a whole based on a number of factors, including the likelihood of occurrence and the consequences of an impropriety? In some markets, bribery may be the greatest risk. In other jurisdictions, money laundering, consumer fraud, environmental issues, or strict privacy rules may require the greatest attention. In others, there may be special patterns of enforcement or a cohort of employees with backgrounds prone to conflicts of interest. This is not to say that any compliance issue can or should be ignored. It is only to say that risk-based prevention systems will necessarily focus on the highest-priority items first and commit the most resources to these problems.[5]

After process mapping and risk assessment, then the General Counsel, again working with other compliance-oriented staff and with the business leaders, must build specific mechanisms for *risk abatement* that are aimed at the process points of greatest concern and that are adapted to the specific circumstances. Risk abatement techniques are numerous and can obviously be used in varying combinations. Such mitigation techniques may involve special targeted education for employees handling sensitive employment data carefully in a jurisdiction with stringent privacy rules. They may involve express checks and balances requiring different levels of review and sign-off for pricing strategies that raise competition law issues. They may involve creation of large data sets of testing information to ensure that complex products—like aircraft engines—are being manufactured according to government certifications. They may involve a computerized system for tracking plant operations against the multitude of environmental, health, and safety requirements. They may involve monitoring sales calls to ensure fair disclosure and avoid undue pressure.

In light of process mapping, risk assessment, and risk prioritization, these risk mitigation techniques—special training, checks and balances, information aggregation and control, computerized tracking, and many others—must apply at various points across the whole panoply of company functions from manufacturing and engineering to sales and marketing to M&A and sourcing. The CEO must require the deep involvement of business leaders and operational staff in designing risk mitigation techniques that are both effective and seamlessly integrated in business processes. The General Counsel, as a peer of those leaders, has a central role in working with those operational managers and with other key staff leaders to connect law and business.

The challenge of prevention is, of course, exponentially greater in emerging markets with limited rule of law, endemic corruption, rampant conflicts of interest, money laundering, unscrupulous local competitors, and hard-to-assess legal (and economic and political) risk. Here, especially, a laser-like focus on process mapping, risk assessment, risk abatement, and over-arching controllership is required. The General Counsel must argue for these essentials and *against a dangerous corporate tendency to tell emerging market business leaders—where economic returns are not clear—to hit stretch revenue and profitability goals, but then fail to give them the resources to address dangerous emerging market compliance issues.*

One of the most pervasive—and most widely recognized and discussed—issues is that posed by third parties associated with the corporation: the legion of consultants, agents, distributors, advisers, joint venture (JV) partners, and service providers that stand between the global company and the customer (be it the government or private parties). These third parties pose a clear and present danger because of the potential—the propensity?—to undertake bad acts as an agent of the company: from bribes to money laundering to misrepresentation to extortion to fraud. There are a variety of techniques multinationals should employ to prevent problems with the range of third parties. Request for use of such parties from within the company should be in writing, with clear terms of reference defining scope. That request should be approved, again in writing, by a senior country or regional officer. Extensive due diligence should be conducted with the third party on its qualifications: financial resources, personnel, commercial experience; formal business documentation;

etc. Similarly, due diligence through above-board checks should also explore the third party's reputation: cross-matches with terrorist lists; references in the business and diplomatic communities; public record searches for misdeeds. These third parties must be retained by a written contract that includes provisions regarding specification of work, fee within a reasonable range (2 percent, not 20 percent), identification of subcontractors, payment in country, audit rights, training in the corporation's integrity values and processes, a certification of compliance with the global corporation's policies, and representations of no bribery. And, to prevent problems after the contract is signed, the company must monitor performance through its audit and other contractual rights. Company employees must also have their "eyes wide open" for warning signs such as unusual requests for cash, inflated invoices, or informal requests for additional partners or subcontractors. Finally, the company should have a unilateral contract right to suspend (or terminate) for misdeeds (although enforcement against third parties in the host country can lead to politicized countersuits).[6]

On other common emerging market issues, the company can prevent problems by setting clear limits. For example, corporations can institute a bright-line rule against "facilitating payments"—paying officials to conduct routine, ministerial (nondiscretionary) acts of a minor nature, like allowing goods to be unloaded at a custom dock. Such payments, while common, are often violations of the host country's antibribery laws, which are, however, erratically enforced (if at all). Real facilitating payments are, however, allowed under the FCPA (though not under the UK Bribery Act). Nonetheless, global companies should have clear prohibitions against such payments, despite the "pass" under U.S. law (and should work with both local governments and foreign assistance agencies to improve the professionalism and pay of lower-level public workers). Any exceptions within the FCPA's "safe harbor" must be determined by senior corporate officers for truly routine matters with minor amounts of money and *only under a clear process and under exigent circumstances involving health and safety of customers or others.* To take another common example of preventive bright-line rules: Many multinational corporations set very low dollar thresholds on gifts that can be given and received by employees, even though, in Asia, exchange of expensive gifts is common. This bright-line rule avoids even the appearance of impropriety, but it requires culturally sensitive conversations to explain to customers why they are receiving a book not a Mont Blanc pen. Similarly, companies properly have strict disciplines about approving company reimbursement of travel and living expenses for customers. Yes, they can visit the factory and research center in Pennsylvania. No, they can't stop for a week at Pebble Beach with their wife and children. Or corporations can insist that, when they have majority control, joint ventures should adopt a compliance program that is a mirror image of the corporation's own approach. Or, as another example, companies can sharply limit the amount of cash available to remote business sites due to risk of use for improper payments. These kinds of bright-line approaches will emerge from careful risk assessments based on all the circumstances of a market.

2. DETECTION

Detection seeks to uncover both individual problems that must be resolved and systematic problems with the compliance framework that must be remedied. Detection can be carried out by internal processes or by external reviewers. The monitoring—or verification—processes must be risk based and use a wide variety of systematic techniques for rigorous review and evaluation, including document review, interviews, sampling, and comprehensive auditing.

The *internal processes* include at least the following:

- Giving employees voice as described earlier so that they can report specific concerns.
- "Bottoms up" reviews as also described earlier so that employees can raise more systematic integrity problems regarding the way their division or unit conducts business.
- Regular compliance auditing by the internal audit staff, with protocols designed in conjunction with Legal, Compliance, Risk, and Finance, across a range of business processes, geographies, and legal areas.

- A wide variety of technologically sophisticated digital oversight tools (e.g., monitoring sales calls; looking at data sets) to detect patterns of impropriety.
- Annual surveys and focus groups that probe whether employees believe particular business units in particular geographies or the company as a whole are (or are not) committed to doing business with integrity, are (or are not) cutting corners to make the numbers.
- Regular top down "integrity/compliance" reviews by each major division of the corporation run by the CEO of the business with strong support from the Legal, Compliance, Risk, and Finance staffs. These reviews focus on risks, abatement methods, and results. They should use consistent and systematic compliance metrics that can be compared year over year, often in conjunction with relevant business metrics (e.g., customer complaints per 100 sales calls).
- Regular meetings of top leaders in key staff functions such as Legal, Finance, Compliance, Risk, and HR to discuss challenging individual cases and to put on the table systemic issues that need attention.
- A strong corporate-level compliance review board that receives reports from internal auditors and from the individual divisions after they have completed their annual compliance reviews. This compliance review board often includes the CEO or Vice Chairs as well as the GC, CFO, HR head, and Compliance and Risk leaders. After hearing from the various entities focused on compliance, the compliance review board should set goals and objectives for the company as a whole for the coming year(s)—and approve goals and objectives for the particular business units.
- Regular reports from members of this compliance review board—GC, CFO, or CCO—on the status of the company compliance efforts to the Audit and/or Risk Committees of the board of directors. These reports do not just cover troublesome cases, but present systematic metrics and other evaluation elements so the board can not only understand problems and responses needed for immediate improvement, but can also assess year-over-year trends and more systematic needs.

The General Counsel and inside lawyers, working with Finance, Compliance, and Risk staffs, will help develop the individual detection/evaluation mechanisms; establish periodic dates for recurrent reporting; and ensure that there is a robust set of tools that provide a multi-faceted, comprehensive, coherent, and actionable review format.

External processes for evaluating the health of the company compliance programs involve regular mandated compliance auditing by the corporation's external auditor and special compliance reviews by outside lawyers, consultants, and former regulators on specific, complicated areas such as environmental, health, and safety or financial regulations. Again, the General Counsel and the inside lawyers will work closely with Finance, Compliance, Risk, and HR staffs to design these studies, retain the experts, and ensure the results are fairly reported to top leaders and, as appropriate, to the board.

For me, the important point is that, through these detection mechanisms, corporations build up systematic metrics and methods for gathering and evaluating information. For example, a program evaluation may include detailed analysis of hotline calls, internal and external compliance auditing, completion rates and information retention from employee education and training, comparisons with peer companies when information is available, cross-company analysis of employee surveys to identify problematic areas, or use of statistical techniques if big (digitized) data on repetitive corporate acts is available. In addition, a company may develop a systematic and comprehensive set of "red flags" to detect early a variety of possible compliance problems. For example, in the anticorruption sphere, sophisticated companies not only develop strong routines for vetting third parties, but develop routines for spotting questionable activity in a variety of "routine" business functions (e.g., commissions, sales expenses, write-offs, unexplained "expenses"). There is a growing literature on how to conduct systematic monitoring and verification of compliance programs. Analyses from the consultancy, LRN, and the NGO, Transparency International, are good examples. And there is a growing array of technology platforms for systematically gathering compliance data and flagging emerging issues through digitization.[7]

3. RESPONSE

My mantra for many years inside GE was: "It is our problem the instant we hear about it." When a significant compliance issue is detected that may have company-wide implications—an environmental problem in the Netherlands, the possible misappropriation of funds in Israel, indications of money laundering in Russia—then the top of the corporation must jump on it. The CEO, General Counsel, and other senior executives in the chain of command will be judged on how they perform as soon as they learn of a major problem. *This is senior management's stress test.* After a serious compliance problem emerges, the team, including the CEO, should meet regularly, even on a daily basis, to take the steps described herein until a more detailed plan of action is formulated and staffed. That core team should then receive frequent reports on plan implementation—and constantly make mid-course adjustments. The gravest mistake a leadership team can make—and this is truly a capital offense for a General Counsel—is to simply delegate a major issue back down the line with no understanding of the facts, no action plan, and a vague request for a report-back in a few weeks. Never forget that mantra: "It is our problem the instant we hear about it. And, we will be judged by every action we take, or don't take, from that moment on."

The corporation's *internal actions* are the first dimension of an appropriate response when a significant compliance issue is detected. Here, in broad outline, are some of them.

There is the need to establish the proper team or teams to protect/preserve records and documents and to investigate the facts. If this is a major matter, an independent and credible outside law firm and forensic accountants may be retained. If the matter involves lower-level officers and employees, the General Counsel, Compliance, and Internal Audit may partner with the firms to help them understand the company, to help find relevant materials, and to assess where the evidence leads. If the matter reaches higher in the company, involving the peers or superiors of the General Counsel, then greater autonomy should be accorded the outside investigators, and they may be retained by the board of directors, not by the company itself. The General Counsel may advise outside counsel or review findings, but not partner with

them in the independent fact-finding. Legal issues in overseas jurisdictions—lack of attorney–client privilege, privacy constraints, limits
on document production—are dangerous shoals that require careful
navigation.

There is the need to stop an inappropriate course of corporate
action as soon as it is possible to make that determination. Ascertaining whether the issue is due to wrong-doing must be done with all
deliberate speed. But harm to people or property must be stopped even
more quickly even if it cannot yet be accompanied by a determination
of fault.

There is the need to develop and implement a communication plan
inside the company, including keeping the board closely informed on
a regular basis—with telephonic meetings if the events pose extremely
serious threats to the company. This communication plan evolves over
time—from an initial, necessarily general report to the company and
the board to a final explication of the matter and the lessons learned.

There is the need to deal with the potentially culpable employees
at various stages of the process. This begins with decisions about seg-
regating them from their current activities or suspending them with
or without pay. It raises questions of whether the company should or
should not pay for individual counsel and whether and how the investigators will hear what employee's counsel have to say. If the corporation is able to obtain enough facts for sanctions prior to completion
of the government investigation, it can demote or fire if there is culpability, perhaps after informing the government. Although that may
indicate company liability under agency theory, such an affirmative
step in cleaning up a mess can also help in resolving a case that is so
bad it can't go to trial anyway. And, of course, if there are indictments
of individuals, then the company may suspend without pay pending
disposition of the government matter (or until it has developed enough
independent facts to warrant firing).

There is the need to design and implement appropriate system remedies to address the root causes of the problem inside the particular
business unit or units where the problems arose. Such actions must
flow from a rigorous post-mortem on the root causes of the event—
and address both specific points of failure as well as broader cultural

issues. A further decision is whether some or all of the system remedies that were necessary in the particular unit(s) should be applied
across the corporation or at least in other comparable units in the
company.

The second dimension of response is, of course, how to handle
external relations with those interested and affected parties outside
the corporation. Here are some core steps.

There is a need to create a team broader than the one charged with
the internal investigation to develop facts and craft responses to the
diverse array of external actors who will be making demands on the
corporation: from government investigators at home and abroad to
private plaintiffs to congressional committees to agencies with debarment authority to NGOs to the media.

There is a need to determine whether—and when/how—to make a
voluntary disclosure of the matter to the relevant government authorities if such disclosure is not *required* by law. Regulators say that they
give substantial credit to companies who come forward promptly with
disclosure of wrong-doing. This is, generally, the sound step to take
when the General Counsel determines that the employees of the corporation have engaged in wrong-doing because the company should
not drain time, resources, and reputation litigating a losing case. But
the decision to disclose voluntarily can be much more difficult early
in the life of a matter—when the government gives the most credit but
when the corporation may not have a good fix on culpability. And, of
course, enforcement authorities have no set formula for giving voluntary disclosure credit in most settings: The government assiduously
retains discretion. Yet, with increased government incentives for whistleblowers and increased enforcement in multiple jurisdictions, there
can be serious risk of being "outed by others" if the company waits
to disclose. If bad facts are not clear, if there is smoke but not clear
fire, voluntary disclosure can be one of the toughest calls for a corporation—and for the General Counsel. If my gut told me that there
was likely wrong-doing, my general approach was to disclose, even if I
wasn't sure and even if it would take some time to reach a more exact
determination. This is not exactly an elegant principle. But, there are
any number of moments in the life of the GC, when he has to act on

experience and on educated guesses about what further investigation is likely to uncover, given the speed of events.

There is the related need to determine the degree of cooperation the corporation will offer in order to make the government's task less burdensome—including conducting and disclosing a thorough review of the nature, extent, origins, and consequences of the misconduct, although this may, ultimately, involve waiving attorney–client privilege. Such cooperation can help with a reasonable enforcement authority and be misused by an unreasonable one. The GC has to explain taking a chance on full cooperation to the CEO—and take his own chance that the decision won't work out.

There is a need to decide how quickly to disclose to the government enforcers the internal remedial steps necessary to stop damage and fix problems—from discipline to the systems reform discussed earlier. Doing that prior to the enforcers' decision about how to handle the matter may suggest culpability, but, if there is culpability or likely culpability based on the internal investigation, then moving swiftly to address system problems may bind up a wound in the company and help achieve a less onerous disposition from the government.

There is a need to execute a public communication plan that takes into account the different constituencies and is sensitive to changing facts. The watchword here is that public statements must be scrupulously accurate—or be qualified with "this is what we know now, but our inquiry is not complete." If you don't know, don't tell. Truth in public communications is everything. Spinning half truths is simply stupid. Misstatements can damage reputation as irreparably as the underlying problem. It is better to "no comment" than to "mislead" or give the impression of misleading. With trust in corporations at an all-time low, this communication plan, and its execution, has high stakes for the corporation's short- and long-term reputation (and the value of its brand).

There is a need to make the ultimate decision whether to go to court or to settle—and whether, as is often the case, the company must enter into painful settlement for more than the CEO and General Counsel believe warranted because the risk of trial is so great. Should the corporation try a private product liability case with a good, legitimate defense on the merits—with a win acting as a deterrent and a loss putting blood in the water for more cases. Should the corporation take on the government at trial, with a loss leading to terrible media and limitations on future contracting and a win a resounding affirmation of the corporate claim that the government's case is "without merit"? If there is a high degree of confidence that the government is wrong and if a loss is not a death sentence (relatively low damages, no danger of disbarment), then litigating with the government may be the right approach as GE did in the industrial diamonds antitrust case (see pp. 51–53). The facts on the side of the corporation must be strong and clean—and this determination about the facts should avoid the corporate predisposition to happy talk, self-deception, or even self-righteous chest-beating. But, even then, the irrationalities inherent in adjudication have to be carefully taken into account in making the ultimate risk-reward decision about fighting or settling.

These basic steps in the external response to compliance problems hide extremely complicated analyses that a General Counsel and inside lawyers must undertake and extremely complicated decisions the CEO and/or the board of directors must make with the advice of the General Counsel and the Finance, Compliance, and Risk staffs. *The only consistency for a corporation in these types of compliance matters is to follow the facts.* If there is a culpability or a reasonable probability of culpability, then it is usually best to resolve the issues as quickly as possible because prolonging them will only consume the most precious commodity of a corporation: the time and focus of its leaders. For example, after receiving published reports in Middle East newspapers on a Sunday that showed an Israeli general and a GE marketing manager in the Middle East may have misappropriated U.S. funds intended for the Israel Air Force, I was in the Department of Defense (DoD) on Monday to ask the DoD General Counsel if, from the DoD perspective, this involved a "black" program we needed to keep secret. By Wednesday, when DoD confirmed the problems needed to be aired publicly and when I knew there was already powerful evidence of a serious impropriety, the company went to DoJ to pledge it would investigate the matter completely and share the results with the DoJ. Later the same week, GE informed a very aggressive investigating subcommittee in the House of Representatives concerned about procurement improprieties. The company promptly worked through the issues, gave reports to the Executive Branch and Congress, pled guilty, paid a fine, and testified in Congress, where Jack Welch was congratulated for forceful action, rather than excoriated as an indifferent corporate miscreant.

4. EARLY WARNING SYSTEMS/FUTURE LEGAL RISK

An important complement to the prevent-detect-respond triad in compliance and reduction of legal hazard is creation of regular, systematic, and comprehensive early warning systems on all three issues. This is a fundamental business process that the General Counsel, CFO, Chief Compliance Officer, and Chief Risk Officer should lead with the CEO at headquarters—and that division counsel/CFO and compliance staff should lead in the major divisions of the company. The first step is to gather, on a periodic basis (once a quarter or twice a year), information on emerging developments on the spectrum of compliance subjects. This involves careful review of a variety of sources: new and pending legislation and regulation, formal and informal government investigations, legislative and regulatory agency hearings on emerging issues, industry debates, NGO positions, news stories, and commentary from think tanks and universities. The second step is to prioritize these changing expectations and emerging issues for business leaders at the regular meetings. There, business leaders and senior staff decide which issues have enough possible import to require in-depth analysis and development of options for subsequent action that, if one were adopted, would put the corporation ahead of the compliance curve. Taking action now to avoid future regulations or enforcement actions is, at the very least, worth considering. Robust, regular, and systematic early warning systems make this possible. It is an essential tool for dealing with future legal risk and should be presented to the CEO or to the business leaders of the company's operating divisions.

But systems for preventing and for giving early warnings will not, of course, eliminate legal risk. As I discussed in Chapter 2, inside counsel as experts and wise counselors must deal with obvious situations where the corporate action poses legal hazard in gray areas, where consequential decisions must be made about taking legal risks that are within a reasonable range of discretion but uncertain in outcome because precedent is not clear or decision makers have a particular ideological predisposition contrary to the company's position. A striking example from my experience was the famous Honeywell case where GE faced regulatory risk in an antitrust clearance. It lost the deal but ultimately was vindicated on the law. In 2000, GE announced an acquisition of Honeywell, knowing that the EU's competition law was heavily influenced by industrial policy, contrary to the evolution of U.S. antitrust doctrine aimed at advancing consumer welfare. This meant that EU regulators might use European Community antitrust law to protect competitors, not competition and consumers. But it was an important merger: The deal rationale was to connect Honeywell's avionics business with GE's aircraft engines business (and ultimately sell many other pieces of Honeywell). There was no meaningful horizontal or vertical overlap. The antitrust issue involved legal theories about "conglomerate" mergers where U.S. law supported approval of the deal. The combination would expand/enhance one of GE's premier global businesses. The uncertain risk presented by the EU merger review process was worth taking.

The merger cleared in the United States with virtually no problems but was blocked by the EU Commission's antitrust enforcers, primarily on a conglomerate theory rejected by the United States many years before. Some said that GE had not handled the Brussels clearance process with appropriate *politesse*. If so, blame me. But for those of us in the middle of the fray (supported by a veritable army of European advisors and lawyers), it was obvious from the beginning that the problem was a very fundamental difference on antitrust doctrine that could not be papered over. This occasioned one of the most heated disagreements in history between the United States and the European Union on antitrust issues. The EU courts subsequently rejected the EU Commission's conglomerate merger theory in a case that preceded ours but was decided after the EU Commission had blocked the Honeywell merger. Had the European courts spoken prior to the Honeywell regulatory clearance procedure in Brussels, the Honeywell-GE merger would have gone through with only minor modifications, if any. But judicial vindication of GE's theory came too late. The deal had died.

Still, because we felt we were right on the law of conglomerate mergers (as proved to be the case in the EU courts), we felt it was a risk worth taking because the transaction was so important.[8]

F. DEALS

Strong compliance disciplines are also necessary so global corporations—and General Counsels—can avoid expensive, embarrassing problems in acquisitions. These disciplines inform both the due diligence of target enterprises and then post-closing integration of the acquisition into company operations. Sophisticated multinationals have detailed "deal templates" to reduce cultural, operational, and integrity risks and to increase synergies and performance beyond the deal "pro formas." Deals are broken into many segments: evaluation, initial due diligence, negotiations, initial agreement, further diligence, initial integration planning, closing, acquisition integration, and full transition to operations. And a whole series of tasks are carried through the segments, such as base-lining the target's processes, assessing people, identifying risks, and designing integration of operating mechanisms. Despite these efforts, many transactions yield unwelcome surprises and underperform expectations.

This can be true due to unwonted compliance issues, which carry huge price tags. The acquiring company from the start must, thus, apply its own compliance disciplines in evaluating the target company's systems and process and in uncovering problems of noncompliance and legal hazard hidden all across the globe, especially in emerging markets. The inquiries about systems range from the very specific questions (What kind of provision does the target make for encouraging employees to voice concerns?) to the mid-range issues (What kind of annual compliance reviews does management conduct?) to the large and controlling (What kind of integrity culture does the target have?). Even more important is discovering the actual illegalities and improprieties the target has committed—or is committing.

The fundamental goal is to close gaps and to bring the target company up to the cultural, aspirational, and integrity infrastructure characteristics of the acquirer. But, most directly, the acquirer also needs to address the target's compliance problems, which may be hidden by fraud or simply hard to uncover in pre-closing due diligence because of time and access limitations.

If problems emerge prior to signing, then they can either become part of the price negotiation, or they can kill the deal. For example, when I was General Counsel, GE was negotiating in a less-developed market for a capital equipment industrial business. After initial due diligence, it was clear that the environmental costs would be prohibitive to clean up facilities that were essentially 50-year-old toxic waste dumps. The deal was called off before signing a letter of intent. There was sensitivity to this problem because, at an earlier period—when there was a rush to China—GE had hurriedly purchased a local light bulb manufacturer without sufficient diligence. By the accident of an already scheduled global trip, I was one of the first senior officers to arrive at the site to discover, among other things, that workers, without any protective gear, were using mercury (one of the most toxic substances) in the manufacturing process, with excess amounts running into sluiceways and out into rice paddies behind the facility. Let me just say gently: The amount of money needed to bring the plant up to our environmental standards was far more than contained in the pro formas. The deal never worked for many reasons, including that one.

After the initial agreement, the acquirer needs representations and warranties and a material adverse change clause so that compliance problems with remedial costs that emerge in further diligence can either lead to renegotiation of the price or termination of the deal prior to closing. Acquirers should have deal language that defines specific compliance issues that may emerge before closing.

Alternatively, if the acquirer is only buying a portion of the target, then it can negotiate, or the prosecutors can insist, that, post-closing, culpable individuals and corporate liability remain behind with the rump company, which will cover any costs from those liabilities. For example, in 2014, GE agreed to buy most of Alstom's power turbine and power grid business, leaving Alstom with a large, ongoing transportation business. Although the deal was not to close until 2015, both parties knew that the DoJ had been investigating Alstom for many years about bribing officials to get power contracts.

Late in 2014, DoJ announced plea agreements with Alstom and various subsidiaries. Alstom agreed to pay a record $772 million criminal fine. But, under pressure from DoJ and GE, the remaining Alstom entity, not GE, would take the criminal charge and pay the amount, even though the bribery had involved the Alstom power business GE was buying.

If the acquirer is buying all of target and if there are substantial compliance issues, it may need—perhaps under explicit contract provisions—to require that the target resolve those issues with enforcement agencies before closing or offer a significant price adjustment. Otherwise, the acquirer may, after the close, have a criminal case in its own name. Regulators are now less likely to allow a "good" company to buy a "bad" one and get a complete pass on a criminal problem known prior to acquisition on the theory the acquirer will clean it up. A potential criminal case remains, regardless of who owns it. If the target fails to resolve the matter with the enforcers after a designated period, the acquirer can walk. Cardinal Health paid 10 percent less for an acquisition after the target became ensnared in a bribery prosecution.[9]

Once the deal has closed, the acquirer must act with all deliberate speed to do compliance reviews and uncover problems not known during due diligence, in addition to integrating the target swiftly into its broad compliance culture, systems, and processes. If the acquirer promptly finds and fixes compliance issues, or is making a good faith effort in a complicated company, it may get a pass or a lenient disposition from regulators. But it will need to show it could not (should not) have known of the matter prior to the close. Moreover, if the acquirer does not act with all deliberate speed, then any residual target problems will become those of the acquirer, which will bear full legal and financial responsibility.

G. VALUE OF A GOOD COMPLIANCE SYSTEM: MORGAN STANLEY

A well-designed and strongly implemented set of compliance disciplines can shield a global company from liability for the actions of a "rogue" senior executive. That is the lesson General Counsels should take from a DoJ/SEC decision to give Morgan Stanley a pass under the Foreign Corrupt Practices Act (FCPA) in a China case where a senior executive gave a local government official in Shanghai an improper quid pro quo.[10] The government official obtained investment opportunities in Morgan Stanley transactions and, in exchange, gave Morgan Stanley government business and government approvals. The Morgan Stanley executive, acting on his own, misled the company's compliance personnel when responding to direct questions about compliance risks. He also improperly profited from some of the transactions.

In declining to take action against the corporation, DoJ and the SEC praised various elements of the Morgan Stanley compliance program: broad, well-designed anticorruption policy and practices; extensive resourcing of the program, including 500 compliance officers worldwide with knowledge of local markets and responsibility for addressing hard problems like due diligence or third-party agents; direct training of field employees in person, online, and in writing; constant communications to employees about the importance of anti-bribery policies and practices; and disciplines built into transactions to avoid illicit quid pro quos. Despite this robust set of measures, the Morgan Stanley executive used a series of fraudulent misrepresentations to channel transaction interests, as well as improper cash proceeds, to the Chinese official. The government was convinced that a bad corporate actor had lied to circumvent an otherwise good compliance program.

General Counsels can use this case with their CEOs and other senior executives to show that federal authorities will give credit for good compliance programs when making prosecutorial decisions. Indeed, in their FCPA guidelines, DoJ and the SEC highlighted this case to illustrate the value of strong programs. As I have tried to indicate, there are many reasons for a high performance with high integrity culture beyond influencing decisions by regulators, starting with creating value and trust in the company, in the marketplace, and in society. And, although getting credit with the government is certainly a worthy objective, there is, however, little certainty for corporations because regulators are strongly disposed to retain broad discretion over prosecutorial decisions. Rather than setting clear standards about when companies will get credit for compliance programs, regulators just list general factors to which they will pay attention as they see fit. It is unclear whether the Morgan Stanley disposition, for example, just turns on a very unusual set of facts. But strong programs and active cooperation has helped other companies avoid criminal prosecution.

Federal enforcement authorities should give much more systematic credit to effective corporate compliance programs when making decisions about criminal prosecutions—including non-prosecution or deferred prosecution agreements—and when deciding the scope of civil and administrative settlements. That is the fundamental conclusion of a recent report from an advisory group comprised of law enforcement officials, judges, prosecutors, academics, and compliance experts from companies and law firms (Disclosure: on which I served), which was organized by the Ethics Resource Center. As I have written in detail, I strongly support this conclusion.[11] It applies not just to the DoJ and to the SEC, but also to other administrative agencies. This is a first-order issue for corporate General Counsels. I believe that GCs should work together and with the government to define with more rigor what constitutes a good compliance program beyond the broad general statements of the corporate sentencing guidelines, to develop the governmental capacity to make meaningful assessments and to have government be more explicit about what credit is due when a program passes a certain threshold. To be sure, this is an uphill battle given enforcement authorities' inherent reluctance to cabin their discretion, but it is worthy of serious GC attention. Clearer standards for giving credit when due would enhance corporate compliance among a broad range of corporations.

H. VALUE OF A GOOD RESPONSE TO COMPLIANCE DISASTER: SIEMENS

I have used the Siemens bribery case to illustrate the pressures for corruption inside global companies, a failed corporate culture, and the dire consequences that followed (see pp. 99–101). In the terminology of this chapter, Siemens didn't prevent bribery but, instead, encouraged it by a willful failure—for example, using unsupervised bank accounts for suspicious purposes; entering into consulting agreements that had no legitimate objective on their face; having secret slush funds to provide cash for bribes; failing to conduct serious compliance reviews by senior officers; and, in general, failing to put in place any operational systems, processes, and controls—any checks and balances—that would stop multiple bribes in multiple jurisdictions across multiple divisions. Not only did Siemens fail to detect bribery, but it willfully ignored it—for example, by failing to follow internal complaints, disregarding red flags, making misrepresentations to the company Audit Committee, and failing to investigate reports from the external auditor about suspicious payments.

I revisit the Siemens case here because it illustrates not just the company's utter failure to "prevent" and to "detect," but also the value of an aggressive "response" by new management once wrong-doing had been uncovered by government raids. First, Siemens took extraordinary steps to investigate the issues and share the fruits of that investigation with both the U.S. and German governments. On its own motion, it scoured the globe in all its major divisions to uncover bribes. It employed 100 external lawyers and forensic experts, with 100 support staff, expending 1.5 million hours of effort. It conducted 1,750 interviews in 34 nations; held 800 informational meetings; preserved 100 million documents; and produced 24,000 to the U.S. and German enforcement authorities. In addition, it provided information on third parties as well as sharing forensic analyses. It laid out the pattern and practice of this massive bribery scheme not just in memos, but in countless face-to-face meetings and conference calls. As the DoJ said in its Sentencing Memorandum submitted to the U.S. Federal District Court:

> The scope of Siemen's internal investigation was unprecedented and included virtually all of its world-wide operations, including headquarters components, subsidiaries and regional operating companies. Compliance, legal, internal audit and corporate finance were a significant focus of the investigation and were discovered to be areas of the company that played a significant role in the violations. Finally, the role and awareness of Siemens Managing Board and Supervisory Board in serious compliance failures were the subject of particular scrutiny[.][12]

Second, at the same time, Siemens was taking a number of steps to reorganize the company and to remediate its problems. The DoJ called this effort "exceptional . . . extraordinary . . . a high standard for multi-national companies to follow." The company replaced nearly all top management (Chair of Supervisory Board, CEO, General Counsel, and heads of Audit and Compliance); fired senior line management implicated in improper conduct (heads of major product divisions); reorganized the company to provide more central control over both business and compliance; overhauled and greatly expanded its compliance and audit functions; introduced new anticorruption policies, education, and training; created a new reporting mechanism for employees to express concerns; set up a new disciplinary board to impose consistent, strong sanctions across the company for wrongdoing; evaluated and terminated third-party consultants; changed the process for retaining such consultants in the future; and centralized and strengthened control over funds for third parties. Obviously, these steps together were an admission the corporation had been derelict. But these and other measures led DoJ to view favorably Siemens's commitment "to ensure that it operates in a transparent, honest and responsible manner going forward."

As a result of Siemens's cooperation in the investigation, its swift imposition of discipline, and its sweeping remediation, the DoJ allowed the company, and three of its subsidiaries, to enter an FCPA criminal plea to false "books and records" and inadequate "internal controls" violations, thus avoiding a criminal "bribery" plea. The latter would have raised the possibility that Siemens, which had significant contracts with the U.S. government, could have had those existing contracts suspended and could have been debarred from competing for future contracts. It had approximately $1 billion in annual sales to the U.S. government at the time of the plea arrangement and had hopes to double or triple that amount each year in the future. Far greater sums were at stake in Europe, which has an even stricter debarment regime than does the United States, at least on paper. Avoiding the debarment threat was a major objective of Siemens's extraordinary effort, and it was achieved. The DoJ criminal fines totaled $450 million. Siemens was given credit for cooperation and remediation well below what the federal Sentencing Guidelines called for. But, because the pattern of illegality had gone on for so long and because Siemens had not come forward on its own, this lack of voluntary disclosure prevented a smaller fine. Nor was Siemens able to avoid appointment of an independent monitor for four years, although the DoJ took the unprecedented step of allowing Siemens to employ a German national, rather than an American FCPA expert, as its compliance monitor. The SEC reached an additional $350 million civil settlement with Siemens, also for FCPA books and records violations. This $800 million total financial sanction while large was not, by itself, going to have a material impact on Siemens's operations going forward.

Some have questioned whether Siemens went too far in its global investigation and offered up too much to the prosecutors because neither the United States nor Germany had the resources to conduct such a sweeping and thorough inquiry. At a minimum, Siemens's comprehensive response is a limiting case that can stimulate debate. Given the huge scope of Siemens's real problems and the potential for an endless sequence of separate disclosures, investigations, and proceedings, my judgment is that a refurbished board had to undertake this enormous effort for the sake of the company itself. It had to take out all the cancer it could if the company was going to go into the future with the right values and the right culture. Hiding the crimes and coddling the perpetrators would have led to a schizoid organization uncertain about its future legal and ethical direction. In a world where multinationals are under harsh scrutiny, it would have also led to a likely reprise of the sorry drama when, for example, governments collapse and dirty secrets fall out of bureaucratic file cabinets. In my view, it was the right thing to do. Although the disruption inside the company was great, it allowed Siemens, in the main, to put the scandal behind it.

That it was the right thing to do is reflected in the subsequent decision by Wal-Mart to follow the Siemens playbook.[13] In 2012, *The New York Times* published a story alleging that Wal-Mart Mexico, under the direction of the then-country CEO and his in-country General Counsel, had for many years ordered the bribery of officials to get permits and other clearances for new stores. It then falsified records to cover up the improper payments, according to the story. When a

Wal-Mart lawyer in Mexico blew the whistle in 2005, senior officers both in Mexico and the United States allegedly stopped two attempts by Wal-Mart lawyers and compliance personnel at the Bentonville, Arkansas, world headquarters from starting a thorough and independent inquiry. The charges of the Mexican whistleblowing lawyer were sent back to Mexico and buried. The subsequent 2012 news story caused a sensation (and won a Pulitzer Prize). If the facts in the story were accurate, Wal-Mart leaders in the United States, including senior lawyers, had violated every major principle of good governance. This may have included hiding the whole matter from the Wal-Mart board.

Per Siemens, Wal-Mart did a volte-face after being exposed. It retained three law firms: one for the audit committee, one to conduct an internal investigation, and one to advise on a global compliance review. It paid numerous other law firms to represent 30 Wal-Mart employees subject to questioning in the probe, including senior executives at headquarters. It broadened the investigation to include possible improprieties in Brazil, China, and India. It vowed to cooperate completely with DoJ and the SEC, which, of course, began formal inquiries immediately after the news story. Through January 2014, the company had spent $440 million on the inquiry and estimated it would subsequently spend hundreds of millions more in years to come.

Also, per Siemens, Wal-Mart radically reformed its compliance programs. The company detailed this in a Global Compliance Program Report released in May 2014, almost two years to the day after the *New York Times* story appeared. The report, stemming in part from 20 Audit Committee meetings, detailed important changes in people, policies, processes, and systems. It reads like a compliance best practices manual. It covers everything from unfettered employee reporting to risk assessing markets to checks and balances to enhanced controllership to tying compensation to integrity. The report claimed, for example, that Wal-Mart had 2,000 employees working in compliance around the world. There is little question in my mind that Wal-Mart is giving itself a major compliance facelift because its board was embarrassed and was trying to change radically a malign culture. But it is also doing this because it knows it is likely to be engaged in a tough negotiation with U.S. enforcement authorities and is hoping that its investigatory zeal and its wide-ranging reforms will led to "the least bad result" in a negotiated disposition. The 2014 Global Compliance Program Report did not include any discussion of the bribery allegations and Wal-Mart's internal investigation. We will only know when the case is resolved whether the government finds Wal-Mart's efforts as credible as Siemens, or determines they are just words on paper. But, the value of the Siemens strategy—however great its cost—is reflected in its adoption by Wal-Mart.

I. GC, CFO, AND CHIEF COMPLIANCE OFFICER: FUNCTION NOT FORM

One of the hot issues in the compliance world relates to the respective roles of the General Counsel, the Chief Financial Officer, the Chief Compliance Officer (CCO), and the Chief Risk Officer (if there is one). Much of that debate is on the question of whether the CCO should "report" to the General Counsel/CFO or to the CEO. This issue is far less important than deep, authentic CEO and business leader commitment to compliance. It is far less important than assessing, in the particular corporation, the different strengths the Legal, Financial, Compliance, Risk, and HR staffs bring to the multi-faceted subject of compliance in the context and culture of particular companies in particular industries. And it is far less important than ensuring that these staffs work together seamlessly on the wide variety of different tasks under the broad prevent, detect, and respond mandates. As I have argued for some time, I believe the CCO should report to the GC and CFO but have a vital organizational role and an independent voice. But this is a preference and predilection, not a "no exceptions" prescription. It is based on the assumptions about the lawyer-statesman and partner-guardian role of the GC and CFO in the high performance with high integrity company I have advanced. But, those assumptions may not always hold true, and, on this issue, there are different ways to draw the organizational charts in a successful compliance program. Function, not form, is what matters.

ASSUMPTIONS ABOUT THE GC

To put this issue in perspective, it is thus important, very briefly, to recapitulate first principles as I see them. The CEO, the board of directors, and senior business leaders must create a powerful culture of integrity and, importantly, must enthusiastically encourage the dual role of partner and guardian for senior staff—the General Counsel, the CFO, the Chief Compliance Officer, the head of Risk, and the head of HR—and must want unvarnished views in discussion and debate before making decisions. Working with other legal domain specialists, the General Counsel should, as expert, counselor, and leader, have ultimate responsibility in the corporation, short of the CEO and the board of directors, for making the complex determination about "what is the law" and being accountable for ensuring that the corporation adheres to that law. (The same is true for the Chief Financial Officer with respect to formal financial rules.) Compliance with law is not one substantive subject. It encompasses many subjects that cut across a company (antitrust, tax, accounting rules, labor and employment, etc.). Compliance also involves particular regulatory regimes governing specific industries (health law, communications law, banking law, etc.).

In most corporations, most of the time, the substantive experts on "what is the law" work for the General Counsel. They use that expertise in a variety of ways that create value for the corporation, including, but not limited to, compliance. But it is simply ludicrous to argue as a prescriptive matter, as some do, that law and finance should just be involved in "performance" but not "integrity." It is simply ludicrous to think that the General Counsel should just be a passive figure doing what he is told by CEOs and senior executives (see pp. 46–54). My whole prescriptive approach is based on the independence of the GC as lawyer-statesman and partner-guardian—and overcoming obstacles to performing those roles and advocating for what he believes is the right course of action (see pp. 68–90). *As GE General Counsel, I viewed the absolute core of my role as promoting corporate integrity—as advancing law, ethics, and values.*

ROLE OF CHIEF COMPLIANCE OFFICER

The Chief Compliance Officer's core job is to operationalize the formal rules inside the company through engagement with the GC, CFO, and other substantive staff experts and with business leaders and in business operations. Unless the company is very small and resource constrained, the General Counsel should not be the Chief Compliance Officer. The CCO's core job, in my view, is process integration and organizational rigor. The CCO must meld the legal and financial expertise of the GC and CFO and their staff organizations (as well as the expertise in Risk and HR organizations) with the line responsibility of the business leaders. Because there are so many different substantive areas of compliance, handled by different experts, it is vital that these threads be woven together into a coherent compliance approach. That is the job of the CCO. For example, there must be a single code of conduct and uniform set of policy guides. There must be integrated general education and training for all employees—and for middle managers. There must be an integrated method for tracking, training, and testing individuals who move into high-risk jobs. There must be a systematic and consistent company method to process map, assess risk, and mitigate risk. There must be oversight of the ombuds system to ensure that it is being operated fairly, promptly, and without retaliation. There must be a continuing, energetic search for best compliance practices outside the company. These are the kinds of vital process and organizational tasks for a CCO.

The CCO should, thus, first and foremost have organizational and managerial expertise. He must help create a coherent company-wide framework that cuts across substantive areas, different business groups, and diverse geographies so that there is a uniformity and energy in approaches to prevention, detection, and response. These organization skills are not ones necessarily possessed by lawyers. Moreover, because of his overview of the company's diverse compliance activities, the CCO should be at all meetings with the CEO or senior business leaders involving individual cases or systemic problems. He should have his own independent voice and should view as central to his role the task of asking hard questions whether corporate actions comport with concepts of integrity. His role, in my view, is analogous to the head of the internal audit staff (a position of great prestige at GE). He should report independently on a regular basis to the board of directors, providing his perspective on the strengths and weaknesses of the broad compliance function—or giving his view on individual cases with which he is familiar, offering, at the least, the perspective of process strengths, weaknesses, and areas for improvement. At the end of the day, the role of the CCO in directing process management across the whole compliance system—and making compliance operational—is a central and vital job.

But, as a general matter, there should not be duplication in the CCO function of the substantive expertise about what are the formal rules upon which compliance is built—expertise that normally exists in the Law and Finance functions. That would be a source of confusion, waste, and possible turf-fighting. The GC and CFO have primary substantive responsibility, and the CCO has primary process and organizational responsibility. But, close working relations between substance and process responsibilities are critical. Moreover, those demarcations are not, of course, always bright lines. Certain members of the Legal team may have organizational and process skills. Certain members of the Compliance organization may have substantive expertise in discrete compliance areas. For example, in financial services institutions, there may well be compliance personnel expert in the substantive and detailed arcana of financial regulation, while the legal staff retains substantive expertise in more traditional areas like antitrust, tax, or labor and employment. In these special cases, the General Counsel, the CFO, and the Chief Compliance Officer need to sort out process and substantive responsibilities and make that division clear to affected business leaders and business units.

INDEPENDENCE

Under my view of the General Counsel as lawyer-statesman and partner-guardian, I simply do not buy the idea that the GC is less independent than the CCO. Under a good CEO, both will be respected for their analysis of problems and for their unvarnished views about "what is right." Under a bad CEO, both will be "dissed" and diminished. And let us not be naïve. Compliance Officers, just like General Counsels, are subject to the same financial and group pressures as the lawyers and Finance staff. Like General Counsels, they, too, can be cowed by business leaders and be implicated in improper activities, including some that lead to corporate termination and government indictment.

FUNCTIONAL REALITIES

Far more important than debates about the reporting relationship is creating a strong sense of shared purpose among the various staffs. An effective approach to the many, many dimensions of compliance under the leadership of the CEO and senior business executives will, I must emphasize, turn on the effective integration of Law, Finance, Compliance, Risk, and HR specialists. I hope my overview of compliance functions—prevent, detect, and respond—has indicated the multiple tasks, which require different skill sets, and has underscored the multiparty functional realities of an outstanding compliance program.

Take different dimensions of competition law. With strong legal regimes in different parts of the world, there is the basic question of what the relevant antitrust law is that the corporation's antitrust lawyers must differentiate and explicate. The legal expert on competition law can formulate the key issues that must be covered in a compliance audit; the compliance experts can bring expertise on how such audits have worked across other substantive legal areas; the internal audit team, working under the CFO—and with Legal and Compliance—will develop a work plan; auditors and compliance personnel may carry out the compliance audit; all three functions—Legal, Compliance, and Audit—will review results and determine how to present issues and action items at compliance reviews at different levels of the corporation. In a different context, the competition law specialist working for the General Counsel will propose the critical rules—and the key questions and answers (Q&As)—in the company policy guidelines, but the Chief Compliance Officer and other experts in the compliance organization will help refine that communication, making it both engaging and consistent with other parts of that document. If there is a serious antitrust problem and government investigation, the General Counsel, the inside antitrust leader, and outside counsel may lead the response to the subpoena, but both the Compliance staff and the Audit staff will help work inside the corporation to prevent document destruction, to gather information systematically, and to make sure that employees are responsive but not terrified by a rigorous internal probe. And, in the response mode, the General Counsel, with the approval of the CEO and the board, will either settle or litigate a case after careful consideration of what is "right" given the facts.

Look at the different strengths of the functions. The CCO can create the whole appearance and feel of the company's compliance communications from the code of conduct to detailed policy guide to education and training to web-based information to a powerful video shown to new employees. Together, the CCO, the GC, the CFO, and the Chief Risk Officer can design the template for annual business compliance reviews, with the CCO advising the business on how to sharpen up both the substance and format of its presentation to the corporate compliance review board. The ombuds function can report to the CCO. But determining which experts will investigate which complaints will emerge through a joint discussion among the various staff functions. The GC, CFO, and CCO will all jointly analyze the results from that ombuds system to determine what is most important for business leaders and the board. Following a major compliance miss, the General Counsel, with advice from the CCO and Risk Officer, may develop a plan with the Communications VP and experts in government relations for dealing with external constituencies—from Congress to the Executive Branch to media to NGOs. And I could literally give countless other examples of compliance activity that should be cross-functional for optimal effectiveness.

The fundamental point is that, under the leadership of the CEO/senior executives, the myriad compliance tasks are classic matrix activities, cross-functional efforts that require seamless (and egoless) integration of the general skills of specific staffs and the specific skills of particular individuals in different combinations on a wide variety of issues. It is truly a team sport. It is comprised of many, many critical but varied elements of the protect-detect-respond framework. The leaders and teams responsible and accountable for these elements can encompass a changing mix of people from various corporate staffs. The deep sense of commitment from the various staffs to the importance of compliance *and to each other* is something that cannot be captured on any organization chart. But, without that sense of joint commitment, and the leadership of the CEO, the right compliance approach for particular companies cannot exist. The GC, CFO, and CCO must provide both leadership and a strong ethic of seamless cooperation.

ORGANIZATIONAL FORMALITIES

Thus, it is within this ethos of staff integration and under the broader assumptions about a high performance with high integrity company, that I believe the appropriate model is for the CCO to report to GC and the CFO, with a CCO having vital organizational and process responsibilities and an independent voice on both individual matters and system reforms. Putting the units together under the GC and CFO advances the ideal of staffs operating together seamlessly and avoids waste and turf-fighting because the substantive expertise about the "rules" with which the corporation must comply—and that guide the whole compliance function—is found in Legal and Finance. For purposes of the Sentencing and DoJ/SEC FCPA Guidelines, which require designation of a person responsible for compliance, the board of directors and the CEO should designate the GC and CFO as having ultimate responsibility for ensuring corporate compliance with formal rules and the CCO as having day-to-day operational responsibility for working with the key staff and the businesses to make compliance operational. The Sentencing Guidelines allow flexibility in designation of both overall and day-to-day compliance leadership.[14]

There is one other point in favor of this reporting arrangement. Readers now know my deep belief that being an effective business partner to the CEO gives the GC (and CFO) both the vision into issues and the credibility necessary to be a powerful, effective guardian. It is harder for a CCO, who is dealing solely with compliance issues, to gain that kind of across-the-board trust. And the CCO simply cannot be at all the top-level corporate meetings on strategy or operations where integrity issues, including compliance problems, may arise but are not the main topic. A related point: The credibility of the GC and CFO comes from presenting a range of options for accomplishing business objectives with legitimate integrity alternatives. The CCO may not have the same business exposure or experience and may argue for the "safest" compliance option, which is not the only "legitimate" one.

But, as noted, my view about the CCO reporting jointly to the GC and CFO is a presumption and a preference. It is not an iron-clad prescription. For example, in some organizations, a body of regulation may be so detailed and so controlling—as in financial services or pharmacology—that a CCO may have authority over the substantive interpretation of that body of regulation and thus an independent reporting line to the CEO (while Legal is responsible for substantive interpretation on all other matters of issues of compliance). Indeed, in financial services, the regulators may require this kind of division (at least with respect to financial regulation). Alternatively, a General Counsel may come from the transaction side of the law with the CCO coming from the prosecutorial, regulatory, or private litigation side of the law—and, in such an instance, the CCO may work more effectively in tandem with the GC rather than as a direct report. Despite my preference, I would be the first to say that function is more important than form given the needs of a particular corporation, the realities of staff integration, and the skills of particular individuals. This is truly a case where one size does not fit all.

Let me end with an illustration of the different ways this can work from my own experience. At the GE corporate level, the Chief Compliance Officer (actually called Chief Compliance Counsel) was a tenacious and talented former Assistant U.S. Attorney, Scott Gilbert. He technically reported to the head of litigation and preventive law but often worked directly with me as well. Most of the time, however, he operated with great independence in organizing the compliance function for the company. He had a strong direct relationship with the corporate Audit staff. He did everything from direct and produce the video we showed new employees to lead investigations on some of our most sensitive matters. The whole look and feel of the compliance program was due to his ability to draw on expertise from Legal, Finance, HR, and Audit and his creativity in building the integrity infrastructure across subject matter areas. He came to all important meetings where he had knowledge. And I was able to run interference for him when he bumped up against resource problems or recalcitrant business types. My view of how the GC-CCO partnership can work is doubtless influenced by my close, cooperative relationship with Scott (who then became a national leader in the compliance world as a free-standing CCO at Marsh & McClennan).

Alternatively, we had some serious compliance breakdowns in our Aircraft Engines business, which served both commercial and military customers. I had hired Henry Hubschman—an outstanding lawyer from Fried, Frank—to be GC of Aircraft Engines and help clean up these problems. He and the leader of the business decided that Engines needed a free-standing compliance function and a strong compliance leader. They hired a former two star Air Force general, Ken Meyer, who knew little about law but everything about organization and process—and everything about leadership, which he exemplified superbly. He rehabilitated compliance in conjunction with Law and Finance. He had a seat at the table and the ear of the business leaders. His ideas on integrity organization and process became best practices across all of GE, even though he was not a legal or finance expert. In a peer relationship, he and Hubschman, the GC, were inseparable and reinforcing—and held each other in the highest regard.

J. PEOPLE AND RESOURCES: PLATINUM, GOLD, SILVER, BRONZE—OR NICKEL

The creation of a performance with integrity culture, and the embedding of compliance systems and processes in business operations, will never occur without great people and real resources. A test of board of director and CEO commitment is whether these issues—and all the actions I discussed earlier—are given high priority by hiring and promoting the best people and by providing the necessary funds after financial analysis of organizational needs.

WHY?

The request for people and resources must always be premised on a succinct and powerful argument about why the particular area of compliance is so important to the corporation. The General Counsel should be able to explain to the CEO and senior executives the legal complexity and regulatory trends summarized at the beginning of this chapter. And he should be able to argue why compliance in that area is so important to the mission of high performance with high integrity and to the proper corporate culture, why it both protects the corporation, and creates value in the company, the market, and society. But each area of compliance may have its own particular rationale.

Let's take a common example. What would the General Counsel say to the board of directors and the CEO in support of a strong anti-bribery compliance program? There are broad policy arguments, which I discuss in Chapter 9, about improving global competition, creating rule of law in emerging markets, and reducing global crime such as narcotics and terrorism in failed and failing states (see pp. 326–335). In addition, there are the benefits of avoiding investigation and prosecution under the FCPA and the burgeoning number of anti-corruption laws in other nations. And, as we have seen in the "bad" culture cases, without robust and genuine compliance, corporations can suffer catastrophic costs, loss of reputation, termination of top officials, and an enormous expenditure of time and effort cleaning up the mess that could be better spent on commercial activities. No CEO should want to be the next Siemens or Wal-Mart bribery case.

But, of equal or greater importance, a strong anti-bribery policy creates pride among employees in their company: It joins "what they do" with "who they are" by fusing corporate identity and personal identity. This impact on employee morale has an immeasurable benefit in hiring and retaining people. As long as employees understand that their leaders really do not want them to lie, cheat, steal, and bribe in doing business, they, as a general matter, are highly motivated to win the right way. Major multinationals have the clout—if they have quality products at competitive prices—to do well even in corrupt markets by just saying no. They will lose orders, of course. But, even in nations marked by corruption, there will be government technocrats or private parties who want to purchase on merit (on cost and quality), not on bribes. This is not Panglossian. Of course, corruption poses huge obstacles. But at the time of Siemens's towering bribery scandal and vast expenditure of funds for illicit purposes, GE with a strong commitment to an anti-bribery policy (although hardly free from sin) had equal or better share and margins than Siemens in emerging markets in competitive lines of business like power and health care.

HOW MUCH?

But, if the reasons for compliance are compelling for avoiding problems and for creating benefits inside the company, the marketplace, and broader society, the fundamental question still remains: How much should a company spend on compliance? Here there is a critical distinction between the costs of preventing and detecting and the costs of responding. The prevention and detection costs include direct costs for inside lawyers and their staff, costs for other corporate staff, the costs of business time and effort in education and training, and the cost of reviews and compliance tracking. But, when prevention and detection fail, there are, of course, the (often significant) response costs: diversion of inside resources to address investigation and litigation issues; outside legal costs; other external forensic costs; reserves for legal costs; reserves for potential settlements; the actual costs of fines, penalties, and restitution; and other harms to corporate reputation and brand. Where on the spectrum from platinum to gold to silver to bronze—to nickel—should the corporation be in terms of its financial commitment to prevention and detection? That commitment can range from the capital costs of building a chemical plant that meets environmental standards to significant investment in people who are building and delivering great education and training to implementation of simple financial rules (little cash in remote sites). If no company is ever going to eliminate sin, the devilish (angelic?) question is: How close can it get to the irreducible minimum?

The answer to this question in a practical, resource-constrained world must begin with assessing which compliance risks are most "significant." Again, as with so many other issues in compliance, this can be a joint effort of Legal, Finance, and Compliance as well as line management. "Significant" can mean many things: risk of harm to people, risk of harm to facilities, risk of material harm to financial integrity, risk of enforcement, risk of substantial forensic expenditures, risk of substantial penalties or fines, and risk to reputation/brand. In some areas, compliance must strive, in Six Sigma terms, for "zero defects." An aircraft engine must absolutely meet Federal Aviation Administration (FAA) certified performance and safety specifications in manufacturing and operation. A chemical plant must absolutely operate under environmental requirements. Managers and salespeople in emerging markets must all receive effective and frequent education and training on the many pitfalls in winning orders from government entities. In general, the amount of resources devoted to compliance will depend on the company's size, complexity, industry, geographical reach, and risks associated with the business. And this general principle of risk-based commitment must be applied to prioritizing specific legal and compliance risks.

A detailed financial analysis of the costs of the different elements of the complex prevent-detect-respond framework is an ideal. But it may not be realistic because developing a comprehensive baseline may simply not be possible given the huge variety of activities encompassed in compliance across a multi-business global corporation operating in 100 nations and under hundreds, if not thousands, of laws and regulations. But, if *management* is defined in business terms as "handling complexity," there can be no escape from having a sophisticated methodology that makes a good faith effort in each business and in each region to risk assess the compliance issues and allocate sufficient resources to priorities. And that methodology must be adjusted according to the "evaluate and verification" aspects of "detect"—which assess whether the compliance programs are effective or are faulty and in need of upgrades. These concrete questions about the cost of compliance are difficult. Resources are limited. Priorities should be funded for measurable effectiveness, but less-important areas should receive "best efforts" funding. These are hard questions—very hard. A company serious about compliance simply must approach this vital set of compliance finance issues in a systematic manner using joint staff resources and best efforts. Otherwise, the company is just sticking its finger in the wind and hoping.

One of the hardest issues in this area is, of course, assessing the "benefit" that comes from an investment in prevention. Prevention reduces the risk of a compliance miss occurring or prepares for a change in the legal rules. But how can the avoidance of a cost of something that hasn't happened be measured? What would be the "all-in" cost of a plant explosion or a major bribery scandal or a product class action suit? A pro forma analysis of harms could be constructed. But clearly another important way to proceed is by analogy. Look at Siemens. Look at JPMorgan. Look at BP. Look at Wal-Mart. Developing a database—secondary sources exist—that includes the costs of misses by other, comparable multinational corporations can provide important perspective to business leaders faced with the questions of the "significance of the risk," the "benefits" of avoiding that risk, and how much to spend on compliance programs. Companies cannot meet a standard of perfection, but whether their program should be "platinum" or "gold"—or "nickel"—is a recurring issue. It turns on financial analysis and methodologies that, in my judgment, have not received enough attention in the vast compliance literature. A joint "estimating" team, comprising Law, Finance and Compliance staffs, on this baseline issue of the costs of failing to comply with existing law or failing to anticipate future law should exist, not discreetly, but explicitly as part of the analysis of the need resources for compliance priorities.

BUDGET PRESSURES

Some studies suggest that corporations are spending more money on compliance as the complexity, trends, and risks increase. But there are also indications that suggest strong cost-reduction pressures on compliance budgets exist due to the lingering effects of the financial crisis/recession and due to the inexorable pressures from global competition. When facing such pressures, the General Counsel needs to fight the standard CEO budget edict: "10 percent down." CEOs issue this standard budget season diktat, of course, because they don't want every business and every staff function to engage in trench warfare, fighting every line-item reduction. Swing that meat-ax. With respect to compliance, the complex matrix of activities is rarely overfunded. The scope of the compliance—and the risks of noncompliance—are growing. If the General Counsel can show productivity or genuinely reduce costs in some low-priority activities, great! But, in most areas, compliance is a small part of overall costs—and the risks to reputation and to the balance sheet are large. The General Counsel may not want to draw attention to "being different" to avoid the meat-ax—that is, the GC may not want to stand dramatically, Horatio-like, at the budget meeting bridge—but he must be skilled in the budget wars and not let the compliance function be degraded and greater risk created. This can include going in privately to talk to the CEO, although I worked for one who knew that game well and would say in meeting: "If you have a problem, talk now. I don't want to see you privately later." (Most of the time, he meant it.) Or the GC can work quietly with the Finance staff to move money around. Or, the General Counsel can have private, if risky, conversations with influential members of the Audit or Risk Committees. Welcome to the bureaucracy! I discuss broader issues of budget strategy for the legal function in Chapter 10 on the global legal organization.

General Counsel may also face a different problem in the budget wars: overregulation. There are certainly cases where the government does not understand how business works and, out of an excess of bureaucratic caution, imposes overly onerous requirements. But, if the government is serious about enforcing these rules—thus making the area high priority under a risk-based analysis—then the GC must argue for devoting platinum resources (not just "good faith" bronze resources) to the area. At the same time, he can indicate to the CEO and business leaders that the best way to address the issue is through balanced changes in public policy that acknowledge an important public goal but offer more efficient and effective ways to achieve it.

SMALL AND MEDIUM-SIZED COMPANIES

At virtually every presentation I have given on high performance with high integrity, and on the costs of compliance, I am admonished by the audience: "You worked for a mega-company with a huge balance sheet, but what should a smaller company do?" Here is my answer. Small and medium-sized companies have the same obligation to obey the law as large companies. They must prioritize their compliance risks and spend more where the risks are higher. But they cannot ignore the law. A failure to be compliant can have two adverse consequences. First, if a small or medium-sized company takes a compliance torpedo midship, it can sink when the matter is serious. A Siemens or a JPMorgan can seal the area, fix the engines, and motor on. A major compliance issue can literally send a small or medium-sized company to the bottom of the sea. Second, many small companies want a nice payday by selling themselves to big companies. But due diligence techniques of large acquirers on compliance issues have become more sophisticated. If the acquirer finds a problem, as noted earlier, it may tell the target: "drop the purchase price," "turn yourself in or deal is off," or simply "sayonara." So, not addressing the compliance issues creates deal risk as well as enforcement risk for small and medium-sized companies. Finally, people who run small businesses have to look in the mirror and decide what kind of company—with what kind of employees— they want to operate. One of the great cases in business school is about the Indian founder of Infosys, Narayana Murthy, who simply refused to pay a small bribe to get telephones installed so his new company could start operations. For months, employees in this promising start-up had to go outside the premises to pay phones. Infosys lost orders. But Murthy wouldn't bend because he believed so strongly in doing business the right way. He is a wonderful example of looking in the mirror and deciding on integrity, even at the cost of lost business (eventually he got the phones installed without the bribe).[15]

6

ETHICS: THE COMPLEXITY

Corporations voluntarily decide to adopt ethical standards beyond what formal rules require. Those standards are uniform: They bind the companies and their employees everywhere in the world. They cover large subjects: setting standards for global sourcing; building emerging market facilities to world environmental standards; nondiscrimination in employment in societies without antidiscrimination law; prohibiting bribery as matter of company policy even when no statutory ban; voluntarily reducing greenhouse gases; refusing to do business in Iran; or, generally, vindicating human rights in corporate policies and practices. Once established, these standards are enshrined in the company's code of conduct and then described in more detail in the corporation's core "guide to company policies," which covers both mandated rules and voluntary standards. This process of establishing binding global norms, decided internally, is very different than the process of determining which legal and financial rules, promulgated externally, also bind the company. Setting ethical rules for a corporation involves a combination of prudential and moral considerations. The rationale for adopting one ethical rule (global sourcing) may be different than another ethical rule (voluntary reduction of greenhouse gases). Each decision depends on context and on a different mix of prudential and moral factors. Because binding global standards are so important in defining the corporation and in setting enforceable norms for all employees, the CEO and top company leadership should make these decisions about "ethics," often with the advice or approval of the board of directors.

The General Counsel, as lawyer-statesman, is intimately involved in this process: going beyond asking "what is legal" to the ultimate question for a corporation of "what is right." As discussed in Chapter 2, these questions about ethical positions occur in four broad areas:

- Duties to the corporation and its employees.
- Duties to all other stakeholders.
- Duties to the rule of law and administration of justice.
- Duties to help secure public goods that are vital to societal well-being but that cannot be realized through market mechanisms.

The General Counsel should play an important, often central, role in *organizing the processes* by which the corporation makes ethical determinations, in *generating options* about voluntary standards for addressing specific issues, and in *offering considered substantive views* about what is the "right" approach. The GC role in helping the company decide what global standards beyond law to adopt is another cornerstone of the inside counsel revolution because these standards are an essential element of corporate citizenship (see pp. 317–326).

Once the company has decided to make an ethical standard binding on all employees, that standard becomes operational reality through the organizational structure, systems, and processes described in Chapters 4 on culture and 5 on compliance. Indeed, although the method for determining them is different, the manner in which mandatory formal rules and voluntary ethical standards become part of the corporate culture and become integrated into business operations is the same. The combination of adherence to formal rules *and* to ethical standards is, in combination with core values, the essence of the broader concept of "culture of performance with integrity," which I strongly prefer as a corporate objective to "culture of compliance." "Integrity" is a broader, more aspirational word, and includes law, ethics, and values. It has greater resonance with business leaders and employees.

This chapter, therefore, focuses on how the corporation should voluntarily decide to set enforceable global standards beyond what the formal rules require. *It discusses different processes for surfacing questions about those standards for analysis and decision. It describes the general prudential and moral considerations that may be used in making those decisions, although it emphasizes that the decisions are contextual and multi-factorial.* It then illustrates the reasoning process by focusing on ethical issues in global labor markets and discussing problems raised when national law and a corporation's global standards are in conflict. I address two of the four broad ethical duties—promoting rule of law and helping secure public goods—in more detail in subsequent chapters on citizenship/public policy and on legal organization/law firms.

A. IDENTIFYING ETHICAL ISSUES

Corporations need a systematic, CEO-led process that makes identification and analysis of ethical issues a well-established part of the company's regular rhythms. The topic of ethical issues, for example, could be on the agenda of the quarterly meeting of the CEO, top corporate staff, and top business leaders. The staff work for this quarterly agenda item should be handled by the GC and CFO—and, as appropriate, the Chief Compliance Officer, head of the Audit Staff, Chief Risk Officer, and head of HR. Companies increasingly have a Vice President for Corporate Citizenship, who is responsible for the corporate charitable foundation but also for helping raise and decide these ethical issues.

In outline, the process could work as follows. The staff raises to the quarterly meeting of top executives a list of ethical issues relating to various corporate constituencies: investors, creditors, employees, partners, customers, suppliers, the community. As with early warning systems on compliance issues, these ethical issues will emerge from a variety of sources, including statements of stakeholders, newspaper stories, journalistic and academic commentary, and concerns of public officials. The top leadership group then conducts triage—and decides which of those issues, based on reputational importance and actual impact, should receive more detailed analysis and by which functions/

people in the corporation. After it is completed, the analysis and options are brought back to the senior executive group for discussion and for CEO decision. If a decision is made voluntarily to adopt an ethical standard—for example, to stop sales in Iran, to impose labor standards on third-party suppliers in the supply chain—and if it has a major financial, stakeholder, or reputational impact (like stopping new contracts in Iran), the CEO or other senior executives, including the GC, will often present the issue, options, and recommendation to the whole board of directors for review, either to seek their advice or secure their approval. After that step, the ethical rule is then incorporated in the corporation's messaging and implemented through existing systems and processes as if it were a formal legal or financial rule.

Let me emphasize that this process for *identifying issues* should be embedded in the daily life of the corporation. The issues that are presented on a quarterly or twice yearly basis to the CEO and the group of senior executives will arise out of other company processes and be combined into a master list for top-level consideration. For example, the company processes for establishing culture and for assuring compliance can also be used to surface ethical issues for separate, focused consideration. These processes include the "ombuds" system; the annual "bottoms up" employee review and "top down" business compliance reviews; the regular meetings of the staff functions, which see a variety of company-wide issues in their own disciplines (e.g., experts in environmental or labor and employment); and the early warning systems. But, the corporation may put special emphasis on additional methods of surfacing ethical issues to the senior executive group. Different approaches include the following.

When deciding what formal rules the corporation must comply with, the Legal and Finance staffs can surface ethical questions about whether the company should also comply with the "spirit" of those rules—should voluntarily take steps beyond what those rules require but that are in the broad penumbra of the rules' intended purpose. For example, in commercial financial services, staff leaders (or affected businesspeople) could surface the question of establishing "responsible lending" for low- or moderate-income customers from "wing to wing"—from product development through advertising to sales to disclosures to applications to account servicing to collections and problem solving—that set uniform company standards higher than many of the diverse laws in diverse jurisdictions.

As part of either a compliance review or general business reviews, company divisions can periodically conduct what I call a "common-sense" review of long-standing practices that may be out of date in light of evolving industry practices or common sense. Both key staff and key business leaders should explicitly flag hoary ways of doing business that need a "re-look." The idea occurred to me in my last years at GE due to the difficulties experienced by insurance broker Marsh & McLennan when it failed to disclose adequately that it was receiving contingent commissions on both sides of some insurer/insured transactions. Some argued that the incomplete disclosure of potential conflicts of interest to the affected parties was technically "lawful." But it was clearly a bad business practice that common sense said should be clarified, modified, or stopped. CEOs can ask business leaders to scrub practices that are hidden in the mists of time and might look inappropriate in today's bright lights—and the GC can ask inside counsel in the businesses to help surface such issues.

Corporations can develop systematic outreach to representatives of major stakeholder groups to assess what types of issues beyond legal and financial requirements are of greatest concern. Different staff leaders will relate to different groups. The General Counsel and Chief Financial Officer, through senior corporate counsel and the head of Investor Relations, will canvass shareholders. The head of HR will assess concerns of employees. The head of Marketing in the various divisions will, under the corporate leader, compile the many issues arising from the diverse customer base.

In addition, as I discuss in Chapter 9, most major corporations now publish a "Citizenship" or "Sustainability" Report, customarily following a reporting template (see pp. 354–357). A typical template is the Global Reporting Initiative. It asks companies to report baselines and trends in a wide variety of areas like shareholder engagement, labor practices, human rights, and environmental protection. Companies using such templates may not have actions to report in all categories— but those templates can highlight issues for discussion and debate about whether the corporation should voluntarily initiate action in areas where it is not currently active. Such reporting templates are now numerous and include principles from a new Sustainability Accounting Standards Board (modeled after the Financial Standards Accounting Board [FASB]). The CEO can also ask that senior staff review once a year the practices of peer corporations with respect to employees, customers, suppliers, investors, creditors, pensioners, and communities and bring salient issues forward to the quarterly senior executive meeting for discussion and possible analysis. These practices are easily found in the policy guides or citizenship reports of peer companies that, today, are on the Internet. This effort could include periodic review of the numerous codes of conduct for international business now in circulation going back to the venerable Organization for Economic Cooperation and Development (OECD) Guidelines for Multinational Enterprises to the Caux Round Table *Principles for Business* to the UN Guiding Principles on Business and Human Rights to various codes from groups like the International Chamber of Commerce or the World Economic Forum.

These diverse processes for identifying potential issues for voluntary commitments helps ensure that the doors of the corporation are open to ethical ideas. Obviously, with limited time and resources, the company can only address a priority set of actions, but it must stay flexible in order to address emerging consequential issues. Importantly, when the CEO puts the identification and analysis of ethical issues on the agenda of the quarterly senior executive meeting, she is sending an important message to the top leadership of the corporation. The General Counsel and CFO and others key staff leaders in HR, Compliance, Risk, and Citizenship can organize vibrant presentations that present priority issues in sharp focus, with real options and real impact, and do not become time-wasting "talking shops."

B. SETTING ETHICAL STANDARDS

Corporations should adopt ethical standards if it is in their "enlightened self-interest" to do so. But, of course, invocation of that much-used phrase merely begins—and does not end—discussion. Articulating a single set of criteria for making ethical decisions in a corporation is not possible because, from my long experience with this subject, I firmly believe that these decisions vary greatly and are understood and decided best in specific contexts when multiple factors are considered. Contextual and multi-factorial. Those are my watchwords. That is corporate reality, and it is intellectually challenging even if not always intellectually elegant.

I do believe, however, that these decisions are often a blend of "prudential" and "moral" factors. By *prudential*, I mean the practical, real-world impact of a decision in reducing risk or creating opportunity on an immediate circle of "direct stakeholders" and on a broader circle of "concerned societal actors" like competitors, government officials, the media, NGOs, and other opinion leaders. By *moral*, I mean respect for the "rights" of others, for the "duties" of a corporate citizen, and for the "norms" of society (national or global) that are identified in normative writing (political, philosophical, jurisprudential, etc.) or in aspirational codes of conduct published by international organizations or commentators. But, there is no bright line between "prudential" and "moral." Prudential considerations focus on the impact of corporate actions on affected parties and society. But the real-world impact of a corporate action may affect a stakeholder's perceived "right" or a community's perceived "norm." For example, a corporation may be very aggressive about opposing discrimination based on race, religion, or gender. Such a position may have a strong prudential dimension because it appeals to a diverse workforce in a world of diverse customers, but it may also have a strong moral dimension based on humane values shared by corporate leaders, corporate employees, and corporate customers. Or, even if not legally required, a corporation can, if it makes a mistake, refund customers' money; fully disclose, in understandable language, loan terms for borrowers; or describe side effects of drugs in plain English. These actions can not only help commercial reputation as a prudential matter, but also advance the moral values of fairness or transparency or duty. And, at the end of the day, although we can reason about practical impact and moral rights, duties, and norms, I do not believe there is any single "system" that mechanistically yields ethical decisions for corporations. Such decisions turn on corporate leaders' commonsense judgment and moral imagination—the ability to see the interests and rights of "others"—in light of their assessment of the history, culture, and mission of the corporation. Prudential and moral! Contextual and multi-factorial!

Two other throat-clearing points. First, I view "morals" and "ethics" as nearly synonymous. Put simplistically, *morals* are the principles on which judgments of right and wrong are based. *Ethics* are principles of right conduct. Obviously, morals inform decisions about ethics. Second, corporate law clearly allows boards of directors, CEOs, and other business leaders to make ethical decisions for the corporation that may have costs and that, in a particular accounting period, may reduce profits. "Profit maximization" is not the only goal or purpose of a corporation. Well-considered decisions are clearly lawful when they are in the broad self-interest of the corporation and when they are consistent with the decision process required by the business judgment rule. I take this as an obvious given and will not waste space to rehearse the arguments about why this is so.[1]

PRUDENTIAL CONSIDERATIONS

In thinking about whether or not to adopt ethical standards, *four broad practical questions* should be asked: Will the standards reduce an important risk facing the company? Will they improve the internal operation of the company? Will they have benefits for the company in the marketplace? Will they enhance the standing of the corporation in broader society in ways that, ultimately, help the corporation achieve its mission of high performance with high integrity?

Within this broad frame, decisions about whether to adopt ethical precepts beyond what the formal rules require will turn, as suggested, on a detailed assessment of how they will actually affect that inner circle of key stakeholders: shareholders, creditors, employees, customers, suppliers, partners, and communities in which the corporation operates. But such decisions also turn on assessments of how those stakeholders/societal actors *will perceive that impact and the intensity of that perception.* How important to shareholders is "majority voting" for board members? How will employees view special efforts to increase health and safety in manufacturing facilities? How will proponents of a company's labor unions view a corporation when it requires third-party suppliers in emerging markets to meet certain labor standards? How will a corporation's different constituencies react when it moves jobs to a different location? These prudential questions focus on how affected parties will react, not on the moral question of whether it is "right" for a corporation to impose these consequences.

Of course, the word *stakeholder* only conceals complexity. There is no such thing as "a" shareholder. There are a host of different types of shareholders with different objectives. There is no such thing as "an" employee. There are young and old, salaried and nonsalaried, unionized and nonunionized, domestic and foreign—all with different interests. There is, almost certainly, enormous diversity in the customer base. And, of course, particular ethical actions often require trade-offs between different types of the stakeholders: between investors and creditors, between customers and suppliers, and between new employees and existing employees.

Another level of "prudential considerations" involves the impact of an action—as well as the intensity of the perceived impact—on the reputation and standing of the company with an outer circle of "concerned societal actors" or "influencers" who can have impact on the corporation's future course: members of the legislative branch; regulators and other members of the Executive Branch; the media; NGOs; other commentators and opinion makers; existing and potential competitors; and, perhaps most importantly, certain segments of the public at large. Will taking the proposed ethical action help or hurt other items on the company's agenda with influential actors in this broader political, social, and economic sphere? And, once again, these labels merely conceal the daunting diversity of reactions and views, especially when envisioning the diversity of "concerned societal actors" in 100 nations across the globe.

These framing paragraphs merely set up the three-dimensional chess board of prudential considerations. Any single problem—for example, labor markets in a global economy—unveils the many different actors and forces at play—the varied pieces and moves—on the many complex subjects facing a corporation trying to decide whether to take action beyond what the formal rules require. The chess board not only has three (many!) dimensions, but it does not stay still. One obvious, though difficult, question is: How does the corporation know what the various inner-circle stakeholders and outer-circle influencers "think/believe" now and what they will "think/believe" in the future as ethical actions are announced and implemented? Beyond that "think/believe" question is the question about "possible counteractions" these inner and outer circles actors could take now and in the future in reaction to company action—and about whether will they be motivated to exercise that influence. That is a profoundly political problem, with a small "p."

MORAL CONSIDERATIONS

As suggested, corporate ethical decisions often have "moral" components as well as "prudential" ones. Books about "business ethics" often begin with discussions about systems of moral philosophy: from teleological to deontological, from utilitarianism to natural rights, and from Bentham and Mill to Kant and Rawls. The problem, of course, is that, with extremely rare exceptions, business leaders do not approach questions of global standards from that perspective (to put it mildly!). In my experience with extremely smart business leaders, it was far better to start with a concrete business problem and then begin to work through all the prudential and moral considerations in a practical, not theoretical, way. The business leaders and the board had to believe that a problem implicated either the inner circle of stakeholders or the outer circle of influencers in a very real and important sense before they would begin to think beyond consequences and seriously consider some concrete conception of what was right in a moral, not just a prudential, sense. I was the Senior Vice President–General Counsel, not the Senior Vice President–Moral Philosophy. *But, if not gussied up with too much erudite theory or too many fancy words, issues of "right" and "morality" are of concern to good business leaders, who must make very real choices about what kind of company they want to lead.*

Thus, it was much more important to ask more commonsense moral questions when we got to the "morality" part of the "beyond what the law requires" analysis rather than debating different schools of philosophy. These questions help answer, from a moral perspective, the framing questions of whether the contemplated act will reduce risk or advance company interests internally, in the marketplace, or in society. For example, the ethical framework advanced in a leading business school course on leadership and corporate accountability focuses on three key ethical questions for CEOs and other senior executives: Is the corporation's own identity consistent with the likely consequences of this action? Is the corporation meeting its duties toward, and respecting the rights of, individuals or groups? Is the corporation respecting broader communities (local, regional, national, global) and their norms?[2]

In keeping with this general orientation, most helpful, in my view, were analyses of normative issues that directly enumerated for consideration (1) possible duties of corporations and (2) the rights of direct stakeholders and other societal actors. Such efforts did not solve problems or yield results, but they did act as important "prompts" or benchmarks about moral considerations that companies should take into account in deciding whether or not to take an action beyond what the formal rules required. Two useful examples are the Caux Round Table *Principles for Business* and an analysis of corporate codes around the world conducted by a team at the Harvard Business School (HBS) that identified eight core ethical principles recognized in global business. The HBS study covered the following subjects: fiduciary duties of care and loyalty, respect for property, reliability, transparency, respecting individual dignity, fairness, being a responsible community citizen, and being responsive to the legitimate claims of others. And, in both the Caux *Principles* and the HBS study, there were more detailed issues under these more general ethical subjects. For example, under the dignity principle alone there are these issues: respect for individual, promoting health and safety, protecting privacy and confidentiality, abjuring use of force, respecting freedom of association and expression, and providing learning and development. And, to go one step further, under "health and safety" there is enumeration of these ethical subjects: ensure that products and services sustain or enhance customer health and safety, protect employees from avoidable injury and illness in the workplace, provide a work environment that is free from substance abuse, and prefer suppliers and partners whose work practices respect international labor standards and health and safety. Importantly, in a follow-up study, the authors of the HBS article on ethical principles found that a high percentage of employees they surveyed said the broad principles identified in the first study should be adopted by their companies, but a smaller percentage said that their companies had actually adopted them.[3]

These examples—and subjects found in other codes—are quite useful for General Counsel in shaping discussion about whether the corporation should adopt a global standard. But, each decision will ultimately turn on the best judgment of the CEO and the board under all the circumstances, prudential and moral. My position is summarized by Andrew Crane and Dirk Matten, authors of a well-regarded text, *Business Ethics: Managing Corporate Citizenship and Sustainability in the Age of Globalization*:

> ... normative ethical theories ... in a pluralistic perspective can provide a number of important considerations for ethical decision-making in business. ... [But] it should have become extremely clear that these theories rarely provide us with a clear cut, unambiguous and non-controversial solution. ... [E]thical theories are at best tools to inform the "moral sentiment" of the decision-maker and as such cannot predetermine solutions from an abstract, theoretical or wholly "objective" point of view. Ultimately ethical decisions are taken by actors in everyday business situations. Ethical theories might help to rationalize and structure some of the key aspects of those decisions, but their status can never be one that allows a moral judgment or decision to be made without effectively immersing into the real situation.[4]

On the other hand, a focus on the "real situation" does not relieve decision makers of systematic consideration of the relevant prudential and moral factors. General Counsel have a special responsibility to ensure that personal bias is identified and countered and that as broad a view as possible is developed of consequences, rights, and duties in the appropriate context—whether that be local, national, regional, or global. Professor Lynn Paine, a national thought leader on business and ethics at Harvard Business School, acknowledges possible "conflicts between moral and financial points of views." While noting that there "can be no general across the board resolution to such conflicts," she argues that corporations should address such problems by asking systematic and sequential questions about corporate purpose (beyond wealth creation), company principles (precepts that should guide behavior), people (whose interests should the company take into account), and power (who should decide, according to what authority).[5]

COSTS AND BENEFITS

In deciding whether to adopt a global standard beyond what the formal legal and financial rules require, it may be possible to conduct a relatively conventional financial analysis about future costs and benefits. For example, if the corporation decides voluntarily to invest in "front of the pipe" manufacturing initiatives to reduce environmental cleanup costs at the "end of the pipe," it should be possible to determine both the cost of the investment and the savings in cleanup and other remedial costs. But, in many instances, such predictions may be much harder to make. Investing in operational improvements may reduce customer complaints, lawsuits, or employee injuries. But, it may not be possible to predict the precise reduction in those complaints, suits, or injuries. Thus, a decision to make those improvements may turn on "it is the right thing to do" buttressed by general knowledge of the direction of savings—of "benefits"—but not knowledge of the precise amounts that will actually be realized. Or take the issue of whether to make special recruiting efforts to attract talented women in China and Japan. Although women are highly educated in those societies, they may suffer discrimination from local employers. The costs for a global corporation of seeking out such employees may again be concrete, but the benefits can obviously be significant even if hard to quantify: finding great talent in the host country; developing a global reputation as a good place for women to work; and, even more broadly, promoting general company hiring and retention due to a reputation for nondiscrimination in the workforce.

In assessing the "economics" of voluntarily adopting global standards, it is important to keep several perspectives in mind. First, the outlays for such changes are not just costs, but are *investments* in improving the company. Second, the *benefits* of such investments cannot always have financial precision and cannot always be expressed as having an internal rate of return (IRR). Whether the global standard will enhance the corporation's reputation—and perhaps increase its brand's value—will often turn *as much (or more) on judgment as on financial analysis.* What is the value of taking an action that will avoid public embarrassment from an action perceived as inappropriate, even if not illegal, and the associated costs of making an effective public response, imposing appropriate discipline, and instituting needed system changes? Third, decision makers should take a long view of the relevant *accounting period.* The benefits that may result from an investment in a binding ethical standard may not occur in the next quarter or the next year but may accrue over a number of years. The full benefits of making a special effort to hire highly educated and talented women in China and Japan, for example, may be realized over time, not just in a few quarters or even a few years. Fourth, as indicated earlier, there may be *moral choices a corporation makes that, regardless of cost, are the right thing to do.* A corporate policy against discrimination may fit into the flexible, "good-judgment" framework of investments and "soft" benefits over a long period of time outlined here. But it may also be justified simply and directly on its own terms. There are certain acts of corporations—no bribes—that, in the view of its leaders, are appropriate because they are simply the ethical thing to do.[6]

Because decisions about global standards are not only contextual and multi-factorial; are not only about different combinations of prudential and moral considerations; but are also about less-than-precise views of *investment, benefits, and accounting periods,* they ultimately require common sense, wisdom, and *judgment.* And an exercise of judgment on important matters that will voluntarily bind the company and its employees requires that the CEO or the CEO with the board make the decision. *And it is in this area especially, on the classic "what is right?" questions, that the General Counsel as lawyer-statesman has such an important place in the corporate firmament in helping to conduct the analysis and to shape the options, the discussion, and the decisions that can avoid risk or create benefits in light of the corporation's history, mission, and culture. The intense engagement of the GC and senior company lawyers on this vital set of issues has helped shape the inside counsel revolution.*

To illustrate analysis of global standards, I now offer an overview of ethical issues relating to global labor markets. As additional explication of these issues, I then discuss the vexing problems that occur when national law or lack of enforcement conflicts with a company's global standards and when governments are rogue states that prevent a global corporation from doing business—with integrity—there at all.

C. CHALLENGES IN GLOBAL SUPPLY CHAINS

No complex of issues poses greater "ethical" problems for multinational companies than how to handle labor and other issues in global supply chains. No issue poses greater challenges for the General Counsel as lawyer-statesmen and partner-guardian, given its breadth and complexity. This discussion aspires only to be exemplary because, in the real world, few ethical subjects are as fraught with legal, ethical, policy, and political nuances and require sophisticated analysis.

After World War II, the second great era of economic globalization in the 20th century began (the first ended with World War I and the Great Depression). Initially, companies engaged in "offshoring"—moving basic corporate functions like manufacturing to emerging markets to lower their labor costs. This could involve either full manufacturing or more limited assembly. Starting in the 1980s and accelerating in the 1990s, multinational corporations began a concerted push toward "outsourcing"—moving corporate functions to third-party suppliers, to "buy" not to "make" in overseas markets.

Over time, offshoring and outsourcing covered a wide range of goods and services: finished products (ranging from autos to electronics to toys), components or subassemblies (for both high-tech and low-tech products), food or ingredients for food, drugs or elements of drugs, and an increasing range of services (from accounting to law to health care to finance). These goods and services initially were often imported back into the United States (and other developed nations) because they were less expensive. And, during this period, non-U.S.

companies exported ever-larger amounts of cheaper goods to the United States, undercutting domestic manufacturers and reducing U.S. jobs.

As a result, the well-known debate ensued between free traders (more competition, cheaper goods in the United States, growth in developing markets that then buy U.S. goods) and fair traders (only wealthy benefit, blue-collar job loss, hollowing out of U.S. middle class, exploitive labor standards overseas). The debate heated up during the Great Recession with its high unemployment rate, especially in political years like 2012, when "outsourcing" became a dirty word in many key electoral states and politicians were calling for economic "nationalism." Virtually every direct stakeholder of a major international corporation, both at home and abroad, was and is affected by "offshoring" and "outsourcing" decisions: shareholders, employees, customers, suppliers, and communities. And virtually every entity in the broader circle of "affected societal actors" has an opinion and position on the subject: national labor unions, NGOs/human rights groups, socially responsible investors, politicians, and the media. Economic policy debates rage about how many jobs in the United States are currently being lost due to trade and how the United States can create jobs, stimulate growth, increase exports, improve technical education, invest in R&D, and encourage advanced manufacturing. And, of course, debates also rage about the appropriateness and cost of any governmental initiatives to advance these objectives.

Yet, the imperatives of offshore facilities and employees are—and will remain—central to American companies' international competitiveness. American companies will, for a wide variety of reasons relating to global dynamism and complex supply chains, continue to participate in this transformative era of global economic change by increasing activities and hiring workers outside the United States, especially in fast-growing, less-developed countries. Still, offshoring and outsourcing today are like sex in the Victorian era: often repressed (by business) or criticized (by labor) in public discussion, much practiced in private behavior.

It is therefore vital for global businesses, which may be subject to exacting scrutiny, to defend offshoring with clear positions and clear actions regarding ethical standards abroad and assistance for displaced workers at home. Global companies must be prepared to forcefully embrace the responsible, competitive basics of offshoring and outsourcing—and to articulate those basics clearly to their communities, to their stakeholders, and to other societal actors active in American politics.

1. BUSINESS PURPOSE

Companies should step up and honestly explain why they offshore and outsource business functions and employment in a broad array of product and service activities to compete in a truly global economy. (When is the last time you heard an American CEO defend offshore economic activities to a broad public audience as opposed to the virtues of American exports?) Among the strong (and standard) reasons that non-businesspeople could understand, if properly explained and if supported by clear, accurate statements of facts, are:

- The need to stay cost-competitive with international companies, either through reduced finished product/service cost or through supply chain efficiencies.
- The need to manufacture, assemble, provide services, and perform R&D in order to understand and sell in a local market, and to attract great local talent for jobs that would not ever be offered in the United States.
- The need to have a significant employment or plant/equipment presence in a local market because host governments demand it.
- The need to have such a presence because it can also help pull through a company's high-end exports from the United States.
- The need to strengthen a local market's economy and thus increase U.S. exports over time.
- The need to offer consumers in the United States lower-cost products.

In the last 25 years, a fundamental reason U.S. corporations invested in markets outside America was to grow business there. Indeed, this increasing activity has its own name: "onshoring." For example, foreign auto makers in China (Japanese, European, and American) have roughly 60 percent of a 24 million unit per year market, with production facilities frequently owned with Chinese partners. GM is the leading automaker in China, with about 20 percent of sales (selling more units than in the United States). In 2014 in China, GM had 11 assembly plants and four power-train plants in eight Chinese cities. Thirty-five percent of its revenues came from sales in China. These new jobs in China were not taken away from U.S. workers but were necessary for developing a strong GM presence. For many U.S. multinationals, approximately half their revenues, and 30 to 50 percent of their workforce, are outside the United States, reflecting a primary need to serve overseas markets through "onshoring" overseas.

Similarly, foreign companies have, of course, been "onshoring" in the United States for years to be closer to customers, to develop an "American" identity, and to gain political credibility. Foreign automakers built more than 5 million cars at 16 facilities in the United States in 2013, with 70 percent of Japanese cars sold in the United States made in North America. In that year, foreign automakers had 32 manufacturing facilities, 56 R&D centers, and nearly 10,000 dealerships in the United States. Announcements of acquisitions or new plants in the United States are made almost every day by non-U.S. companies, like Airbus, Siemens, Lenovo, Infosys, IKEA, and Foxconn. Indeed, foreign companies employ nearly 6 million Americans and account for 13 percent of manufacturing jobs and about 18 percent of exports.

Moreover, the supply chains that support global imports and exports across a broad range of national borders from manufacturing or assembly facilities in an increasingly broad range of nations are increasingly complex, with the finished products often having different parts, components, or ingredients from multiple countries. The simple trade model of manufacturing overseas to bring products back is largely a thing of the past, and business leaders need to explain how modern supply chains work to the advantage of many.

2. USE OF REVENUES AND MARGINS

Similarly, companies must be more forceful in explaining the uses of revenues and margins derived from offshoring/outsourcing's competitive cost structures and local appeal. They are key both to cash flow, which finances dividends, and to "net income," which drives stock price that, in turn, benefits shareholders (often, American pensioners). The cash from revenues and margins is also often used to enhance the corporation: to improve its internal operations, productivity, technology, and products or to increase its reach and scale efficiencies through acquisitions.

3. LABOR STANDARDS

One of the traditional arguments against globalization is that multinationals move jobs and facilities to emerging markets to avoid environmental, health, and safety regulations in the developed world. In response to that criticism, international corporations have set—or should set—policies to ensure decent labor standards overseas, both in their own facilities and in the facilities of third-party suppliers.

a) Why? In general, there are three broad reasons a global corporation would adopt binding labor standards both in their own offshored activities and in their relations with third-party suppliers. First, there is the simple equitable argument that workers in a nation should be treated the same by a global corporation, whether employed by the company or by a third-party supplier. This argument applies to the effect of local law. The global company must, at a minimum, comply with local law relating to labor standards, and it would be seen as hypocritical if it did not require local law compliance from third-party suppliers. Similarly, if, as a matter of global labor policy, the corporation goes beyond what the law requires in terms of giving its employees certain benefits in working conditions or workplace protections, the same argument applies about avoiding hypocrisy and requiring the same—or at least very similar—benefits for employees in contracts with third-party suppliers.

Second, requiring that third parties must, at a minimum, comply with local law to qualify as a corporation's suppliers reduces the risk that there will be supply chain interruptions due to enforcement actions. To be sure, enforcement in emerging markets is erratic and often political, especially with respect to worker protections. And even good compliance with local law by third-party suppliers does not provide a guarantee against "political" enforcement actions aimed either at the vendor or at the multinational customer. But such a requirement certainly can help reduce the risk, even if not eliminate it.

Third, large global corporations have an iconic status. They need to refute the arguments against globalization about using offshoring and outsourcing to avoid good laws at home and to adopt bad practices abroad. The GE CEOs understood that the company was a symbol of globalization and needed to adopt good labor standards in offshoring and outsourcing to answer the many opponents of globalization. A regime of labor standards at third-party suppliers can reduce a telling criticism of globalization though not eliminate it.

b) What? Working with NGOs, corporations have developed a set of labor standards over time that should apply at both company-owned operations and at the operations of third-party suppliers. These include non-discrimination in hiring, compensation, promotion, or termination on the basis of gender, race, religion, or other categories recognized in civil rights laws; prohibitions on physical, sexual, verbal, or psychological harassment and abuse; no child labor; no forced labor, including prison, indentured, or bonded labor; recognition of the right to association and collective bargaining; provision of a healthy and safe environment to minimize workplace accidents and injuries; reasonable measures to protect the environment outside the workplace; limitations on both regular hours and hours of overtime; and providing the minimum or prevailing wage and, if that is not sufficient to meet employees' basic needs, providing a wage necessary to do so.

But to list the subjects is only to begin the discussion about "what" means. Is it just requiring in the supply contract that the third-party suppliers comply with their national law? Or should the global buyer require suppliers to follow higher standards—for example, on issues like non-discrimination or freedom of association that may not be recognized in law of the supplying nation. And if standards beyond the law of each individual nation are sought, should the labor standards both for own employees and for third-party suppliers still vary by nation or region, or should they be uniform across the globe in detail and scope? These are the broad issues with which global corporations—and General Counsels—must wrestle by creating options, understanding costs, exploring trade-offs, and detailing implementation issues.

c) Why and What? Child Labor[7]   The ethical complexity of these offshoring and outsourcing issues is reflected in the problem of limiting child labor at third-party suppliers. Basic issues include the age below which children cannot work; how that age relates to the age when compulsory schooling in the relevant community ends, both in theory and in fact; whether the age of the child varies depending on how dangerous is the industry; how working children can be protected from physical, sexual, and psychological abuse; and whether indentured child labor (employed to pay off parental debts) should be banned.

Answers to these questions are found in international conventions that countries may or may not sign and may or may not implement—for example, the International Labor Organization's Conventions on Minimum Age (1973), Worst Forms of Child Labor (1999), or the UN Convention on the Rights of the Child (1989). The conventions are directed at countries, not companies, and are precatory only, lacking any enforcement mechanism and relying only on "naming and shaming" reports directed at nations. Child labor standards that buyers impose on third-party suppliers may also be found in the differing laws of relevant countries—for example, China and India—although emerging markets are notorious for not implementing child labor laws on the books. Or they may be found in industry codes established to monitor supplier practices—for example, the labor standards of the Fair Labor Association established in the late 1990s by the apparel industry. Choosing one high global standard from among these various sources may be the best combination of preventive ethics and administrative simplicity—for example, no child under a set age (15 or 16) will be employed in any emerging market regardless of local law.

Constraints on child labor seek to avoid serious economic, physical, psychological, and other harms to young people. But limiting child labor at third-party suppliers poses the perplexing question of what happens to children who are not allowed to work for global companies or for their third-party suppliers. These children may live in poor communities. They may be working because their families need the income and because meaningful secondary schools may not exist. If children are not allowed to work for global corporations or their suppliers, then there is concern that they will be forced into more dangerous industries or be lured into the sex or drug trade.

Put another way, when global corporations adopt child labor standards, they may be doing it to protect their global reputation—No Child Labor!—but they may be exposing the impoverished child to a worse fate. This may especially be so if, as noted previously, the corporation, out of an excess of caution, chooses a high age (say, 16) below which employment of a child constitutes prohibited child labor. GE chose that number due to both an excess of caution and to the need for administrative simplification in the supply chain. But such an approach then raises the issue of whether the global corporation has an affirmative, ethical duty to deal with the social welfare problems of the region. Companies like IKEA have worked with UNICEF and the World Health Organization, in regions of India where rugs are sourced, to create programs that educate children who do not attend school, to provide health care for mothers and children, and to create programs of microfinance to help families improve their economic lot. IKEA refused to join a retailer coalition that promised rugs sold by developed country retailers were not made with child labor. IKEA felt it could not verify that commitment. Instead, it believed this social welfare program—with a cost of roughly $140 million per year—would address the underlying issues of poverty and poor institutions more directly. This type of program reaches only a tiny fraction of the children in India, yet there is obvious value in helping even a small cohort of children. But such a program involves resources, time, effort, and expertise, which many corporations—however well intentioned—are not prepared to deploy or simply do not have.

So, corporations must ask whether in banning child labor they are protecting their reputation but harming children. Yet, corporations are not social welfare agencies and have limited capacity to effect broad economic and social change in emerging market communities. Can they combine safe work and decent education at their sites or at the sites of third-party suppliers? Global corporations cannot employ "underage" children, but forcing third-party suppliers to stop child labor, without health and education alternatives for the children, is a difficult, morally ambiguous choice. I felt that GE could not employ child labor but that the company was not competent to conduct social welfare programs in emerging markets. GE could use modest amounts of philanthropic funds to support child welfare organizations in emerging markets. But this was clearly a limited response and was not a comprehensive answer to the very real issues of child development. Part of GE's justification for this limited approach was that most of our products were in the capital goods sector and didn't involve much, if any, child labor by third-party suppliers anyway. But, companies like IKEA struck the balance differently, illustrating the sharp dilemmas with respect to child labor.

d) How? As a corporation, and its General Counsel, go through the process of deciding "why" and "what" with respect to labor standards, it must also consider the host of questions on "how" the company can implement such a commitment. A first issue is how the company would build this set of disciplines into the global supply chain processes. Where would ethical supply chain issues fit into the organization? Who would have responsibility/accountability? Who would staff the effort? What kind of training would be necessary? How would suppliers be qualified—with what kind of information on the labor standards issues? How would suppliers be trained (should companies make special effort to help third parties meet global standards)? How would suppliers be audited and requalified? What is the role of external auditors—if any? How should corporations communicate their program to stakeholders—with what kind of detail?

Here, again, straightforward questions hide more than they explain. For example, in the qualification process of third-party suppliers, how is the complicated question of environmental health and safety assessed? By trying to assess local law or apply more stringent company global EHS standards? If global buyers require suppliers to follow local law regulating wages and hours, how exactly is the supplier's duty under the contract ascertained if the rules are not opaque (not published) and if there are not clear rules of decision? Or, how is the age of children determined when applying child labor precepts? Are suppliers really going to have birth certificates of workers? How prevalent is the practice—which occurs in China—of fraudulent papers of young workers or phony work study programs that are exploitive not educational?

Another set of implementation questions about labor standards is what rights and duties should be included in the supply contract. Should the corporation have inspection rights; audit rights; unannounced visitation rights? Should it have a unilateral right to terminate upon finding a violation—or should it have to give the supplier notice and a reasonable opportunity to cure? Should suppliers be required to certify that they are in compliance with local law and with global corporation "standards" or "expectations"—and is that requirement meaningful?

And what about second- and third-tier suppliers? Should the first-tier supplier be responsible for ensuring that the lower-tier sub-suppliers are following the labor standards? If so, how does the multinational know that this is happening, or is it just a formalistic cop-out? Alternatively, does the global company itself have the willingness and the resources to impose and assess labor standards at these second- and third-tier suppliers? Or should it adopt a middle position and leave supervision to the first-tier supplier except in special cases—for example, when the company has recently moved work from the home company and is under special scrutiny or when the company has an equity interest in the first-tier supplier and has a higher degree of responsibility?

One thing is clear: A corporation should not set labor standards for third-party suppliers unless it is prepared to answer all these "how" questions—and is prepared to implement with rigor and discipline. For example, despite rhetorical commitment to standards at third-party suppliers, Apple was raked over the media coals for several years for the poor labor standards practices of Foxconn, its huge third-party supplier in China. It was forced to hire an independent auditor, the Fair Labor Association (FLA), to monitor Foxconn. When the FLA found widespread violations of labor standards—including far more hours worked by employees on average than allowed under Chinese law—both Foxconn and Apple promised and then implemented significant changes. But, due to its initial failures and its huge profits, Apple's supply chain, involving hundreds of third parties, is now scrutinized with care by the international media and is routinely the subject of outsourcing stories.[8]

4. QUALITY

It is imperative that global companies assure quality in their offerings that are made in whole or in part in foreign supply chains. This assurance can result from compliance with legal requirements or from following self-imposed quality standards. Serious safety and quality concerns in offshored or outsourced components, ingredients, and products have now emerged front and center in the globalization debates. Lead paint in toys, antifreeze in toothpaste, tainted ingredients in blood-thinner medicine, and unsafe food (for people and even pets)—these events have led consumers, parents, patients, and regulators to question whether products using global suppliers are of sufficient quality and safety to protect end-users in America and elsewhere in the world from grievous harm. China has, in the past, been the cause of some of the most dramatic headlines. Baxter International halted sales of its blood thinner Heparin because Chinese manufacturing problems were allegedly associated with death and injury in patients. Mattel had to recall 500,000 toy cars with lead paint and 18 million toys with loose magnets children could swallow that were "Made in China." There has been much debate about the adequacy of regulatory structure and resources both in supplying countries and in the United States.

But companies must themselves proactively address these profound questions of quality assurance in global supply chains and go beyond what the law requires. A central purpose of global supply chains is "deverticalization"—the creation of goods and services through "buy" rather than "make" techniques. When companies had integrated vertical processes for making products (from mining the ore to the finished steel tube), they were responsible for what went out the factory door to the customer. But deverticalization does not change the ethical responsibility for quality and safety of ultimate products even if materials or ingredients or components or subassemblies come from third parties and even if there are nominal quality assurance regimes of government inspection and control. The global corporation must assure tight contracting and a vigilant oversight "system" for the safety and quality of the items it sells in the global marketplace. Standards, systems, and processes must avoid defects that threaten functionality or, more importantly, that risk impairing health and safety. The grounding of the 787 Dreamliner due to fires in ion-lithium batteries supplied by a Japanese company is a symbol of supply chain deverticalization risks. It happened in a world-class company, Boeing, and symbolized a series of supply chain challenges the company faced in launching a new state-of-the-art aircraft—challenges that all global companies must address in their supply chains.[9]

5. CATASTROPHIC PLANT SAFETY ISSUES[10]

Beyond regular workplace health and safety issues, global corporations, and General Counsels, must also consider the potential for catastrophic issues at the facilities of third-party suppliers. These tragic—and challenging—issues are symbolized by two horrific events in the Bangladesh garment industry, issues that pose profound ethical problems for global companies. In December 2012, 112 workers died in a garment factory fire near Dhaka. In April 2013, more than 1,100 workers died in the collapse of a factory at Rana Plaza, and nearly 2,400 were injured. The backdrop for these deadly events is the growth of the garment industry in Bangladesh. For much global trade, labor costs are only one part of the business equation. But in some spheres, like apparel, textiles, and toys, cheap labor still is a large component and is still vital. As one of the poorest nations in the world (Bangladesh, a nation of 160 million, ranks 192nd in terms of per capita income), the minimum wage for the 3.5 million garment workers is about $38 per month (one of lowest in the world). As wages in China have risen, international buyers have shifted attention to Bangladesh, where approximately 5,000 garment factories produce between $20 and $25 billion in goods annually, which constitute about 80 percent of the nation's export volume and 10 percent of gross domestic product (GDP). Approximately 60 percent of garment exports go to the United States or EU through brand-name retailers.

The factory fire and the factory collapse—and other health and safety problems in Bangladesh and around the world—pose some immediate, real-world problems: Who will compensate for individuals' deaths and injuries? Who will set decent standards? Who will inspect the thousands of factories to ensure that they are structurally sound and protected against fire? Who will pay to bring those factories up to "standard" after the inspections reveal the gap between what is and what should be? For example, estimates put the cost of bringing all the garment factories in Bangladesh up to acceptable standards in the range of $2.5 to $3 billion.

The problem is that many weak or indifferent actors must play a role: the Bangladesh government, the factory owners, the garment buyers (including many international brands), consumers across the globe, and developed world governments that have allowed preferential treatment for Bangladesh imports (using "trade" in lieu of "aid"). A global retailer—and its General Counsel—must find an ethical path through this maze of confusing roles. The government exemplifies a huge *regulatory deficit*: corrupt officials, broken political systems, inadequate laws, virtually no enforcement, greater concern about business than safety, and lack of government programs for workers killed or injured in industrial accidents. The Bangladesh garment makers/ factory owners exemplify a *compliance deficit*: inadequate money spent to meet inadequate laws, bribes to stop enforcement, subcontracting to second-tier garment makers with little review of safety, and indifference to upgrading facilities (before accidents, there were estimates that only 1 percent of the facilities met basic minimal safety standards). The workers are saddled with an *organizing deficit*: Neither the government nor the factory owners allow the employees to take collective action through unions or worker associations to protect themselves. The international retailers exemplify a *buyers' deficit*: These companies—including world brands such as Adidas, Benetton, Primark, GAP, Wal-Mart, L.L.Bean, and Target—have standards they may not enforce, and they buy on low cost and sell on low price. The end-users represent a *consumers' deficit*: Customers enjoy the low prices and have yet to organize serious consumer movements or boycotts to change retailer behavior. And developed country governments like the United States and United Kingdom exhibit a *policy deficit*: They give trade preferences to Bangladesh imports (although not to garments particularly) without demanding any health and safety protections for workers.

The most direct solution for these interrelated problems is for individual global retail corporations, which buy the garments for resale in the developed world, to take matters directly into their own hands and act on their own. They can concentrate their efforts on a few third-party suppliers and ensure that labor standards are met; structural protections are followed (whether the local building codes or global standards established by the company); subcontracting to anonymous, out of code manufacturers is not allowed; inspections are regular; and workers can organize. Alternatively, a company could "make" not "buy." It could build or buy its own facility, where it could ensure all important standards are met. Or, it could form a JV with other responsible global brands to share the costs of select owned and operated facilities (in a manner consistent with competition laws). Obviously, this approach must overcome the hurdle of cost (does this make economic sense because consumers will pay an appropriate price that provides an appropriate margin?). So, too, this approach must overcome corruption, both in government approvals/regulation and in the construction process itself. Companies like Disney and Levi Strauss left Bangladesh after these catastrophes, but many NGOs have pleaded with international companies to stay and do a better job because the garment industry, with all its manifest problems, can offer workers (80 to 90 percent are women) a way out of abject poverty. Wal-Mart has made such an attempt.

Nonetheless, an individual company approach—if global corporations are willing to engage on that basis—still leaves unaddressed the huge systemic problems I described earlier—not just in Bangladesh, but in other emerging markets with large garment industry presence (or with other low-cost products). As with the discussion of child labor, the underlying conditions are complex and interrelated, and their solution involves significant social, political, and economic change. Is that the responsibility of an individual global corporation alone? After the Rana Plaza collapse, two different consortia of global companies—one organized in Europe, the other in the United States—emerged to deal with the broader problems of inspection and remediation across a wide number of factories. These efforts have made some progress on broader problems, including payment to the injured or deceased and funds for more factory inspections. But the fundamental issues of government dysfunction and corruption and rogue third-party suppliers remain, as does the cost of upgrading health and safety practices across the broad universe of garment factories. As with child labor in India, plant safety in Bangladesh poses deep systemic problems of government failure that corporations cannot solve and broad issues of bringing hundreds of plants up to safe levels that corporations are not willing to fund. Of course, these serious plant safety issues in the garment industry, and other low-cost industries, exist in other poor countries with, as yet, no coordinated industry response. If corporations want to make a systematic difference, they need to face the broader citizenship questions of changing public policy and building public institutional capacity in a broad coalition effort. If not, then they need to ensure that the factories they use are truly safe and sound, either through rigorous supplier qualification and monitoring or through owning and operating facilities themselves.

6. WORKER TRANSITION AT HOME

Global corporations must also address the domestic dimensions of international labor markets. How should they provide for workers laid off in the home country when jobs move overseas? Whether driven by the obvious political considerations of helping U.S. workers affected by global trade or by moral considerations of fairness to workers, American multinational companies need to focus on four issues for their displaced workers: good severance pay, transitional health benefits, meaningful retraining opportunities, and job outplacement services. The vivid stories of American workers laid off and communities affected due to offshoring and outsourcing have given critics of globalization much of their momentum. Acting humanely toward those affected is important as an act of citizenship, but also as an act of politics. The steady decline in manufacturing, and resultant loss of manufacturing jobs, is not solely due to offshoring and outsourcing but to other factors, too, such as the information revolution, increased productivity, robotics, and a shift to a service economy. As a result of these broader factors, a company may be wise to have a consistent policy toward all workers displaced, for whatever reason. Labor agreements may, in fact, have such provisions providing transitional benefits to laid-off workers, but the numbers of unionized workers in the private sector is only about 12 percent, down from more than 30 percent decades ago. If labor agreements do not cover workers, then the company should simply adopt a policy for worker transition covering the key elements of severance, health, training, and outplacement.

7. PUBLIC POLICY

Such company-specific efforts can be coordinated with—and can supplement—governmental safety net programs. For example, the Trade Adjustment Assistance Act is aimed specifically at training, job placement, income support, and health care for workers laid off due to international trade. This 50-year-old program enjoys bipartisan support in both the House and the Senate. Since its inception, the Labor Department has certified about 4.8 million workers as hurt by global trade, and about 2.2 million eligible for the program took advantage of it (at a 2013 cost of about $750 million). But it has often been criticized: Its funding is not adequate; it needs to be coordinated/consolidated with other programs for displaced workers (like unemployment insurance); its effectiveness in placing workers is questionable. But, in addition to programs for their own displaced workers, corporations should support *effective* public policy to assist those American workers adversely affected by accelerating global technology change and global competition. Corporate support was important in 2015 when the Trade Adjustment Assistance Act was reauthorized with some improvements.[11]

Support for enhanced worker adjustment legislation and funding only highlights that many of these ethical issues relating to global labor markets have public policy cognates. As I discuss in Chapter 9 on citizenship, the General Counsel, wearing her policy hat, needs to assess whether to devote company resources and engage in the many governmental debates on global labor or other supply chain issues—for example, Chinese labor law reform, improvements in global product safety and quality standards, enhanced environmental standards, better enforcement in emerging markets, labor and environmental standards in trade agreements, or disclosure requirements on "conflict minerals" (extracted from certain nations beset by, inter alia, civil war violence and use of child soldiers).

IN SUM

I have chosen to illustrate (if hardly solve) the multiple problems of corporate ethical standards through this discussion of global supply chains. As I warned, it is only schematic. But, more importantly, it is incomplete, not just in its treatment of this subject, but because there as so many other ethical issues facing corporations. Such assessment of multiple dimensions could be directed at the host of demands for global companies to take actions beyond what the law requires (e.g., privacy or environmental stewardship or governance). But, I hope, this example illustrates the type of analysis in which a company must engage—and in which a General Counsel must have a vital part.

D. CONFLICT BETWEEN GLOBAL STANDARDS AND NATIONAL LAW

A fundamental principle for multinational companies is compliance with the law of all nations where they do business. But a recurrent dilemma is what to do when a corporation's global standards (e.g., "oppose censorship" for a global media company) collides with national law (e.g., China's extensive state censorship). As companies globalize and nations regulate ever more, this vexatious problem for General Counsel is not esoteric but recurring. A decision that a company's global standards conflict with national law raises a range of options: obey the law, be civilly disobedient (a very uncomfortable, often untenable, position for global companies dedicated to rule of law), try to change the law, or stop doing business in that nation.

In thinking through this dramatic issue, I have found it helpful to posit two limiting cases. At one end is the ethical obtuseness, even complicity, of American companies in Nazi Germany in the 1930s. Although the detailed history is complicated, many U.S. and UK multinationals—for example, IBM, Kodak, GE, DuPont, GM, Ford—had either wholly owned or majority interest subsidiaries operating in Germany from Hitler's assumption of power in 1933 to the outbreak of war in 1939 (and some thereafter). These subsidiaries continued to operate in Germany despite increasing discrimination in "law" (e.g., the Nuremburg Laws of 1935) and enforcement of those laws against religious groups (primarily Jews), ethnic groups (gypsies), political opponents (Communists), and other minorities. The American subsidiaries stood by as harassment, violence, and imprisonment occurred. Moreover, a number directly or indirectly aided the Nazis, either in developing weapons of war or in the horrific acts against oppressed peoples. There were many reasons American companies were so obtuse, inert, or complicit—for example, desire for profits; support for Germany in the face of Communist threat from the Soviet Union; their own weak ethical standards in that period, including their own anti-Semitism; and unawareness or indifference (more likely) in pre-war America to the growth of Hitler's dictatorial powers and the inhumane "principles" and practices of the Third Reich.[12]

At the other end of the spectrum is South Africa in the 1980s.[13] American companies, after long quiescence, became more vocal in opposition to apartheid. This was due to strong anti-apartheid sentiment in the United States—sparked by the moral power of the civil rights revolution of the 1960s in America—and to the widely publicized attempts by the South African government to put down protests against discrimination with violence that echoed repressive acts by the Southern states in America. By the mid-1980s, more than 125 American companies had signed the "Sullivan Principles," which committed these global corporations not to discriminate in the workplace and to achieve greater pay and supervisory roles for black workers, through training, employment practices, and pay adjustments. The principles were the 1977 brain-child of Leon Sullivan, a black minister who was on the board of General Motors (then the largest employer in South Africa). The implementation of the principles was not uniform, and their impact is a subject of continuing debate. But those companies that did implement them in their South African operations ran the risk of violating far-reaching apartheid laws. And implementation of the principles was, for some years, the benchmark by which U.S. companies were judged in determining whether investors both in the United States and around the world should divest.

To many critics, however, the Sullivan Principles only meant that international companies continued to operate in South Africa and, in so doing, continued to support the economy and to sustain an apartheid government. By the late 1980s, a combination of international economic sanctions against South Africa, vocal divestment campaigns at visible shareholders like universities, and continued protests and violence in South Africa led many international corporations, including most American global companies, to exit South Africa. Apartheid ended in 1993.

But, along this wide spectrum of corporate failure to oppose Nazi discrimination and atrocities and corporate opposition to apartheid are a range of possible actions when national laws are in clear conflict with a company's global standards. The poster child today for this set of problems—and ranges of response—is China. At one extreme, despite their support for the civil rights and civil liberties of traditional market economies, most multinationals headquartered in developed nations are willing to do business in China's autocratic, corrupt, and repressive political regime. They seek revenues and profitability in a huge, growing market. They may believe economic liberty (if not political freedom) is increasing. They may hope (or pay lip service to the hope) that China is capable of moving toward greater rule of law over time, in contrast to the sclerotic apartheid regime. They may be influenced by general U.S. government support for economic engagement with China—despite many specific disagreements about currency or piracy or cyber-security or human rights violations or islands in the South China Sea. Moreover, there is no strong anti-China sentiment in the United States due to more diffuse and abstract feelings about deprivation of civil rights and civil liberties—even when dissidents are jailed—compared to South Africa's demonstrably racist regime.

Despite a general ethos of multinational engagement in the Chinese economy, businesses must tread carefully when Chinese law conflicts with a corporation's global standards in a very direct and immediate way. In my own experience at GE, we were faced with a Chinese law enforcement demand to review the contents of all employee computers at a GE facility with several hundred local Chinese workers. One of those workers had been arrested in Tiananmen Square for demonstrating against the government as a member of Falun Gong (a quasi-religious group the Chinese view as a threat to stability and security).

The authorities informally wanted to determine if other GE employees at that workplace were members of Falun Gong.

This matter reached my desk within hours. GE told Chinese authorities that such a broad request, without some clear evidence of an issue in the workplace, would violate our employees' right to privacy and religious freedom. The company also noted that, like most major companies, it had a worldwide policy against proselytizing for political or religious causes inside the company, although we supported an employee's right to advocate for political causes outside the workplace perimeter. GE never had to decide whether to resist the request (or insist on being served with a formal subpoena). On a private basis, the company was able to convince the enforcement superiors that a public dispute over this potential hot-button issue, in these circumstances, did not make sense. The information request was not withdrawn, but it was never pressed and simply went away. But we recognized that such a result, which avoided a potential conflict between local law enforcement and GE global standards, was possible only because there had been no public attention to the matter and because it involved only one facility with several hundred workers.

By contrast, Google's decision on whether to accept Chinese Internet censorship, despite its general global position for free speech and against government intrusion, was going to receive international attention.[14] It involved operations of a famous company across all of China. It highlighted in stark terms a deep conflict between Google's belief in an open Internet and the Chinese belief that the Internet was a threat to order and to Chinese Communist Party control. As discussed in Chapter 2, Google in 2007 had at first decided to operate under a Chinese license that accepted government censorship, contrary to its global standards. In addition to obvious commercial objectives, it did so in the hope that giving the people of China access to some information was better than no access at all. In 2010, after hacking incidents, disclosure of private e-mails, and theft of intellectual property, Google reversed course. It decided it would elevate global standards for free speech above China law and announced it would no longer accept Chinese censorship. It knew that the Chinese authorities would close down Google China, which it did. This is a striking contemporary example of the tension between a company's ethical standards and national law.

Yet, different responses by other Internet companies show the complexity of these issues. Microsoft's Bing search engine continues to operate in China, with that iconic global company accepting censorship. But it does not censor voluntarily and has a set of internal principles that require a legally binding order in writing from the government before it will disallow content. Those principles also require that users be informed that the information they are receiving has been censored by the government. Bing has virtually no China market share, so Microsoft attracts virtually no international attention for taking a position different than Google's. One can only speculate why Microsoft would act differently. Perhaps, so long as it has a formal government order in writing, it is willing to accept China's Great Firewall against Internet freedom because "search" is such a small part of its activities in China (in contrast to Google) and because of other Chinese commercial interests, which it doesn't want to jeopardize in a confrontation with the government: significant sales of basic software in China (despite constant threats of intellectual property theft) and important R&D efforts that tap China's intellectual capital. Similarly, LinkedIn recently sought to expand in the China market and said that it would accept Chinese censorship. Here, too, it made a judgment that complying with local law, which it deems odious, is consistent with a commercial strategy to grow in China. And even Google is seeking to participate in the Chinese market through smartphone operating systems and apps that, for now, do not alter its opposition to Chinese censorship and e-mail hacking.[15]

These issues of free speech in China also affect mainstream news media. *The New York Times* in 2012 published a story on the enormous wealth accumulated by China's then-ruling family (for which it won a Pulitzer Prize). The Chinese government then shut down the *Times* website in China. Other news organizations—*The Wall Street Journal*, Reuters, and Bloomberg—have also had websites shut down due to stories the Chinese government disliked. These organizations have chosen to stay with their global news-reporting standards and take the website hits. But the question that cannot be answered here—but that doubtless occurs every day in China—is how far those principles of news-gathering can be pushed, because the Chinese have many other means at their disposal for punishment. For example, the Chinese can revoke the residency visas of U.S. reporters. The tension between robust reporting and Chinese sanctions—whether the news organizations need quietly to self-censor or at least soften tone—is a clear and present danger.

Moreover, the Internet issue of ethical standards v. national law, of course, exists outside of China. Google and other Internet companies, despite global commitment to free speech and the free flow of information, face thousands of demands a year for censorship from governments all across the globe. Some nations say that content deriding religious figures is prohibited. Others ban information on the private lives of government leaders. Others want the Internet free of hate speech or child pornography or web gambling or neo-Nazi propaganda. Google, and other Internet companies, accept this much more targeted censorship of national law, sometimes voluntarily and oftentimes when ordered to do so by government authorities. Free speech advocates say Internet companies should resist such censorship and only accept it when there is a final legal order from competent authorities. Established in 2008 by Google, Microsoft, and Yahoo!, as well as civil society organizations, investors, and academics, the Global Network Initiative (GNI) seeks to establish standards for what Internet companies should do when confronted with government demands to suppress speech. But, if there is a "valid" censorship order from authorities that follows local legal process, GNI does not require that the affected entity disobey. For example, in the second half of 2014, Facebook, a GNI member, removed more than 9,000 pieces of content for violating local laws (most arising in either Turkey or India).

This is emblematic of the duty of the General Counsel to anticipate and resolve recurrent tensions between the global corporation's ethical standards and the demands of national law. This conflict across a range of matters has been important in the past and will, in my view, be increasingly important in the future as globalization proceeds apace and corporations seek to establish ethical standards culture that are uniform across the world but that inevitably—and constantly—bump into contrary national law.

E. ETHICAL PROBLEMS WHEN THERE IS NO NATIONAL ENFORCEMENT

Ethical problems also arise when a nation does not enforce its own law. A striking example is the use of ultrasound technology to aid in sex-selection abortions in China and India. In both societies, there are cultural preferences for male children and pressures to restrain population growth, with (until very recently) a one-child policy in China. As a result, despite national laws prohibiting *physician use* of technology to aid sex-selection abortions, parents and doctors use ultrasound imaging to favor live births of male babies and prevent births of female babies. However, in both China and India, there is a growing movement of advocates who seek to change the cultural practice favoring male children and who demand enforcement of the laws prohibiting use of ultrasound machines for sex selection.

The dilemma for a global company that sells relatively inexpensive and portable ultrasound machines is that the technology has many important medical uses, especially in emerging economies. Ultrasound helps address such medical problems as breast cancer, uterine fibroids, cardiac disease, and gynecological disorders. It also has the capacity to aid early detection in such fields as fetal disease, anesthesia delivery, cardiac surgery, and sports medicine. Ultrasound has great potential because other imaging techniques (CT scans, MR scans, or PET scans) are often too expensive in emerging markets. What should a multinational manufacturer of ultrasound equipment do? There is great opportunity for sales that address serious medical issues. There is great risk that the equipment will be used for the legally impermissible purpose of aborting a female fetus based on gender (in contrast to the lawful parental or maternal choice to use abortion, under specified circumstances, to avoid having a child of either sex). The company faces three options: not enter the ultrasound market; enter the market and defer completely to parents and doctors; or enter the market and try to "minimize" use of its ultrasound machines for sex-selection abortions, which are nominally against the law.

In China, GE originally adopted a "minimization" strategy. It chose not to sell to the Family Planning Commission, which reportedly used ultrasound to enforce the one-child policy and aid sex selection through abortion. Instead, it focused sales on the Ministry of Health, which used ultrasound in many medically appropriate applications. GE also put labels on the equipment warning that it was a violation of Chinese law to use ultrasound for sex selection. Its product manuals highlighted the legal strictures. It sought to educate physicians on the law and to sell only to licensed doctors. And it made sales data available to government authorities if they were interested in enforcing the law. Obviously, GE could not guarantee that its ultrasound machines were not used for sex-selection abortions, but it could point to good faith efforts to avoid that practice.

The rationale for the minimization strategy had a number of strands. It was an attempt to avoid being an "aider and abettor" of violations of Chinese law, not in a technical legal sense, but in a practical sense. It was an attempt to respond to activist communities both in China and around the world that opposed sex-selection abortions. And, it was also a moral decision that it did not want to participate in profound discrimination on the basis of gender, which offended a fundamental global, corporate commitment to gender equality. There was no question, however, that there would be "leakage," even with a minimization approach. Unless and until the Chinese government chose to enforce the law against using the technology for gender selection, some GE ultrasound machines, especially as they became cheaper and lighter, would be used by some physicians for that purpose. GE gave up important revenue and market share. But it was not prepared to give up 100 percent by not participating in the market at all and by not having many of its machines used for important medical purposes.

In India, the circumstances were more complicated *because not just physicians but manufacturers were made legally liable.* In 1998, India enacted a law that prohibits any person or organization from using equipment or techniques for the purpose of detecting the sex of an unborn child. Practitioners and clinics conducting these tests must both register and display a notice about legal prohibitions on fetal sex detection. In 2004, the law was amended to make manufacturers and distributors also responsible for assuring proper use of ultrasound. Manufacturers must confirm that the customer/practitioner has a valid certificate and has signed an affidavit stating that the equipment shall not be used for sex determination. Manufacturers also must provide the government with a quarterly report disclosing to whom the equipment has been sold. Violations could lead to criminal sanctions. But the law was not enforced energetically.

GE followed the China minimization strategy but went further in India, taking steps beyond what was required by the law. It began more extensive mandatory training on the Indian legal requirements for salespersons and distributors. It used customer magazines and websites to advertise and otherwise communicate about legal prohibitions on fetal scanning for gender. It added explicit warnings to terms and conditions in all sales contracts. It made noncompliance with the Indian law an explicit basis for termination of dealer contracts. It instituted a quarterly audit of both direct and dealer sales—from signing the contract to installation—to make sure that 100 percent of customers had a valid certificate of compliance before they used the technology. And confirmation of appropriate certification on the part of the user is required before GE will service the ultrasound machines. GE also began a major public service advertising campaign about the importance of the Indian law.

Not surprisingly, in their dealings with medical users of ultrasound technology (physicians, clinics, and hospitals), GE's manufacturing competitors often did not take such a systematic approach to implementing the spirit and letter of the law. As it instituted tougher customer requirements, GE began to lose market share. As a result, the company sought to work across industry groups to improve industry standards. It also sought to increase government enforcement. But nonenforcement of law is still a serious problem in India. As in China, the ultimate answer to these problems is for government to take seriously its own laws against use of ultrasound for sex-selection abortions. But making that happen, especially in an emerging market, is far more difficult than for a corporation to take action on its own, even if that action is not wholly effective and comes with reduction in market share.

F. EXITING ROGUE STATES

Global corporations have not customarily spent time comparing nation states on scales of good and evil. Their job is to sell goods and services in every nation so long as national or international law permits, the commercial risk is acceptable, and they can act with integrity—however questionable the regime or the nation's general economic and political system. But, today, it is more difficult to avoid these "ethical" questions about "rogue" states. Nations sponsor terrorism, develop weapons of mass destruction, engage in intra-country genocide, overthrow legitimate governments, launder money, abuse human rights, practice breath-taking corruption, deal in drugs, and otherwise make themselves pariahs on the international stage. Failed, failing, and fragile states exhibit a host of serious problems that not only make economic development problematic, but can create serious national security and foreign policy issues. These kinds of problems are not new. What has changed is global communications. These issues are much more salient to much wider populations—and the role of corporations in relation to such states is much more subject to question.

Multinational corporations now more frequently face the ultimate discretionary decision of whether they should do business in a country at all. (Mandatory legal prohibitions prevent business in some nations like Syria or North Korea.) The problem is not whether the corporation's global standards conflict with national law in a particular line of business nor whether nonenforcement of national law requires the corporation to adopt its own ethical standards. Instead, the question is whether the nation is so fundamentally lawless or otherwise flawed that it is not possible to engage in commerce there at all with integrity and with safety for employees. Making such a voluntary determination is extremely taxing for global corporations not normally in the business of force-ranking nation states on geopolitical factors. The General Counsel should be in the center of such decisions that pose profound choice for global companies and that, perforce, have a presumption for doing business in nations all across the globe. Several examples from my experience follow, but every multinational faces these questions today.

Before the international community imposed a significant sanctions regime, GE decided in 2004 to stop taking new orders in Iran. At the time, the company had sold compressors to help international companies move oil and gas through pipelines. GE also had other Iranian sales, primarily of medical diagnostic equipment. All told, the company's annual revenues from business in Iran approached $500 million. Even in 2004, direct U.S. sales in Iran were barred under the U.S. Iran-Libya Sanctions Act. But under that law, sales were allowed if carried out through a wholly owned foreign subsidiary and if there was no involvement of U.S. citizens and minimal U.S. content. A GE subsidiary in Italy, exempt from the Iran-Libya Sanctions Act, had the successful compressor business. Its customers—most of the major oil and gas companies—did business in Iran, using the subsidiary's equipment. Similarly, another GE subsidiary in Europe made medical equipment.

The problem the company faced was that Iran, even then, was the subject of significant criticism from the U.S. government for supporting the jihadist insurgency against U.S. and Iraqi armed forces after the overthrow of Saddam Hussein. The U.S. government also sharply criticized Iran for its avowed aims of developing nuclear weapons and of destroying Israel as well as for a range of terrorist activities. A variety of shareholder groups aimed a steady drumbeat of criticism at GE. As the war in Iraq dominated the news, the media barraged the company with questions about why we were doing business with Iran, a nation supporting fighters who were killing U.S. soldiers and frustrating U.S. foreign policy aims. The company became increasingly uncomfortable with its twin answers: "everyone else is doing it" (many European competitors were active in Iran) and "it is legal" (under the narrow exception to the Iran-Libya Sanctions Act). But, discomfort about the public rationale for sales in Iran ran into a deep commercial concern about GE's long-standing relationships with international oil and gas customers. Couldn't they fairly ask whether we were partners they could trust if we left them in the lurch in Iran? If Iran, then why not China or Myanmar—what was the basis for making distinctions? Leaving Iran thus risked not just the tens of millions in sales there, but credibility with customers and billions of dollars of sales to those major companies around the world. Not surprisingly, the head of GE's compressor business in Italy was strongly opposed to ceasing business in Iran (and losing a significant percentage of his sales and a certain amount of credibility with his customers).

Jeff Immelt, GE's CEO at the time, felt we should exit, however. This business issue, with major geopolitical overtones, was discussed at a series of board meetings. Ultimately, GE decided to take no new orders for equipment destined for Iran due to a variety of prudential considerations: U.S. foreign policy opposition to Iran, the increasing hostility of important institutional investors, the unfavorable coverage and commentary on our hyper-technical legal justification, and the possibility that Congress would eliminate the wholly owned subsidiary exception and make it impossible to supply and service customers anyway. But there was also the moral reason that the company simply did not want to support the economy of a nation that was fueling the insurgency and killing and wounding American soldiers. GE did agree to complete orders already on the books. And it said it would try to find other vendors to service the GE equipment in Iran but would provide the service if that effort failed (the company was able to find substitutes in most instances). GE was still pilloried in some quarters for fulfilling existing orders, but at least the company could now hew to a clean line, with credible reasons, that it was taking no new orders in Iran. While we worried at the time that the European oil field companies would make gains in other global markets with our oil and gas customers, GE was fortunate that, in this case, it was on the right side of history. In the ensuing years, the international community imposed a broad array of economic sanctions on Iran that sharply curtailed, as a matter of international law, the activities in Iran of both customers and competitors, from both the United States and Europe (sanctions that will be relaxed under the 2015 nuclear agreement).

If this decision, like many other ethical ones, was driven by both prudential and moral factors, other determinations to leave a nation altogether were either largely prudential or largely moral. The company also decided in 1996 to take no new orders in Myanmar where it had a tiny amount of sales. One reason was moral: the illegitimacy of the military government, which in 1990 had overturned an election won by the party of Aung San Suu Kyi, who had been placed under house arrest (and who subsequently won a Nobel Peace Prize). But, an important factor was prudential. Strong protests against the Myanmar government had become a staple on U.S. campuses, where students targeted recruiters from companies doing business there. Because the amount of business and the size of the market were so small, the company decided, in part, to stop doing business in order to avoid being controversial in the United States and suffering an adverse effect in recruiting.

Bad as Myanmar's military dictatorship was, it was hard to distinguish from other dictatorial or autocratic regimes (e.g., China). U.S. domestic pressure was a key factor in the pull-out decision. When an international company wanted to develop the oil fields off Myanmar's shores and use GE compressors, GE declined, giving as its reason the voluntary withdrawal from Myanmar business. When the customer said that GE could pass title to the products in Europe, GE again declined to enter into contract talks because it would be a transparently hypocritical work-around of its self-imposed ban. Aung San Suu Kyi was released from house arrest in 2010 and participated in the government reforms from 2011 on, until winning an electoral victory in 2015. Like many other multinationals, GE renewed commercial activities in the country as a result of these developments.

In other instances, however, GE decisions were driven primarily by ethical concerns. As the number of people kidnapped in Colombia rose during the 1990s, the company pulled out of the country for several years in the interest of protecting its employees. Due to pervasive corruption that made it impossible to do business without either bribes or money laundering, the company also at various times refused to do flow (cash) businesses in Russia or to do any business at all in Nigeria. In these cases, the CEO and senior leaders determined that it was simply not possible to do business in those locales without compromising company integrity.

G. COST: SMALL AND MEDIUM-SIZED COMPANIES

A recurring question is whether small and medium-sized companies should approach the question of adopting ethical standards in the same fashion as large multinationals. I have argued that, when it comes to compliance with formal legal and financial rules, all companies, whatever their size, have such a duty (see pp. 176–182). But, I think it is only realistic to recognize that small and medium-sized companies may not have the resources to *voluntarily* adopt global standards that necessarily require cost in formulating, implementing, monitoring, and readjusting. For example, a small company that is buying only 2 percent of a third-party supplier's output may have neither the market power nor the resources to have a sophisticated global sourcing program. If it owns a small manufacturing or assembly factory, it may have resources to comply with local environmental, health, and safety laws but not the resources to implement higher, more expensive global standards. No generalizations are possible on this subject. The CEO, General Counsel, and senior executives of these smaller companies will have to assess the relative strengths of prudential considerations relating to stakeholders and other societal actors and to conduct their own "look in the mirror" gut-check on moral aspects. If possible, major corporations could, for a reasonable fee, allow smaller and medium-sized companies to venture with them in facilities or sourcing or other commercial processes so that they can take advantage of the multinationals' higher standards. Of course, such arrangements would have to be lawful (e.g., not violate competition laws) and sensible (not aiding a competitor).

H. VALUES

I have left one of the most important subjects on compliance and ethics to the last. The values of honesty, candor, fairness, reliability, and trustworthiness are the third dimension of my concept of integrity: law, ethics, values. When employees embody these values, the corporation may have a virtuous cycle of high morale and high productivity. When they do not, the corporation can have the vicious cycle of back-biting and turf-fighting that leads to dysfunction. Similarly, when employees embody these values in their relations with the world outside the corporation, they help create the fundamental trust among direct stakeholders and affected societal actors that is the watchword of a sustainable, high performance–high integrity company. These values are hardly the exclusive province of the General Counsel, but their inculcation inside the company is surely an essential element of the GC's domain.

Not only are these values profoundly important, but I deeply believe they can only exist in a corporation that is dedicated to adherence to the formal rules and to adoption of binding ethical standards. Corporate compliance and ethics are built on corporate values, but these core values cannot exist without compliance and ethics. Although these values are embedded in adherence to formal rules and ethical standards, they, of course, apply in a far broader set of internal and external interactions. Where is the line between improper lying and proper tactics in negotiations? How balanced should a contract be between buyer and seller? How candid—and in what ways—should managers conduct personnel reviews? Should a company have a congruent approach to how it treats receivables and payables? The questions are recurrent and insistent in daily life in a global corporation. *Not every application of good values can be enshrined in binding ethical rules for the whole company, but core values surely should be the subject of discussion, debate, examples, education, and consistent practice across the company.*

Core company values—covering performance as well as integrity—always find their place in the code of conduct. The challenge—and many companies do little more than pay lip service to it—is to make sure that these values come off the page and actually are alive in company relationships and operations. That is why, as indicated in Chapter 4 on culture, the core company values, not just the legal and ethical rules and not just sound risk management, must be vividly communicated by company leaders and effectively embodied in the education and training of every employee up and down the organization. Making values a meaningful dimension of company operations must also be on the daunting "to do" list of the General Counsel—and, of course, of all senior executives.

7

RISK AND CRISIS MANAGEMENT

Simply stated, the subject of risk covers all adverse events that can impair a corporation's high performance or its high integrity. Legal/ compliance failures and ethical misses—the subjects of Chapters 5 and 6—are critical areas of risk that are of special concern to the General Counsel. But risk, of course, involves a broad array of significant topics, beyond those two issues. Cutting across all risk issues, as I underscore later, is the fundamental point that a "safety culture" in aid of sound risk management is an essential component of the imperative corporate culture—a culture of high performance and high integrity. Despite all the appropriate attention to the specifics of risk assessment and risk mitigation, sound risk practices inside a corporation only occur when people "feel, think, and behave" in support of those goals, when these essential cultural perspectives are incorporated into their daily business lives.

A successful corporation must take risks—it must be creative and innovative. But it must also bound these risks with discipline. What the balance should be between risk-taking and risk management—the proverbial "risk appetite"—should turn on a careful, thought-out set of decisions by corporate leaders, including the GC. That balance can only occur if the corporation is capable of the intellectual breadth, analytical rigor, and operational excellence needed to assess and address constantly the diverse, indeed mind-boggling, set of risks facing a global corporation in a sound, but not musclebound, safety culture. The central role of the General Counsel and other inside lawyers in helping to create an appropriate safety culture and helping to assess and mitigate a broad range of risks beyond legal and ethical hazards is another characteristic of the inside counsel revolution.

After the business and natural disasters of the past 20 years, risk has become a subject of great moment for corporations—and a subject of much writing. My goal in this chapter, as in others, is to give an overview of core ideas, including important examples, but not provide an exhaustive account of the subject. Very distinguished and thoughtful people have recently written or edited books on risk and crisis management. There have also been numerous illuminating commission reports and books analyzing some of the great risk failures of recent decades from the *Challenger* accident to 9/11 to Hurricane Katrina to the tsunami that disabled the Fukushima nuclear plant to the explosion of the *Deepwater Horizon* drilling rig in the Gulf of Mexico to the great financial crisis of 2007–2009. I refer those in search of a more detailed discussion of risk to those sources.[1]

A. SCOPE

Today, every major corporation has a program of enterprise risk management (ERM). In plain English, this means a *comprehensive* assessment of the diverse types of risks facing the corporation—a corporation-specific assessment requiring imagination and judgment, not just running through a checklist. Although there are many typologies of "risk" (e.g., financial, operational, and strategic), a straightforward approach is to divide risk into *economic risks* and *noneconomic risks, each of which requires analysis by a multifunctional group of experts and all of which, depending on circumstances, may need to be seen in synergistic interaction with each other.*

Although there is no magic in the following categorization, *economic risk*, in broad outline, can include the following subjects: *financial risk*, which includes such subjects as capital adequacy, liquidity, leverage, creditworthiness, and limits of risk modeling; *commercial risk*, which denotes risk associated with current competitors, customers, suppliers, and markets; *future product risk*, which includes the ability to replenish goods and services to meet future market needs; *operational and technology risk*, which involves the corporation's capacity to execute on its business plans using increasingly complex technologies, integrating employees from diverse cultures, managing a wide array of third-party suppliers, and handling acquisitions/dispositions in multiple jurisdictions; *entitlement risk*, which involves the corporation's capacity to meet employee health care and pension costs; and *macroeconomic risk*, which affects all the other corporate economic risks and involves the uncertainties with fiscal and monetary policy and associated questions about growth rates, interest rates, and currency rates in nations and regions across the globe.

Again, in broad outline, *noneconomic risks* can include the following subjects: *compliance and litigation risk*, which includes regulatory enforcement actions and private lawsuits; *ethical risk*, which includes failing to meet current or changing societal expectations in a fashion that can affect reputation, brand, and operations; *quality or product risk*, which can include adverse effects of a corporation's goods and services on the corporation's customers, suppliers, or the general public; *externalities risk*, which includes problems created for society from the by-products of company activities in such areas as accidents, pollution, waste, and use of energy/water; *security and safety risk*, which includes threats to the corporation's people, facilities, information, and supply chain from internal failures, natural disasters, or acts of terrorism, including cyber-security; *public policy risk*, which includes adverse changes in the global, national, or province/state public policy architecture—in law and regulation—across vital areas like taxes, trade, competition law, environmental law, and privacy; and *geopolitical or country risk*, which includes revolution, other regime change, expropriation, corruption, or political animus toward international companies (and which can also encompass macroeconomic and public policy risks identified separately above).

In clearing the ground for risk analysis, it may also be important conceptually to divide the causes of both economic risks and noneconomic risks into *internal* and *external* because this distinction will further delineate the types of experts involved in risk analysis and the nature of the corporation's response. Many corporate decisions and actions create risk, from products to financing to resource allocation to competitive strategies. With respect to external causes, the corporation must, as noted, address a wide variety of threats—macroeconomics, public policy, regulatory enforcement, private litigation, natural disasters, terrorism, cyber-sabotage. The General Counsel can play an especially important role in helping to find appropriate domain specialists for external risk—who are likely to reside outside the corporation—such as the potential for political violence or economic distemper in nations important to the corporation. But specialized expertise also can be critical in trying to assess the potential causes and adverse impacts of risks created by company products or processes in such varied areas from new drugs to possible pollutants discharged in manufacturing to financial models. And here, too, the GC has an important role in making sure that the right analysis of potential internal risks is undertaken.

Moreover, risk analysis must seek to understand the interaction between both economic and noneconomic factors. Assessing potential synergistic effects is yet another daunting problem. But, whatever the intellectual difficulty, these risks, singly or in combination, are a subject of surpassing importance because, if handled badly, they pose serious threats to people and to property; to communities and to the environment; and, ultimately, to the fundamental trust in, and even viability of, the corporation.

B. ORGANIZATIONAL PRINCIPLES

Like "compliance" and "ethics," risk has infinite variety and requires many different approaches. Stress testing a financial services firm for a liquidity problem is completely different than scenario planning at manufacturing facilities to address potential accidents. Handling an aggressive regime of regulatory enforcement is completely different than ensuring that products are safe before being put into the stream of commerce and establishing a sound system of post-market surveillance. Each company is going to have its own risk profile. Each company, for sure, is going to have its own form of organization for handling the diverse range of risks it faces.

But, despite such diversity, there are some broad organizational principles that, in my view, apply to all corporations. These principles, which the CEO must make clear and the GC can help articulate, provide foundational guidance to business/operations leaders and to the varied corporate staff actors who have a role in risk—for example, Legal, Compliance, Finance, Treasury, Controllorship, Audit, Planning, Marketing, Credit, Insurance, Quality, Customer Service, and Public Affairs, as well as all those who have the word "Risk" in their title. Most importantly, the implementation of these principles should help create an organization dedicated to sound risk management where transparency, awareness reporting, collaboration, discussion, escalation, and sharing of information instills an abiding sense of personal responsibility for risk in the many and diverse corporate actors who must integrate risk considerations into corporate decisions and operations.

- Given the complexity and importance of risk, there should be a corporate Risk Committee, chaired by the CEO, that brings together in one place—to compare and contrast, to prioritize, and to resource—all the different threads of economic and non-economic risk. In this area, like Compliance and Ethics, the CEO must take all the steps necessary to ensure the necessary systems, processes, resources, and talent for risk assessment and risk mitigation exist. The company's Chief Risk Officer (CRO) should co-chair the committee and ensure the various risk areas are covered both at corporate and in the business units with appropriate expertise. The Chief Risk Officer also ensures that the independent voice of risk analysis is heard at important corporate- and business-level decisions. The CRO could have the status of Vice Chairperson.
- As discussed in the next chapter on governance, the board of directors should oversee both the corporation's approach to risk management in general and the highest priority risks facing the

corporation in particular. Given the diversity of risk issues, different board committees will have jurisdiction over different issues of economic and noneconomic risk (e.g., Audit over SEC requirements, Governance over shareholder issues, Risk over financial soundness, Public Responsibilities over country risk). These board committees will initially review the first-priority issues on their way to full board review and will alone oversee second- and third-priority risk issues that will be the subject of shorter reports to the board as a whole. The CRO will have a direct connection to the board to provide independent reports on the risk function.

- For those economic and noneconomic risks considered important to the corporation, the CEO must, at the corporate level, clearly denominate discrete "risk" leaders and separate "cross-functional" risk committees to oversee *each* area. These discrete leaders and committees must have a firm-wide perspective and must thus oversee all issues in that area as they manifest themselves at all levels of the corporation. For example, discrete risk subjects/committees at the corporate level in a financial services firm could cover market, credit, liquidity, financial modeling, regulatory, country, and product risk. Business leaders, in conjunction with the various corporate risk leaders, should appoint cognate, discrete "risk leaders" and cross-functional risk committees for each key risk area that is relevant at the business division–level of the company. The division-specific risk committees will advise business leaders but also report up to—and coordinate with—the corporate-wide risk committee in each particular area.

- Legal, Finance, Compliance, and Risk staffs perform essential risk functions and should be represented on the different risk committees at the corporate- and business-unit levels. In broad strokes, Legal and Compliance may be primarily concerned with noneconomic risk, especially legal and ethical risk. Finance and Risk (depending on how the corporation defines it) may be primarily concerned with various aspects of economic risk (market, credit, capital, liquidity, etc.). But there should be no rigid rules, and all the staffs should be invited to all the different risk committee functions at the corporate and business levels. The CEO should provide direction about which staff leaders have the coordinating and leadership responsibilities, but this demarcation should include a request that the composition of particular committees should be fluid and permeable because of the overlapping skills on the different staffs and the imperatives of cross-functional integration.

- The CEO must make clear to senior staff and senior operational executives that sound risk assessment and sound risk management is, like integrity, at the core of what they do—and they will be held just as accountable for risk misses as for performance or integrity misses. These senior corporate leaders must understand that they need to ensure that there is appropriate risk expertise in their functions or divisions. These senior leaders must also understand their responsibility to allocate necessary resources to manage the risk process; to mitigate discrete identified risks; and to have high-quality, periodic reviews of the overall risk function. They must, in short, understand that risk assessment and mitigation should be an integral and respected aspect of all decisions and all implementation. Senior leaders must know they will be rewarded, promoted, and sanctioned for their actions on risk resources, systems, processes, and results.

- Most importantly, the CEO must make absolutely clear to the board and senior leadership—and to the whole corporation—that each of the leaders on economic and noneconomic risk needs to present their unvarnished independent views on decisions made both at corporate and in the business divisions. It is important to have leaders responsible for risk analysis *inside the business units* (whether in legal, finance, audit, compliance, risk, or other units). But such individuals *must have a responsibility, recognized by the CEO and senior executives, to report on a direct or dotted line basis to a senior risk leader at corporate*, to whom they can elevate an important issue if they believe it is not being fairly and fully considered by the business-unit decision makers. Risk is a control function. *In an enterprise built on risk-taking, risk concerns do not—and should not—necessarily hold sway, but they need to have independent standing—to be candidly articulated and honestly confronted and, if necessary, elevated—in corporate decision making.*

- The Chief Risk Officer should institute a robust, repeating process to review the structure of the various risk committees as the corporation's activities evolve so organizational *rigor mortis* does not set in and so new committees or new combinations of existing committees may be formed to address emerging risk issues.

- The General Counsel should have a place of prominence at the top of the corporation in handling the broad array of risk issues. For the noneconomic issues, the GC, as a guardian, either should be a risk leader or a key member of the top-level, cross-functional risk committees. For many of the economic issues, as a partner and a guardian, he can be a member of the senior team discussing and debating risk issues, which will be decided by the CEO or other high-level business leaders. And when, as is often the case, risk issues have interrelated economic and noneconomic dimensions, then he should either be co-leader or a *key member* of the risk team. For example, questions of environmental protection or product safety will often have a powerful cross-functional dimension (e.g., creating a safety culture and safety processes for dangerous deep sea drilling with significant legal and regulatory dimensions). Legal, compliance, technology, safety, and operational perspectives will necessarily, and importantly, be intertwined.

C. FRAMEWORK QUESTIONS

Although corporations face very disparate risks, there are, in addition to the organizational principles, a sequential set of basic questions that are the framework for assessing and, as appropriate, mitigating risk. *As with compliance and legal risk, corporate risk processes are aimed at preventing, detecting, and responding.* Being deeply involved as a broad thinker and partner in the debates and discussions on this framework set of questions—which go far beyond legal or ethical issues—is a test of whether the General Counsel can truly serve the company as broad-gauged lawyer-statesman and partner-guardian.

1. ISSUE IDENTIFICATION

The first task in the different areas of economic and noneconomic risk is to create an *inventory of threats* that can adversely affect performance and integrity in important ways. Creating and refreshing this inventory must be a continuous, repeating process that occurs at regular intervals. In the broad, here are some of the techniques for surfacing these potential risk issues.

There can be process mapping of the corporation's fundamental systems and processes, as with compliance, to pinpoint areas where risk can occur if operations do not proceed as envisioned. There can be benchmarking of company data against peer companies on any number of financial, commercial, operational, technology, or other parameters—or review of other company best practices in risk assessment and risk mitigation activities. There can be systematic early warning systems not just on legal and ethical issues as discussed earlier (see pp. 144–159), but on literally every type of economic and noneconomic risk deemed important in light of the corporation's product and geographic profile. There can be focus groups exploring risk issues raised by corporate constituencies, especially employees. There can be retention of outside experts to assess the economic and noneconomic activities of the corporation from a risk perspective. There can be structured debates to surface risks through a variety of techniques: stress testing, scenario planning, or war gaming to explore key assumptions.

There can be a list of "red flag" issues that demand immediate focused attention: not just the possibility of legal (especially criminal) violations, but also the risk of financial harm, serious injury to people and property, or threatened harm to the environment. There can also be special attention to specific, clearly identified types of institutional stress that can create risk, such as major cost-cutting, which, while necessary for productivity and enhanced margins, can eliminate needed checks and balances and damage employee morale and values; poor financial performance in business units, which can lead to pressure to make numbers and take excessive risk; excessively good performance, which really can be "too good to be true" and be built on slipshod processes and disregard for risk; excessive compensation, which can create incentives to ignore risk disciplines in hitting pay-out metrics; mergers or joint ventures, which may involve incorporating and changing cultures, systems, and processes that are, initially, below corporate standards; or use of third parties, which can involve actors indifferent to company risk disciplines. A dramatic example of "too good to be true" risk in my experience was the false profit of $350 million in routine trading of treasuries by Joseph Jett of Kidder Peabody (then a subsidiary of GE) in the early 1990s: Jett's supervisor, the head of the Kidder fixed income division, failed to ask hard questions about how these striking profits could possibly be achieved in a routine, low-margin activity and was forced to resign after a company-sponsored investigative report by the former head of the SEC's enforcement division.

The methods of raising risk issues will turn on the nature of the corporation and the markets and nations in which it operates. Developing and following a checklist of issue-generating techniques is important, but equally important—and this is true of all the risk questions—is the imagination, creativity, and breadth of those responsible. They should not let their imaginations run wild—no "chicken littles" here—but a fast-moving corporation and a fast-changing world are so complex that the risk leaders/risk committees must not be enslaved by existing techniques and organizational structures but always thinking beyond them.

2. ISSUE IMPORTANCE

Once the issues are identified, then it is necessary within each risk category to assess their importance. This process involves understanding the various possible *causes* of the adverse event identified by the risk team. This is an especially tricky business. Establishing precise "cause," in a scientific sense, may be difficult in many cases. Effects of a pollutant on the public or a drug on a patient may present themselves as problematic "associations" or "correlations," not as scientifically proven "causes." As I have emphasized, sophisticated expertise is needed to understand possible causal or associational relationships. But, beyond identifying potential causes of adverse effects on performance and integrity, the task of determining issue importance involves assessing the *likelihood* that the adverse event will occur as a result of those possible causes. This probabilistic determination can arise from statistical models at one end of the spectrum or from reasoned judgment at the other end—or from some combination. The conceptual difficulties of honest risk analysis is a theme that runs through the myriad internal and external threats companies face—a theme of special importance to the General Counsel.

There must, in addition, be an assessment of the likely *scope* of the adverse event: How many parts of the company or the community will the event touch and with what types of effects? Finally, there needs to be an evaluation of the *severity of impacts* on the corporation or the community from the adverse event.

In determining issue importance through analysis of cause, likelihood of occurrence, scope, and impact, there will be varying degrees of uncertainty. This uncertainty raises the fundamental problem of where on the spectrum between worst-case and best-case evaluations of importance—of likelihood, scope, and severity—the corporation wishes to place the issue for the purpose of allocating resources for prevention and response. And there is the related problem of taking the very different kinds of risks—using different methods of assessing importance and different degrees of uncertainty—and then prioritizing them for purposes of resources allocation from a holistic corporate perspective: first-, second-, third-, and fourth-order risks across the range of hazards. Helping to develop sophisticated methods for assessing how to view an issue's importance and then how to prioritize all the key risks facing the company is a core General Counsel function.

3. PREVENTION/RISK MITIGATION

Once risk issues have been identified and a good faith, if necessarily uncertain, attempt has been made to assess the importance and priority associated with risks, then one of the most important steps is to have an honest, complete discussion in which risk management issues are posed against risk-taking issues. Especially with respect to first- or second-order economic issues, these risk-taking v. risk management choices should be elevated to highest levels of the corporation so that the business unit leader who will benefit from the risk-taking does not have the final word on risk management. In some instances, the ultimate decision maker—the CEO, a senior executive, the GC, the CFO—will decide that the risk should be taken and the economic action will continue. It some instances, the opposite may be true; the risk should not be taken and the economic action will be stopped. For example, in the early stages of drug development, a pharmaceutical company may determine that, based on either laboratory or early clinical trials, it believes that the safety or efficacy risks are too great to continue the trials or to put the product on the market. Or, in a financial services company, the top leaders may determine that exposure to a particular sector of the economy with a particular type of instrument is outsized, and they will stop further activity in that area.

When deciding to take internal risks or when facing external hazards, the question facing the corporation is how to prevent the adverse event from occurring—or mitigate the probabilities or effects of such an event before it occurs. These "prevent and mitigation" actions will customarily involve *concrete systems and processes*, which must be implemented with genuine commitment. These actions can include "safety" management checks and balances during operations—whether in the corporate treasury or in a dangerous chemical plant—in which key safety/quality parameters are constantly measured and checked before further action can be taken. These actions can include redundancy and default (fail-safe) mechanisms. They can include detailed deal integration protocols that attempt to systematically and promptly adapt the target corporation to the culture, standards, and behaviors of the acquiring company. These prevent-and-mitigate techniques can involve scenario planning with respect to external events so that the corporation is ready with a proper crisis management organizational structure and a set of actions that should be taken (even if the details will depend on the event). They can include simulations of adverse events so the corporation is prepared to respond to a real event and minimize impact. Prevention and risk mitigation can include systematic feedback from prior problems to improve the risk reduction function going forward. It can include careful planning to provide financial protection against risk through such mechanisms as reserves or insurance (in a host of areas from events to products to credit to political risk). Just this brief discussion illustrates the enormous variety of systems and processes companies may use to prevent or to mitigate risk. But two things are clear: Measures to prevent and respond must be developed by the different, discrete teams for each type of risk but endorsed and supported by the business leaders. And, importantly, endorsement must mean those risk systems and processes are effective in practice and are not paper plans in a drawer.

In addition to concrete systems and processes that, in effect, are checks at various points in diverse company processes, there are the important set of mitigants aimed at *company culture* and the *attitudes and behavior* of key corporate actors regarding risk. Because this subject is so critical, I must at least underscore here that the essential steps a CEO, aided by the General Counsel and other top leaders, must take in creating a performance with integrity culture (see pp. 91–128) all apply to creation of the companion "safety/risk" culture. For all employees, this entails serious, continuous, and impactful education and training, both on the general importance to the corporation of properly addressing risk in the context of risk-taking and on the specific risks presented in the particular function or operational unit. It entails making risk management a concrete and discrete part of compensation, especially for executives, including "claw-back" provisions if people who manage large resources fail in their risk duties (see pp. 300–307 on compensation). It entails making risk management an important criterion in promotions. It entails a variety of forums, meetings, and communications across the company on real issues and real misses—on the real importance of this subject.

4. DETECTION/MONITORING

Closely related to effective prevention and risk mitigation is a system of monitoring to detect if the adverse event is occurring or is about to occur. Again, given the plethora of economic and noneconomic risks, such mechanisms come in many shapes and sizes. The point here can only be that monitoring and detection are a key part of a system of risk management. Examples of such mechanisms include safety/quality/soundness auditing by internal or external auditors/experts; defining red flags that, when certain facts emerge, require a hard stop of an activity until the situation can be analyzed and remedied; using technological or statistical techniques such as post-market surveillance of large populations or products to spot problems; constantly reviewing reports from remote diagnostics of high-tech products like gas turbines or aircraft engines; regular business reviews at all levels of the corporation on the different types of risk issues; using the mechanisms for employees to report legal and ethical concerns—the ombuds system, the bottoms up business reviews—to also report "concerns" about other types of risk; using a risk "miss" in one part of the corporation to prompt inquiries into whether similar issues are occurring in other parts of the company; and using focus groups to explore particular issues in some depth.

These discrete techniques should comprise parts of a periodic, comprehensive review of the company's risk processes and failures that ask questions about whether risks have been ignored and why; whether risks have been improperly measured and how; whether risks have not been monitored and why; whether risks are changing and require different expertise; whether statistical risk models have been based on the wrong assumptions and how to improve model performance; whether risk information is up-to-date or lags so far behind current events as to be of limited use; and whether those in critical risk-sensitive positions have the right attitudes about imagining and addressing risk.

5. RESPONSE

The final dimension of risk management within the corporation is a systematic approach to responding when the adverse event occurs. This response should typically be carried out by a cross-functional team trained in crisis management. For each type of risk, part of the risk planning process is to have that core team denominated to handle such events. There are at least five recurrent elements of an appropriate response.

First, the response team needs to address the immediate company product, system, or process that has created the problem if it was caused internally by the corporation. This may require a very time-sensitive set of immediate decisions to protect employees, the public, or property. For example, the result may mean removing a product from commerce or modifying it or stopping pollution from a newly discovered corporate source.

Second, there must be an inquiry "with all deliberate speed" into what happened and why, including a wide-ranging, in-depth analysis of organizational, behavioral, technological, and other relevant root causes. The results of this inquiry can lead to a variety of actions after immediate, emergency steps are taken. It may mean fixing the systems to include enhanced checks and balances that are better integrated into business operations. It may mean taking those fixes across the company to other aspects of operations. It may mean ensuring that the results of compliance or safety or quality audits are promptly addressed and closed out. It may entail substantial corporate finance actions to address balance sheet problems.

Third, if fault is involved (negligence, gross negligence, intentional acts), the persons responsible for the adverse event should be held accountable through firing, demotion, lack of promotion, lack of pay increases, or compensation recovery of granted or vested financial benefits.

Fourth, depending on severity of event, there should be an *action plan* for addressing external parties that accompanies the steps for fixing internal problems as promptly as possible and for holding those in the company responsible. These external parties range from those injured to government officials to shareholder activists to other stakeholders to communities and, of course, to formal investigators, regulators, and litigants. For major, potentially catastrophic events whether caused by internal failures—like a plant explosion—or *external* events— like natural disasters, terrorism, huge geopolitical or macroeconomic transformations—special response planning is necessary, as discussed immediately below. A key part of the action plan is a *risk communications plan* for both internal and external parties that is consistent and, if an inquiry is ongoing, that does not speculate or "spin" but is candid about what is known and not known. A systematic, recurring process for updating the communications is a key part of any plan. Although there can be obvious tension between honest and complete risk communication and keeping facts under wraps as part of a litigation or regulatory strategy, when the risk communication is necessary to prevent consequential impact on people, property, and communities, it must trump litigation or regulatory tactics and be given priority.

Fifth, for important adverse events, the CEO and the board of directors need to step back and ask broader questions about culture, systems, processes, and organization across the whole enterprise. Are there deeper issues that caused the event and that must be addressed to prevent a recurrence? Are there lessons learned that should be disseminated across the whole company? This dimension of responding to a specific event should be integrated with the periodic comprehensive review that should be part of a regular process to detect and monitor.

6. JUDGMENT

The organizational principles and the framework questions of issue identification, issue importance, prevention/risk mitigation, detection, and response require high-level expertise, commitment, and analytics. But they also require judgment at the top of the company. Although there are now many ERM systems and many tools for conducting risk assessments, the amount of risk and the methods for addressing it across the broad range of a company's economic and noneconomic issues turn, ultimately, on the corporate culture and on sound judgment of the CEO and senior management, with carefully focused board oversight. Of course, no company will last long with a culture so conservative that all risk is avoided or so undisciplined that untoward risk is the common practice. But where to strike the balance? Like performance and like integrity, risk assessment and management must be a fundamental pillar of the company. The CEO and senior executives, including the GC, must create a culture where performance, integrity, and risk are constantly in view: where decision making candidly—and systems and processes continually—takes account of all three fundamentals.

D. CATASTROPHIC EVENTS AND CRISIS MANAGEMENT

The financial crisis, the *Deepwater Horizon* explosion in the Gulf of Mexico, and the damage to the nuclear reactors at Fukushima are now years in the past, with Hurricane Katrina and the implosion of Enron and WorldCom even further back in time. But all these events occurred in this century. It is human nature, and the nature of time and memory, for these events to recede in mind as they recede into history. But, knowing when to expend special time and effort preventing—and responding to—catastrophic events is now, more than ever, one of the hardest and most important risk management problems for businesses to address.[2] A catastrophe occurs, of course, when the event has a high impact, directly causing widespread damage to people or to property or to communities or to the environment. But, one might also call an event high impact—as in the case of the Siemens bribery scandal or the GM ignition switch failures—when it inflicts very significant but not immense injury or damage but demands a huge mind-share of corporate leadership or outsized corporate costs and when it has a profound—some may say catastrophic—impact on the corporation's reputation and brand.

Calling out the special nature of catastrophic events is not morbid thinking or gloom-and-doom prognosticating, but rather a crucial planning feature in a turbulent world. As the distinguished political scientist Francis Fukuyama has written: "Anticipating and dealing with what were thought to have been very low probability events have clearly become central challenges for policymakers in public and private sectors alike all over the world." The key question for all organizations when it comes to catastrophic risk is how to make the critical planning and spending decisions for such events, which are often characterized as "low probability/high consequence." Such high impact can occur due to corporate failure (Enron, the Gulf explosion, and the financial meltdown), natural disasters (Katrina and Fukushima), or acts of terrorism (9/11). Unfortunately, however, the benefit of hindsight, reflected in the extensive literature on past disasters, provides guidance but not answers for leaders today trying to make best-efforts judgments on which potential problems or events in the future may require extraordinary current action.

To be sure, the organizational principles I described earlier apply with even more force in thinking about catastrophic events. So, too, all the framework questions must be asked and answered. But, corporations, and General Counsel, must overcome some oft-noted obstacles if they are effectively to perform the risk assessment and risk mitigation functions in the context of potentially catastrophic events. First, there is the problem of cognition, of having the imagination to see that the "models" of the way the world works—which are held by a dominant "group" in the company—may be incorrect or in the process of being eroded. Second, there is the problem of resources. How much should a corporation spend today to prevent, mitigate, and then be prepared to respond to low-probability, high-impact events in the future. Third, there are the recurring cultural and institutional issues of creating a "safety/risk culture" across a huge, multifunction (and multi-business?) company that integrates different functional perspectives truly to risk assess and risk mitigate in both an imaginative and rigorous way *so that employees scrutinize with care small details with potentially explosive impact.* This is the ultimate challenge of a safety culture. These problems are exacerbated when a future adverse event is not a risk (which can, in theory, be assigned a probability, however low and however questionable the methodology) but an uncertainty (which may not lend itself to probabilistic analysis at all).

In *addressing the problem of low-probability but high-impact adverse events*, it is important to note that most are "predictable surprises," to use the phrase of Bazerman and Watkins. In answering the framework risk questions of issue identification and issue importance, the corporation must consciously think creatively and challenge basic assumptions in creating a *special list*—constantly updated—of possible high-impact events that are plausible, even if not likely. It must then make a hard set of decisions about which of those high-impact events it is going to address. And it must design the preventive systems— and spend the necessary resources—to reduce the risk to as close to negligible as possible. As Bazerman and Watkins write: "To prevent predictable surprises, leaders must enhance the capacity of their organizations to recognize emerging threats, prioritize action and mobilize resources to mount an effective preventative response."

To take a simple example, if a corporation has operations in an earthquake zone, it would identify that type of natural disaster as a "predictable surprise." It should thus only occupy or build facilities that meet earthquake-resistant standards and have plans for employee protection and business continuity. Or, if a corporation was doing business in New Orleans prior to 2004, it could have identified the vulnerability of the city's levees to a Force 4 or Force 5 hurricane from numerous prior studies. It could thus have sought collective public–private action to mitigate the danger to the city or moved to high ground or moved away from the location altogether. If a corporation operates potentially catastrophic equipment, like a nuclear plant or a jet airliner, it will, working with the regulators, have strong safety protocols that take into account a wide variety of scenarios that could cause catastrophic accidents and that are constantly updated. It will have a robust system for transforming lessons learned from mistakes or problems into preventive changes, which is why both the U.S. nuclear industry and aviation industry have generally decent safety records.

Two separate issues relating to the airline industry demonstrate both the opportunities and failures of preventing high-impact events. On the plus side of the prevention ledger is a story that began more than 25 years ago when engines on two 747 jetliners were severely damaged in Indonesian airspace due to an eruption of volcanic ash from Java Island. Over the next decade, other incidents of engine damage from volcanic ash were reported. The industry learned that ash particles, which may not be visible to the naked eye or to radar, stick to the hot parts of a jet engine's turbine; form a dangerous coating; and thus restrict air flow through the engine, which can cause in-flight shut-downs. The industry—regulators, airlines, and plane and engine manufacturers—developed protocols to avoid flying near such ash clouds whatever the commercial cost. In 2010, this policy led to a cessation of air traffic over the Atlantic Ocean after a volcanic eruption on Iceland. Identifying this catastrophic risk—and taking preventive action—was consistent with general (though hardly perfect) industry practice of analyzing all flight-related safety incidents, detailing root causes, and continuously revising safety practices. On the negative side of the ledger was the reluctance of the airline industry to support or implement important on-the-ground security and safety measures to ensure baggage was matched to passengers before take-off and to screen passengers for weapons. This foot-dragging, combined with other failures, is considered a likely contributing factor to terrorists' 9/11 hijackings, subjugation of flight crews, and attacks on the World Trade Center and the Pentagon.

In *responding to high-impact adverse events*, a critical anticipatory step is to create a high-level, multifunctional crisis management team of senior executives under the direction of the CEO or other senior executive. These teams will, with great intensity and focus, carry out the "response" steps previously described. But, the high-impact event poses special problems because of its complexity and dynamic qualities, which require extraordinary real-time coordination among the various parts of the corporation—for example, Legal, Finance, HR, IT, Operations, Technology, Communications, Public Affairs. This coordination, led by the CEO or other top executive, may initially occur on a daily (or hourly) basis until the impact is contained, a complete response plan of action is developed, and the parts of that plan are clearly delegated to company leaders. Some high-impact events may be recurring. A crisis management team and a response plan can be fairly complete before the fact. For example, an extensive subpoena from a government investigator will trigger a relatively clear set of actions from securing documents to making decisions about affected employees to beginning an internal inquiry to informing the board. The dimensions of other high-impact events, like a terrorist attack on people or facilities, are much harder to predict, so a general outline of response elements will require constant adjustment as the crisis unfolds. Similarly, the specifics of crisis management planning will vary from the relatively simple—identification of teams; contact phone or e-mail lists; specifying a command center— to the much more complicated—providing high-level guidance to on the ground employees; evacuating employees under certain conditions; shutting down operations (finance or manufacturing); striving for business continuity; using alternative supply chains; activating redundant resources; and, most importantly, responding appropriately to human death, injury, and suffering and to continuing threats to people, property, communities, and the environment.

Although response planning is protean in its complexity, there are certain keys based on my experience. The top leaders of the company own both the response process and the actual crisis management when an event happens ("it's our problem the moment we hear about it"). Coordination in a war room across a range of simultaneous actions is vital. Developing facts with all deliberate speed is essential, but it must be complemented with absolute honesty about what is known and not known, both internally and externally, and about clear processes for developing crucial facts as promptly as possible. There must be a culture in which employees concerned about risk—especially catastrophic risk—can come forward, even if they may have made a contributing mistake, to seek help in resolving problems before they become worse. Conducting practice exercises and simulations prepare people psychologically for the emergency; plans that exist only on paper are not internalized or remembered—and are close to worthless. And, scenario planning by a cross-functional "Blue Team" for different types of high-impact events—to peer into the future and to explore options and inform choices—should be complemented by a review and critique by a similar "Red Team," a subject to which I now turn.

E. FUKUSHIMA: DEBATING DISASTER[3]

Believed to be one of the largest seismic events in recorded history, the Tohoku earthquake occurred early in the afternoon on Friday, March 11, 2011, off the coast of northern Japan. The quake caused a tsunami that swept over the shoreline and caused a loss of onsite and offsite electricity at the Fukushima Daiichi Nuclear Power Station, leaving it without any emergency power for several days. This sustained loss of power led to an inability to cool the reactor cores at three reactors, and the ensuing meltdowns and hydrogen explosions caused a release of radioactive materials to the region surrounding the site. This, in turn, caused a mass evacuation of approximately 300,000 people. Tokyo Electric Power Company (TEPCO) and various regulatory authorities blamed nature for the damage at Fukushima Daiichi.

But the official report of the Fukishima Nuclear Accident Independent Investigation Commission concluded bluntly:

The earthquake and tsunami of March 11, 2011[,] were natural disasters of a magnitude that shocked the entire world. Although triggered by these cataclysmic events, the subsequent accident at the Fukushima Daiichi Nuclear Power Plant cannot be regarded as a natural disaster. *It was a profoundly manmade disaster— that could and should have been foreseen and prevented.* And its effects could have been mitigated by a more effective human response. (Emphasis supplied.)

The report was commissioned by the Japanese legislature. The Commission found that, despite information developed in recent years suggesting an increased risk of a tsunami in the Fukushima region and despite changing world standards on risk assessment, TEPCO failed to take sufficient measures to prevent the possibility of tsunami flood waters destroying the electricity needed for reactor cooling systems: "researchers repeatedly pointed out the high possibility of tsunami levels reaching beyond the assumptions made at the time of construction, as well as the possibility of core damage in the case of such a tsunami." The Commission's findings are echoed in other independent reports on the Fukushima events, which discuss TEPCO's failings in design, management, approach to risk, operations, and response to the accident.

My purpose here is not to deal with the many issues arising from the Fukushima incident. Instead, I want to focus on the core causes of the Fukushima catastrophic problems as a vivid example of the need for robust scenario planning and for a vigorous debate inside corporations (and between corporations and regulators) about safety-critical occurrences. The underlying cause of this human error, according to the Commission report, was a failure of debate and discussion, as, among other things, new information about tsunami risk became available to TEPCO: the "fundamental causes are found in the ingrained conventions of Japanese culture; our reflexive obedience; our reluctance to question authority; our devotion to 'sticking with the program'; our groupism; and our insularity." Said the Commission: we "found ignorance and arrogance unforgiveable for anyone or any organization that deals with nuclear power." This set of problems applied both inside TEPCO and in the relationship with its regulators, according to the report. But such problems are hardly confined to Japan.

Scenario planning requires a group of cross-functional experts (the Blue Team) to construct possible impacts of potential catastrophic events—earthquake, tsunami, both together—and then, with an understanding of possible scenarios, to recommend preventive and response steps to mitigate the effects of such an event or events were they to occur, including the cost of necessary changes. For truly high-impact events, an important companion of scenario planning is a "Blue Team/Red Team" debate. Drawing from a military war-game tradition, this involves forming a multidisciplinary Red Team to critique the Blue Team's scenarios and its prevention and response plans. A recent, riveting example, in a book by the former Deputy Director of the CIA, describes the use of a Red Team to scrub a Blue Team intelligence analysis that concluded there was a reasonable probability that Osama bin Laden was hiding in a compound in Abbottabad, Pakistan. This "fact"—a likelihood but not a certainty—was the premise for the President ordering a dangerous special forces night raid, which killed bin Laden. Both Blue and Red Teams should include operational business leaders as well as risk-focused technology, policy, compliance, risk, and legal experts. Having these distinct perspectives present on both teams helps ensure that the process of point-counterpoint will illuminate hard issues hidden in the shadows of lazy thinking—and that the teams are not talking past each other. This debate between Blue and Red Teams should occur in front of top leaders, including the General Counsel, who should ask hard questions, challenge key assumptions, and, perhaps, bring to the table some of the recurring organizational failures exhibited in other catastrophic events analyzed in public reports and books.

Neither the regulators nor TEPCO had had *recent debates* about international practice; about the development of more modern tools and information about tsunami risk; or about worst-case scenarios involving flooding and sustained loss of power, which are central dangers at a nuclear plant. The plants had been in operation since the 1970s. Had there been a periodic Red Team/Blue Team process to update scientific information and risk assessment techniques as applied to older plants, some fairly obvious alternatives could have been available even for a predictable, but very low, probability of a large tsunami and subsequent flooding. A set of generators, with water-proofed electrical connections, could have been built in more secure buildings away from the affected plants on higher ground as existed at other reactors built later on the Fukushima site that did not lose cooling capacity. Alternatively, the utility could have invested in mobile power units stationed away from the plant that might have become available by emergency airlift. The expense might have been modest in an absolute sense and miniscule compared to the ultimate cost of the reactor meltdowns due to loss of electrical power. As the Commission report underscores, the reactor damage was a preventable event, given the enhanced knowledge of tsunami risk that had become available to TEPCO over the 15 years preceding the accident.

Scenario planning—and a Blue Team/Red Team debate—could also have revealed the deep flaws in the response plan. These included lack of attention to detail: only one stretcher, one satellite phone, no guidelines for getting outside assistance, a single fax machine, inadequate connection to first responders, and no large-scale drills on emergency events. But, more fundamentally, the command structure within the company and between the company, the regulator, and the central government was, in the early days, dysfunctional. Poor lines of authority and poor communication caused confusion on, among other things, the extent of the evacuation and public announcements about an evacuation policy in flux. In fact, the number of deaths actually attributed to the mass evacuation far exceed the number of deaths predicted from any radiation exposure. The problems surrounding another natural disaster, another "predictable surprise," that occurred six years before the Japanese earthquake—Hurricane Katrina—were very similar: failure to do scenario planning or take an identified risk seriously, ill-thought-out response plans, confused public–private responsibilities, a scrambled command structure, inadequate resources, and failure to simulate. Good scenario planning at TEPCO would have included consideration of all widely reported problems of prevention and response in a natural disaster in New Orleans that had occurred just a few years before and that was widely reported around the world.

In sum, I believe strongly that scenario planning and Red Team/Blue Team debates need to be at the core of the risk management processes focusing on potential catastrophic events. Business leaders must give strong support and encouragement to the constructive tension created by competing teams. General Counsels, experts in finding truth through competing viewpoints, can help structure this process. *Without debates about disaster, the risks of inattention, complacency, and failure to examine key technical, financial, or other assumptions can lead to a corporation being overwhelmed by events.* Of course, scenario planning *plus* a Red Team/Blue Team process is only appropriate for the highest priority concerns. But it is a core "must do," not a "nice to do," for those issues and should, selectively, be part of the annual cycle of risk reviews when the highest impact events, even if low probability, have been identified for assessment. The lessons from past catastrophes are vitally important, but a continuous and robust process for genuine, detailed exploration of future risks by rival teams is as important—to business and to society. When it comes to catastrophic events, the past is only partly prologue.

F. BP AND THE GULF: "EXHIBIT A" FOR CATASTROPHIC COSTS OF FAILURE[4]

On April 20, 2010, an explosion and fire on the deep-sea oil rig *Deepwater Horizon* killed 11 and injured 17. The rig sank 36 hours later. A sea floor gusher of oil flowed into the Gulf of Mexico for 87 days until it was ultimately capped on July 15, after an estimated 3.2 million barrels of oil escaped (more than ten times the size of the 1989 Alaskan spill from the *Exxon-Valdez*). The oil spread toward the Gulf coastline of five states, stimulating a variety of response and cleanup activities that sought to contain burgeoning damage to marine and wildlife, the fishing and tourism industries, other businesses in the region, and the whole Gulf ecosystem. The *Deepwater Horizon* explosion caused the largest environmental injury in U.S. history. It revealed deep flaws in BP's approach to safety culture, safety processes, and safety management. It underscored BP's stark failure to learn lessons from another plant explosion five years earlier and to create a uniform global culture for all hazardous activities. This failure raised profound questions about BP leadership at both the operational and staff levels.

The *Deepwater Horizon* case should be "Exhibit A" for every General Counsel who has to convince business leaders about the importance of a safety culture and about expending resources on low-probability but high-impact events. The theory of the case is never as powerful as an actual case. And, for an actual case, BP and the Gulf is about as bad as it gets.

1. THE TEXAS CITY EXPLOSION

The critical backdrop for BP's fault in the Gulf explosion occurred five years before. In March 2005, an explosion at BP's Texas City, Texas, oil refinery killed 15 workers, injured more than 170 others, and caused more than $1.5 billion in damage. There were two independent investigations of the event in addition to an internal BP inquiry. One was by the U.S. Chemical Safety Board (CSB) that, in a fall 2006 preliminary report, identified the immediate cause: a geyser-like release of highly flammable liquid and vapor onto the grounds of the refinery, which was ignited by an idling pickup truck. But the CSB found much broader causes, citing "organizational and safety deficiencies at all levels of the BP Corporation" and noting that BP had ordered cost-cutting at the refinery and ignored its own reports calling for new expenditures to upgrade safety features. The CSB also asked the BP board to appoint an independent commission to look beyond the particulars of Texas City and to examine and recommend needed improvements to BP's corporate safety culture and safety management systems and processes.

This group, chaired by former Secretary of States James Baker, issued a blistering report in January 2007. The Baker Commission identified the following BP failings: lack of consistent risk assessment, inadequate risk abatement, lack of effective early warning systems, lack of effective education and training, lack of employee voice when problems arose, inadequate dissemination of lessons learned, inadequate senior management oversight, lack of leadership consistency, and lack of uniform safety culture. For example, the Commission noted: "BP did not effectively incorporate process safety into management decision making." And the Commission concluded: "BP has not instilled a common, unified process safety culture among its U.S. refineries . . . significant process safety issues exist at all five U.S. refineries . . . BP has not adequately embraced safety as a core value." In the aftermath of Texas City, BP paid millions in personal damages. It also agreed to pay the federal government approximately $137 million in criminal, civil, and administrative environmental, health, and safety fines related to process safety violations at the Texas City refinery.

As a result of the Texas City explosion, BP's iconic CEO John Brown was forced by the BP board to move his retirement forward. A critical reporter from the *Financial Times* wrote that Brown was leaving with "his reputation tarnished, besieged by problems . . . overshadowed, above all, by the explosion at BP's Texas City refinery . . . he is accused of presiding over a culture of slack practice and corner cutting." In a less hyperbolic tone, Brown's successor as BP CEO, Tony Hayward, said: "The top of the organization doesn't listen hard enough to what the bottom of the organization is saying . . . we have lived too long in the world of making do and patching up this quarter . . . [we have] quite a bit to do to ensure a safety culture." Although Texas City involved a refinery explosion in the "downstream" part of the business, the broad issues of safety processes and safety management described in the accident reports required a uniform, global approach to all aspects of safety culture in the oil and gas business, including the "upstream" activities in exploration and drilling—as on the *Deepwater Horizon*.

2. THE DEEPER CAUSES OF THE GULF EXPLOSION

The high-impact explosion on *Deepwater Horizon* could have been prevented. But it wasn't because, remarkably enough, BP did not learn or effectively apply the vital lessons about safety culture that rained down on them after Texas City, especially in the Baker Commission Report. BP's failure to apply the lessons from Texas City may be inferred from the fact of the catastrophic accident itself. But it can also be inferred from the silence of senior BP management. In all the *Deepwater Horizon* post-mortems, BP never sought to make a concrete case—with actions, timelines, and resources—that senior management had effected major changes after Texas City and that the Gulf explosion was just a tragic exception to those changes. In fact, when Tony Hayward's bumbling response to the disaster led to his replacement in

July 2010, his successor, Bob Dudley, criticized Hayward's company, in an ironic echo of Hayward's criticism of Brown's BP. Said Dudley in September 2010: "There are lessons for us relating to the way we operate, the way we organize our company and the way we manage risk." No kidding. Almost a year after the explosion, Dudley was more direct: "BP is sorry. BP gets it. BP is changing."

In simplest terms, the explosion was caused by a sequence of events on an oil rig drilling in 5,000 feet of water. BP was seeking to cap and temporarily abandon the Macondo well, which was being drilled another 13,000 feet below the ocean floor. Cement and valves at or near the ocean floor did not prevent hydrocarbons from flowing up a steel pipe known as the well-casing. Engineers misinterpreted tests on whether there was gas improperly flowing toward the rig. Not recognizing the improper flow, the crew did not divert it overboard. A cloud of explosive gas enveloped the rig, and systems to prevent gas from igniting failed to shut off, leading to the explosion. After the explosion, a device called a blowout preventer on the ocean floor failed to close the hole in the ocean floor so that oil gushed, unconstrained, into the Gulf. BP was the leaseholder and operator of the Macondo well and was ultimately responsible for operations there. It subcontracted with Transocean to operate drilling on the *Deepwater Horizon*; it contracted certain exploration services from Haliburton, including the task of putting cement around the well on the ocean floor, and it contracted with Cameron for the blowout preventer that did not function after the rig explosion. *But this narrow sequence of events does not address the broad cultural and safety management issues that led to the disaster. And a variety of sources point to those broader factors—those lessons not learned—as being critical.*

3. BP'S OWN REPORT

In September 2010, five months after the explosion, BP released its own report on what happened. It described the sequence of events and placed much of the blame for the event on its subcontractors. But, while the "blame-game" aspect of the report was dismissed by many as self-serving, the report also contained 25 recommendations for future action—buried in a back section—that were, in fact, an indictment of BP. The recommendations covered such subjects as:

- Developing better, clearer standards and processes for a range of activities in deep-sea drilling from cementing to testing for leaks to well control and general risk management.
- Employing better safety processes for ensuring latest design and operational improvements are implemented.
- Significantly improving education and training of BP personnel to enhance capability and competency.
- Strengthening BP audit processes to improve close-out and verification of actions to remedy deficiencies found in safety audits.
- Implementing much greater oversight of contractors' current practices relating to cementing, well control, rig process safety, and blowout preventer design and safety.
- Requiring contractors to develop and implement auditable safety processes, including identification of key indicators—processes BP can review.

Although BP said that these recommendations should not be read as causal factors, they are so basic to an appropriate safety program that they indicate a failure to respond to issues raised in the Baker Commission report three years earlier. The recommendations are hardly a complete account of what went wrong, but they are clearly indicative of broader, systemic problems. Chief among them is the responsibility of the "owner" in high-risk projects to closely coordinate with high-tech contractors and to ensure that everyone is operating under robust, coordinated, and comprehensive safety processes and safety standards established by BP.

4. SUBSEQUENT REPORTS

BP's failures to learn the lessons of Texas City and have a strong safety culture at the Macondo well are substantiated in the library of reports written after the accident by, among others, a Presidential Commission, the Chemical Safety Board, the Interior Department, the Coast Guard, the National Academy of Engineering, and the National Academy of Science. These reports fixed blame on BP, and the contractors under its control, across a broad range of systemic issues: from poor risk assessment to failure to use best methods and technology in well design and operation to inadequate education and training to absence of fail-safe systems to lack of coordinated and integrated systems, leadership, and decision making. Said the National Academy of Engineering:

> The actions, policies, and procedures of the corporations involved did not provide an effective system safety approach commensurate with the risks of the Macondo well. *The lack of a strong safety culture resulting from a deficient overall systems approach to safety is evident in the multiple flawed decisions that led to the blowout.* Industrial management involved with the Macondo well–Deepwater Horizon disaster failed to appreciate or plan for the safety challenges presented by the Macondo well. [Emphasis supplied.]

The National Academy, for example, noted that, as with TEPCO at Fukushima, BP did not take into account up-to-date developments: "alternative completion techniques and operational processes were available that could have been used to prepare the well safely for temporary abandonment . . . [and BP failed to make] effective use of real-time data analysis, information on precursor incidents or near misses, or lessons learned in the Gulf of Mexico and worldwide to adjust practices and standards appropriately." Like the Baker Commission report, the National Academy concluded that there needed to be a major cultural shift at the company to improve "the overall safety of offshore drilling in the areas of design, testing, modeling, risk assessment, safety culture, and systems integration."

Similar themes were sounded in the report of the Presidential Commission. It said: "The explosive loss of the Macondo well could have been prevented. The immediate causes of the Macondo well blowout can be traced to a series of identifiable mistakes made by BP, Halliburton, and Transocean that reveal such systematic failures in risk management that they place in doubt the safety culture." Most fundamentally, it concluded that deep-water energy exploration and production, particularly at the frontiers of experience, "involve risks for which neither industry nor government has been adequately prepared" as investments in safety, containment, and response failed to pace with deep-water activity.

5. CRIMINAL PLEA AND CIVIL GROSS NEGLIGENCE

Finally, BP's plea to criminal charges and a court's finding of gross negligence in a Justice Department civil case also underscore BP's failure to fix its culture after Texas City.

In November 2012, BP pled guilty to 14 *criminal charges* and agreed to pay approximately $4 billion in criminal fines ($1.256 billion) and in other criminal recoveries ($2.777 billion). The plea was to 12 felony charges (11 relating to the death of workers and one to obstruction of Congress) and to two misdemeanors (under the environmental laws). BP agreed to the charges that BP well-site leaders were negligent in their handling of the pressure test that showed that gas was flowing up the well but that, despite contrary indications, they chose to interpret as showing the well was safe. This negligent act, BP acknowledged in court papers, was the proximate cause of the explosion, the deaths, and the environmental damage. In addition to the unprecedented payments, BP also agreed to a series of mandatory safety steps that mimicked the Baker Commission report from five years earlier, including hiring process safety and ethics monitors, increasing oversight of contractors, enhancing education and training, developing new safety technologies, and creating a safety organization with the authority to stop operations. As a result, BP was debarred from federal contracts until March 2014.

In September 2014, the District Court hearing the Justice Department's case seeking *civil recovery* from BP under the Clean Water Act ruled that the company had been "grossly negligent" in conduct relating to the explosion on *Deepwater Horizon*. This meant that the company had engaged in an extreme departure from reasonable care under the circumstances with foreseeable adverse consequences. The result of this ruling was that BP was subject to treble damages under the Clean Water Act ($4,300 liability for each barrel spilled rather than $1,100 for simple negligence). The District Court concluded that there was gross negligence because the pressure test results were handled so badly and because of the "chain of failures" through a series of negligent acts in a drilling operation that was behind schedule and over budget, acts that "taken together, evince . . . a conscious disregard of known risks." Certain decisions, said the judge, were "primarily driven by a desire to save time and money, rather than ensuring that the well was secure."

6. RESPONSE

Once BP had failed to implement the lessons about a safety culture and safety processes and had failed to prevent the explosion and oil spill, it faced short-term, medium-term, and long-term response problems of unparalleled complexity. A brief comment on BP's problems in responding is a companion cautionary tale.

In the days and weeks after the explosion, BP had to address two immediate issues: first, finding and updating vital facts, and, second, devising and updating crisis-response actions. The priority fact-bound issues were apparent from the early days of the spill: How much oil is flowing from the broken well? How can that oil flow into the Gulf be stopped? Where is the oil going—on the surface and subsurface—and at what speed? How can both surface and subsurface oil be contained or removed? What natural and human resources are in harm's way? How can damage to them be eliminated or mitigated (chemicals, booms, cleanup, berms)? What damages to human activities (loss of jobs or commerce) require immediate monetary compensation?

But BP failed to have clear, transparent processes that explained how, in cooperation with the government and other experts, it would continually develop critical facts on those questions and how, in light of evolving facts, it would take and, as necessary, modify crisis-response actions. It needed to be clear about what it knew, what it didn't know, how it was trying to improve its knowledge, and on what timetable it would make the improvement. Such clarity in process and responsibility was especially important in a crisis like this one, when the scientific and technical facts were complex and constantly changing and when, literally, the whole world was watching. Consistent with candor about how it was trying to develop the facts, it needed to be equally clear about what actions it was taking for which purposes, what actions it was contemplating, and what evaluations it was conducting of those crisis-response actions to modify them quickly for increased effectiveness.

Rather than being ahead of issues in this fashion, however, it was reactive: from fumbled attempts to stop the flow of oil to initially ignoring the fish and wildlife impact to taking more than two months to provide emergency payments to seriously affected parties to grossly misstating the amount of oil flowing into the Gulf—publicly claiming 5,000 barrels per day when its own internal estimates were at least ten times that amount—for which it ultimately paid a $500,000 civil penalty to the SEC for misleading disclosure. As a result, BP's reputation—already at risk due to the mere fact of the explosion—was even more severely impaired by its mishandling of the immediate response to the disaster. This impairment was reflected by the sacking of CEO Tony ("I'd like my life back") Hayward within three months of the accident. But clearly the whole BP upper echelon in corporate headquarters was broadly responsible. Six weeks after the explosion, a Harvard Business School professor said BP had flunked any test of leadership: failing to state or face facts, minimizing the problem, promising action that couldn't be delivered, and blaming others.

BP did not fare much better in subsequent analyses, which found that what appeared to be the case in the early days of the crisis was true: BP was woefully unprepared across key parameters of crisis management and crisis response. It was not organized to decide, implement, evaluate, and modify on needed actions as the facts evolved. The only saving grace on the "embarrassment meter": the federal and state governments were equally unprepared. As with so many other "disasters," what happened at the Macondo well was not implausible, but there had been no serious scenario planning to address the implications of such an event. Said the Presidential Commission: "[T]he events that unfolded in subsequent weeks and months made it dismaying[ly] clear that neither BP nor federal government were prepared to deal with a spill of the magnitude and complexity of the *Deepwater Horizon* disaster." The problems existed on at least three fundamental axes: better response planning for a large-scale, difficult to contain spill in deep water, including cooperation between public and private entities and the prime contractor (BP) and its subcontractors; better technology for stopping oil flow from under the seabed; and better technology for containing the oil either on the surface or below the surface once it was released in the ocean. Yet all these planning problems required resources. The Gulf explosion and spill exemplify the stark consequences of not paying for adequate preparation to address a low-probability/high-impact event.

7. "EXHIBIT A" FOR GENERAL COUNSEL

I have taken some space to discuss BP's problems as a result of the *Deepwater Horizon* explosion because, as I have indicated, it is Exhibit A for every General Counsel who has to convince business leaders about the importance of a safety culture and about expending resources on low-probability but high-impact events. Some fundamental arrows for the GC's quiver follow:

First, companies must approach lessons learned with great seriousness. I have tried to outline the case that BP's failure to follow the lessons of Texas City are the backdrop to the Gulf disaster. But, even if there is not an event and report directly on point, GCs and others concerned with risk can use a host of analogies with their business leaders to illustrate lessons learned about corporate failures to prevent and respond to high-impact but low-frequency events. They can start with the Gulf explosion.

Second, coordinating an immediate, honest response will have an outsized impact on the corporation's credibility and reputation. The company must develop a coordinated command structure because it must deal with a clamoring host of actors: personal injury victims, those with property damage, investors, partners, contractors, state and local governments, executive departments, regulatory agencies, Congress, and the media.

Third, if a corporation is responsible for a catastrophic event, the legal and policy response stemming from a catastrophic event will bedevil the company for years to come because of the variety and complexity of claims made against it. BP was simply overwhelmed by a variety of lawsuits: demands from federal agencies that BP remediate the Gulf, pay natural resource damages, pay civil fines, and pay criminal penalties for violation of environmental laws; demands from state governments on a variety of environmental and tort theories for economic injury; demands from investors and the SEC for failure to disclose material facts; demands from its contractors for indemnification (as well as BP countersuits); demands from BP to its partners for cost-sharing; demands from individuals and businesses suffering property damage; demands from individuals (not on the rig) suffering health injuries; and derivative suit demands. After the event, BP faced more than 250,000 claims (and more than 90 plaintiffs' law firms). Moreover, BP was also beset by demands to respond to formal investigations: from Congress, official commissions (Presidential, Coast Guard, Chemical Review Board), and expert study groups (National Academy of Engineering). Finding appropriate outside counsel/outside experts for all these matters and coordinating their efforts with the efforts of inside counsel/inside experts is a problem of surpassing complexity for the General Counsel—but also for the CEO, senior management, and the board who had to be involved in a complex morass of cases that, together, truly constituted a "bet the company" situation.

Finally, a catastrophic event can truly have a "high impact" financially. By the end of 2014, BP had set aside approximately $43 billion (pre-tax) to cover a variety of direct costs, including $14 billion for environmental cleanup, $4.5 billion for criminal and SEC claims, $3.5 billion for Clean Water Act penalties, approximately $12 billion paid to people and businesses suffering economic harm, and more than $1.5 billion in outside forensic fees. In October 2015, BP reached a global settlement agreement with the federal government, the Gulf states, and 400 local governments, which pushed BP's direct costs of the disaster to about $55 billion. The 2015 settlement amount was $20.8 billion to be paid out over 15 to 17 years, but about $8 billion of that total had already been included in BP's prior $43 billion total direct cost estimate. With one exception, the 2015 settlement was deemed by BP to end all litigation: It covered Clean Water Act penalties, Natural Resource Damages, and economic damage suffered by states and localities. The exception is the category of claims for additional economic damages sought by private parties: as of July 2015, BP had set aside $10.3 billion for such claims, but the actual amount it will ultimately pay is estimated to be at least $2 billion more than that number. In addition, BP has had to sell $38 billion in assets to cover the costs of the explosion and spill (12 percent of its reserves, half its pipelines, 35 percent of its wells, and some refineries). And its stock price has languished, down 30 percent since the accident as of January 2015, while the FTSE 100 was up approximately 30 percent and Shell Oil Company was up 20 percent in the same period.

But BP and the Gulf is also Exhibit A for underscoring the GC role as part of the top management in dealing with multi-faceted risk. The issues that preceded the explosion and that then ensued were not just legal (the myriad environmental, maritime, common law doctrines) and technical (the evolving and complex issues surrounding ever deeper ocean drilling), but ultimately involved how to combine rules and technology in operations under the umbrella of powerful safety culture, safety processes, and safety management—which should have been taken with deadly seriousness not just in company statements, but on a deep-water rig in the Gulf of Mexico.

G. A COMMENT ON GEOPOLITICAL, TERRORISM, AND CYBER RISK

A discussion of the risks facing global companies requires at least a "tip of the iceberg" comment on three extremely complex, difficult, and risk-laden subjects that will increasingly demand the attention of senior executives, including the General Counsel: geopolitical/country risk, terrorism, and cyber-security.

The history and culture of foreign nations—and their legal, political, social, and economic systems—present significant but varied risk issues for global corporations. Global aerospace, defense, and energy companies are accustomed to evaluating a broad range of geopolitical risks. But, too often, other corporations look narrowly at commercial risk in nations around the world without considering the potential problems of *country risk or broader, multination geopolitical risk.*[5] As with other risk issues, the GC should be a key actor in developing processes for identifying country or geopolitical risk; assessing its importance; and deciding whether to accept, avoid, or mitigate. Indeed, I would offer a fervent injunction that General Counsel in an international company devote significant time and effort to this ever-important subject.

Approaching the country risk issue turns, of course, on the nature and scope of current and future activities of the corporation. If it is an industrial company, what are its plans: building a manufacturing facility; building an assembly plant; conducting research and development; serving the local market through goods and services created in-country or goods and services imported from out-of-country; using the local presence to export to other countries; sourcing parts or sub-assemblies or finished product from third-party suppliers; acquiring major local companies? If it is a financial services company, what are its activities: sovereign debt finance; fixed debt; commercial loans; project finance; resource-based lending; trade finance? A wide variety of a nation's economic, social, legal, and political problems can pose risks, which is why this is such a fascinating and difficult set of issues: decline in its economy; corruption in its legal system; violence and disorder in its political system; demographic changes in its social system. These can, in turn, lead to a wide variety of direct adverse effects on company economics and operations: cancellation of contracts or licenses; expropriation; nationalization; devaluation; currency controls; discrimination against foreign corporations; secular changes in the market itself.

Assessing the nature of the risk and the probability of its occurrence requires expertise from a variety of in-country and out-of-country sources with their own generalist or specialist perspectives: academics, consultants, former government officials, experienced businesspeople, experienced lawyers, and sophisticated journalists. Worry about a nation's fiscal policy might yield one set of experts. Another set of experts may be appropriate for assessing protectionist risk, money laundering risk, currency risk, regime change risk, or the risk of war with neighbors. The disparate views must be analyzed and synthesized. Whenever I traveled as senior GE executive, I met routinely with foreign leaders in my role as corporate diplomat for the exchange of platitudes and cups of green tea, sitting on huge armchairs and talking in stilted phrases through interpreters discretely hidden behind the floral arrangement. And I would always meet with senior businesspeople and lawyers from other companies. But I found that constantly useful sources of information were key journalists from *The*

New York Times, The Wall Street Journal, the *Financial Times,* or other major media organizations whom I often sought out. If they had been on the beat for some years, they were skeptical of the received wisdom and knew the nitty-gritty. One of my favorite recollections was having breakfast in the mid-1990s at a Jakarta restaurant with John Burns, a three-time Pulitzer Prize winner at *The New York Times.* He observed that seeming strongman President Suharto was actually in an increasingly precarious position and, without giving business advice, said that reliance on Suharto and his Minister for Research and Technology, H. J. Habibie, could prove misplaced—men whose policies and power had been central to many of GE's Indonesia plans. Burns, of course, was right. Suharto left office a few years later, and Habibie had only a short tenure as his successor.

In addition, there are a host of consulting and econometric firms more than willing (for a price) to provide broad risk assessments of the nation's economic, legal, social, and political systems, ranging from standard economic modeling of the future course of the national or regional economy to deep think from former Secretaries of State and former National Security Advisors who have formed consulting firms. Moreover, if the company involvement is important enough, corporations can pay for scenario planning based on past events: What would happen to the company in a particular country or region if, for example, an event occurred that mimicked the Gulf War, the Second Iraq War, or the Arab Spring? Or such planning could be based on possible future events: significant Sino-Japanese tensions, the break-up of the EU monetary union, further Russian incursions in Eastern Europe, or excursions in the Middle East.

In addressing defined risks, global corporations have three broad choices. They can simply accept the risk and take their chances. For example, although there is a non-trivial risk of an India-Pakistan border war or even a doomsday nuclear exchange, corporations generally accept that risk, do business in India (less in Pakistan), and assume (perhaps mistakenly) that these events are simply remote or that they can somehow adapt to them (at least to an India-Pakistan non-nuclear war). By contrast, corporations can simply avoid the risk by choosing not to do business in a nation, at least for a period of time. For example, immediately after Tahrir Square, Egypt faced political and constitutional uncertainty, but its economy was also in a shambles and its direction uncertain because of conflicts between the "statism" of the military and the "free market" reforms of businesspeople, some of whom were seen as corrupt by many segments of the populace. Making investments at that turbulent time—or, today, in the Ukraine or other areas of conflict or regime change—could be deemed too risky.

Between acceptance and avoidance are a variety of alternative ways corporations can mitigate risks. They can make sure that their supply chains exhibit spread of risk across geographies so a problem in one country will not shut down lines of business. They can choose not to put plant and equipment in China but, instead, to enter into JVs where the Chinese company would build the plant and the global corporation would provide the technology (which would not, if possible, be the most up-to-date because of risk of theft). They could seek to reduce use of third parties in government procurements or hold them to strict standards. They could evaluate four countries in Southeast Asia for plant location and choose the nation with the greatest political and legal stability rather than the riskier country that offered higher incentives and was better on the pro forma economics. These were all issues I faced as GE's General Counsel.

Without question, these questions of accepting, avoiding, or mitigating country risk were among the most interesting and most difficult when I was General Counsel of a company doing business in more than 100 nations around the world. Dealing with these boundary-busting issues requires intense curiosity and broad knowledge. And this fascinating challenge should continue to preoccupy General Counsels of global corporations as far into the future as the eye can see.

Of equal and related difficulty is the problem of dealing with the risk of *terrorism*.[6] The 9/11 attack was a wake-up call in many ways. For corporations, it made them think much more systematically about risks to global operations. The GE CEO asked me, the CFO, the head of HR, and the IT leader to work with our top staff and top business leaders to draft and implement a new company policy on security and crisis management. The working group focused on how to handle a range of threats—including chemical, biological, and nuclear terrorism—to four assets: people, facilities, information, and supply chain. The policy was discussed widely within the company, changes were made, and then it was adopted. GE hired, for the first time, a Chief Security Officer, who was formerly the State Department's Assistant Secretary for Diplomatic Security and before that a Brigadier General in the Air Force. Every unit of the company developed a detailed plan for implementing the policy that was reviewed by a corporate task force and audited periodically thereafter.

As a result of this dramatic change in approach, we also developed more in-depth relationships with outside security experts, who had knowledge of different regions in the world and different types of problems and different modes of attack. We developed a list of the 25 most serious company risks and developed special protocols for reducing threats. One facility on that list might be a chemical plant in the Netherlands for its risk to a densely populated urban area, but another might be the Today Studio at Rockefeller Center for its symbolic and reputational value. We sought to mitigate risks in a variety of ways. For example, we simply pulled all employees out of Colombia, where some of our people had been kidnapped. Unlike nations, a company cannot say it will not negotiate with terrorists but has to seek to protect or bring back its people (which occurred after the hardest negotiation of my career). We beefed up personal security—much to the dislike of almost everyone—in particularly dangerous locales. We requested that people on travel stay—and hold meetings—in less ostentatious hotels (after a bombing at a luxury hotel in Indonesia injured some of our employees). We tried to extend the perimeters and "harden" certain facilities, knowing it would not be possible physically to stop a terrorist rocket heading toward a factory (other preventive measures must work).

Importantly, we required emergency practice sessions at every business and in every locale around the world so that people could actually "live" their plans. When possible, business units did joint exercises with local first responders and other governmental authorities, a critical aspect of any terrorist event. These sessions are crisis management 101, but, as I have already indicated several times, it is very hard to get people to do them. One way is to appeal to their experience. The best unit at GE was our Aircraft Engines Division, in part because they had military customers and were accustomed to dealing with emergencies to support equipment in combat zones. Another way is simple embarrassment. I confess to that. Our new Chief of Security called a mock emergency at corporate headquarters. The CEO and senior executives were supposed to go to a new underground command center. The only problem: We (including me, an architect of our new policy) didn't know where it was. That got our attention. Of course, at the end of the day, we had to audit all staff and business units on this critical element of security and crisis management and send to the whole company a list of the good, the bad, and the ugly.

When I was involved in developing a security and crisis management policy immediately after 9/11, the words *cyber-security and cyber-terrorism* were barely in the corporate lexicon. The main IT concern then was to have redundant information systems. Today, the director of the CIA says that one of the greatest threats to both national and industrial security in the next 50 years will be cyber.[7] Individuals, corporations, industries, governments, and NGOs with responsibility for parts of the Internet are struggling to keep up with an exploding array of issues and need special cyber risk groups at corporate and in the business divisions. The threats facing companies are profound: theft of their information, sabotage of their information or their operating systems, violations of the privacy of their employees or customers, and resolving the dilemma of cooperating with law enforcement authorities without becoming arms of the state. These threats arise in the increasing array of IT modalities: employee desktop or laptop computers; mobile devices, conventional servers, cloud computing, customer digital relationships; other third-party relationships; and software asset management. Company-specific actions range from identifying key assets to setting policies to training to monitoring to constant updating to data recovery to cyber-insurance. In addition, there are cyber risks in virtually every infrastructure system on which business depends, and often contributes—from the power grid to air transport to financial services to basic telephone and data transmission (to name but a few). Moreover, this is an era when cyber-spying and cyber-war and cyber-counter-war are of profound importance to governments all over the world. The unexamined, perhaps unimagined, knock-off effects of new cyber weapons and cyber warfare may rival the dawn of the nuclear age in both their destructive power and the absence of as-yet-well-thought-out strategies to constrain them.

These problems can be addressed by companies acting alone, by companies acting together, by informal public–private cooperation, or by mandated national or international policy. But, as noted political scientist Joseph Nye has pointed out in a ground-clearing paper, the governance for managing global cyber-activities is pluralistic and fragmented. Individual companies can do their best at keeping secure the intra-company world, but that may be ineffectual and may be just a fraction of the real risk problems they face in an interconnected world. Few subjects pose greater future challenges for General Counsel. Managing cyber risk for companies is a witch's brew of evolving technology, malignant actors, limits on intra-company approaches, but a lack of consensus—and indeed conflict—about an appropriate role for national governments and multinational actors in providing safety and security in such a ubiquitous, unruly medium.

H. THE NEED FOR SPECIALIZED KNOWLEDGE

The risk issues surrounding cyber-security—which depend heavily on an understanding of the science and engineering issues relating to the Internet—highlight a deep theme running through this section on risk, and indeed throughout this whole book. What kind of scientific and technical "literacy" can or should corporate decision makers possess? How can they understand the state of the specialized knowledge—scientific, technological, economic, sociopolitical—before using it to make decisions about corporate actions? Where is that specialized knowledge on a spectrum from "consensus" to "debated" to "new and uncertain"? How does the corporation sort out conflicting views among experts on that state of knowledge? Are corporations willing to spend the time and effort to make that difficult determination? And, depending on the answer about that question—about the degree of uncertainty in knowledge describing the reality in these vital specialized domains—how then should corporate leaders use it to decide what action to take? This is a huge challenge for all senior executives, but especially for those, like the General Counsel, who will be either leading or counseling the corporate effort to address the broad scope of risks identified at the beginning of this section. The ability to understand the state of specialized knowledge, to be able to interrogate and question the assumptions of experts, and then to use the state of knowledge appropriately in decision making is one of the "complementary competencies" that, I argue, a lawyer-statesman should possess.

Let me end this risk chapter with three very brief examples about technical subjects outside law that pose challenges for General Counsels. The examples illustrate a spectrum from fields of knowledge the General Counsel "should know" to areas where it is "nice to know" but probably not "necessary to know."

- When a company makes a product than can kill people—like a car—it should have a robust statistical process for tracking experience in the field and separating a "signal" that raises important questions about product or manufacturing defects from the "noise" of accidents caused by drivers, weather, or other factors. A predicate for such a statistical method would be a systematic method for gathering accident and near-miss information from a variety of sources (consumer complaints and concerns, suppliers, public safety institutions, other governmental sources, lawsuits). And one implication of such a method would be a clear set of review levels for a full and fair examination of whether the product posed a safety threat to the public—as indicated by statistical analysis or discrete but troubling patterns of cases—and what additional studies or actions were promptly warranted. Protecting consumers from real safety threats must be put ahead of protecting the corporate fisc.[8] Of all the failures in the GM ignition case, this threshold issue was a striking one: the failure to have or to use properly a technical, statistical, or other system that "separated the signal from the noise" with promptness and that raised genuine safety questions quickly to high levels the company must address because lives are at stake. Because of the consequences, I would submit that the General Counsel should develop enough knowledge to understand such systems and be able to join in a high-level discussion of whether it is appropriate for the task at hand and, if so, how to use it to protect lives.

- A new drug must be deemed "safe" and "effective" by the Food and Drug Administration (FDA). These regulatory conclusions are, of course, based on the basic science of the particular pharmaceutical agent as reflected in a variety of animal or human scientific studies. How well-versed in the science of safety and efficacy should the General Counsel be in order to raise challenging questions and participate in a variety of decisions: Should the drug be submitted at various stages for approval? What kinds of additional studies should be conducted? What is the fairest way, in the public interest, to present the safety and efficacy evidence to the regulatory agency? When must new science be reported to the FDA? These are matters of great consequence. For example, GlaxoSmithKline pled guilty to a crime and paid a penalty of $242 million for failing to report data about the increased cardiovascular risk of Avandia, its diabetes drug. It also paid $657 million to settle government civil charges of false claims relating to Avandia in federal health care programs.[9] Acquiring scientific literacy in this kind of specialized, mixed scientific-regulatory decision making is, again in my view, a "should do" for General Counsels in a pharmacology company.

- The 2007–2009 financial crisis had many origins. But a major one was the assumption inside financial services companies that the housing market would never decline. This led to creation of lower credit standards, derivative instruments, excess leverage, and inadequate liquidity, which were at the core of the financial meltdown when the bubble of increasing housing values burst. These problems have been described in numerous books and articles.[10] There were tremendous pressures inside financial institutions, in the deathless words of Citigroup CEO Chuck Prince, to "dance til the music stopped" and to continue to create these toxic housing-related instruments (e.g., collateralized debt obligations [CDOs] and synthetic CDOs). But there were also strong dissenting voices from highly regarded experts suggesting that a dangerous bubble existed. Financial services institutions suffered severe consequences, in part, from ignoring those dissenting voices and failing to scrub their financial risk models—and because they had soothing credit ratings for derivative instruments that they paid for and that were bogus for the same reason. Even though not at the core of his expertise, is it too much to expect that the wise General Counsel who was part of leadership would, at least, have raised hard questions with top management about the validity of the underlying economic assumptions and the unhealthy concentration of risk in the housing market? Such questions could have stemmed from a variety of sources: from an attention to core risk issues and an understanding of key risk assumptions as part of a general risk management role; from a general prudential rule that when companies are minting money, then that is the time to give business models a hard scrub; from asking the obvious question (in retrospect) about concentration of risk in housing-related financings; and from questions raised by the outside and inside lawyers who were creating all the instruments that collapsed— who should have been trained to think about worst-case scenarios that could occur with the legal instruments they were drafting. I would acknowledge that this was a "hard to do" for a GC because this set of financial risk questions was at the core of what other businesspeople and top management were being paid enormous sums to consider. But the risk went far beyond "finance." The financial crisis poses a critical problem of whether the GC and inside lawyers could have at least raised key issues for CEOs and boards so their companies could have pulled back, rather than having the music stop when the dance hall's ceiling collapsed and crushed the piano (and the companies).

The General Counsel will surely be at the center of a corporation's approach to legal, ethical, public policy, and country risk. But, as wise counselor and leader in the corporation, the GC must also, in my judgment, constantly ask whether he needs specialized knowledge that allows him to ask hard questions—and understand and critique technical answers—about the highest priority issues in the broad array of economic and noneconomic risks facing a global corporation.

8

GOVERNANCE: THE BOARD RELATIONSHIP

At its core, corporate governance addresses two related subjects: the purposes of the corporation and the respective powers and roles of shareholders, the board of directors, and management in carrying out that corporate mission. This subject has spawned great controversy in the past 30 years: ownership v. control, principal v. agent, managerial capitalism v. investor capitalism, short term v. long term, shareholders v. directors, shareholders v. stakeholders, focus on stock v. focus on products, shareholders as activists v. shareholders as stewards, and directors as puppets of management v. directors as wise leaders of the company. In addition, poor corporate governance is seen as a cause of striking corporate failures (especially since 2000) and has led to increased federal regulation in Sarbanes-Oxley and Dodd-Frank, which have significantly supplemented traditional state law primacy on corporate governance issues. The purpose of this chapter is not to explore these debates in any detail or to argue for more or less public sector regulation, although these issues are certainly backdrop. Rather it is to offer my prescriptive views on a limited set of core governance issues that are essential for people who lead companies and that seek to cut through much of the fog created by new regulation and by the ever-expanding corporate governance industry. These issues are also essential for General Counsel engagement, highlighting where the GC needs to be closely involved in the board of directors and management relationship.

Indeed, because it involves interpretation and implementation of norms derived from both public policy and private ordering, the General Counsel's role in corporate governance is central and her relationship with the board of directors fundamental. As governance issues have assumed greater importance, this sphere of activity is another dimension of the inside counsel revolution. For purposes of this chapter, the General Counsel, as a partner-guardian, helps define and carry-out a "right-sized" role of the board in providing constructive and critical oversight of the CEO and other senior business leaders— and helps define a constructive company relationship, if possible, with that vast and diverse menagerie we call shareholders.

A. THE THREE DIMENSIONS OF GOVERNANCE

In broad outline, there are three dimensions of corporate governance:

- The relationship between the shareholder and the company (both the board and management).
- The relationship between the board and the CEO/senior corporate leaders.
- The relationship between the CEO and the company—how the CEO "governs" the corporation—which I have termed the "third dimension of governance."

Since the takeover wars of the 1980s, a veritable corporate governance industry has grown up in business associations, consulting groups, governance watchdogs, and academia. The focus has primarily been on how boards of directors can avoid CEO "capture" and provide independent oversight. But going back to Adolf Berle's and Gardiner Means's 1932 masterpiece, *The Modern Corporation and Private Property*, governance experts have also been struggling with how to give shareholders more voice, how to overcome the core problem in the modern corporation of the separation of ownership (shareholders) and control (board and management). A related and recurring issue is "for whom" corporate power is exercised: to increase shareholder value or to optimize the legitimate interests of competing stakeholders—like employees and customers—*to achieve both the short-term and long-term best interests and sustainability of the corporation.*[1]

In my view, the action is in the third dimension of governance—the actual day-to-day governance of the company from the CEO in her corner office down to the corporation's shop floors across the globe. Despite the enormous outpouring of writing and debate, a basic truth remains: The shareholders and the board cannot lead or manage the company. The board of directors can be a check on management. And the shareholders can be a check on the board and on management. They both can make suggestions. The shareholders obviously select the board, and the board obviously selects the CEO. The board oversees/approves strategies and major corporate actions. But neither the shareholders nor the board can effectively initiate strategies or affirmatively manage the company—they cannot actually get things done. For a company to achieve high performance, to act with high integrity, and to exercise sound risk management, the leadership of the CEO, the management by senior executives, and the actions of all the employees must make it happen. I think it is equally obvious that, in seeking to manage "in the best interests of the company," the CEO and senior executives will make fine-grained trade-offs among the interests of the various corporate constituencies—employees, customers, suppliers, creditors, shareholders. This entails seeking to optimize the interests of all of them, often in different combinations over the short, middle and longer term. Attempts to reduce this complex set of decisions and trade-offs to simplistic and formulaic phrases (maximize shareholder value)—across different companies with different sizes and different histories in different time frames, in different industries, and in different geographies—are folly.

This is where the General Counsel has critical influence and why the first seven chapters of this book have been about how she operates in the context of a complex global organization. This emphasis on the "third dimension" of governance from the CEO down into the company reflects my experience—my governance bias—after nearly 20 years in senior management: bias both as to how power is exercised in the corporation and for what purpose. The attention paid to share-holders and boards acting as a check on management is fine, but it simply overstates, in my view, their importance in relation to devising and executing a constructive, affirmative corporate agenda on performance, integrity, and risk. So, too, a focus on "shareholder" value as corporate "purpose" is vacuous, or worse, without considering in a constructive way *all the constituent parties* who are essential to the success of the corporation.

Thus, in this chapter I focus primarily on *six essential tasks* the board should discharge *in conjunction with* the CEO and senior executives to provide strategic direction in a high performance with high integrity company. These are tasks the General Counsel should work on with the board *and* management. These are the tasks essential to a "right-sized" and realistic role for a board of directors that only meets eight to ten times a year. At the end, I discuss how shareholders—who are of all shapes and sizes, with a variety of conflicting goals—can have a constructive but more limited role.

B. THE FRAMEWORK OF FORMAL RULES

But first a word on the importance of compliance with the formal rules on governance—the rules demarcating the roles of shareholders, boards, and corporate managers. One set of rules involves private decisions the corporation makes. The General Counsel is at the epicenter of this first, private-ordering effort. The corporation's articles of incorporation and by-laws provide the governance framework corporations establish under the relevant state's general corporation law. But beyond the articles of incorporation, corporations are, increasingly, publishing detailed corporate governance principles that state formal commitments on governance issues and that are either binding in practice or binding in law if they are subsequently translated into formal by-laws. These governance principles/by-laws cover such basic topics as board functions, board independence, board size, board selection process, types of committees, functions of committees, board meetings without the CEO, agenda-setting, board self-evaluation, board compensation, and board interaction with operating business leaders. Some corporations also have a companion set of interpretive guidelines that describe how these governance principles work in practice. After the collapse of Enron and WorldCom, I worked intensely, like many other GCs, with senior company management and the GE's Nominating and Corporate Governance Committee in 2003 to recast significantly GE's governance principles and to write public governance guidelines. As part of that rewrite, the board, the CEO, and senior management promised an annual governance review in the future to consider what emerging governance best practices the company might voluntarily adopt.[2]

In addition to a central role in developing the private-ordering rules that structure corporate governance, the General Counsel, as technical expert and wise counselor, must, of course, determine for the company the scope and impact of the second set of formal governance rules set forth in state and federal law that add to or modify the corporate decisions reflected in the by-laws, governance principles, and governance commentary. In addition to basic corporation statutes establishing the context for corporate governance, states also define basic corporate law doctrines—usually through evolving judicial decisions—such as the fiduciary duties of care and loyalty. Judges also shape the parameters of the business judgment rule that, depending on context, gives varying degrees of deference to reasonable, informed, good faith board decision making in the best interests of the company. Moreover, starting in the 1930s, the securities laws and the Securities and Exchange Commission have created a companion body of federal law and regulation on aspects of corporate governance. Every reader of this book knows that, because of two waves of corporate failures, two waves of federal regulations on corporate governance have swept over the corporate community in this century, seeking more disclosure and more checks and balances. Broadly speaking, Sarbanes-Oxley sought to provide board checks on management. Subsequently, Dodd-Frank sought to provide shareholder checks on boards and management with respect to financial services institutions but also, in some cases, for all public companies. These laws covered a variety of subjects, including disclosure of risk management, valuation of equity awards, independence of compensation committee members and consultants, claw-back of windfalls due to improper accounting, and nonbinding shareholder votes on executive compensation. Listing requirements for national stock exchanges follow these rules and may impose additional governance requirements.[3]

As discussed in Chapter 5, the General Counsel has the lead responsibility for determining what law applies to the corporation and what that law means in practice. In no area is that responsibility more important than corporate governance. The GC's credibility with the board, the CEO, and the senior executives is based on understanding the complex array of federal, state, and stock exchange governance requirements; explaining them crisply and clearly; and assuring that the top echelons of the corporation are not embarrassed—or made liable!—by failures to follow laws and regulations that apply directly to them. Especially in large corporations, it is important to have clear distinctions, for example, between decisions involving material matters requiring board approval and delegated decisions on which the board may exercise oversight. On either type of matter, the General Counsel must ensure that the board of directors has followed an appropriate process, has appropriate information, and has taken appropriate time to ensure that its approval or its review is well within the parameters of the business judgment rule. Given the attention corporate governance commands, General Counsels need expert advisors—either on the inside legal staff or in law firms—to help ensure that the "i's" are dotted and the "t's" crossed. And, given the importance of this subject to the board, the CEO, and senior executives, General Counsels are well advised to know the rules in this area in detail themselves. *A major mistake on the basic state and federal rules of governance is a career-ender.* Rather than relying on PowerPoint presentations or oral briefings, which can be both imprecise and difficult to follow, General Counsels are also well advised, on fundamental governance issues, to write careful, succinct memoranda so the board can digest the substance carefully and ask hard questions.

C. THE SIX ESSENTIAL TASKS OF BOARD–MANAGEMENT LEADERSHIP

The business community continues to face a corporate governance crisis in confidence. It has many origins. During the Great Recession,

major financial institutions (banks and investment banks) and industrial companies (autos) went bankrupt with significant injury to all
stakeholders. Important financial service companies contributed
to the credit meltdown and severe recession (through, among other
things, poor risk management, high leverage, inadequate liquidity, creation of ill-understood products, and ill-secured credit default insurance). For these travails, JPMorgan's CEO, Jamie Dimon, said: "I blame
the management teams 100% and no one else" (not the Federal Reserve
[Fed], other regulators, Fannie/Freddie, credit rating agencies). High,
poorly structured corporate compensation has, in particular, drawn
sharp criticism as a cause of excessive risk-taking and as being out
of proportion to good judgment and common sense. Said Goldman
Sachs's Lloyd Blankfein in 2009: "the past year has been deeply hum-
bling for my industry . . . the loss of public confidence will take years to
rebuild . . . decisions on compensation . . . look self-serving and greedy
in hindsight . . . [m]eaningful change and effective reform are vital."
Moreover, since the financial meltdown, there is a constant drumbeat in the news about outsized commercial pratfalls and about legal
and ethical scandals in both the financial and industrial sectors (see
pp. 95–108).[4]

One answer to this lack of confidence, of course, has been more
public-sector regulation, primarily through Sarbanes-Oxley and
Dodd-Frank, to limit private-sector self-governance either in the
financial sector or across all publicly held corporations. The second
complementary answer is more broad-gauged, transparent, and effective private-sector leadership through enhanced corporate self-governance at all publicly held companies, a view advanced throughout
this book. At the board–management interface of self-governance, I
believe that there are *six essential governance tasks that are seamlessly
interrelated and that are the touchstone of essential corporate governance and accountability.* Operating inside the framework of formal
public laws, regulations, and judicial decisions, these six tasks provide
an affirmative, *actionable private ordering schema* that boards and
business leaders can apply, as appropriate, in their own corporations.

General Counsels must help boards of directors and business
leaders in publicly held companies carry out these six fundamental,

interrelated governance tasks if those business leaders want to give lie to the claim that yet more public regulation of governance is needed and if they want to regain the vital trust upon which business is based. The six-task framework also seeks to provide focused prioritized answers, in the this period of economic upheaval and change, to the common board lament of too many conflicting demands, too much complexity, and too little time.

The long-standing proposition that the board of directors sets the corporation's broad direction and oversees implementation—and that the CEO and senior executives lead and manage the corporation itself—continues to apply. Too much of the governance writing, especially since Enron, has emphasized the board's role in being a check and balance on management, as if they are necessarily in perpetual opposition. But—*and this must be emphasized*—if the board correctly defines the jobs of the CEO and top business leaders and chooses the right people, the primary relationship should be a questioning but affirmative partnership. *That partnership critically but constructively tests the reasonableness of both the fundamental systems and processes instituted by management and the high-priority decisions and results flowing from those systems and processes.*

1. REDEFINING THE MISSION OF THE CORPORATION

Corporate mission statements are usually a forgettable (and unreadable) mish-mash of pieties and platitudes. But, boards and managements, with General Counsel involvement, need to address the realities of core corporate objectives in a cogent statement from which action flows. *Such a statement needs to set down markers that corporate purpose has three dimensions: high performance, high integrity, and sound risk management.* Just saying that would be an advance on many existing statements that speak vaguely and verbosely in a laundry list of disconnected ideas. Each company will find its own way to rethink and rearticulate its mission. But, I believe, to summarize all that has gone before, that a mission statement should cover the following subjects (in words appropriate to each company) if it is to have operative impact.

The ultimate goal of the corporation is the fusion of high performance with high integrity carried out with appropriate risk disciplines of prevention and response. The *goal of high performance* should be about creation of long-term, sustainable economic value that benefits all stakeholders and, in so doing, benefits shareholders over time. The company must invest in products, in employees, in customers, in creditors, in suppliers, and in its communities. It must optimize the legitimate interests of all those stakeholders so that value is created for all of them. It should explicitly state that maximizing short-term shareholder value is not its only goal—and individuals and institutions should not invest in the corporation if that is what they seek. The *goal of high integrity* involves, as readers know, robust adherence to spirit and letter of the formal rules; the adoption of global ethical standards that bind the company and its employees; balanced public policy positions that fairly balance the private and public interests; and employees who embody the core values of honesty, candor, fairness, trustworthiness, and reliability. The *goal of risk management* involves appropriate investments in people, systems, and process to find a balance between risk-taking (the creativity and innovation so essential to the growth of our economy) and economic risk management (the financial, commercial, and operational disciplines so essential to the soundness and durability of business institutions). It also involves investment in appropriate people, systems, and processes to mitigate effectively and appropriately the integrity and other noncommercial risks (safety, quality) that can threaten a company's health. Through these and other actions the corporation seeks to be a good corporate citizen in the short, middle, and long term by devoting systematic attention to business-in-society issues: how society can and will affect the conduct of business, how business has an impact on society, and how business leaders should shape and communicate the alignment of business with societal interests.

I am part of the legion of critics who believe that far too much emphasis has been placed in recent years on the single corporate goal of maximizing short-term earnings per share, stock price, and total shareholder return.[5] I have never understood this focus other than simple greed of certain groups of shareholders. As one who sat at the top of a huge global enterprise, it was obvious to me that the ultimate success of a corporation depends on investing money or time in all its constituencies and to acknowledge their vital role in corporate success. Different constructive and productive goals for all these constituencies are vital. There is nothing ordained in corporate law that exalts a short-term focus on shareholders over a focus on all the other aspects and relationships of a corporation and on all the different ways it creates values for its various constituencies. CEOs need to have well-thought-out and balanced strategies and the strong support of the board and long-term shareholders to withstand the passing squalls of the short-term investors in the stock market.

The history of Apple is one example that demonstrates why the diktat of "maximizing shareholder value" is so empty by itself and why a focus on other issues and constituencies—in Apple's case, customers—make so much more sense in the real world of corporate operations. The shareholder value shibboleth stemmed from the famous Michael Jensen and William Meckling article in 1976 that argued the solution to the principal-agency problem—where business leaders advance their own interests, not those of shareowners—was to make the goal of the corporation the highest return to shareholders and to align shareholders and business leaders through stock option grants. It was a rebuke of "managerial capitalism" that, in theory, focused on all the corporation's stakeholders but to critics just led to the agency problem of ignoring shareholder interests. In recent years, the pendulum has, however, swung again; there have been numerous critics of this focus on shareholders and stock options.

One of the most trenchant critiques comes from Roger Martin, dean of the Rothman School of Management at the University of Toronto, in his 2011 book, *Fixing the Blame*.[6] Martin argues that agency theory and the goal of maximizing "shareholder value" have had many harmful side effects. Pressures from institutional investors for stock price increases as well as business leaders gaining outsized wealth through stock options have led many business leaders to manage the "expectations market" of the public stock exchanges, which, in turn, has led to short-termism, accounting manipulation, cutting of ethical and legal corners, failures to invest for the future, and the financial crisis. Martin argues instead that the primary purpose of the corporation should be constructive action in the "real market," not the "expectations market," and that this means "customers are the focus, and the central task of companies is to find ever better ways of serving them." Martin's manifesto is: "We must shift the focus of companies back to the customer and away from shareholder value. In other words, we must turn our attention back to the real market and away from the expectations market. This shift necessitates a fundamental change in our prevailing theory of the firm." Martin cites Thomas Edison and Henry Ford as people who created customer value through "innovations in products, services, and business models." And he was echoing Peter Drucker, who famously wrote: "The purpose of business is to create and keep a customer."

No one exemplifies the focus on the "real" market better in our era than Steve Jobs, whose fundamental credo was that Apple existed to "delight customers." There can be little question that, from 2000 on, Jobs focused the company on making innovative, robust, and beautiful products consumers loved. Apple reshaped whole markets in areas like personal computers, music, cell phones, and tablet computing. There can also be little question that Jobs was not focused on shareholders or short-term actions to maximize shareholder value. Under Jobs, Apple paid no dividends, held tens of billions in cash, and didn't do stock buybacks. He looked with dismay at the dot. com entrepreneurs in the late 1990s who wanted to make a quick profit on exit strategies. "It is such a small ambition and sad really. They should want to build something, something that lasts." And, of course, Apple shareholders have done spectacularly. At the beginning of this century Apple was not even in the top 100 companies by market cap. When Jobs died in 2011, it was tied for number 1 with ExxonMobil. As I write this in mid-2015, it is the most valuable company in the world with more than $650 billion in market cap (although, with a huge cash pile, it has started stock buybacks). An important part of Jobs's legacy was his focus on products and customers and his ability to withstand short-term "shareholder value" pressures. Indeed, Michael Jensen, observing what he had wrought, had second thoughts. Writing 25 years later, he observed: "Short-term profit maximization at the expense of long-term value creation is a sure way to destroy value."[7]

2. REVAMPING THE LEADERSHIP
DEVELOPMENT PROCESS

Stimulating education and training for all employees is a foundation stone for building a performance with integrity culture (see pp. 121–125 in Chapter 4). But executive development—the second key task—takes that education and training to a whole different level. For individuals with high potential, corporations often provide highly specialized training in a wide variety of business skills such as finance, sales, marketing, IT, business development, manufacturing, engineering, and product or technology development. They also may provide less specialized, more general training for P&L (profit-and-loss) managers, who are promoted from positions of narrow expertise to assume broader operational responsibilities. Such general manager training customarily focuses on leading cross-functional teams to achieve commercial goals in different, challenging environments.

But, with oversight from the board of director's Compensation and Development Committee, the CEO and other top business leaders must institute leadership development processes for corporate P&L and functional leaders that, at early stages in their careers, put strong emphasis not just on developing specialized expertise or on achieving commercial goals, but on developing the experience and skills to do this through balanced risk management and performance with integrity. This emphasis on risk management and on integrity should be a talent–management imperative as individuals rise within the corporation and face increasingly broader challenges requiring integration of all three dimensions of corporate mission. This wide perspective on corporate performance, risk, and integrity can be delivered in *broader and different educational courses offered by the corporation during an individual's career.* Such courses may be offered inside the company or in executive MBA or executive education programs. But a rethinking of such courses, both in the company and in academia, is critical, given a broader definition of the CEO and business leader role and the robust debate about necessary changes in business education as a result of recent business failures.[8] Although GE had an outstanding internal business school, one of my failures as General Counsel was to develop such a course for rising executives who were moving from functional to generalist leaders just below the very top leadership ranks.

Such leadership development will also entail *giving high-potential individuals a broader range of assignments earlier in their careers*—for example, working on a team scrubbing a new product line for its risks; being integral to a major internal investigation of potential wrong-doing; helping to ascertain the geopolitical issues, as well as the business issues, in locating a new manufacturing facility in one of three or four Southeast Asian nations; and assessing supply chain risks and opportunities in emerging markets. From the mid-1990s on, my peer staff officers as CFO and head of HR had distinguished themselves in a major integrity matter when they were head of the Corporate Audit Staff and leader of HR in the affected business. Jack Welch and the board of directors promoted both of them for many reasons, but their outstanding performance, when working in the business and across the company on this tough, tense matter, was clearly an important factor. The General Counsel and senior lawyers can help define some of these essential cross-functional risk and integrity assignments—and provide perspective on individuals' performance—as part of a well-thought-out Compensation Committee and CEO development process. But they must be asked—or seek to insert themselves in the process. This contribution from the GC is not currently a staple of the executive development processes at corporations.

3. REFOCUSING THE PROCESS FOR CEO SELECTION—AND FOR OTHER PROMOTIONS INTO HIGH CORPORATE POSITIONS

Most would agree that the board's most important act of governance is choosing the CEO. The ultimate result of the initial tasks—redefining the mission of the company and revamping leadership development—should be a CEO-succession process that expressly searches for, and then selects, a new leader for the company whose personality and career reflect the combination and integration of the necessary performance, risk, and integrity dimensions.

The need for core economic performance skills—financial, commercial, operational, and strategic—is as important as ever in the

CEO and top business leaders in a rapidly changing global economy. Nothing said here is intended in any way to diminish the primacy of high economic performance in a business organization. But failures of business leadership in the recent past have frequently been due to serious weaknesses in risk assessment and management or to serious lapses in adhering to legal, financial, or ethical standards. These failures have had significant, even catastrophic, impacts on shareholders, creditors, employees, customers, suppliers, and communities. They have, over time, eroded the trust upon which successful conduct of business depends. A contemporary CEO must have proven skills in risk management; in creating a culture of integrity; and in understanding business-in-society issues that pose both threats to, and opportunities for, the corporation. Strength in commercial operations and strategy is absolutely necessary, but not sufficient, in today's business environment.

As it begins this succession process, the board of directors should restate and reiterate the mission of the company in a company-specific articulation of purpose aimed at both inside and outside audiences. It should make clear that candidates will be assessed according to capacity for leading the company into the future on economic performance but also on high integrity and sound risk management. Ideally, the board should be able to choose the next CEO from a strong talent pool inside the company who have undergone proper leadership development. But if the board needs to go outside the company for CEO succession, it must ensure that the candidates clear a high bar not just on performance capabilities, but also on deeply engrained talent for managing risk and promoting integrity in a leading corporation under challenging conditions. This approach should also guide joint board–CEO promotions to senior corporate leadership positions. General Counsels should be among the group of select senior executives who interview candidates in the CEO succession process in order to provide *confidential* perspective to the board of directors alone. Again, this is not a practice uniformly followed in major corporations today.

4. FORMULATING PRIORITY OBJECTIVES FOR PERFORMANCE, RISK, AND INTEGRITY

How the company measures commitment to its fundamental mission over the short, middle, and long term is a critical decision that drives desired behavior and sets the terms for corporate accountability. The board of directors, of course, approves the two or three major strategies the corporation will seek to follow in the future. But, within that strategic framework, boards of directors and business leadership must together define a concise, comprehensive, and robust set of priority operational objectives across the dimensions of economic performance, high integrity, and risk management that can be clearly communicated inside and outside the company. Those objectives can be milestones on the path to the strategic objectives. Or they can be vital stand-alone goals on their own. This process of translating the mission into operational objectives requires great care and sustained attention. It should articulate measures that can be tracked over time. It should measure both financial and nonfinancial factors. The General Counsel should be a strong participating member in this important governance process.

A best practice, in my view, is to have an explicit board discussion toward the end of every calendar (or fiscal) year about priority operational objectives for the following year. The key is to sort the top issues facing the company according to the three critical parameters of mission—performance, integrity, and risk—and according to short, medium, or longer time frame. The board and management together should then prioritize these risks and opportunities. First-priority issues, which should probably number no more than 15, are those on which the board of directors as a whole "will touch bottom" with management—will learn in significant detail—whether an "approval item" or a close "oversight" matter. These first-priority items will be scheduled out over the course of the next year's board meetings and covered in depth—sometimes at sequential, not just single, meetings. Some of these first-priority issues will be vetted first in board committees, but their first-priority status means the board will take time to dig into them as a whole. The second-priority issues will be covered in significant depth by committees of the board—Compensation, Audit, Governance, Risk, Technology, Public Responsibilities—with summary reports to the whole board. A third-priority set of issues across performance, risk, and integrity will be identified and objectives set but will be delegated to the CEO and the management team who will summarize results during the course of the year but not discuss in detail (unless those third-level items move up the priority list due to changed circumstances). Of course, as the next year unwinds, new issues will emerge that should be stratified—and addressed—as first-, second-, or third-level priorities.

This process of issue identification, stratification, and objective setting must be based on energetic and candid discussions between the board and management on which subjects should become the first-, second-, and third-order priorities. Other than choosing the CEO, nothing—nothing!—is more important than this comprehensive board perspective over short, middle, and longer term on the major performance, integrity, and risk issues facing the corporation—on establishing priorities and setting objectives. As a close advisor to the board, the General Counsel should assist management and the board both on the process and substance of this critical end-of-year interactive exercise.

Types of performance, risk, and integrity objectives, which draw on prior chapters, are summarized here simply to illustrate the range of operational goals boards and managements can consider. These objectives can be expressed in direct company results or in the construction of necessary systems and processes to address basic, recurring issues.

a) Achieving High Economic Performance. These measurements should be insulated as much as possible from book-keeping manipulation and short-term stock price fluctuations.

- Portfolio structure—the mix of businesses, the relative capital allocated to them, and spread of risk.
- The efficient use of capital through such measurements as return on assets and return on invested capital.
- Operational excellence as reflected in cash flow or operating margins or productivity increases.

- Strong connections to customers, through such measures as trends in market share, increases in revenues, repeat customer percentages, assessments of customer satisfaction, new products as percentage of offerings, and brand strength.
- Employee motivation, satisfaction, and individual productivity.
- The more traditional performance measures of net profits, earnings per share, stock price increases, total shareholder return, and return on equity. While these metrics of economic performance should not overwhelm all others, they should be in the mix. One of the challenges is how to give them their due, not make them dominant, and thus put them in context with the many other measures of economic performance that make for a strong, vibrant company.
- How, and to what degree, changes in new technologies, new products, new acquisitions (or dispositions), and new geographies positively affect economic performance.
- Performance against peer companies in all the measurements mentioned above whenever possible.

b) Promoting High Integrity. In promoting the high performance with high integrity corporation, nothing the board of directors does can be more important than identifying and prioritizing the specific operational objectives in promoting integrity it will use in evaluating the CEO and senior executives whom it follows closely in executive personnel reviews. Here, especially, the General Counsel should play an important partnering role with the board and management in establishing the metrics for first-, second-, and third-order integrity priorities that are reviewed by the whole board and/or by board committees.

Here are examples of how to assess integrity priorities. Have leaders, for example:

- Adopted key principles such as consistency and commitment in both words and actions; embedded integrity disciplines in business operations; had systematic processes for surfacing, analyzing, and deciding ethical issues; given employees voice to express concerns; and protected company security?

- Adopted key implementing practices to make those foundational principles a reality (risk assess/risk manage fundamental business processes; ensuring systems for preventing, detecting, and responding to integrity issues are robust across businesses and geographies)?
- Performed well when monitored by inside and outside reviewers (corporate compliance review board; internal and external auditors; other third-party compliance auditors; ombuds system reports)?
- Created an affirmative culture of integrity where employees are not just afraid of violating rules but affirmatively want to do the right thing? In addition to evaluating whether core systems and processes exist, boards of directors can assess culture through a number of techniques, including anonymous internal surveys, external reputational surveys, 360-degree evaluations of key leaders, and focus groups.
- Performed well against peers (comparisons to external peer companies in, e.g., environmental compliance or, for senior executives, comparisons to other divisions inside the company)?
- Established and met specific annual goals and objectives (hard problems handled, key people hired, identified weaknesses remedied, number of formal governmental inquiries reduced, number of law suits reduced, customer complaints about legal or ethical reduced)?

c) **Managing Systematic Risk for Economic and Noneconomic Issues.** As discussed in detail in Chapter 7, the board of directors can evaluate the CEO and top business leaders on the most important areas denominated from the set of economic and noneconomic risk issues (see pp. 230–232). Economic risks that require explicit attention include *financial* (e.g., risks associated with capital adequacy, funding capacity, liquidity, leverage, creditworthiness, off-balance sheet entities), *commercial* (e.g., risks associated with current competitors, customers, suppliers, creditors, and the health and future of company markets), *future product and technology* (e.g., risks associated with replenishing in the future the corporation's goods and service offerings so they can succeed in context of future competitors, customers, suppliers, creditors, and markets), *operational* (e.g., in addition to all the risks noted earlier, the risk that the company cannot execute internally on its own strategic plans), *entitlements* (e.g., the future, predictable, and controllable costs of health care and pension obligations), and *macroeconomic* (e.g., risks for all the other economic risks associated with issues like GDP growth rates, interests rates, currency rates, different fiscal, and monetary policies either in different regions/markets or in the global economy as a whole).

Noneconomic risks that require explicit board attention in setting operating objectives for the CEO and top leaders include *geopolitical or country* (e.g., revolution, coups, other political upheaval, corruption, and discrimination against multinational corporations); *security and safety* threats from internal failures, natural disasters, and acts of terrorism, including cyber-security; *public policy* (e.g., adverse changes in the global, regional, or national public policy architecture—law and regulation—in key areas like taxes, trade, antitrust, environmental protection, and privacy); *compliance and other legal hazard* (e.g., increased and different regulatory actions in areas that are critical to the company's economic health like taxes, trade, antitrust, and anti-corruption, as well as risk of private lawsuits); *ethical* (e.g., changing expectations and demands that can impact the company's operations, reputation, and brand); *quality and products* (e.g., risks for customers, suppliers, and the public associated with company products and services); and *other externalities* (e.g., risks created for company and for society from its business processes such as pollution, waste, and excessive use of water/energy).

In sum, explicitly establishing and prioritizing these basic, interconnected operational goals and measurements across performance, risk, and integrity dimensions are essential for the board of directors to carry out its fundamental management direction and oversight functions—to ensure accountability on the most important issues facing the corporation. It is essential to put responsibility clearly on the CEO for the third dimension of governance—for making it happen all the way down in the corporation.

5. REVISING COMPENSATION FOR CEO, SENIOR EXECUTIVES, AND OTHER KEY EMPLOYEES

The fifth essential governance task—the proper approach to compensation—flows from the first four relating to corporate mission, executive development, CEO selection, and setting priority operating objectives. The broad purpose is to incentivize short-, medium-, and long-term value creation attained with sound risk management and high integrity. The purpose of compensation is, of course, to attract and retain talent but *within* that balanced framework. Boards and management must respond to the well-founded criticism that executive compensation, by focusing too heavily on share price and total shareholder return, bears little relation to the detailed, long-term drivers that create and protect value. To address this problem, boards and management should structure compensation to discourage improper "short-termism" that takes undue risk and aims primarily at enriching executives rather than creating a strong, sustainable company. The GC has an important role in this discussion because of shareholder and public policy focus on executive compensation. Properly structuring executive compensation flows from the following principles that have clearly emerged in recent years and that, I believe, command assent from many boards of directors.

First, compensation for the CEO and top business leaders should turn on actions and results in achieving priority operational objectives across the performance, risk, and integrity dimensions. Each dimension should be a discrete element in a comprehensive pay regime that then uses them in combination to determine total awards. This fundamental principle focuses on pay for real, company-specific performance with real, company-specific risk management and real, company-specific integrity—measured, where possible, against peer companies.

Second, compensation for any one year should, in important part, be delivered in subsequent years in order to take account of the impact, over the middle and long term, of decisions made in Year 1. Of course, top business leadership will receive substantial annual cash compensation in a particular year. But a significant proportion of the compensation for that particular year should be in grants of *both* deferred cash and deferred equity. Both deferred cash and deferred equity will be paid out or held back over time as performance, risk, and integrity objectives are met, exceeded, or missed—and as the impact of decisions and actions can be more fully evaluated. Deferred cash has the advantage of avoiding stock price manipulation and providing necessary liquidity to individuals. Deferred equity has the advantage of tying employees to the long-term creation of shareholder value, but only if also tied to particular positive corporate actions and not just to appreciation of the company stock as part of general market appreciation.

Third, tying deferred compensation to a key set of prioritized operating objectives gives the board the option to adjust deferred cash compensation or deferred equity upward or downward in the out-years based on objective results. Future outperformance on the key goals could, if it passes a high, objective threshold, lead to a percentage increase in the out-year cash payment. Significant underperformance could, on the other hand, lead to a diminution in the out-year deferred cash compensation. This increase or decrease in deferred compensation must be explicit in the Year 1 grant of the award, and the "factor" that will be measured for a proportional increase or decrease must be important, objective, and clearly defined.

Fourth, in the event certain adverse events occur, either caused directly by grantees or due to failures of the corporation or their division, deferred cash or equity may either be "held back" (not allowed to vest) or "clawed back" (recovered from the individual after vesting). These "compensation recovery" policies—whether mandated by public policy or imposed by private ordering—are an important disincentive to bad behavior but are usually decided on the facts of the case. The scope and design of such policies are important but complex and are discussed in more detail later.

Fifth, boards and top management must risk assess jobs below the CEO and senior executives and apply new compensation design for individuals with the ability to commit resources with significant long-term opportunities and risks for the corporation (e.g., those who sell instruments creating long-term obligations for the company). Compensation design will turn, in important part, on specific performance, risk, and integrity parameters applicable to those individuals and will take into account the "tail risk" of trades or deals that have apparent success in Year 1 but have embedded within them poor performance prospects over time. Here, too, "compensation recovery" policies should apply for bad results stemming, in part, from bad acts. But solo contributors should also have part of their compensation built on company and division results to help create a strong and loyal culture.

Sixth, for the key staff officers who are front line partner-guardians—GC, CFO, CCO, CRO, HR head—tailored compensation packages should have special focus on rewarding independence, integrity, and risk management (see Chapter 3, pp. 75–81). Compensation should provide some reward for overall company economic performance but minimize the appearance that these key staff officers would shed their independence on risk and integrity to promote commercial success that will line their pockets—the standard concern about the integrity of inside Legal, Finance, and HR leaders who are employed by the company.

Application of these principles would sharply reduce two problematic compensation mechanisms that, in the view of many analysts and commentators, drive the short-termism and excessive risk-taking that are important causes of the corporate governance crisis in confidence: the "naked" stock option that rewards a simple increase in share price disconnected from attainment of priority operational goals and the huge annual cash bonus awarded without regard to risk consequences in the out-years. Such a compensation redesign—like establishing measurements for risk, performance, and integrity accountability—began to occur after the scandals, financial crisis, and major industrial bankruptcies in the first decade of this century. But this subject is so important that constant review—and constant GC focus—is warranted. One difficulty is devising multi-factor measurements (performance, risk, integrity) in the right proportions that reflect the mission of the company but that are not so complex as to be confusing—nor so opaque nor so simplistic as to be distortions of reality. A second difficulty is ascertaining when company leaders or individual performers have made a difference by their efforts—the kind of differentiation that should be at the core of all compensation—or whether exogenous conditions have affected results, either on the positive or the negative side. Leaders and key employees should not be penalized for events beyond their control, but neither should they be rewarded excessively for such occurrences.

6. REALIGNING AND REDEFINING THE BOARD'S OVERSIGHT FUNCTION

The critical oversight function of the board of directors should be aligned with the performance, risk, and integrity operating objectives that control whether the company will deliver compensation to the CEO and top business leadership over a multi-year period. This alignment should help directors focus, in their limited time, on what is essential. Broadly speaking, "corporate strategy" is not just "commercial strategy" but is defined by that annual effort—repeated each year—to identity and define the first-, second-, and third-order goals in all three dimensions of mission over the appropriate short-, middle-, and longer-term planning horizon (three to five years).

An independent board chair or presiding director, working with the CEO and the GC, will help ensure that these priority issues are, in fact, covered in depth during the course of the year either at the full board or in the relevant committees. In preparing for board meetings, the General Counsel can work with the CEO and senior executives to ensure that the core trade-offs and key considerations are fairly and candidly discussed with the board (whether in written materials, oral presentations, or some combination). Rather than just giving the board a proposal for approval or oversight, good corporations will explain to the board the choices among different options that underlie priority courses of action—and will try to share their thinking and reasoning in order to stimulate open and candid discussion. Hard decisions are often 51–49 percent propositions. The board should understand the key assumptions and determinants in order to understand different ways to assess the choice. Exposing, not hiding, the critical dimensions of difficult decisions or complex systems in clear, succinct terms allows the board to ask good questions—on the basis of their own relevant experience—and helps it avoid getting lost in the details. A related best practice is to have more than one board meeting on a key topic, if time allows: to introduce it, discuss it later in more depth, and then have a final decision meeting. Structuring sequential discussions of complex and important issues also allows the company to "feather in" appropriate background materials. An overview of the issues at the first meeting can lead to more in-depth presentations to respond to board questions, rather than overwhelming it with unreadable phone books at the outset. Quality, not quantity—and absolute candor on the hard issues, not vague descriptions of the decision—is the ideal. The General Counsel can help the CEO and senior executives achieve it on almost all issues. An example of such a sequential discussion was the multi-meeting consideration by the GE board of whether or not to stop taking orders in Iran early in the 21st century (see pp. 222–225).

At the end of each year, the CEO and business leaders should prepare a report for the board of director's review on how the company has performed on the various core performance, integrity, and risk measurements.

Communication and Accountability. To increase accountability, the board of directors and business leaders could consider how to make a Core Goals and Objectives Report available to the public at the end of the year that, in clear, concise form, discusses progress toward that year's strategic and operational objectives; indicates how that progress directly affects the compensation of the CEO and senior executives; and sets forth the first-, second-, and third-level priorities across performance, risk, and integrity for the following year. The company would also need to make the case that this summary is a meaningful alternative to the reductionist, often misleading, metric of short-term share price as an indicator of company value and performance. Such a systematic look-back, coupled with the agenda-setting look-forward exercise for the next year, can require significant board attention in the fourth quarter.

It is hard to imagine a better use of board/management time. Such a review may also require intense discussions between the senior director and the CEO in advance of the board meeting to improve the candor and completeness of the presentation. At present, discussions at end-of-year analysts' meetings, in Proxy Statements (e.g., on executive compensation), and in Annual Reports (CEO letter/Management Discussion and Analysis) may not present a clear, comprehensible account—in plain, understandable language—of the key company priorities: past goals, present record, and future goals across the performance, risk, and integrity dimensions. A new joint board–CEO statement or recasting of the CEO's letter to the shareholders in the Annual Report could constitute such a pointed, analytic, but "plain English" report on the essence of management's efforts. Competitive and other confidential information will be omitted, but a significant public effort to link operating objectives, compensation, and board oversight in a concise, coherent document could constitute a vast improvement over much of current over-lawyered, poorly written, and hard-to-understand "corporate-speak."

This Core Goals and Objectives Report should stand alone as a straightforward annual statement of corporate success and failure in achieving top priorities. But, it should be consistent with—and integrated in—two broader reports: the standard Annual Report and the now almost standard Citizenship Report (discussed in Chapter 9, pp. 354–357).

*****

The board of directors and business leaders must candidly confront difficult, real-world issues that can undermine a corporation's will and ability to discharge the six seamless and essential tasks of corporate governance in a meaningful way. These include competitors in the labor market for top executive and other business talent that can defeat structured compensation schemes by throwing money at valued individuals; the limitations of many current compensation consultants who may not understand the underlying business reality of specific companies well enough to help design the operational performance, risk, and integrity objectives upon which compensation should rest; and the short-termism of many institutional investors who do not act as owners of individual companies or care about company fundamentals but, instead, respond to fund manager incentives to beat aggregate benchmarks (like the S&P 500).

But strong, energized boards and business leadership dedicated to discharge, in good faith, the six essential tasks—and to communicate them effectively—can address the governance problems of the era and provide a clear, credible, and powerful private-sector response to the corporate governance crisis in confidence. Put more harshly, the unvarnished reality is that business organizations must be designed by boards and management to check greed, stupidity, and corruption and to channel capitalism's "animal spirits" into sustained, durable creation of real economic value within the framework of financial and risk disciplines and of law, ethics, and values. Implementation of this "six task" framework can create a clear template for accountability and, in so doing, can bind business leaders, board members, long-term shareholders, and other stakeholders on a fundamental set of issues and thus create a reasonable opportunity of withstanding the self-serving market churn caused by many (though not all) short-term or super-short-term shareholders.

D. SPECIAL PROBLEM: EXECUTIVE COMPENSATION

1. HOW MUCH?

The six tasks provide a framework for a much more sophisticated and appropriate approach to "pay for performance with integrity." But they do not directly address a companion issue—"how much" compensation the CEO and senior executives should receive. In the past 25 years, the pay of the CEO has grown at a rate of increase more than ten times the rate of increase of average worker pay. CEOs' compensation is many multiples of the companies' average pay today, 300 times as much in some cases. That multiple is many times larger than it was in the past. (A new SEC rule requires companies to disclose the ratio of CEO pay to median compensation of their employees.) *And* CEO compensation has grown, on average, at a much faster rate than increases in company profits or share price. The gap has also widened between CEO pay and pay for other highly compensated executives listed in the Proxy Statement—with ratios of 4:1 or 5:1 now common. And, of course, with the famous "top 1 percent" commanding more than 25 percent of national income, the broader issue of "inequality" is now—and is likely to remain—a significant issue in national (global) political discourse and will continue to contribute to the low trust accorded corporations in public opinion surveys. The head of the UK's Institute of Directors has said: "What has done the most damage to the reputation of business and the free market in recent years . . . It has been the greed of those who demand and secure rewards for failure in far too many of our corporations." His views prompted a *Financial Times* columnist to conclude: "Chief executive pay is a scandal. It is too high, too complicated and has badly damaged the image of business. Even fervent defenders of free markets think top pay is out of control."[9] This fundamental issue of governance is one that deserves the serious attention of the General Counsel as part of the board–business leader team.

Although the issue of "how much" is, of course, driven in part by the market for executive talent, boards can consider dealing not just with timing (deferral), but also amount in order to address serious concerns. There are *business arguments* for addressing the "pay gap" and limiting absolute amounts: Such action would enhance employee engagement and productivity, would reduce reputational harm to particular firms, and would arrest plummeting general trust in business. There are *economic arguments* for limiting pay: Action would promote economic growth (society cannot grow when the rich receive disproportionate amount of income and when the middle class stagnates), would reduce economic instability (in pursuit of personal wealth, business executives take excessive risk), would address sectoral imbalances (due to high pay, financial sector is drawing talent disproportionately and is not financing the real economy), and would improve social mobility (middle class with lack of real income growth cannot provide opportunities for children). Finally, there are *social/political arguments* limiting pay: Such action would reduce societal instability (to the extent wealth disparities reflect lack of opportunity, this can lead to social unrest) and would redress, in part, the undue political influence of the wealthy (who, it is argued, have outsized access and voice in shaping public policy). The General Counsel can work with the board and management to assess the degree to which these and other company and societal concerns about executive pay are supported by evidence and how important these concerns are to the corporation when weighed against the need to attract and retain executive talent. The possible importance of this issue is reflected in the recent, conscious moderation of the size of compensation packages (still huge amounts) given to top Wall Street CEOs.[10]

The General Counsel can also help the board and management to go beyond current process stratagems for addressing the "how much" issue, such as detailed Proxy Statement disclosure on top executives' compensation package and advisory "say on pay" votes by shareholders. Consistent with writing a "plain English" account of mission, objectives, pay criteria, and oversight, the General Counsel could work with the board to transform the Compensation Committee Report in Proxy Statement from anodyne, predictable rhetoric to a discussion not just of the "how" and "why" of CEO compensation but also "how much" and "why that much." This could involve explaining that the amount depends greatly on meeting performance, risk, and integrity goals over time. Rather than just concluding that the pay package has a certain size "to be competitive," as the Proxy Statement bromide goes, the compensation report could show that, in fact, an important dimension of deferred pay is actually to be "competitive" over time on a series of important metrics compared with other companies—not just stock price or total shareholder return. The task of more completely justifying not just "what" and "why" but "how much" has always been necessary, not naïve. But it certainly is much more important now due to mandated "say on pay" votes.

2. COMPENSATION RECOVERY POLICY

In addition to helping design compensation structures that reward important achievement of operational objectives on performance, risk, and integrity, the General Counsel has a pivotal role in designing the corporation's "compensation recovery policy" that allows the company to hold the CEO and key corporate officers financially accountable for wrong-doing or excessive risk-taking. Such a policy addresses when, why, and how the corporation should hold back non-vested benefits or claw back vested benefits owned by the executive. Properly designed, and in conjunction with other forms of employee/officer discipline (see pp. 108–115), these compensation recovery policies—adopted in some form by more than 250 of the *Fortune* 500 companies— provide a needed deterrent to improper individual behavior. Properly implemented, these policies answer, in part, the criticism that too often individual corporate wrong-doers do not pay a price for the injury they have imposed on their companies. These policies can be far broader and far more flexible than the provision of Dodd-Frank, which mandates claw-backs of incentive-based compensation for a specified group of officers in *any publicly listed* company if it has material financial restatements.[11]

A properly designed compensation recovery policy could incorporate the following ideas. Covered individuals should not just include the current and past executive officers (defined by the SEC as certain named officers and others with "policy-making" authority), but also other important, highly compensated employees who have the capacity to injure the corporation with regard to performance, risk, or integrity. The claw-backs/hold-backs should cover both deferred cash and deferred equity as well as long-term incentive and compensation deferral programs. There should be a section describing the claw-back and hold-back powers of the company in contracts covering employees' hiring and/or the grants of deferred compensation. There should also be a clause stipulating that any disputes will be resolved in arbitration, which is far preferable for these sensitive matters. Directors and officers insurance should be carefully written to exclude coverage for acts the company brings against officers and employees under this compensation recovery policy. The board of directors makes compensation recovery decisions regarding the CEO and senior executives—usually with assistance of special outside counsel—because involvement of the General Counsel would give the appearance of a conflict of interest. Otherwise, the senior management can carry out the compensation recovery process, with board review.

The act of malfeasance that can lead to a hold-back or claw-back should be far broader than a material misstatement of financials—and should encompass acts that lead to serious financial or reputational injury to the corporation. Actual intent or gross negligence (recklessness) should be necessary to trigger compensation recovery. But, an individual's negligence could give rise to sanctions in certain circumstances. For example, senior business leaders should be subject to compensation recovery if they have negligently failed to create a culture of integrity in their units that led to widespread and long-standing compliance violations. Similarly, the policy can address windfalls obtained by senior executives through the malfeasance of others. Claw-backs are especially relevant when a senior official is terminated for acts in the past but holds substantial vested benefits received when those past acts occurred. The inevitable, real-world variation in possible circumstances for compensation recovery means that the board and management, working with the General Counsel, should have discretion to find the facts and make appropriate individual hold-back or claw-back determinations. This discretion should be applied to determining the nature of the harm, the level of intent, and the appropriate amount of damages—how much unvested variable cash or equity or other long-term awards should be withheld.

Such broad, flexible, circumstance-based compensation recovery policies do, however, require accommodation with Dodd-Frank's mandatory claw-back requirement. That mandate is narrower than the approach just described (it applies only to financial restatements due to "material noncompliance"), removes discretion from the board (recovery must be sought), does not require fault of individuals from whom monies are clawed back (both present and past employees), specifies and limits those individuals ("executive officers"), specifies the amount of recovery (the percentage of incentive compensation, including equity awards, in excess of what would have been paid without the restated results), and has a narrower purpose (prevents windfalls for the many who had no role in the material misstatement). But, because the trigger to Dodd-Frank Section 954 is a financial restatement due to material noncompliance with reporting requirements, this is just one type of malfeasance within the broad framework suggested earlier. In any voluntary corporate hold-back/claw-back policy, such restatements will have to be treated separately due to regulatory requirements. But that does not prevent the corporation from adopting the broader approach outlined here. Such a flexible, fact-based approach is an appropriate complement to the Procrustean legislative mandate of Dodd-Frank, if (a big if) companies take design and implementation of their own policies seriously as an important method of holding business leaders and employees accountable for balanced behavior but also not penalizing appropriate, disciplined risk-taking, which is the life-blood of the corporation. The important role of the General Counsel in design and implementation of these policies is self-evident.

3. COMPENSATION RECOVERY AND JPMORGAN CHASE

A good example of a broad compensation recovery policy, and its application, is found in JPMorgan Chase's (JPM) handling of the $6 billion derivative trading losses in 2012 by the London "Whale."[12] The JPM policy in effect at the time stated in part:

> Equity awards ... are subject to the Firm's *right to cancel an unvested or unexercised award, and to require repayment of the value of certain shares distributed under awards already vested* if:
> —the employee engages in conduct that *causes material financial or reputational harm to the Firm or its business activities,*
> —the Firm determines that the award was based *on materially inaccurate performance metrics, whether or not the employee was responsible for the inaccuracy,*
> —the award was based on a *material misrepresentation* by the employee,
> —and for members of the Operating Committee [an elite subset of firm's executive committee] and Tier 1 employees [senior employees with significant responsibility], such employees *improperly or with gross negligence fail to identify, raise, or assess, in a timely manner and as reasonably expected, risks and/ or concerns with respect to risks material to the Firm or its business activities.* [Emphasis added.]

Under this policy, and as a result of its internal investigations, JPM has stated that for the London Whale matter it clawed back or canceled $100 million of compensation under these policies. This included two years of "total annual compensation" from the London traders involved: Bruno Iksil (the "London Whale"); another trader, Javier Martin-Artajo; and their boss, Achilles Macris. All three left the firm with no severance pay. In addition, the global supervisor of the London office and the former head of the firm's Chief Investment Office (CIO), Ina Drew, gave up two prior years of salary, the "equivalent to the maximum clawback amount," according to JPM CEO Jamie Dimon. Media reports put the amount of Drew's loss at $15.5 million. Due to long service with JPM, Drew was allowed to retire and retain other vested benefits. The JPM board also cut CEO Dimon's compensation in half—from $23 million in 2011 to $11.5 million in 2012—as a result of "Whale-related" failures. Drew's unit reported directly to Dimon, and its purpose, obviously not followed in this instance, was to invest a pool of funds conservatively in order to have financial resources to offset losses elsewhere.

After initially downplaying the problem, Dimon acknowledged that the trading strategy was "flawed, complex, poorly reviewed, poorly executed and poorly monitored . . . violated our own principles . . . It puts egg on our face, and we deserve any criticism we get." Various company, board, and congressional reviews found fault in London, in the Chief Investment Office, and in the company-wide finance and risk functions: doubling down on bad trades, hiding poor results, not giving enough scrutiny to the level of risk, ineffective risk management, insufficiently detailed risk limits, and use of the wrong risk models for the type of investment. Given this litany of problems, "compensation recovery" in this matter was an appropriate remedial step (one of many taken by the bank under board and regulator pressure) and is a good case study for GCs.

But, if JPM deserves two cheers for its claw-back and other compensation actions, it doesn't deserve three. And herein lies a less favorable lesson. The precise amounts of money clawed back from the London traders were not disclosed—nor the type of compensation affected (salary, bonus, equity). The company did not indicate which compensation recovery policies were the basis for that recovery—nor the policy that pressured Drew to voluntarily give back compensation. Nor did it indicate who made the decisions (other than the board's decision about Dimon) and according to what process (what was the role of GC in causing the problem or in finding the facts that led to compensation recovery?). Also on the debit side was the decision to double

Dimon's compensation in 2013, after cutting it 50 percent in 2012, without adequate explanation, even though JPM's cultural failings, which extended far beyond the "Whale" and for which Dimon was ultimately responsible, had led to settlements in the multiple billions and to continuing regulatory problems (see pp. 102–106). Although the compensation recovery aspect of the "Whale" matter is a powerful teaching moment for business, boards, CEOs, and GCs will have to fill in the answers in future cases to these unanswered questions in the "Whale" matter and to the broader rationales omitted by JPM in dealing with compensation recovery decisions amid major cultural breakdowns.

E. BOARD INDEPENDENCE AND LEADERSHIP

Meeting the governance challenges described in this chapter requires independence and leadership of the board of directors. It is hard to carry out the six tasks well. It is hard to grapple with the broad issues of "how much" and "compensation recovery" in executive compensation. The traditional critique of the board of directors has been that they are chosen by the CEO, are deferential to him, and enjoy being in the directors' "club" rather than working hard to find that constructive, yet critical, "right-sized" role. But, in the wake of this century's dramatic corporate governance failures, boards of directors in major corporations are, in general, surely aware of these criticisms. Outstanding directors know that certain key actions are necessary to secure the board independence and board leadership upon which the proper balance between board and management depends and that is necessary for corporate health and accountability. The General Counsel has an important role in assisting both board and management in securing this balance through the following actions.

The board needs to exercise control over the selection of new directors to ensure that at least a majority of the board is independent as defined both in law and in the corporation's governance principles. (For example, a director is not "independent" if the person works for the company or has a family member who is senior executive in the company.) As important, there needs to be a robust process in the nominating committee—and then at the board as a whole—that truly defines and implements the kind of diversity in skills, industries, geographies, and personal characteristics the board should exhibit. There needs to be a search that listens to CEO ideas, but is hardly limited to them, that uses head-hunters but reaches out to other sources, especially the board's broad network, to generate a robust list of candidates. Board selection decisions must proceed from a clear case on the merits of potential substantive contribution to the board. But, as with all personnel decisions, there needs, of course, to be an assessment that the candidate's personality will "work" both with the board and with the CEO, that there will be mutual respect and regard all around. This is not "clubby-ness" but the condition for a constructive and critical relationship. Moreover, in major companies, I believe that the governance principles or commentary should restrain "over-boarding"—that directors should only be able to serve on one or two other for-profit boards of directors.

The functions of the lead director should be well understood both by directors and by management. One of the good developments in governance has been an increased focus on the need to have a *primus inter pares* director on the board—a first among equals who can help provide leadership, independent of the CEO, to a group of powerful individuals. But one of the least productive corporate governance issues—on which there has been endless and needless debate—is whether to split the roles of board chair and CEO. Function matters here, form doesn't, as in so many other organizational issues relating to corporations. In my view, this debate about titles has wasted much time and effort because it matters little whether the senior director is "chairman of the board" or "lead director" or "presiding director." Working closely with the board and the CEO, the GC can help define in governance principles or commentary the key substantive elements of the actual role of the lead director, whatever the title. These include chairing meetings of directors alone, without the CEO, before or after regular board meetings; following up with the CEO on the issues raised in those meetings; leading the annual prioritization and agenda-setting exercise with management; setting agendas for particular board meetings in the subsequent year in light of that process;

ensuring board materials fairly and clearly set forth basic issues for decision making or for information; ensuring that discussions at board meetings address the key issues and trade-offs in a decision; leading a board self-evaluation process; assessing the CEO and senior executives against operating objectives in setting and awarding compensation; evaluating overall leadership of CEO and top executives; and, ultimately, making sure that the "six tasks" are diligently and energetically discharged.

This is a critical *internal* position, not primarily an *external* one. To avoid confusion, the CEO should generally be the company's public spokesperson And, if the top director needs to speak or meet with corporate constituents or to the media, the role of the lead director, not the title, provides functional credibility. Such an external director role to provide additional company perspective may be increasing as activist investors are ever-more vocal and persistent in their governance and strategy critiques of CEOs. I personally favor the CEO as board "chair" and senior director as "lead" director because I think the CEO should be both the internal and external leader/spokesperson for the company and because a presiding director of stature can ensure that all the key board functions are discharged But either formulation can work as long as there is clarity on the elements of board leadership for the lead director.

Director compensation should have a significant element of deferral to encourage a long-term perspective (although board compensation for many directors, while not trivial, is also often not a big part of their income/net worth). Compensation should also be simple and transparent. One typical example is GE's post-Enron governance revisions, which still apply today. Forty percent of director compensation is delivered in cash during the year. But 60 percent of comp is in "deferred stock units" (DSUs), which are granted each year at the then-current stock price and which also accumulate dividend equivalent payments (invested in more DSUs). The cumulative value of all these deferred stock units—determined by stock price at retirement—is paid out to directors one year *after they leave the board.* There are no meeting fees. And directors have the option of taking some or all of their cash compensation in deferred stock units.

F. SHAREHOLDERS: STEWARDS AND ACTIVISTS

1. PROBLEM OR SOLUTION?

For boards and CEOs trying to develop a short-, medium-, and long-term strategy on the interconnected issues of performance, risk, and integrity, "shareholders" pose a fundamental issue: Are they part of the problem or part of the solution?[13] Can shareholders be long-term "stewards" who support a well-grounded strategy properly developed? Or are shareholders short-term "activists" who care only about immediate financial return for themselves and not about the long-term health of the investee company? This is a fundamental issue for General Counsels as well because part of their governance responsibility is to work with boards and management *on the two key issues relating to shareholders: the appropriate governance provisions relating to shareholder powers and the appropriate substantive corporate strategy to advance shareholder interests.*

There is, of course, no simple answer to the question of whether shareholders are part of the "problem" or "solution" because of the oft-repeated fallacy that there is such an entity as "a shareholder." Over the last 25 years, institutional investors have owned an increasing share of public equity markets—more than 70 percent of the largest 1,000 companies in the United States today, for example. But, in addition to a wide variety of individual shareowners, these institutional investors come in all shapes and sizes, with a mind-numbing and often conflicting array of goals, strategies, and governance structures. They are as diverse as hedge funds, pension funds, mutual funds, insurance companies, and endowments of nonprofits such as universities and foundations. Moreover, there are hundreds of different entities, with different purposes and strategies, within each of those broad categories.

Historically, shareholders had a limited set of vehicles for communicating concerns: withholding votes for directors, offering proposals for shareholder votes, voting on proposals ultimately included in the proxy statement, selling their shares, or waging a proxy contest for control of the board. To counter the failings of corporate governance, Congress, the SEC, and shareholder advocates in recent years have pushed for a stronger shareholder role. These initiatives include elimination of staggered or classified boards, majority votes in uncontested director elections, disallowance of broker votes in uncontested elections, shareholder advisory votes on compensation ("say on pay"), and shareholders' ability to nominate directors ("proxy access") or augmented shareholder authority to call special meetings. In addition, the historic debate about "maximizing shareholder value" in the near term as opposed to optimizing stakeholder interests over the longer term—and a variety of views along that spectrum—continues, with various members of the "shareholder" menagerie taking various positions.

From the point of view of the board and management (and the General Counsel), there are some critical issues about this recent move toward greater shareholder involvement. These issues should also be of concern to public policy makers and governance gurus because research and analysis of many institutional investors has lagged far behind the research on investee public companies. Such research is now gaining momentum.[14] Let me note these issues briefly as backdrop to thoughts on how boards and management should orient their efforts toward "shareholders."

First, do fund managers for institutional investors advance their own interests, not the interests of the beneficial owners or of investee companies? Such problems for individuals who have capital in institutional investors may occur whether the individuals are pension fund beneficiaries, mutual fund investors, insurance beneficiaries, or hedge fund investors. The question is the classic "principal/agent" problem: Do those who manage the trillions of dollars of other people's money advance the objectives of the ultimate beneficiaries—who may be dispersed and disengaged—or are they intent on achieving their own self-regarding objectives? And, with institutional investors often having portfolios with a large number of diversified stocks, do the managers of those institutions have any detailed knowledge or interest in the mission of the investee companies beyond fluctuating share price and their long, short, or short-long positions?

Second, is the first problem compounded because these fund managers in institutional investors contribute significantly to "undesirable short-termism"? A number of commentators have argued fund-manager incentives are geared to short-term strategies (e.g., beat composite indices), short-term compensation (based on performance during quarter or year), and other competitive factors (i.e., continually outperform peer investors, not just indices). The argument is that such investor short-termism adversely affects the attempt of investee companies to achieve balanced long-term investment, risk management, and integrity. But, of course, there are often problems in investee companies that require immediate action and that may, properly, lead to short-term investment strategies.

Third, can institutional investors become more effective "stewards" of publicly held investee corporations, and how does that "stewardship" role differ from the role of boards of directors to oversee the direction of companies? Although many fund managers, overseeing large portfolios, have no time or interest in really understanding the details of particular investee corporations, other active fund managers do seek such detailed information. However, if corporate directors face challenges in truly trying to understand the operations of a complex corporation, how can a numerous and widely diverse set of institutional investors have access to the board and managers without taking up huge amounts of time CEOs and senior executives should devote to running the company? And how can the select investors have such access without violating securities law strictures under Regulation FD (Fair Disclosure), which requires making material information available simultaneously to all investors in publicly held companies? (An exemption to Reg FD allows corporations to give nonpublic information to institutional investors under an agreement to keep it confidential and not to trade unless and until the information is public.)

How then should corporations, and General Counsels, navigate through these potential problems of institutional investor self-interest, shareholder short-termism, and problems of information sharing, even with shareholders who have a longer-term, stewardship orientation?

2. SHAREHOLDERS AS STEWARDS

Recognizing the problems of narrow investor focus on "short-termism" and "maximizing shareholder value," some major institutional investors are trying to define a "stewardship role" that seeks to support longer-term corporate strategies that take into account performance, risk, and integrity. Whether pension funds or endowments or insurance companies or mutual funds, such investors seek to have a constructive dialogue with investee companies in order to justify a longer-term hold of the stock. As Roger Ferguson, President and CEO of TIAA-CREF and a respected thought leader in the institutional investor community, has said: "Better to engage management on governance and strategy issues before problems arise and shareholder value plummets."[15]

In response to these shareholder concerns, engagement with these major holders on business strategy, to the extent consistent with Reg FD, is not only desirable but a long-standing practice. But these discussions must weave together the threads of performance, risk, and integrity. They should focus not just on shareholders, but on the importance of sound investments and on broad benefits to other stakeholders—employees, customers, supply chain—as essential to the long-term financial well-being of the firm. The Apple example discussed earlier speaks volumes. If the corporation is articulate and as explicit as possible about the six tasks, either in written documents or personal engagement or both, then the institutional investors know what they are buying. And companies can articulate the kind of shareholder they hope to attract. This is a basic benefit of the sharply focused annual report on Core Goals and Objectives I recommend earlier. Having constructive engagement with the *major institutional holders* on strategy is more important than ever, given the volatility and short-termism of other parts of the market. For example, corporations need to make the case—in this era of mandated "say on pay" votes—for the structure and amount of executive compensation that, in my view, should flow from the seamless "six tasks" orientation. Not too long ago, a CEO of a major corporation told me: "The stock market is a storm tossed sea. I can't figure it out. All I know is that I have to develop the right strategy for the company. I have to persuade the directors it is right. But I also have to persuade my major institutional, long-term investors. They are my rock in a storm."

From the perspective of the corporation's board and management, engagement on questions of corporate governance, not just business strategy, is not just desirable but, increasingly, feasible in this day and age. Major institutional investors—for example, BlackRock and Vanguard—have encouraged investee corporations to discuss governance issues directly. Many major asset managers have decreased their reliance on proxy advisory firms—like Institutional Shareholder Services and Glass Lewis—which, to the long-standing consternation of most corporations, take formulaic, box-ticking positions on many governance issues, often elevating form over substance in the view of critics. Short of the CEO, the GC, CFO, and head of Investor Relations should engage with these major shareholders to separate the governance wheat from the chaff. The CEO, GC, and CFO—and the board—need to be flexible and responsive on formal governance measures that give shareholders an opportunity to have their views heard through advisory votes or to seek ballot access for long-term holders with a reasonable percentage of a company's stock (proxy access). Sensible measures allow shareholders to express themselves without threatening management prerogatives, much less portending the chimera of "shareholder democracy" that would convert vital, substantive company decisions made by senior executives and boards into binding plebiscites and bruising political fights among shareholders with diverse, often conflicting objectives.

3. ACTIVIST SHAREHOLDERS[16]

The dual perspectives of governance issues and business issues are also useful lenses for viewing "activist" shareholders. As to governance, many different types of shareholders may have strong views. Typical activists on governance issues are: union-backed or educator-based pension funds, "socially responsible investment" funds, certain hedge funds, and individual investors with strong personal beliefs. The GC and her chief corporate/securities lawyer will typically meet with these activists and should be open to discussions on the merits. GE always tried to have good relations with the union funds, for example, even though we didn't necessarily agree. When they were pressing a change to a majority vote in board elections, it seemed reasonable, and the board and management approved the change. On the other hand, with the help of major institutional holders, the company defeated what I viewed as a formalistic shareholder proposal, sponsored by unions, to take the Chairman of the Board title from the CEO and confer it on the lead director whose significant duties the company had already explained publicly in its corporate governance principles and commentary.

With respect to strategy, "activist" shareholders are generally hedge funds who seek immediate economic gains for shareholders through share buy-backs or special dividends or divestitures or serious cost cutting (e.g., in employees or in R&D spending). Their short-term goals are often reductionist: increase margins and earnings per share and, hence, stock price (assuming the stability or expansion of the price-to-earnings [P/E] multiple). These efforts can elevate the short-term interests of certain shareholders over the broader, longer-term efforts of the corporation to create value by optimizing stakeholder interests across the performance, risk, and integrity dimensions. It may, thus, be appropriate for the board, management, and longer-term share-holders—with the in-depth involvement of the GC—to oppose such measures. Yet, it is also possible that the "activists" have focused on a genuine inefficiency or other valid issue in the management of the corporation. And, in such cases, major institutional investors may side with the activists. In trying to assess both the merits of the charge on business strategy and the appropriate response, the GC may find herself in that difficult position between the board, which might be inclined to negotiate with the activists, and management, which may feel defensive about the activist claim.

9

CITIZENSHIP AND THE PRIMACY OF PUBLIC POLICY

A corporation's success and durability is ultimately built on trust—of shareholders, creditors, partners, employees, customers, suppliers, communities, government, media, societal "influencers," and the general public. Durable trust is ultimately built on corporate citizenship: on how the corporation acts toward, and has impact on, society, on how it addresses "business in society" issues. As discussed, these "business in society" issues involve four fundamental corporate responsibilities: responsibilities to the corporation and its employees; responsibilities to all other stakeholders; responsibilities to the rule of law; and responsibilities to help secure public goods, which are vital to societal well-being but which cannot be realized through the market. As with governance, these four citizenship duties are carried out, across three essential, interconnected elements: high performance, high integrity, and sound risk management. In other words, discharging these four duties of citizenship turns on balancing the essential business risk-taking of entrepreneurship, innovation, and creativity with the disciplines of law, finance, ethics, and risk management. With limited corporate

317

resources, discharging these duties also invariably involves trade-offs in optimizing the near-, medium-, and longer-term legitimate interests of diverse stakeholders—all of whom are important to the success of the company.

Whether shaped by rules mandated by government or by decisions taken voluntarily by the corporation, the core subjects of prior chapters—culture, compliance, ethics, risk and crisis management, and governance—are foundational elements of the four citizenship duties to company, stakeholders, law, and society. Each of these subjects requires sound judgment and a strong sense of what is "right" assessed through the performance, integrity, and risk lenses. Each of these subjects involves the board of directors, the CEO, and senior executives. And each of these subjects requires the General Counsel, as a senior executive, to exhibit the technical expertise, wise counseling, and accountable leadership of the lawyer-statesman and partner-guardian to help his company fulfill those responsibilities. The GC's active role in helping a corporation define citizenship for itself is at the core of the inside counsel revolution.

The word *citizenship*, I believe, is a better way to convey the four broad "business in society" responsibilities of a corporation, especially a major global corporation, than the phrase *corporate social responsibility* (CSR), which has often been narrowly defined as voluntary ethical actions by corporations acting *alone* on *social* issues. As I define it, corporate citizenship is broader. It focuses on high performance, not just high integrity. The societal impact of a corporation's business processes and its good and services is obviously enormous. Corporate citizenship focuses on compliance with law, not just on ethics. In this day and age, adherence to the legal and financial rules in jurisdictions across the world is a challenging and compelling need of a corporate citizen. Corporate citizenship also focuses on corporate values, not just ethics. A corporation cannot have an ethical precept for every situation, and thus core corporate values are essential to guide appropriate behavior. Corporate citizenship focuses on resolving problems of "protecting public goods" through collective action—either in voluntary associations or through public policy—not just on the voluntary ethical acts of a single company. The political processes corporations follow and the substantive positions that they take in public policy debates is of paramount importance in a democratic society—and in societies with a democratic deficit.

Corporate citizenship, ultimately, focuses on creating culture, not just on a host of discrete elements, and requires the knitting together of the elements I have identified in a conscious, coherent, and comprehensive effort. That is how to secure lasting trust. Without getting into an exegesis or history of the words, I thus believe "citizenship," because of its comprehensive, inclusive nature, is preferable to other concepts like "corporate social responsibility" or "sustainability" that, depending on the usage and context, may focus on a single corporation's voluntary ethical acts or sound environmental practices (important though those subjects are) and may not clearly address other key elements of citizenship: economic performance, compliance, values, public policy, or culture.

In limning the basics of citizenship for the General Counsel, this chapter will not repeat, but incorporates by reference, the prior discussion. For example, adopting ethical standards beyond what the formal rules require, discussed in Chapter 6, is an absolutely essential element of citizenship, but one I will not reprise here. Instead, I will explore the essence of four other core citizenship issues: philanthropy, responsible commercial activities, a sound approach to public policy, and an obligation to adopt an integrated approach in reporting on all citizenship activities.

A. PHILANTHROPY

Philanthropy is a subset of the "ethical" actions corporations take beyond what the formal rules require. Charitable contributions usually do not include a corporation's *own direct actions* on economic performance, integrity, or risk. Instead, philanthropy involves providing funds or in-kind contributions or voluntary efforts of employees/retirees to third parties in order to benefit the society in which the corporation operates and thus indirectly to benefit the corporation. These donations to third parties can address any of the four duties: matching charitable gifts by employees, giving equipment to current or potential customers in need (computers to students; health care equipment to the ill in developing nations), designing and implementing rule of law initiatives, and providing public goods to society (cleaning up a local lake; aiding elementary and secondary schools; scholarships in science and engineering). Traditionally, corporations have supported a wide variety of charities in their local communities—for example, gifts to the symphony, to the local hospital, to a child welfare organization, and to beautification of parks. The purpose is to strengthen local nonprofit institutions, be a good citizen of the community, and enhance corporate reputation. Courts have viewed these activities as well within the legitimate purposes that advance the best interests of a corporation and, if arrived at properly, well within the business judgment rule.[1] All good.

But, in my judgment, corporations also need to take a significant proportion of their available philanthropic funds (40 to 50 percent?) and focus on a few innovative and important activities. These structured charitable programs can define objectives; seek systemic impact; measure outcomes; and, if the program works, create models others can replicate to make a dent on important societal problems. This is consistent with other efforts at programmatic voluntarism carried out by foundations or nongovernmental organizations: provide systematic assistance but also explore innovative programs to effect needed change other public or private institutions can adopt. These systemic charitable efforts will generally have some relationship to the corporation's lines of business and are easily justified as in the corporation's broad interests.[2] General Counsels should sit on the board of their corporate foundation. They may even chair it. They have an important lawyer-statesman role in helping to define these innovative broad-impact and high-priority philanthropic efforts.

Concentrating some significant proportion of charitable giving on high-impact projects is not new, but it is an important task for General Counsel as trustees of corporate foundations. Examples abound where corporations spend tens of millions of dollars on such focused, impactful programs. Concerned about the devastation and suffering from hurricanes and tornadoes and floods, Home Depot has a special program for providing disaster relief to homeowners after nature has wreaked havoc on communities. Concerned about the poverty that drives underage children into improper child labor, IKEA worked with UNESCO in India to develop social welfare programs that provide education to children, health care to both mothers and children, and microfinance to women to grow the local economy. Concerned about community development, PNC, a regional bank, focused its charitable activities on early childhood education and school readiness activities. Concerned about hunger in America, Wal-Mart donated food to local food banks and hunger relief organizations, provided meals for poor children, and taught cooking and shopping skills so that individuals could make meager food budgets go further. Concerned about lack of skills to fill open jobs, JPMorgan Chase started a five-year initiative ("New Skills at Work") to connect employer needs with innovative education and training in concrete community settings and to then research best practices for broader replication. Concerned about lack of management skills in charities, McKinsey provided free consulting services to social, educational, and artistic nonprofits. Concerned about the importance of math and science education, GE—for more than 30 years—spent substantial funds and substantial volunteer employee/retiree mentoring effort to improve the graduation rates and science and math education in inner-city high schools.[3]

General Counsels also have a role in assessing the overall corporate philanthropic effort, both absolutely and compared to peers. Third-party evaluations of individual company programs help make the case that an innovative approach can be—and should be—replicated by others. A periodic assessment of the total philanthropic activity is also necessary. For example, the median total corporate philanthropy (cash, in-kind, pro bono hours) as a percentage of pre-tax profits for all companies in a survey was a shade more than 1 percent in 2013. But this percentage has been steadily declining over the past 30 years, from a high of 2.35 percent in 1986.[4] A way to start such an assessment is a longitudinal accounting of overall corporate expenditures on ethical standards beyond what the law requires (e.g., ethical sourcing by third-party suppliers) and on efforts to meet the four ethical responsibilities as a percentage of total corporate cost. The cost trends of the corporation's philanthropic effort can then be viewed within that larger citizenship frame to provide a more comprehensive accounting.

B. BUSINESS ACTIVITIES

Strong, sustained economic performance provides significant benefits to a broad array of corporate constituents, and performance failures can devastate those interests. Too often, advocates of corporate citizenship ignore or downplay the "high performance" dimension of that concept. They may not give appropriate weight to the benefits of a corporation's goods and services to customers and of payments to employees, retirees, creditors, suppliers, and communities in which the corporation is located. Too often, business leaders pitch their business case to investors and fail to make a compelling business case to other stakeholders and to the public—they just hype it in short-form sales pitches or in TV ads with *Mad Men* slogans and arresting images. Indeed, there is a surfeit of corporate PR in the form of "institutional advertising" or, on the front-of-mind subject of sustainability, a surfeit of "green-washing," where claims of environmental citizenship are hyped but not supported. But, the business activities of the corporation are, after all, the core of its existence. There are many ways to make the case for the beneficial societal impact of these activities to the general public. Doing this in meaningful ways, devoid of deadening corporate-speak or glossy TV ads, is an enormous challenge for CEOs and senior executives, including, of course, the General Counsel. Being credible and being heard is a daunting task. Let me briefly summarize *five different themes* that corporations, and General Counsels, can use to express the positive effects of their core business activities—but only when supported by hard facts.

1. BENEFITS OF CORE ECONOMIC ACTIVITY

There are two dimensions to the economic impact of current core business activities. First, what are the beneficial societal effects of the company's goods and services? What is the concrete benefit of gas turbines, iPhones, a cancer drug, low-cost retailing, a commercial airliner, or small business lending? For example, GE has more than 18,000 aircraft engines with superior performance records on 8,000 commercial airliners flying nearly a billion people around the world each year. It has an installed base of more than 10,000 turbines, providing one-third of the world's electricity. More than 40,000 of its CT scan and MRI machines provided health care scans for more than 100 million people every year. Second, what are the beneficial effects of a corporation's fundamental economic activities on other stakeholders? How many "family" members are supported by direct company employment (often three or four dependents for each employee)? What kind of economic support through local taxes and direct expenditures does the corporation provide in discrete communities (as opposed to some vague and unintelligible global aggregate)? What are the multiplier effects of the tens of billions of dollars a year spent on suppliers of materials, components, subassemblies, ingredients, and services? What kind of benefits does the company provide to retirees who, either individually or through institutional investors, hold company stock that appreciates or provides a growing dividend or both? How does the company's business activity help grow the economies of emerging markets, which can then import other company goods and services? There should be innumerable ways to tell the story about core economic activity with honesty and authenticity for a good company. But, too few do it—or do it as a PR exercise lacking in credibility.

2. MEETING SOCIETY'S FUTURE NEEDS

A second theme is that business activities meet society's emerging needs, *with regular profit margins*, through new technologies, new products, new markets, or new responses to regulation. An emerging theme in current business writing is about the potential for corporations or other commercial entities to address profound societal problems through their core provision of goods and services. Such problems include an aging population; lack of low-cost/high-quality health care; the looming impact of climate change; the multiple problems of lower-income communities, both at home and abroad; the search for less expensive, more efficient energy sources; or the general demand for infrastructure improvements in developing nations.[5] But this is really old news (very old news—the steam engine? the mechanical reaper? the sewing machine? the light bulb? the automobile? the radio?) because good companies are always trying to find the future with products that address societal problems. One way to express this effort is through the corporation's research and development expenditures, both basic and applied. Explaining the profound importance of these outlays both in general terms and in terms of specific technology issues being explored is a critical counterweight to pressures from short-term investors to cut such costs and an important point for all stakeholders with an interest in the long-term growth of the company and in solutions to societal problems.

Another way to explain this effort is through suites of new products or new commercial approaches that are explicitly aimed at solving specific and significant societal problems. For example, CVS recently made a decision to stop selling cigarettes at its 7,700 locations nationwide. It also rebranded itself as CVS Health in an attempt to become a health care destination for millions of consumers by providing such basic services as blood pressure tests and flu shots and by creating a series of medical clinics to provide fast, low-cost service for relatively minor problems. IBM has developed new programs for "smarter cities" that, through data analysis and management tools, can improve such fundamental services as law enforcement, emergency management, transportation, and social services. GE's ecomagination effort, which began more than ten years ago, sought to increase the number of products that were certified by an independent third party as reducing greenhouse gas pollution and being more energy efficient. By 2014, the company had invested more than $13 billion in R&D on more environmentally friendly technologies, focusing on its big infrastructure businesses. It created new aircraft engines, gas turbines, and hybrid locomotives, which, in turn, created nearly $30 billion in new revenues over this time frame.[6]

3. REDUCED MARGIN BUSINESS

The first two themes of business-activity citizenship—the benefits of current goods and services and developing new ones to meet society's future needs—seek normal profit margins. But to deal with communities and people in need, companies may also provide goods and services at *reduced margins*. Costs are covered, but because of inability of customers to pay full freight or because of a desire to increase volume, the corporation decides to take less than full profit. For example, a variety of offerings are possible in finance, such as microfinance in developing nations, favorable rates to small business to stimulate economic growth, below-normal-rate financial advice to the disadvantaged, or reducing the cost of capital for trade in "sustainably" produced raw materials. Similarly, technology companies can sell new or refurbished equipment in the developing world on favorable terms (if they chose not to donate such equipment as part of their philanthropic efforts). So, too, health care companies can sell pharmaceuticals or medical equipment at less than full margin to ensure greater access to needed products in poor nations.

4. REDUCED EXTERNAL IMPACTS OF BUSINESS ACTIVITIES

An important aspect of the business citizenship case is the continuous process of reducing harmful externalities in the company's own operations. Many of these issues are covered under prior discussions: ethics, risk, quality, and safety. The fundamental challenge is a never-ending process for using less energy, fewer materials, and less water in basic business operations, including manufacturing, either through technological change or through other efficiency measures or through straightforward conservation. The General Counsel should be at the center of this affirmative effort. This conscious approach to externalities means reducing air and water pollution. It means generating less greenhouse gases to the extent that they are not regulated pollutants. It means creating programs for product and materials recycling, recovery, or reuse. It means creating less waste, especially hazardous waste, in production processes. It means reducing risks from product quality or improving product safety. It means focusing on all these issues through an assessment of the environmental impacts of selected products throughout their life cycles. In sum, it means having a systematic and comprehensive program of assessing external impacts of products and processes that harm society. It means taking concrete, measureable steps to reduce those impacts over time. It does *not* mean knowingly installing "defeat devices" in engine software that spew excess emissions on the road after deceitfully passing muster on the test bed, a stark, even grotesque, Volkswagen example of flunking citizenship through knowing misleading acts.

5. STAKEHOLDER BENEFITS

A fifth theme relating to the citizenship dimensions of a corporation's business activities is the company's voluntary effort to benefit stakeholders as discussed in the chapters on ethics and risk. These voluntary stakeholder enhancements, which are primarily aimed to strengthen the corporation's economic performance, risk management, or integrity, cover a large array of possible actions. There can be better, clearer disclosure to shareholders. There can be greater education and training or better health care or more robust wellness programs for employees. There can be training for individuals in the community to improve the transition to work, which will create more and better employees or customers for the company. There can be assistance to veterans across the employment spectrum—training, job search, placement, and retention—which helps place people in real jobs in the company itself. There can be ethical sourcing, which establishes labor quality and safety standards at third-party suppliers. There can be humane treatment of laid-off employees through fair severance, meaningful retraining, and effective outplacement. There can be generous parental leave policies for couples with newborns. There can be the corporate requirement that suppliers provide paid sick leave for workers, a cost the corporation will bear through higher supplier costs. There can be purchases from alternative energy sources at company facilities.[7]

Establishing systematic and comprehensive processes for identifying, deciding on, implementing, and explaining actions under these five "business activity" themes is at the core of corporate citizenship. It, therefore, is a set of tasks that must be led by the CEO and senior executives, with the General Counsel having a central role in decision making and then in making an accurate, credible, and contextual case.

C. COLLECTIVE ACTION: ANTICORRUPTION[8]

Much of the thinking about corporate social responsibility or sustainability emphasizes voluntary ethical actions by a single corporation. Yet, there are many problems that require collective action of corporations and other societal actors. The reasons are straightforward. The problem is too complex or pervasive or expensive for one company to solve.

Or, partial responses by some companies create the potential for free-riding by others. General Counsel, especially, must help sort out those problems his corporation should address through collective action, not just unitary voluntary action.

A striking example of such a problem is "grand" corruption. This involves bribery, extortion, and misappropriation involving public officials who make major "discretionary," governmental decisions under the malign and improper influence of personal pay-offs rather than through good faith effort to advance the public interest under relevant law and regulation. Because this problem illustrates both progress and problems for corporations seeking to address major global issues, I discuss it in some detail. In 1977, in response to widespread U.S. corporate bribery of foreign officials, Congress enacted the U.S. Foreign Corrupt Practices Act (FCPA). The FCPA's anti-bribery provisions, among other things, prohibit U.S. and foreign public companies listed on U.S. stock exchanges from making corrupt payments to foreign officials to obtain or retain business. The FCPA's accounting provisions require issuers to make and keep accurate books and records and to devise and to maintain an adequate system of internal accounting controls—and these provisions prohibit knowing falsification of those books and records or knowing failure to establish or follow internal controls.

1. "LEVEL UP"

Shortly after I became General Counsel of GE in 1987, I received an entreaty from a group of *Fortune* 100 GCs. They asked if GE would join their companies in seeking to repeal or weaken the FCPA because, at the time, other nations did not prohibit corporate foreign bribery. They argued that U.S. companies were thus at a "competitive disadvantage" in overseas sales. These GCs wanted to even the playing field by "leveling down."

Corruption has deleterious effects in host countries, especially in emerging markets. It distorts markets and competition; breeds cynicism among citizens; stymies the rule of law; damages government legitimacy; corrodes the integrity of the private sector; and impairs development, economic growth, and poverty reduction. It perpetuates the power of corrupt elites, who block needed change. Corruption also has baleful effects internationally. It undermines economic globalization by impairing predictability and stability, which are necessary for foreign investment and foreign operations. And it helps perpetuate failed and failing states, which are incubators of terrorism, the narcotics trade, money laundering, human trafficking, and other types of global crime. These failed and failing states pose significant foreign policy and national security problems. Finally, corruption is completely antithetical to an integrity culture inside a corporation and to the core corporate values of honesty, candor, fairness, reliability, and trustworthiness. Asking employees to comply with law and ethics generally but to make an exception for bribery is hypocritical and counterproductive. Indeed, it is simply unthinkable if a company is serious about integrity. Even if there were no FCPA, a prohibition on bribery by company employees in any foreign market should be a first-order global ethical standard for multinational corporations because corrupt payments are so corrosive to a real integrity culture and because companies can, in any number of instances, win on cost and quality in the marketplace (though some orders would, of course, be lost to corruption).

For all these reasons, I called my colleagues back with a suggestion. "Why don't we level up, rather than level down?" The idea was to create the level playing field by seeking an international convention signed by all the developed nations that prohibited bribery of foreign officials by their corporations. This initiative was already being discussed in Europe. A group of U.S. companies, as well as many other important actors, then took this position to Washington. As a result, the Executive Branch, at the request of Congress, began to negotiate an international agreement in 1988 through the Organization for Economic Cooperation and Development (OECD). Companies in OECD countries had bribed for years and, in Germany, could deduct foreign bribes as a business expense. Yet, widely publicized corruption scandals in several important OECD countries—including France, Italy, Germany, and Belgium—combined with a renewed U.S. effort and strong leadership, led the national ministers of the OECD to conclude in the spring of 1997 that a convention making foreign bribery a crime made sense. The finished product was signed in December of that year and, after ratifications, it became effective in 1999. Today, the 34 OECD member countries, as well as seven non-member countries, have adopted this Convention and, importantly, enacted national legislation prohibiting their domestic corporations for engaging in foreign bribery. The signatory countries are responsible for approximately two-thirds of world exports and almost 90 percent of total foreign direct investment outflows.

Collective corporate action, combined with many other important political actors and forces, had worked to "level up" the law of the developed world, although it had taken from 1988 until the turn of a new century. In 1993, in a closely related collective action, a new NGO, Transparency International (TI), was founded in Germany, with the leadership of a former World Bank regional director, Peter Eigen, and with the strong support of a core group of U.S. multinational corporations. The organization comprises national chapters (more than 100 exist today) that monitor, and publish reports about, political and corporate corruption at both country and global levels. Transparency International-USA, also founded in 1993, has strong support from U.S. global corporations that believe in the leveling up agenda and support the OECD Convention.

2. THE ENFORCEMENT ENIGMA

But there were major obstacles to making effective the national anti-bribery laws required by the OECD Convention. Most importantly, the signatory nations all want their national champion corporations to win orders in international economic competition, to employ as many workers in the home country as possible, and to improve the nation's balance of payments. This deep economic and political desire runs directly counter to prosecuting those corporations for bribery in foreign markets. The symbol of this problem was the 2006 decision by British Prime Minister Tony Blair to stop dead in its tracks the long-running UK investigation of serious bribery allegations involving British Aerospace Systems' (BAE) lucrative Al Yamamah multi-billion-dollar contract for sale of British fighter planes to Saudi Arabia. Blair ostensibly made the decision for "national security" reasons, even though there is no national security exception to the anti-bribery mandates of the convention. In reality, the decision to kill the inquiry sought to preserve the sale, protect jobs, and avoid embarrassment for BAE, for the British Defense Ministry (allegedly helping arrange payments), and for the Saudi royal family.

In addition to succumbing to trade and jobs pressures, signatory nations may not enforce their anticorruption obligations because they don't have the resources and skills to investigate and bring enforcement actions involving complex global crimes with intricate facts. Another problem: Nations may have political appointees making initial investigation and prosecution decisions rather than civil servants who may be more knowledgeable and more effective. Also, the OECD itself cannot sanction laggard countries. A respected and professional OECD Working Group on Bribery monitors enforcement and issues reports on progress and issues. But these reports are highly technical; do not compare the performance of the signatories; and, because of comity among OECD member states, do not engage in highly publicized "naming and shaming."

As a result, only a minority of signatory countries have active enforcement programs. This is according to Transparency International. It issues an annual report that, in contrast to the OECD Working Group, compares and contrasts national efforts. The results have not changed dramatically over the years (with the exception of Great Britain, which, after the Blair fiasco, subsequently enacted a new anti-bribery law and began more active enforcement). In its 2015 report, TI concluded that there was "active" enforcement in four nations with 23 percent of world exports (United States, Germany, United Kingdom, and Switzerland); "moderate" enforcement in six nations with 8.9 percent of world exports; and "limited, little, or no" enforcement in 30 nations with 33 percent of world exports. Thus, almost three-quarters of the OECD convention's signatories are still not "active" in carrying out the Convention's anticorruption goals. Over the period from 2010 to 2013, the United States had about 25 percent of total investigations, even though it had about 10 percent of world exports. In early periods, the United States had an even higher percentage of enforcement actions.

The failure of many nations to meet their commitments under the OECD Convention creates a substantial disadvantage for corporations subject to the jurisdiction of the United States and other actively enforc-ing nations. This disadvantage can be acute during a global economic downturn when there is a desperate scramble for global orders and sales. Nonenforcement by nations seeking to promote national cor-porate champions is, in fact, pernicious protectionism. In 1988, there was the hard "leveling up" problem of putting laws prohibiting foreign bribery on the books in the industrialized world. Today, there is the hard "leveling up" problem of having those laws enforced energetically and uniformly. This is a quintessential strategic problem of citizen-ship for General Counsel of corporations in the "active" enforcement nations. They need to seek collective action of like-minded corpora-tions, but they also must enlist other political actors like labor unions, international financing institutions, and NGOs concerned with cor-ruption, transparency, development, and human rights. They need to develop strategies to encourage their host governments—especially the United States—to exert pressure in bilateral relations with laggard nations (like Japan who relies heavily on the United States) and in multilateral forums like the G20 and the OECD itself. (The OECD, for example, should make the reports of its working group on bribery more comparative and pointed.) They need to enlist like-minded cor-porations in laggard nations—where they may have a significant busi-ness presence—to press for fair enforcement of anticorruption laws. This is possible, if not probable. As a result of being caught in a huge bribery scandal, Siemens, for example, has gone from being a major bribe-giver to a proponent of enforcement in Germany and Middle Europe. Using pressure in states and in congressional districts, corpo-rations can also pressure Congress to hold hearings on the anti-bribery practices of major foreign corporations doing substantial business in the United States and to require reports (as it has done in the past) from Executive Departments (Justice, State, or Commerce) on com-parative enforcement of anti-bribery strictures by the signatories to the OECD convention.

3. THE BROADER ANTICORRUPTION AGENDA

In considering other venues in which to combat global corruption and where to spend resources on collective action, corporations face a number of choices beyond making their own internal programs as effective as possible and beyond seeking to have more balanced and uniform enforcement of the OECD convention. To encourage better and more comprehensive programs in companies under U.S. jurisdiction, they can focus on U.S. policy and seek to have more formal recognition and credit by enforcement authorities of voluntary disclosure and "good" anti-bribery compliance programs. They can seek enforcement of cognate anti-bribery conventions, like the UN Convention Against Corruption, which is signed by 175 nations but includes many developing countries that have serious rule of law issues. They can work with prosecutors to name not just the corporate bribe-giver, but also the government bribe-takers.

They can seek anticorruption procurement provisions in trade talks, especially the important bilateral and regional negotiations that have, for the moment, supplanted global talks at the World Trade Organization. They can work with international financing institutions like the World Bank or the Asian Development Bank to prevent bribery in those institutions' procurements, grants, and loans or to provide technical assistance for building national institutional capacity. They can work with national development agencies—such as the UK's Department for International Development or the U.S. Agency for International Development (AID)—on the same set of issues. Importantly, AID must also work with the Defense and State Departments in addressing the intractable program presented by counterinsurgency doctrine in conflict-ridden failed or failing states—such as Iraq and Afghanistan. Counterinsurgency theory places emphasis on building civil institutions in the midst of war and using private corporations to facilitate this complex task. But this goal is often frustrated by profound, endemic corruption, symbolized by the expensive "narco-tecture" in wealthy areas of Kabul built with proceeds from the opium trade. Thus, this element of the key national security doctrine of counterinsurgency—which can involve global corporations—is of great importance but also great difficulty due to global corruption and to limited U.S. capacity in either the Defense or State Departments to address corruption with sophistication and effectiveness.

4. HOST-COUNTRY ACTIONS

Global corporations can also themselves take actions against corruption in emerging market nations. Combating corruption, at the end of the day, requires developing nations to create durable, transparent, and accountable institutions, which can order fundamental economic, political, and legal affairs free from illicit influences. The set of forces that will start and sustain this process of changing culture and building institutions will turn on each nation's history, culture, and potential for a shift in power from exclusive, extractive elites to a more inclusive political and economic institution. Experts on development don't agree about much, but the current consensus today is that meaningful change must begin from within each nation or region, although there is no consensus on what constellation of in-country forces and conditions will produce effective reform movements. Outside pressure for modernization or democracy or social engineering is not likely to work. Outside assistance can only be useful when local actors seek it as part of a larger process of self-initiated social, political, and economic change.

But, despite these outsized problems, corporations, nations, and multilateral institutions can all have incremental effects, even if not transformative ones, through affirmative actions in host nations. Acting on their own, global corporations, as global citizens, should perform with integrity in difficult emerging markets. Although this may mean losing some orders, clean corporations—if they have technology, cost, and quality—can still do business in these difficult markets by just saying "no," as I have argued in detail (see pp. 161–168). This is especially so if a global corporation is helping an emerging market meet basic needs (like infrastructure) with superior products. In "doing business with integrity," transnational corporations can send an important message to local and international business. Major individual corporations can also, as GE did, serve as "management schools" in these markets, working with both sympathetic commercial and government leaders to impart business and integrity disciplines. In GE's case, this included bringing both public-sector and private-sector leaders from China for a month-long training course at the company's business school in Crotonville, New York. Corporations can also use philanthropy either for humanitarian assistance to gain a measure of credibility and goodwill (at least with central government technocrats) or to support anticorruption programs for business students or businesspeople at the nation's universities. Corporations can carry out these initiatives through ad hoc cooperative efforts with other global companies.

Corporations may also seek to forge alliances to address corruption issues in emerging markets. Business sectors have either issued guidelines for in-country behavior or committed to greater transparency (e.g., disclose payments to government). These sectors include extractive industries, banks, other financial services institutions, oil and gas producers, and aerospace and defense industries. Alternatively, corporations support a variety of "rule of law" efforts in emerging markets—the American Bar Association's Rule of Law Initiative is a flagship program—that cover a range of related topics from direct anticorruption/public integrity reforms to reforms in areas like access to justice, the judiciary, the administrative process, alternative dispute resolution, and professional standards. These voluntary in-country collective efforts face two problems. To the extent that they are "associational efforts" and require individual industry participants to disclose information or take other actions, there are the classic problems of a voluntary association's capacity to verify and hold those actors accountable and to sanction free-riders. Such programs always face the risk that rhetoric far outruns reality. More importantly, for the reasons just stated, law reform initiatives by outside actors, even when collaborating with some dedicated local nationals, face the problem of not being part of broader political social and economic change required to effect real and systemic change. Nonetheless, targeted, corporate anticorruption efforts, especially in concert with other companies, can be important acts of citizenship in effecting incremental change that can make a real, if not transformative, difference.

The huge issue of corruption is thus a paradigmatic one for global corporations and for General Counsel. It is of surpassing importance to international business. It is of extraordinary complexity and intractability. Other than having their own high-integrity anticorruption program, global corporations' actions alone can have limited impact.

Collective action is necessary to begin to address the issues. But, even then, the impact may be limited. For example, the OECD Convention is a vital symbol of the developed world's change of view from being complacent about corruption to being active in opposition. It has led to major cases against international companies. It thus serves as a deterrent to bad behavior and as a spur to creation of good internal programs. But, even within its own framework, implementation in the developed world is not uniform. And the problems of corruption in the developing world will hardly be solved even if corporations from the developed world stop bribing. Thus, it is an important step forward in the long war against corruption, even if not a decisive one. General Counsel, working within their corporations, must continuously make decisions about devoting time and effort to collective action on major global issues that affect corporations, as anticorruption efforts exemplify and as I illustrate next in a discussion of public policy.

D. PUBLIC POLICY

Under the broad themes of promoting economic growth, protecting workers, promoting consumer welfare, and promoting public welfare, each nation in which a global corporation does business has enacted a broad array of detailed legislation and regulation that shapes what companies can and cannot do. These regimes of public policy are constantly subject to revision and augmentation as corporations face proposed changes that have positive and negative effects. A corporation's approach to public policy—organizationally, substantively, and procedurally—is a key reflection of its broader approach to corporate citizenship. *And it is obvious: Public policy and governmental issues are a key part of the General Counsel's role.* They afford him a signal opportunity to contribute to the company if he has the critical *complementary competencies* of the lawyer-statesman (see pp. 41–46). In particular, these issues of public policy and government pose striking problems in balancing public and private interests, not least in the **process** *of making public policy*, where corporations should, as I will discuss, consider a set of "golden rules" to address corrosive problems in our dysfunctional political system.

To meet the broad challenge of ever-changing public policy across the globe, transnational corporations need a systematic, forward-looking, and balanced approach to government and public affairs, but many don't have one. Although governmental decisions significantly affect global business success, many corporations and legal staffs are only involved in defensive, short-term, or narrowly self-interested "government relations." Fewer companies have sought to make sophisticated public policy formation and implementation an important dimension of their business's global strategies. They haven't evolved from a narrow reactive to a broader proactive approach. This step is necessary, given the vital and increasing global interaction between government and business, not just in the United States but around the world.

1. BROAD SCOPE OF DIRECT-IMPACT ISSUES

The range of issues in a comprehensive corporate approach to government and public policy across the globe is striking. Major corporations will have a broad portfolio of public policy issues that *directly* affect their business. These issues can arise in the legislature, the executive, or regulatory agencies, but they can also arise in litigation, transactions, business development, or adoption of ethical standards that, among other things, may seek to preempt formal policy proposals. These can be cross-cutting issues that affect the whole corporation (e.g., taxes, trade, IP, labor/employment, or competition law) or more discrete issues that affect specific divisions within the broader company (e.g., telecommunications, food safety, health care, aerospace, or energy/environment). These "direct-impact" policy issues can be beneficial to the corporation and be part of an affirmative agenda, or they can be harmful to the business and be part of a defensive agenda. And, of course, they can arise in every nation across the globe. Examples of items on an "affirmative" agenda include:

- Stimulating policy paradigm shifts—for example, putting more emphasis on early diagnosis and prevention in health care or on carbon constraints and renewable fuel sources in energy.
- Within those paradigm shifts, obtaining government support for whole new markets, like wind or water, through tax incentives,

grants, or loans, if it is clear that these markets are in the public interest and that these boosts are needed temporarily before moving to a state of competition without government involvement.

- Approving new products and new technologies after ensuring they are safe and effective.
- Streamlining regulatory systems to advance public goals more efficiently and effectively (although one person's sensible "deregulation" is another person's "demolition" of public interest protections).
- Improving global competition by reducing national tariff and nontariff barriers to trade and treating cross-border investment in a nondiscriminatory manner.
- Establishing company-to-country partnerships with less-developed nations to help define infrastructure needs and to provide a range of needed goods and services; and, in this regard, when seeking orders, making a genuine case for how the technology, cost, and quality will serve both the near-term and long-term public interest.
- Gaining approval in major cross-border transactions from antitrust and other governmental authorities in multiple nations.

Beyond these major affirmative issues, there are countless smaller, daily interactions (licenses, permits, approvals, contracts) with government that corporations must undertake. And, of course, there can be an equally long and important list of "defensive" issues that corporations may seek to defeat or modify. Such defensive issues, in broadest outline, could occur when proposed policy does not properly balance equity and efficiency or properly balance governmental oversight with necessary private decision making. And there may be issues that have both affirmative and defensive dimensions. The aftermath of crises like the Gulf explosion, the Fukushima nuclear problems, and the plant collapse in Bangladesh stimulated intense public policy debates about deep-water drilling, nuclear power scenario planning, and improving health and safety in emerging market plants that could be either helpful or harmful to business. So, too, there is the temptation to seek short-term advantage from government without any (or very weak) policy basis: *This is the "crony capitalism" of unnecessary—but hard to repeal—concessions, franchises, tax exemptions, subsidies, regulatory loopholes, monopoly rights, public works contracts, and rights on public lands.* Addressing with integrity this daunting set of affirmative, defensive, or mixed issues—and, in good conscious, not pigging out at the trough of crony capitalism—is, of course, even more challenging in emerging markets.

2. INTERNAL APPROACH: THE IDEAL

A global corporation's approach to government and public policy must start with the CEO's commitment to strategic and operational processes that explicitly include a public policy dimension. *The CEO must make clear both to division business leaders and to senior corporate executives that their annual plans should include and integrate three dimensions of global government issues: desirable policy (policy formulation), feasible policy (policy enactment), and how enacted policy can become effective (policy implementation).* In annual strategic reviews, business leaders should present a prioritized agenda of offensive and defensive policies relating to their industry or line of business on matters all across the globe. Senior corporate executives should do the same, covering broad area like taxes, trade, labor, and employment. With strong involvement and advice from the GC, the CEO makes strategic decisions on priority policy formulation and resource allocation for policy enactment or implementation across the whole corporation—both on industry-specific issues in the divisions and on company-wide issues at headquarters. To underscore the importance of these priority policy matters, the CEO and business leaders should hold regular reviews—either as part of general business reviews or as stand-alone sessions—to determine whether milestones are being met in the processes of enactment and implementation.

This corporate process depends on two kinds of experts inside the corporation: policy experts and political experts. The *policy experts* are located with corporate and business unit leaders. They have broad understanding of the relevant substantive policy areas and the relevant government institutions. They need to help devise the policy that should be enacted and the strategy for ensuring governmental implementation. These people are experts either in specific industries (e.g., health care, energy, communications, security, finance) or in specific cross-cutting subjects (e.g., antitrust, taxes, trade, environment, labor and employment, intellectual property). Each business should have such an expert in the public policy of the particular industry. That policy expert should be a key inside member of the business team and lead an important part of the annual strategic review identifying priority policy issues that will have an important impact in the years ahead. Similarly, cross-cutting subject matter experts will be located with the senior corporate executives at corporate headquarters (and will often be the senior specialist lawyer). Whether in the businesses or in headquarters, these policy experts need to have both an aptitude for business and a keen sense of politics beyond their own specialized knowledge. This is the person who, through knowledge, experience, and networks, understands the trajectory of policy debates and can spot and develop policy issues with the corporate and business unit teams. Ideally, this senior policy person has had experience in government and so understands the interplay of policy, politics, and governmental process.

The *political experts* are located not at corporate or division headquarters, but in the political capitals. Their "clients" are the decision makers in the legislature, the executive, and the regulatory agencies. They need to have the intellectual ability to understand, in depth, all the moving parts of complex substantive issues. These experts need to help perform the difficult task of translating the desirable, from both a policy and business perspective, into something feasible whether that involves a broad communication plan or a detailed one-on-one lobbying plan. Their expertise is knowledge of, and sensitivity to, global political and governmental politics and processes and an understanding of how to get things done with integrity in Beijing, Brussels, Budapest, or Boston. *Just as the policy experts must have an aptitude for politics, the political experts must also have an aptitude for policy (and both need an aptitude for business).*

The integration of policy and politics is the sina qua non of success. And the interaction between the two types of experts is vital. When the policy expert is working with the business or corporate leaders on issues of policy formulation in strategic reviews—on the substantive agenda—he must be in constant touch, as well, with the political expert to make sure that the proposed policies have a reasonable chance of becoming law and being implemented in the real political and governmental world. When the political expert is trying to get the policy enacted, he needs to be in constant contact with the policy expert and businesspeople to assess the continued desirability of the changes that will occur as the governmental decision-making process follows its inevitable twists and turns. The political expert will also selectively want the policy expert and business leaders to make a substantive case to government officials. And, on implementing policy by the executive departments or regulatory agencies after enactment, the policy and political experts will often work closely together.

The person with overall responsibility for integrating public policy and politics into business strategy across the whole company, short of the CEO, can be the General Counsel. This role for the GC is an important aspect of the inside counsel revolution. I had this responsibility at GE. Policy, legislation, regulation, and (as necessary) test case litigation are about public institutions mandating meaningful rules and achieving their intended impact through effective implementation. When hiring GE's legal specialists (tax, trade, IP, etc.), who reported directly to me, I almost always sought a person who could skillfully handle GE's myriad operational issues but who also had served in government and thus had policy expertise. My hires included individuals who had served as senior officials in Justice, Treasury, Defense, State, the U.S. Trade Representative (USTR), Commerce, Health and Human Services, and key regulatory agencies like the SEC or the Federal Communications Commission (FCC). I also sought, though I did not always succeed, to have the business units hire policy experts in addition to the General Counsel if the GC did not have policy expertise in the relevant industry (e.g., energy, aerospace, communications). I also oversaw the political experts in Washington and other capitals. At any moment, the company might have more than 150 policy matters on which it was engaged. I would have the top 10 on my personal "to do" list. I had to know issues in depth and was personally responsible for helping to shape them and to monitor them closely. But, although the General Counsel will always have a major role in public policy, some GCs may not have enough background in governmental issues to provide overall leadership on policy and politics. Some companies may choose to hire a senior person to work at headquarters on "government affairs," overseeing both the policy and political experts. Such a separate head of governmental affairs, typically a former senior government official like Deputy or Under Secretary of a major Executive Department, often reports directly to the CEO and coordinates closely inside the corporation with the GC and the substantive policy experts in the company.

I must stress that systematic policy development across a global company is a difficult, multi-faceted task. Take the example of GE's global energy business. It has many different product lines that raise first-order energy and environmental issues in virtually every nation: gas turbines, coal gasification, nuclear, wind, solar, hydro, and transmission/distribution, as well as services for those products. The annual business review process systematically looked at all these businesses in each region/country (the United States, Europe, the Middle East, Asia) and asked a set of systematic policy-related questions: What is the policy environment? What emerging issues, policies, laws, and regulations in energy and environment could affect performance in the next three years and in the longer term (usually a ten-year time period)? From this extensive offensive and defensive issues list, what global policy actions are priorities according to both near-term and longer-term impact/precedent? What are the substantive positions? What should be the level of GE involvement/resource commitment? Who are the key governmental and interest group actors, and what are their positions? More broadly, how do these priorities looked at from a company perspective align with the trajectory of public policy in the jurisdiction and with broader issues in the political culture? And, for enacted policies, how can the corporation aid in effective government implementation? This process—covering multiple product lines across more than 100 countries—just involved one division in a global company!

The annual CEO decisions on policy, with significant involvement of the General Counsel (among others), must be based on a sophisticated understanding of policy and political processes and the varying cultures in diverse nations, with different political and economic systems, all across the globe—as well as the contingent nature and variable time horizon of investment in these issues. Not all priorities will be short term. Not all will be winners. Integrity must *never* be compromised. But the financial investment in policy and political experts is small compared to the potential importance of these policy issues. There should also be no misunderstanding: Although the monetary expense may not be large compared to a corporation's significant capital projects, the time required to make any meaningful change in public policy is substantial because of the complexity of political and governmental processes. This time commitment is especially great in open societies like America's, where myriad interest groups, constitutional separation of powers, traditions of federalism, a competitive party system, and media outlets mean that enormous effort is required on both policy and politics to move the needle on any issue of consequence.

3. INTERNAL APPROACH: THE GAP

Sophisticated public policy work is not a natural act for many corporations. There is often a significant gap between the concept of a proactive policy process and actual practice. Even with strong CEO support, subordinate business leaders who are crucial to its success may not share the commitment. They may have only a short-term view or may not want to invest in the necessary resources to perform quality policy analysis or effective public communications. They might not have a balanced or realistic understanding of public policy and governmental processes. Their business school education and their experience of rising initially within narrower company functions (marketing, manufacturing, finance) may leave them unprepared. This is why effective CEO exhortation and explanation—and the broad leadership development discussed in the prior chapter—is so important.

Moreover, hiring, retaining, and promoting policy and political experts inside the company is an extraordinary challenge in global markets outside the United States and the European Union. Broad roles for lawyers may be underdeveloped outside those areas. Public policy schools may not exist. The transition from working in government to working in the private sector on substantive issues (rather than to just get a pay-off) may also not yet be a strong practice. And, while there are a burgeoning number of think tanks that create a pool of policy experts, here, too, there may not be a tradition of going "in-house" in emerging markets, in contrast to the United States and EU. Moreover, hiring policy and political experts, especially in emerging markets, requires great sensitivity about whether the person has the skill to act effectively and ethically; whether the person has credibility with decision makers or has political enemies; and whether, to put it bluntly, the person is clean and trustworthy as well as effective.

The need for such experts is paramount, however, because of the complexity of opportunities and threats in overseas jurisdictions. China, of course, is a prime example. China's trade balance, currency, IP, and growing military issues garner U.S. headlines. But its society is also in the midst of fundamental policy debates: about creating genuine competition between state-owned and privately owned enter-prises; about creating a balanced energy policy; about constructing and financing a social safety net (health, disability, pensions); about generating growth through consumer finance and consumption, not just through investment and export; about achieving cleaner growth with more environmental protection; and about establishing a rule of law while preserving the power of the Communist Party. But, beyond all these debates and dilemmas is the ever-changing view of top Chi-nese leadership about international business. Early in the 1990s, China wanted developed-world companies to invest in China in order to learn about management, technology, and innovation and to have businesses in-country that were capable of working at the upper levels of the value chain. But, over time, China sought to move its national corporations up that value chain; to license, steal, or develop more advanced tech-nologies; and to supplant global companies with national champions. Global companies may be forced to partner with Chinese companies to have market access, but they do so at their peril in terms of losing their technology to their "partners." And one of the most vexing ques-tions facing a company and its GC is whether government policy and government agreements that seem to encourage global corporations to invest in China are, in fact, durable or enforceable. Arbitrary change to advance China's national interests is always lurking on the horizon.

Most of these (and other) debates have significant implications for business. Indeed, at least half of the challenge of doing business in China is understanding how the Party and the government affect the conduct of business by international companies. Yet, many business leaders are simply untrained in this dimension and need the assistance of policy and political experts. Finding a bicultural, bilingual in-house expert is key. One of GE's best hires was the daughter of a justice of the Chinese Supreme Court who received a Masters in Law (LLM) at Yale University and was an expert in environmental policy. Returning to China as a GE lawyer, she developed a broad network within Chinese government and industry and had influence both on environmental policy and compliance. Such expertise is necessary for complex policy issues, but it is especially important in a society where governmental decision making can be opaque because it involves behind-the-scenes relationships and rivalries between local and central government, between ministries and upper levels of government, and between government and the Party.

Additionally, outside advisors—whether in law firms, consulting firms, think tanks, or academia; whether in the United States or overseas—have a critical role in carefully defined circumstances. A company cannot possibly hire enough internal resources for these matters, given the variation in national processes and the complexity of the issues. But vetting outsiders is key not just in terms of integrity, but in terms of whether they have hidden agendas that are not in the corporation's interest. Corporations need to take the initiative in defining their own issues and projects and not just hand them off blindly to so-called outside experts. Ideally, these experts are not just well-connected door openers but actually provide important policy and political advice. On important retainers of important experts in important countries on important matters, the judgment of the General Counsel is often vital.

4. INDIRECT IMPACT: ADDRESSING BROAD CONCERNS

As corporate citizens, global companies also have a potential role in addressing a host of broader policy issues that more *indirectly* affect the company. Such policies, in theory, secure public goods that cannot be resolved by market forces and that enhance a nation's social, economic, political, and institutional well-being. In so doing, these policies also create the conditions under which capitalism can flourish. Such policies include such basic governmental activities as assuring the fair operation of markets, providing for the national defense, securing internal order, protecting important environmental or consumer impacts not properly addressed by corporate activity, providing a social safety net for the vulnerable, improving opportunity through public education and training, and creating conditions for global competition.

Under these broad categories, a list of more specific, and contentious, contemporary issues would include tax reform; improved elementary and secondary education; improved education at all levels in science, technology, and mathematics; enhanced research and development; infrastructure modernization; homeland security and counterterrorism activities; adjusting to an aging population; dealing with global migration and national immigration; formulating effective methods of cyber-security; promoting global health and preventing global pandemics; dealing with climate change; reducing poverty and inequality; advancing rule of law and anticorruption; and removing or modifying outmoded or ineffective regulation. When corporate social responsibility advocates cannot enact public policy in the legislatures or at regulatory agencies on these types of issues, they may press to have corporations take individual action and bear individual company costs to secure such "public goods." But the best competitive solution, if the cost of individual action is high and a free-rider problem is real, may be for corporations to seek a collective public policy solution on these "indirect" issues that addresses an important "non-market" problem, that levels the playing field for concerned companies and free-riders alike, and that is also enforceable (which voluntary action or industry agreements are not).

Corporations thus may wisely choose to participate actively in policy debates on these broader issues. Some respected commentators have, in fact, urged that, in today's world, CEOs need to become advocates for public policy that addresses the broad *indirect* societal threats to market capitalism, not just promote public policy that *directly* affects the company.[9] But, given all the other issues that face CEOs and General Counsels, such advocacy is very difficult, even in just one or two of these policy areas. The issues are large and complex; there is great difficulty in developing uncontested "facts" that underlie any policy prescription; there are strongly contested views about what is the public interest among a variety of political actors; usually (almost always in my experience), there are sharp divisions within the "business community" itself; there is a risk of being caught in partisan wars; solutions often have an uncertain effect; and the time required of top company leaders is extensive and can crowd out a host of activities that more directly affect the company and its stakeholders. The standard operating procedure on these broader issues is thus to work through a business association: the Chamber of Commerce; the Business Roundtable; the National Association of Manufacturers; or the literally thousands of trade associations clustered in Washington and summarized as "K Street." The problem with this approach is well known: Such associations often simply arrive at "lowest common denominator" positions that are heavily slanted toward business or are a vague collection of business bromides or both.

In my experience, if a global corporation wishes to have an impact on these broader issues, which have an important impact on society and an important indirect impact on the corporation, it must form a "coalition of the willing" who want to commit time and resources to the effort. Such coalitions need not just be of like-minded corporations. Indeed, it is best if they are, in fact, broad based. Here are three examples from my experience. One I have already discussed—the effort to "level up" not "level down" in the anticorruption area by agreeing to, and then implementing, an international convention under the auspices of the OECD. A coalition of like-minded corporations, labor organizations, and activist NGOs have pursued this issue for almost 30 years. A second example is the U.S. Climate Action Partnership (CAP), which was formed in 2007, to develop legislation to address use of greenhouse gases. It had a broad membership: power generation manufacturers, industrial users of energy, automobile companies, utilities, and environmental groups. To the surprise of many, it worked assiduously and developed a statement of cap-and-trade principles. To the further surprise of many, it then developed a set of policy prescriptions and turned those prescriptions into actual legislative language. Bills heavily influenced by this detailed proposal were introduced in Congress in 2009, but, in the midst of the economic downturn and a lack of national consensus on climate change, the proposal did not pass. A third example was an asbestos trust fund to take asbestos injury cases out of the court system (where 70 percent of funds expended were directed to lawyers or other transaction costs); provide quick recompense to workers injured by asbestos exposure; and provide a measure of certainty to a large, looming future cost. GE was part of a coalition of select industrial companies—which had an insurance industry counterpart—to work through this enormously complicated issue. After several years of work, the legislation died in the Senate with 59 votes in favor, but *one vote short of cloture needed to defeat a death-dealing filibuster.*

From the GE perspective, anticorruption, climate change, and asbestos trust fund efforts were aimed at very broad societal problems that were important generally but also affected the company. Moderating corruption would help GE in international competition. Capping greenhouse gas emissions would make GE's environmentally friendly power generation equipment even more attractive economically. An asbestos trust fund would direct corporate expenditures quickly to injured workers and provide a degree of predictability to burgeoning asbestos litigation costs. But all of these policy efforts were high risk. All required substantial effort. Anticorruption has had important, although hardly complete, success. Climate change legislation, for now, is stalled. So, too, an asbestos trust fund, once close to moving in Congress, now lies dormant. But all are examples of good faith initiatives to deal with serious societal problems and, in my view, represent important efforts of corporate citizenship though corporate leadership of diverse coalitions. But they are also emblematic of concerted, coordinated, and selective private-sector engagement necessary to address broad issues of the type described earlier that have both direct and indirect impact on corporations.

5. GOLDEN RULES?

In their role as corporate citizens, major corporations have special responsibilities relating to the *process of developing public policy*, responsibilities that should be the special province of the General Counsel. Most fundamentally, and as discussed many times, corporations should, of course, never bribe public officials to influence policy or other governmental decisions, despite widespread corruption in many capitals around the world. Period, full stop. But there are other, less bright-line, more nuanced *process* responsibilities—I call them Golden Rules—that are of great moment and that require serious debate in the corporate community. This is so because trust in corporations is generally low—especially so with respect to their participation in politics and policy. Each of these responsibilities is worthy of a chapter or even book on its own. But I believe deeply in their importance and so want, at the least, to flag them as important elements of citizenship that the General Counsel should raise with the CEO and the board of directors (presumably through the Public Responsibilities Committee in the first instance). These Golden Rules are key elements of a precious commodity: corporate credibility in the political world of elected officials, media, and NGOs. These issues have special moment in the United States, but they have analogues in other nations across the world.

First, there is the way corporations spend money to participate in the political process—from financing campaigns at one end of the spectrum to spending enormous sums on detailed lobbying or agency rule making at the other end. The amount spent to finance election campaigns for federal office in the 2012 campaign totaled $6 billion. In 2014, the total cost of "lobbying" at the federal level totaled $3.24 billion, although this is but a fraction of amounts spent on preparing public positions and does not include the vast sums spent in the administrative process on regulations. One of the salient issues of our time is how badly our political processes are distorted by the use of money. There is the profound issue of the undue influence of money in political campaigns, which has always existed but has gained even more salience in the wake of the Supreme Court's decision in *Citizens United v. Federal Elections Commission*. Although direct contributions from corporate and union treasuries to candidates are still prohibited (and limited expenditures from employee/member funded political action committees allowed), *Citizens United*, in the broad, held that election campaign expenditures from those corporate and union treasuries on "independent" advocacy are protected speech under the First Amendment if not coordinated with the candidates. Also protected is "independent" spending by privately held corporations and wealthy individuals. Is this spending "unfair" because it favors those with resources? Is this spending potentially "corrupt" because its possible use can, without much imagination, be used to signal requests for an improper quid pro quo bargain with legislators? Does the absence of *substantive* limitations to address these issues of unfairness and corruption pose serious governance problems? Is now-unlimited independent spending an important factor in the diminished public trust in the integrity of the electoral and legislative processes and in government generally? These are important questions that used to engender bipartisan concern but have now become sharply politicized.

There are also profound issues about the *disclosure* of sources and uses of funding. Although disclosures for contributions to candidates from employee/member funded political action committees (PACs) are mandatory, contributions from corporate treasuries to certain types of trade associations organized as "nonprofits" under Section 501(c) of the Internal Revenue Code need not be disclosed. IRS rules historically have not required nonprofit organizations to disclose contributors. Thus, these nonprofits are a political black box and can be used by publicly held corporations, privately held corporations, unions, and individual donors to fuzz up or hide their role, both in financing campaigns and in shaping public policy. A number of major corporations do voluntarily provide detailed disclosure about both their direct financial support and positions taken in campaign finance and lobbying in their annual "citizenship" reports or in other public communications. And this disclosure may include a discussion of whether or not corporations use trade associations in political finance—and if so how and why. But this is hardly a universal and, where it is practiced, that practice is hardly consistent. Moreover, the non-PAC sources of independent money in campaigns often comes from wealthy individuals and privately held corporations, not from publicly held companies.

One of the supreme acts of corporate citizenship today is candidly facing the problems of excessive money in politics and making a serious effort to address those issues to the extent constitutionally permissible. This can and should occur through increased *voluntary company action* to clearly disclose financing actions and policy positions both in elections and in lobbying, both directly and through trade associations. It can also occur in adoption by the SEC of a petition requiring corporate disclosure of political expenditures (a matter currently stalled at the Commission). But, as noted, the problem of money in politics is far broader than disclosure of expenditures by publicly held corporations. The greater challenge for corporate leadership is to develop a broad, bipartisan coalition to effect *public policy*, imposing substantive expenditure limits in elections and requiring better disclosure in both elections and lobbying, not just on corporations but on all funders who are disbursing vast sums of money to "independent" PACs and trade associations. Although some might disagree, I view this as a nonpartisan, good-government issue that would not disproportionately favor one political party. Finding a sensible way to address these issues is, of course, constrained by First Amendment prohibitions against substantive limits on organizational free speech and by the current political dysfunction that impedes serious debate on problems and solutions. Some near-term incremental steps are conceivable (if not likely)—for example, restructuring the deadlocked and feckless Federal Election Commission; forbidding about-to-be candidates from receiving "independent" super-PAC money; tougher rules on, and oversight of, prohibited "coordination" with "independent" donors when a person becomes a candidate; more timely public reporting of contributions to independent political committees (not created under IRS rules) that do have to disclose donors; various public financing "opt-in" measures; and more complete disclosure of the costs of formal representation to government (e.g., testimony or comments on regulations). However challenging it is to devise appropriate measures, it is surely a worthy citizenship effort to help form a broad, bipartisan coalition to seek both short-term incremental changes and more long-term structural solutions to the problems of money in politics in our new Gilded Age.

Moreover, in many emerging markets, corporations should have strict rules prohibiting corporate contributions to political campaigns or charities associated with candidates because of a recognition there— if not here—that such finance is often used for corrupt purposes. And many do. It can be dangerous for companies to be too closely identified—especially through questionable financial support—with the personalities and politics of a particular regime. In many emerging markets, the pendulum can swing wildly, with disastrous results for the careless, unethical corporation. This point is vividly illustrated by the huge corruption scandal involving Petrobras, Brazil's state-controlled oil company, which is implicating leading figures in the company, in government, and in other business (who allegedly bribed for contracts).[10]

Second, there is the question of developing "legislative," "regulatory," or "litigation" facts. Obviously, there is a long tradition of allowing formal adversary systems (litigation) or more political contests (regulation, legislation) to determine what facts are relevant to a policy decision. But corporations should examine whether there are ways— especially in legislation and regulation—for all the parties, including business, to be less prone to slant the facts to their advantage (using their outsized resources) and to seek, with others, to establish at least a core set of agreed-upon facts to inform debate. This would then help highlight where legitimate factual and policy disagreements occur, which may be based more on assumptions (that can be debated and tested) than on conclusively established facts. This effort is especially important when so much policy is built on complex "facts" from the social and natural sciences and when so many policy makers and lawyers are not literate in the relevant disciplines. And it is especially important because our political discourse is now awash in "opinion," untethered to facts, through cable news shouting matches or the unedited profusion of the Internet commentary. Although there will be legitimate debates about facts as well as policy, the extreme "politicization" of facts—and the use of special interests, including corporations, to create one-sided "facts" in addition to the troubling emergence of "Red" facts and "Blue" facts—is an issue of great consequence.

Third, there is the question of balanced policy. Corporations should not advocate slap-dash policies intended (transparently) to bolster the bottom line or otherwise so patently and narrowly self-interested and unbalanced as to deserve the "crony capitalism" appellation. It should be possible for corporations to acknowledge that there are legitimate considerations or values on both sides of most regulatory and legislative debates and to make a good faith effort (rather than just pay phony lip service) to reconcile the values in conflict—for example, finding a balance between the verities of equity and efficiency in social welfare legislation; or among access, cost, and quality in health care legislation; or between expedition and safety in drug approvals. It should be possible for companies, in forging their public policy positions, to try more explicitly (and genuinely) to explain the values in conflict and to balance public concerns and private interests. Unless "victories" can be won by brute money and power, most policy debates and decisions involve a compromise between legitimate values in conflict. I believe deeply that a corporation's credibility and effectiveness—its reputation in politics—turns on candidly discussing those conflicts and seeking those types of equitable, balanced resolutions. That may entail forging alliances with other interested parties prior to formal consideration of an issue, rather than through 11th-hour compromises in, dare I say it, smoke-filled rooms.

Fourth, there is the question of whether corporations should work hard for bipartisan solutions and seek to be nonpartisan in national politics. Broadly speaking, the corporate community has an interest in avoiding hyper-partisanship, gridlock, and dysfunction in the United States' political culture. In an era of intense partisanship and conflict, corporations that represent a broad array of stakeholders and have roots in many communities can play a constructive role by seeking to dampen the distemper affecting the political parties. To be sure, for some companies, the differences in ideas espoused by the parties (as opposed to the naked quest for power) may comport with their particular view of the world, and no action may be preferable to action. But even for those corporations, the question is whether it is in the broader national interest to seek more durable bipartisan approaches—which can clearly demarcate and privilege both public and private spheres of action—and to avoid partisan involvement in partisan fights.

These potential "Golden Rule" responsibilities of corporate participation in the political and policy processes—use of money, development of facts, balancing of values, and seeking bipartisan solutions—are as potentially controversial as substantive policy positions. Some companies will use any lawful tactic to advance their short-term public policy interests, even if such tactics increase the polarization and fragmentation in our political culture and feed the public's low esteem of corporations. Moreover, some of the gridlock in our polity today is due to very different and honestly held views about the role of government. And, given populist traditions in the United States, no matter what corporations do, there will inevitably be criticism and distrust among vociferous sectors of the electorate. Certainly, some will say that I am naïve even to raise them (but it is a "naïvete" based on 40 years of involvement in the political system and watching it degrade).

The ultimate question major corporations need to ask is whether, in seeking to advance their interests, they can do so in a way that focuses on these "Golden Rules" and helps to heal, rather than exacerbate, the ills in our political system and political processes. Beyond that, can corporations find common cause with other segments of society to focus on reforms in our political system in any number of areas, including such issues as tougher rules for ensuring no coordination between independent donors and political campaigns, protecting the right to vote in elections or nonpartisan primaries, or better salaries for government staff so that they can resist (at least for a while) the blandishments of revolving out the door to cushy K Street jobs? I can imagine no more important "what is right" question for a company as corporate citizen or for a General Counsel as lawyer-statesman. This is a fundamental subject corporations should evaluate with an eye to the maintenance of a healthy constitutional democracy and mixed economy, which depends on the private sector for balanced growth. These possible "Golden Rule" issues relating to their participation in policy and political processes should be central to a company's future debates about what constitutes, for each entity, being a "good corporate citizen." This subject is too vast for a single corporation, but it is a good example where a broad-based "coalition of the willing"—extending far beyond corporations—could be formed.

E. REPORTING[11]

Virtually every major global corporation today publishes a "Citizen-ship" or "Sustainability" Report. Many follow the template of the Global Reporting Initiative (GRI), which covers environmental, social, and governance issues. GRI lists a host of specific items a Citizenship Report should address (e.g., strategy, organization, governance, eco-nomic performance, product and service impact, product and service responsibility, anticorruption efforts, environmental impact, approach to labor and human rights, compliance, and public policy). These cor-porate Citizenship Reports often have an appendix listing whether and how the GRI issues are addressed. In addition, given the importance of climate change to some corporations, they may also address issues set forth in the CDP Template (formerly the Carbon Disclosure Proj-ect). And there are other citizenship reporting templates as well. Most corporations' Citizenship Reports are separate from their standard Annual Report (although the first will cite the second). The Annual Report is issued according to accounting standards and is aimed primarily at investors. The Citizenship Report is issued according to voluntarily adopted and loosely followed GRI (or other template) standards and is aimed at all stakeholders. For example, companies as diverse as GE, JPMorgan Chase, and Wal-Mart follow this bifurcated approach, issuing hefty Citizenship Reports that are 100 to 200 pages long in addition to their detailed Annual Reports.

There is a growing movement to merge the financial and citizenship reports into a single report under the rubric of "Integrated Reporting." The rationale for this approach is that it gives shareholders and other stakeholders a holistic view of the company. It recognizes the intercon-nection among economic performance, integrity, and risk that I have advocated in these pages. And, importantly from my perspective, it can explicate and illuminate the trade-offs companies must make in optimizing the interests of various stakeholders in the "best interest" of the company. United Technologies and Southwest Airlines are early adopters of the "One Report" approach. There is also a movement to bring greater systematic rigor (standards for accurate reporting) and timeliness (quarterly updates) to the nonfinancial dimensions of cor-porate reporting through the work of GRI and a new Sustainability

Standards Accounting Board, modeled after the Financial Accounting Standards Board (FASB). General Counsels and CFOs should be deeply involved in shaping the approach their corporation takes to citizenship reporting—whether bifurcated or integrated—because these reports will feature all the issues on compliance, ethics, risk, governance, and citizenship raised here.

First, GCs and CFOs need to work with the CEO and other senior executives to decide the purpose of this reporting for his company. Is it to develop a list of current issues on which the corporation will make commitments, to provide current information for stakeholders and "counterparties"—from investors to employees to customers to partners to regulators—who interact with the corporation, to engage with stakeholders and receive their views about future issues the corporation should consider, to enhance the corporation's reputation generally, or all of the above?

Second, as emphasized in the governance section (see pp. 280–300), GCs and CFOs need to assist the board and management in setting the highest first-, second-, and third-priority objectives across the dimensions of high performance, high integrity, and risk management, which will form the basis for executive compensation and core board oversight. These objectives should be reflected in a shorter, essential Priority Goals and Objectives Report (an "accountability" report) from the board and management at the end of each year, setting forth the strategy and the priority goals for the subsequent year, including milestones toward longer-range objectives. This report is different than the broad Annual and Citizenship Reports. It proceeds from a belief in the importance of integrating the main risks and opportunities across all dimensions of corporate activity and, through such a prioritizing exercise, to provide an important measure both for CEO and senior executive compensation. It proceeds from the further belief that articulating the results of this exercise will more clearly advance core company accountability than the numerous commitments and initiatives described in the hundreds of pages of Annual and Citizenship Reports. Reporting fairly about risk is an especially challenging task. The longer reports, issued subsequently, can articulate the essence of the shorter Priority Goals and Objectives Report in the broader company context.

Third, GCs and CFOs should work with Legal, Compliance, Finance, Risk, and the Audit Staff to ensure that reporting is accurate, even if there are not yet sustainability accounting standards. Part of this accuracy is ensuring that "material" issues meet legal definitions of materiality, and that other important, non-material issues are identified as "significant" or "important." Mistakes here are a torpedo in the side of the corporation's reputation. They should also work with the CEO and senior executives to determine whether there could be more regular, timely, and systematic reports on important citizenship developments, even if those developments are not technically "material" under the securities laws and need not be disclosed.

Fourth, GCs and CFOs should work with others in the company to find a variety of avenues to engage corporate constituencies on issues raised by corporate actions, including those covered in either the bifurcated annual reporting (finance and citizenship) or in integrated reporting. Although the Citizenship Reports are now lengthy, the reality is that they are covering a vast array of subjects in "headline" and "short news story" form. The corporation has to solve a puzzle: how to go beyond the report language and discuss its many activities in some depth with important constituents while not getting overwhelmed by the sheer number of interrogators. In addition to having a board of independent advisors to critique the citizenship (or integrated) report, there are a variety of ways the company leaders can engage, including focus groups, community consultations, investor meetings, and social media options. One of the best sources is employees—they interact with all the other constituencies. Information gained through these processes should be prioritized and fed into early warning systems and into the quarterly meeting on emerging ethical issues chaired by the CEO and staffed by the GC and CFO (see pp. 183–188). The corporation will hardly sign on to every constituent's wish list, but it surely can listen.

Finally, and perhaps most importantly, GCs and CFOs should struggle to make the reporting more meaningful. Too many Citizenship Reports read like extended press releases, touting achievements and reciting numbers *without any sense of problems, context, or impact.* The report should candidly discuss positions on controversial issues (wages in the supply chain, stem cell research, privacy, climate change). It should describe mistakes and prescribe remedies, if it can do so without creating additional legal liability. Trend data from the company's own efforts is obviously important. But, beyond that, it is important to explain the context of the reported item. How does the reported item fit into broader company strategy? How much does it cost in terms of overall firm economics? What key trade-offs did the company make? Far too often, Citizenship Reports present information in an economic vacuum without sizing it in terms of other corporate actions or societal problems. For example, external efforts are often just described with "outputs" that fail to convey both successes and limits. When describing the program to help veterans, the company should give some sense of the universe of people coming out of the military, how many have issues in transitioning to civilian work, and how the corporation is working with other companies (if it is) to make a significant impact on the problem.

F. REPUTATION

If the essential trust among corporate constituents turns ultimately on citizenship, then citizenship turns ultimately on reputation. And, if reputation is perception, that perception, over time, turns ultimately on the reality of what the company does. Yes, that reality should be fairly represented in company reporting. But it must, of course, be far broader. Corporate reality should be reflected in a genuine culture of high performance with high integrity and sound risk management. Fusing the benefits of great goods and services of high performance with the benefits of adherence to law, ethics, and value of high integrity is the surest route to a potent business organization and strong corporate citizenship.

PART THREE

THE GLOBAL LEGAL
ORGANIZATION
IN THE FUTURE

10

LEADING THE LAW DEPARTMENT[1]

Developing and implementing a vision of the global legal organization is the General Counsel's acid test as a leader of the inside counsel revolution.

A. MISSION

Uniting lawyers all around the world on a core mission—that is not just platitudes—is the bedrock of the law department. At GE, I tried, in best business style, to reduce the essence to a single slide. Of course, I emphasized many of the themes I have sounded in this book. The fundamental task of inside counsel at all levels was to be lawyer-statesmen in helping the company achieve high performance with high integrity. "Help GE Be Fiercely Competitive with Highest Integrity" read the top of my one-chart "Vision for GE Legal."

Our mission was to be "proactive," not just reactive: in business growth, compliance, preventive law, ethics, crisis management ("quick decisions on process, then deliberate speed on substance"), public policy ("advocate and effect balanced change"), and citizenship. But our mission was also to integrate not just high performance with high integrity, not just partner and guardian, but also the past and the future, offense and defense, law and ethics. Importantly, the legal organization should fuse specialists and generalists, lawyers in corporate and lawyers in the businesses, lawyers in the United States and lawyers across the globe, and lawyers exemplifying both individual and cultural diversity.

Finally, I stressed that the legal organization should be a true global partnership. It should, to the greatest extent possible, be collegial, not hierarchical. It should be an organization in which teamwork is highly valued, information is widely shared, common purposes are emphasized, and leadership respects individuals through engagement and participation of all. Like most major corporations, GE had (and still has) a mind-numbing set of HR categories for white-collar employees: officer, senior executive band, executive band, professional band, etc. Each of these "stations in life" then had different levels of not just pay, but benefits and deferred compensation. This created inevitable "status anxiety" across the company. Whenever I could, I tried to deemphasize this bureaucratic stratification and to emphasize that GE Legal worked in task forces that put value on substantive contribution and not on title—that, despite being in a company organized on hierarchy, we had the chance to be a truly collegial law partnership, to truly celebrate each other's victories. If we could share our expertise and knowledge on complex problems, if we could work across different specialty areas, different businesses, and different geographies, then we had tremendous potential power and reach. Paradoxically, I would say, collegiality in the legal organization was a key attribute to gain my support in urging promotions for individuals in the corporate hierarchy imposed on GE Legal.

Delivering this core message was imperative outside the United States. Although the inside counsel revolution is going global, as I discuss in Chapter 12 on future trends, it is still the case that many inside counsel in Europe and Asia have a very limited, even passive, view of their role. Legal may report to the CFO, not to the CEO. It may have a custodial and secretarial function, not the broad role advocated here ("don't speak out, unless spoken to"). Inside lawyers may not be able to avail themselves of the attorney–client privilege. To address these problems, the General Counsel and other senior leaders must be relentless in communicating the organizational vision to *all lawyers*. In new lawyer orientation, we tried to explain this much different and more capacious view of inside counsel. But, driving home the basic vision, ideals, roles—and problems—of the legal organization needs to be done continuously, not just in orientation when new lawyers, especially from other countries or companies, are, frankly, disoriented. This is critical when, as is increasingly the case, 30 percent or more of a global corporation's inside counsel will be from non-U.S. jurisdictions. This training should be based, in part, on hard cases that explore, for example, how to handle pressure from business leaders to cut corners or to approve a course of action that is not in the corporation's interest. The heuristic power of this training could be increased if some of the cases—and some of the training—demonstrated cooperation among Legal, Finance, Compliance, Risk, and Audit staffs and the innumerable issues in which they are involved together. Although I advocated the broad concept, another of my failures was not to have this kind of sustained, sophisticated, and structured discussion on my vision of the inside counsel role—especially the nuances of the partner-guardian fusion—for all lawyers in GE Legal throughout their careers.

B. HIRE THE BEST

For the inside counsel revolution to scale the corporate ramparts, the General Counsel must follow a basic dictum: hire the best. The key to the Legal function's credibility with the CEO and senior line executives is to seek broad-gauged lawyers who are outstanding technical experts, wise counselors, and effective leaders to occupy the top specialist jobs in the company and to be General Counsel in the main operating divisions. Placing the best people in senior lawyer positions across the company also has great ripple effects as these individuals, in turn, build their specialty or business legal groups through other outstanding hires. Top business leaders will say that they spend a significant portion of their time—up to 40 percent—on hiring, compensating, promoting, and retaining people in top jobs. That absolutely must be the case for the General Counsel, and her senior peers, in a large, complex company.

1. THE SPEC

An endless list of the attributes a GC should seek in her senior lawyers can be drawn up. In my nearly 20 years of hiring great people, one attribute was common to all applicants. They had to be outstanding technical lawyers—absolutely at the top of the profession with up-to-date knowledge, tremendous analytic ability, and the judgment to get to the guts of a matter. This was, of course, true when they were being hired as specialists—as head of corporate tax or litigation or environment or trade or labor/employment or IP or M&A. But it was also true for individuals who would be General Counsels of an operating division. If that division was highly regulated, I was disposed to hiring an outstanding litigator; if it were primarily commercial, I had a preference for an outstanding deal/business lawyer. But, these preferences were always trumped by unalloyed quality. Whenever possible, I wanted a person with a sterling professional reputation as a great technical lawyer, with domain expertise in general areas like litigation and transactions or in the many other specialty areas important to the company (tax, IP, antitrust, etc.).

But, on the roles of wise counselor and accountable leader, I also was looking for people who had the "complementary competencies" I described in Chapter 2 on the lawyer-statesman. This often means seeking certain kinds of experience for both specialists and generalists: experience in government, in leadership positions, on business issues, and in international matters. The reasons for leadership, business, and international experience are obvious. But, for me, government experience, if possible, was also important because I believed that working *inside* government gave people a "finger-tips" understanding of broad issues with dimensions far beyond narrow legal questions and a feel for how public-sector institutions worked that they couldn't acquire as easily (although it was not impossible) from representing clients *before* government—in legislative, regulatory, or judicial venues. And virtually all the specialty areas and virtually all the operating divisions were going to have important, if not controlling, governmental dimensions both in the United States and abroad, even those businesses that were not highly regulated. The lead lawyers needed breadth of vision or the ability to develop it fast. An outstanding candidate didn't need to have experience in all those areas, but that is what I was looking for.

As part of the search for people with broad "complementary competencies," I also looked for three key personal characteristics when I was recruiting for the top jobs and especially when I was interviewing the final candidates. I wanted people who had *breadth and creativity*. Innovative problem solving is so important because the beauty of inside lawyering is that it offers endless opportunities to improve the legal function and the corporation, but this requires breadth of knowledge and experience. I wanted people who, in my judgment, had the *chemistry* to work in a complex business environment, both in relating to leaders and in relating to peers on the inevitable cross-functional teams. Most of all, I wanted people with *authenticity and integrity* who were, in their souls, concerned about the quest for what was "right." It is not surprising that I, therefore, was looking for people who could be both partners and guardians. Although I might use a head hunter to develop a list of candidates (sometimes, especially in the early years, I just used my own contacts to generate names), I did much of the reference checking for these top hires myself in personal phone calls. I often asked candidates for people who had been on the other side of cases or deals because I wanted to talk to them, too. My interview with the final candidates was to get a feel for the kind of person they were: The résumés were all outstanding, and so were the references. But I had to make the personal judgment about motivation, character, integrity, and potential chemistry in different corporate settings.

2. THE PITCH

At the beginning of my tenure, I recruited lawyers almost exclusively from law firms and government because the pool of strong inside counsel was not as broad and deep as it would become by the late 1990s and the beginning of this century. The case I made to highly talented "outside" lawyers for becoming senior lawyers "inside" the corporation remained consistent during my time as GC (see pp. 10–15). They would become enmeshed in the fascinating world of global business. They would be part of top business teams, working on business problems. They would join a high-quality, collegial, legal partnership. They wouldn't have to worry about getting business, generating revenue, and filling in time sheets. They would learn more than they could imagine about leadership, business, the world. They could, in important ways, define priority issues for their organization, rather than having their workload dictated by client preferences. They would have significant independence from me. But, they would work as hard or harder than they had in their prior jobs: There are an infinite number of initiatives that can be taken to improve a huge global corporation. (None of my Type A hires ever thought an "inside" job was easier than one "outside"—and they were right, of course.) This pitch worked virtually every time as the inside counsel movement gained momentum in the early 1990s.

But the argument to lawyers who were outside corporations began to have even more purchase as more and more corporations decided to upgrade their legal teams and as more and more lawyers joined those teams from the outside. People began to realize that becoming a senior inside counsel significantly broadened career opportunities. I always told people "give me three or four years in place" but soon enough the "head hunters will come calling" and I would be fine if they then wanted to move on. Specialists could build path-breaking units and be even more prominent in their fields—not just for nationally recognized legal expertise, but for their knowledge and skill in translating that expertise into a highly complex business setting. Lawyers could come into a company as specialists and then become either division GCs or GC of the whole corporation. Generalist GCs in corporate divisions could move to become GC in a larger division within the company. Or they could be hired away and become GCs of major public companies. Senior company lawyers, whether generalists or specialists, could cross over inside the company and assume business roles, from being the senior company person in a foreign country (head of Japan or China or India) to being head of a major business unit (GE Aircraft Leasing) to being head of another staff function (strategic development). Or they could become senior business leaders in other corporations, including CEO. Lawyers I hired at GE followed all these career paths.[2]

3. THE MONEY

In "hiring the best," a recurring question is whether the corporation can match, or come close to, compensation for successful law firm partners. This question also applies to senior government officials who, as they leave their jobs, will likely have a choice between law firms and corporations. And it will surely apply to outstanding lawyers already employed by other corporations who may have substantial deferred compensation (in equity or cash grants) that vests in the future. I always told candidates they should join the company for the challenge, not for the money. But I also said they had a chance to develop more net worth in the company than in a firm. The financial proposition was straightforward. We would try to match law firm draw with cash: a combination of salary and bonus (with the bonus guaranteed in the first year). Both salary and bonus would rise annually, assuming good individual performance and good company (or business unit) performance.

But an incoming senior lawyer would also receive a significant piece of equity either in stock options or restricted stock units, and again assuming good performance, the lawyer could expect an annual equity grant too. Senior lawyers could also participate in longer-term incentive programs (programs that were based on three or more years of sustained company performance). This package had obvious risks. One law firm partner, having agreed to join GE, called to say he had forgotten to ask me one question: "How long is my contract?" My response: "One day." At this level, at least at GE, we were all "at-will" employees. We were making a personal bet on our skills and a financial bet on the company.

Not all global corporations, even major ones, want to "meet market" for senior lawyers in the way I have described. In fact, this issue may be more fraught today than it was in years past. In an attempt to keep revenue producers and participate in the "free agency" market, law firms, of course, have focused on increasing profits per "equity" partner (see pp. 402–406). "Stars" in the 35- to 55-year-old range (a target area for senior inside counsel) can obviously be expensive, with annual profits per equity partner in the top firms exceeding $2 million. Outstanding inside counsel at other companies will be well aware of the different elements of a corporate compensation package and can also pose difficult "meet the market" issues. Indeed, there is evidence that there is increasing competition for outstanding lawyers who are already serving inside companies. To deal with these pressures to "meet market," whether law firm pay or seasoned inside counsel compensation, corporations may ask candidates to take less in annual cash remuneration (not meet the annual law firm draw) and take more risk on future equity appreciation. But these compensation packages for senior lawyers must be structured by boards of directors to reward integrity and severely penalize its absence through hold-backs or clawbacks and other compensation recovery policies. Obviously, I believe that outside legal costs—and overall legal spend—can be reduced by enormously creative and productive lawyers inside the company. For the right lawyer, meeting market is a smart economic as well as legal move.

4. THE CEO

The support of the CEO was the key to any success I may have had in meeting market and hiring great lawyers. Both Jack Welch and Jeff Immelt understood the value of top talent and the need to open the doors and windows of the company to people who had a breadth of experience. Indeed, with Welch's blessing, the Legal function was one of the first at GE to look systematically outside the company for lateral talent. When sending a candidate forward to the CEO, I personally wrote an extended justification, attaching both the bio and my summary of reference checks. I sought to explain my vision of the job and why the candidate was the right fit. Here, our size was an advantage. It was not hard to make the case for a terrific person with a sizable compensation package when a Division General Counsel would be serving in the equivalent of a *Fortune* 25 or *Fortune* 50 company if it stood alone. Nor was it hard to make a case for the specialty leaders. GE had huge, complex tax issues with billions at stake. GE faced multi-billion-dollar environmental issues and, because of its longevity, had more Superfund sites than any corporation in America. GE was a leader in the number of annual patents granted, and the Intellectual Property function was critical to a company with a wide array of cutting-edge technologies and one of the leading R&D functions in the world. GE had major cross-border lawsuits and mergers. In small or medium-sized companies, GCs must assess where they need the best inside lawyers—it may well *not* include all their senior reports—and then make the case to the CEO and top executives. Although GE was unusual, arguments like these can and should be made in any company, if not for as many key players, at least for some.

A vital aspect of CEO support for hiring the best was the willingness of Welch and Immelt to interview candidates for the top 40 to 50 Legal positions in the company (the top specialists; their deputies; division GCs; and, at times, key lawyers in those divisions). The CEOs wanted to judge for themselves what kind of person these candidates were. Both Welch and Immelt had a lot of confidence in their ability to appraise people, whatever the job. Once they had completed the interview and if they liked the candidate, then the compensation issues were almost always resolved with relative ease, even if the market price was high. Indeed, if the CEO was convinced, then he could be creative in order to bring someone aboard. In one case, for example, a candidate with superior government and superior practice experience was going to cost more than the head of the business where he was going to be GC. To avoid a problem, the CEO himself suggested that the company nominally pay him less in salary and bonus than the division CEO but give him a slug of restricted stock units (RSUs) that would fill the gap. These RSUs would be approved by the head of HR for the company and by the comp committee of the board of directors but would be visible neither to HR in the business unit nor to the business head. (The person went on to have an outstanding career at GE and then as a leader in another corporation.)

A great advantage of these initial CEO interviews is that, because he had personally been involved in the hire, the CEO felt comfortable having direct personal relationships with one of my direct line or strong dotted line reports. These relationships often led to real mutual respect and admiration. To me, that was great. It expanded enormously the reach and influence of the legal organization. And the last thing I wanted was to have every communication from the senior lawyers to the CEO go through me. The company was simply too big: I trusted my top colleagues, and I knew I would be involved on any major issues. GE was hardly a frictionless utopia, however. Once we moved past the most senior lawyers, then the specialist leaders or division GCs had to make a strenuous case for people to their business leaders because they had to manage budgets and costs closely. Seeing the CEO example and seeing contributions that new senior lawyers made to the company, senior executives were often willing, however, to work with their own senior lawyers to bring more talented junior lawyers into the company.

5. PROMOTING FROM WITHIN

When I became GC in 1987, I had 33 direct line or strong dotted line reports. I replaced 30 of these with lawyers from outside GE within my first three-plus years. At my first and last "all lawyers" meeting (we became too big), I announced a simple principle about personnel: "We will look inside and we will look outside, and we will hire the best." Until then, if GE lawyers stayed long enough, they had slowly migrated up the organization chart by virtue of seniority because there was no lateral hiring for top positions. Not any longer. Until there was a critical mass of new lawyers I had hired, my "hire the best" speech caused significant discontent in some corners of the legal organization among GE veterans because, initially, I went outside the company for talent. To ameliorate this problem, when I let people go and when they were not of retirement age, I tried to place them as "of counsel" in our law firms and give the firm some business. I tried to give them as dignified an exit as possible. I didn't want to unnecessarily create animosity among their friends who remained. But exit it would be. I had learned from my prior mentors in large organizations that you had to move fast to put your people in place. Despite seeking a soft landing for senior lawyers who were leaving, I was resented within a legal organization that, when I started, numbered about 500 people who felt blocked from top jobs. And, for the most part, they were.

But promoting from within is obviously important for morale, *if quality standards are maintained*. So, another advantage of hiring superb senior lawyers is that they, in turn, could hire other superb younger lawyers into their organizations. My senior lawyers used roughly the same pitch I made about the advantages of working inside a company, and together they created a whole new pool of superior but more junior lawyers in the company. When the first generation of my senior hires moved up in GE or outside to major jobs, I was then able in many cases to promote the next level of new inside lawyers to those senior posts because the senior lawyers had remade their legal organizations. But not always. I tried never to lose my "hire the best" ethos for every position. And, although we had the usual corporate "succession planning" chart for annual HR reviews, I didn't follow it in a rote manner because filling a major Legal job depended greatly on the circumstances facing the function or the business. Still, in later years, we could more often (but not always) promote from within.

6. PUBLIC COMPANY LAWYERS?

It is great that, with the inside counsel revolution, there are now many excellent lawyers working inside corporations. But I do not believe that CEOs, HR departments, and head hunters should focus solely on "public company lawyers" when trying to fill senior positions. Over the years, I have had innumerable calls from head hunters or corporate HR departments looking for talent. Increasingly, they say the search is limited to people currently in corporate legal departments. That is a mistake. Hire the best!!! And lawyers in firms, in government, and in NGOs may be great people/great athletes with visions broader than a corporation—may be the "best" on the criteria I described earlier. If they have had prior organizational experience, they can figure out a major corporation's rhythms and learn the law of "public companies" (or get good advice at the outset until they do). It is a serious mistake to limit the field of view in seeking GCs and other senior inside counsel.

C. DELEGATION

When hiring outstanding people, I felt it was important to explain my view of delegation—of how we would work together. I would first say that because I had so many direct and strong dotted line reports—and had to deal with hyper-kinetic CEOs—that I "couldn't meddle." But, more importantly, I truly believed in giving them substantial autonomy, letting them succeed or fail on their own. They would have control over internal hiring (though I would help as needed), they would choose outside counsel on almost all matters, they would develop and defend their own budgets, they would have "face-time" with the CEO and senior executives, and they would create as strong a professional and public presence in their specialty or their industry as they wished.

Most importantly, I tried to convey both in the hiring process and subsequently in our working "partnership" how delegation on "matters" worked. At the beginning of the year, senior lawyers—specialists, division GCs, and senior lawyers in Europe, Asia, and the Middle East—would send me a four- to five-page outline of goals and objectives, with relatively little prose (minimal paperwork!). The outline would cover high priorities for the coming year in the following categories: deals, disputes, compliance, ethics, CEO initiatives (or their business leaders' demands), public policy, other risks, personnel, and organization. I would then try to have a four- or five-hour conversation to go through the list, in person if possible but via phone or webcast if necessary.

On most of the matters, I might share thoughts or give suggestions, but I would basically say: "These are solely your issues, let's have an update at the six-month mark, but no other reports, unless the matter takes a serious turn for the worse." On five or six of the issues, I might say: "This has consequences for the company as a whole, let's touch base every two months (or less) so I can have a sense where this is going, but these, too, are your matters to manage." On two or three issues, I might say: "This is an issue that is of such importance to the company, the CEO, and the board that I need to be involved on a regular basis. In fact, you and I are going to partner on this; I need to touch bottom and really understand in depth; and, although I want you to have air-time, I may have to present this issue to the CEO and the board." Sometimes, there might not be such top priority issues; sometimes there might be more than two or three. And, finally, I would have my own priorities, where I would ask senior lawyers to work with me—for example, on organization, policy, risk, or CEO initiatives.

During the course of the year, I would try to stay with this plan, although, obviously, new issues might emerge and older ones might drop down the list of priorities. Also, I would interact with the senior lawyers on a special personnel review of their whole organization that was part of the annual HR review conducted across the whole company.

And I would see them at the annual compliance reviews presented by their business to the company-wide compliance review board (on which I served). But I also learned early on to be "careful what you ask for" because nothing drives people crazier than burdensome information requests that then are ignored by the sender (namely, me).

At the end of the year, these senior lawyers would send me the initial goals and objectives list, with brief descriptions under each heading of how they had fared (and descriptions of progress on issues that had emerged). I used this information, as well as many other data points (like talking periodically to their business leaders), in setting compensation (salary, options, bonus) for my direct reports (the company specialists and senior international lawyers). I also used it to participate at the corporate level with the Senior Vice President of HR in reviewing an "affinity" list of all senior lawyers—my indirect reports and other key lawyers—at various compensation decision points: salary adjustments, stock option grants, and bonus determinations. If I felt that the compensation recommendations of the business leaders were out of line (too high or too low), then I had an opportunity to make my views known to my peer at corporate HR and to the CEO (if that important). All this information also went into evaluations of how far in the company the lawyers could go (including moves to the business side). By having a strong personal role in setting compensation and evaluating performance for the top lawyers both at corporate and in the businesses, I hoped to strengthen the legal organization culture so that lawyers would focus on the broad interests of the company and have a voice in resolving possible tensions between the narrow interests of a particular business and the broader interest of the corporation.

Let me stress that this "delegation framework" was trumped when there was a serious emerging problem in a function or in a business division. Then the "reporting up" process I described in Chapter 3 on partner-guardian tension kicked in: The senior inside counsel and the GC were then in constant communication until they had defined that new issue; reported (as necessary) to the CEO/board; and established a process for handling the matter, either in the function/division itself or with my personal involvement (see pp. 71–74).

D. ACCOUNTABILITY: CENTRALIZED OR DECENTRALIZED MODEL

A fundamental, recurrent question for inside lawyers—especially senior inside lawyers—is who holds them accountable for their substantive work: the General Counsel or the business leaders with whom they are working? This question of accountability is closely related to money. Does the corporate Legal function or the business unit pay for the inside lawyer; the outside lawyers; and any settlements, fines, or penalties? It is also related to who hires and fires. The answer to these questions depends, to some extent, on whether a corporation's Legal department is "decentralized" or "centralized."

But it will hardly surprise you at this point if I say that, at the end of the day, *function matters more than form. Let me give my conclusions at the outset, before explaining them.* Regardless of whether the legal organization is centralized, decentralized, or some hybrid: *(1) Inside lawyers should be accountable* **both** *to the GC/corporate Legal function and to the business leaders in the divisions. (2) It is vital for inside lawyers to have a close partnership in the business units with the business CEO and business unit staff and operating leaders. (3) Nonetheless, the GC and the corporate Legal function must protect lawyers working closely in the businesses so that they can carry out their role as guardians. (4) The legal costs of outside lawyers and settlements/fines/penalties should generally be borne in the business division where they arise, but corporate Legal should oversee the budgeting of first-order legal matters important to the company as a whole to ensure that the business unit is not being short-sighted and disapproving the costs needed for an appropriate legal responses to serious problems.*

In a *decentralized legal organization*, the lawyers in the various divisions—whether division General Counsel, other generalist lawyers, or lawyers with specialties (like Litigation, IP, Antitrust, Labor, and Employment)—report on a solid line directly to the CEO of the division. The business units pay for the inside lawyers, outside lawyers, and any settlements or sanctions. In my vision of this decentralized model, the lead lawyers in the business have a strong dotted line to the corporate General Counsel or to the lead specialist lawyers in corporate headquarters. In a *centralized legal organization*, all the lawyers report on a solid line directly to the General Counsel (or her corporate specialist leaders) and serve the divisions or smaller business units on a dotted line basis. Corporate pays for the lawyers. But, for purposes of internal book-keeping, the business pays for outside lawyers and for sanctions because the matter arose in that unit. A *decentralized-hybrid legal organization* is also possible. It can have at least two forms: (1) The specialist lawyers *work in* the business but are "corporate" lawyers reporting to the senior corporate specialist (head of tax, head of litigation, head of labor and employment, etc.) and are on corporate headcount/payroll. The generalist lawyers in the division *work for* the business and are paid by the business. (2) In some foreign markets there may be a cadre of corporate lawyers—both generalists and specialists—who serve all the businesses in that particular geography because none of those business units have the scale to support first-rate lawyers alone. In both hybrids, the businesses pay for outside lawyers and for sanctions arising from their activities. Needless to say, there are many variations of this brief typology.

Whether the legal organization is decentralized or centralized, depends, in important respects, on how the corporation is organized from a business perspective. Some global multinational corporations (MNCs) operate in international markets on a "centralized" business model with a corporate CEO—president MNC Japan, president MNC Middle East—having operational control over all the different business divisions operating in that country or region. Other global corporations have a "decentralized international model," where business divisions go directly to market in foreign nations with operating control in a person employed by the business division (President MNC Medical Japan, President MNC Power Middle East). Often in this decentralized approach, a country executive—who is a corporate, not business division, employee—will facilitate cooperation among the business units and provide a corporate face to the government and the public. But that country executive doesn't have the authority to tell the country business leaders what to do. I have been around long enough to see the pendulum swing back and forth—and back again—between centralized and decentralized international business models.

In the centralized foreign business model, a corps of inside lawyers, employed by corporate, will work for the corporate country CEO and provide services for all the businesses in the area. In a decentralized foreign model, if a business division has scale, it may have its own "in-country" legal staff. If it doesn't have scale, the legal staff in a country may be all "corporate" and serve all the businesses as a "center of excellence" per the decentralized-hybrid type described earlier.

When I was GC, GE went to market globally on a decentralized platform, and GE Legal was primarily decentralized, too. More than 90 percent of the 1,200 lawyers—both generalists and specialists—worked directly for the business divisions. The specialist leaders at corporate headquarters—"the lawyers' lawyers"—worked directly for me, but led cross-company practice groups of all the specialists working in the businesses. In nations where individual businesses had a major presence, they would have their own lawyers—for example, GE Aircraft Engines had its own lawyers in Japan. In global markets where divisions didn't have scale, we would have legal centers of excellence that served all the businesses and that were comprised of corporate lawyers working under a regional General Counsel who reported to me. Under this decentralized-hybrid organization, the General Counsel in the business division and her legal team were accountable directly to the business CEO, who controlled the Legal budget and initial decisions about lawyer compensation (often, I had defined the hiring package if senior lawyers were coming from outside the company). But they were also accountable, *on a dotted line basis*, to me or to the specialist leaders who worked directly with me (Tax, Litigation, Trade, Antirust, etc.).

One key to this strong dotted line relationship of business GCs to GE's GC (or the strong dotted line between the top specialists in the business units and the top company specialists at GE headquarters) was the shibboleth: "Both hire, either fire." That meant that, with respect to hiring division General Counsel—and other top lawyers in that entity—I or my senior corporate colleagues created a slate of three acceptable candidates for the senior legal position in the particular business. The business leader chose from that applicant list (and, often, the GE CEO would bless that decision and the compensation package). However, either the business leader or I could "fire" the business GC or the senior business lawyer if either the business leader or I (or my senior corporate leaders) felt that the senior business lawyer was sub-par in performance. However, despite the "either fire" principle, I could stop a business leader from terminating a top lawyer in the business if I felt it was unjust because the business lawyer had stood up to the business leader on an important issue. I then had to convince the business CEO that the business lawyer had been operating in good faith and try to repair the business lawyer–business leader relationship. If this didn't work, I had to decide if the problem evinced by the business leader was so severe that I had to talk to head of corporate HR to help—or even go to the CEO. Luckily, the very, very few times I faced this problem, I was able to work it out so the lawyer stayed on. I occasionally faced a slightly different problem where the "chemistry" between the business leader and the GC was not good based on personality. I would ask the business leader to give the GC a specific "performance improvement" opportunity, with explicit tasks. But, if that didn't work out and if there were just poor relations, and not a *causus belli* that put the leader in a bad light, then I felt the business CEO should have a lawyer she could trust and I would help outplace the division GC (or other senior business lawyer) either elsewhere inside the company (the advantage of GE's size) or outside. This kind of problem between a senior business lawyer and a senior business leader—which happened rarely, but did happen—is one of the most sensitive a GC will face in a decentralized model. But protecting business lawyers who stand up for integrity is an absolutely critical task for the GC.

I also, as noted, had a significant role at corporate headquarters in assessing salary, stock options, and bonus set for the senior field lawyers employed in the business divisions. Because I was perceived as having a solid professional relationship with the CEO, senior lawyers in the business divisions knew that I could be helpful with the CEO who, even in a decentralized company, was a powerful figure in shaping an individual's compensation and career. Finally, because I had hired most of the senior lawyers over time, I had a strong personal relationship with all of them. They came to GE to be part of the whole company and its Legal group—and easily could understand broad company interests not just the interests of their business unit.

At least for the senior lawyers, I was never concerned about having my voice heard or about their exhibiting independence and courage with their business leaders. I knew that they would come to me privately if there were problems with the business leaders. But, fortunately, because so many of the business lawyers were so capable, they were viewed—almost universally—as major assets by business leaders in the divisions. Many of the factors that applied in my experience will apply to other GCs if they lead a decentralized legal organization.

Within this framework of accountability to the General Counsel and to the company as a whole, I believed strongly in this decentralized-hybrid for the legal organization in a company that goes to market on a decentralized basis. *The fundamental reason is at the core of this book: I wanted most of the inside lawyers to work directly in the operating businesses. They had to be part of the conversations; they had to be at the coffee pot; they had to be liked and trusted by the business staff and business operating peers. Otherwise, they didn't really understand the issues and risks. I didn't want the lawyers to be "corporate." Only when they were part of the business did I think that these lawyers could truly be partner-guardians, could achieve the essence of being an inside lawyer. But I had to be in the background to protect them.*

Of course, as discussed in detail in Chapter 3 on the partner-guardian, there was always the risk—especially as division lawyers were further out in the field with rising, ambitious, and often young P&L leaders— that those lawyers would be asked to do the wrong thing or be unable to make wayward businesspeople do the right thing. But with a strong business division General Counsel and with my injunctions to every lawyer in the company to "call home" (reach out to me directly) if under undue pressure, I felt that the Legal organization could counter those pressures and protect the field lawyer and the company (most of the time). There was also risk that to keep costs down, businesses would under-resource the legal function. But a strong business General Counsel and strong specialty leaders in headquarters overseeing specialty needs in business units could provide counterpressure on this issue too. And they could—and would—elevate serious problems to me. Most importantly, *if the corporate culture was right*, business leaders from division CEOs on down understood the importance of performance with integrity and of addressing legal, ethical, and policy risks. They understood that, if they failed to resource properly and if systemic problems occurred, it could lead to their termination. Here, the CEO warning to top managers—"one integrity miss and you're out"—was essential. At the end of the day, the CEO and the board must hold business leaders responsible for adherence to law and ethics, and this is clearly a direct and essential condition for inside counsel to be both strong partners and also strong guardians. For me, the integration of the inside lawyers into the business units was essential to my vision.

Even if the company's international business operations are organized instead on the centralized model described earlier or if the whole legal organization operates on a centralized model, with the General Counsel hiring all the lawyers and carrying them on corporate headcount, the GC must devise methods for "embedding" most of the inside lawyers in the business organizations. This can be accomplished by ensuring that there is a strong dotted line from the relevant business leaders to the lawyers who have a straight line to corporate legal. In effect, this is the mirror image of the dual relationship for a business lawyer when she reports directly to the business leader but has a strong dotted line to the GC or the company specialist leader at corporate. And, again, both the GC and the business leader "hire" in the sense that the business leader should interview, approve, and work closely with the Litigation (or Tax or M&A or Labor) lawyer serving the business. Similarly, "either can fire" in the sense that the General Counsel must give deference to business leaders dissatisfied with the performance of lawyers serving the business so long as the GC is satisfied that the dissatisfaction is on the merits (and not code for improper business leader views on integrity or risk issues). Moreover, even in the centralized model where the lawyers work directly for the General Counsel, the business leaders should provide meaningful evaluations of the lawyer and have a meaningful say on the various components of lawyer compensation during the annual cycle of setting salary, options, and bonus. Even in a centralized legal organization, co-location of "corporate" lawyers within business is also essential on the powerful "one coffee pot" theory.

In short, whatever the formalities of overall corporate or corporate legal organizational structure, whether decentralized or centralized or hybrid, the functional reality should be that inside lawyers directly serving the business on a day-to-day basis have a partner-guardian relationship with leaders in the business division and a relationship of accountability (and protection!) with the General Counsel and senior leaders in the corporate legal organization.

E. GLOBAL INTEGRATION

The integration of the law department across the world is vital with either a decentralized or centralized model of global legal organization. Global integration increases *esprit*, breaks down cultural differences, helps leverage knowledge sharing, and *instills among lawyers a sense of accountability to each other.* Creating a global legal community is a key aspect of the GC's organizational leadership, unleashing power that is more than the sum of the parts and creating a culture of mutual support among lawyers in different units. The mantra is: Respecting many cultures, creating one culture.

An obvious technique is to have different types of meetings that reflect the complexity and diversity of the company. But these must have real energy by addressing real issues in a productive way. A business division can have regional or global sessions. The company Specialty Practices Groups can do the same—for example, all the tax lawyers or all the litigators both at corporate and in the businesses. All the lawyers in a country, cutting across specialties and business units, can meet periodically—MNC Legal in France, MNC Legal in China. The same is true across regions—MNC Legal Europe, MNC Legal Asia. There should be new lawyer orientation, both in the unit where they work immediately and then, periodically, at the cross-company level to drive home messages about expectations and culture. Finally, Legal leadership—business GCs, the specialty leaders, and the GCs for regions—can meet periodically on a wide variety of topics. (I held such meetings once a quarter.) Despite the cost limitations imposed on travel and living (T&L) expenses, I always hoped most of these meetings could be live because the coffee and sachertorte in Vienna or the group dinner at some funky neighborhood restaurant in Hong Kong were so important to building a culture. These were some of the best memories of my tenure at GE. Obviously, video or telephonic conferences or web-chats may be necessary some of the time. Because T&L is one of the first targets of corporate budget cuts, the GC has to fight hard—and selectively—so these meetings can occur in person, even if not as frequently as she would like.

But, underneath the meetings, there should be vibrant and deep activities that cut across the company. For example, the Specialty Practice Groups, which unite corporate and business specialists, can create a set of shared materials, training, best practices, newsletters, bulletins, discussion groups, and web-chats, just like a Practice Group in a law firm. Similarly, lawyers in a region can do the same thing so that, for example, lawyers in the EU or in China can have a host of activities and materials to share collectively in order to increase their sophistication and reach. The Legal leaders below the GC—corporate specialists, division GCs, regional GCs—need to take responsibility for the breadth and depth in the different substantive, business, or geographic groups in the global legal organization. And, this was one important dimension on which I would continuously evaluate my senior lawyers. (We always had to be sensitive to schedule phone meetings at times that were convenient for lawyers in Europe and Asia, not just in the United States.)

Hiring outstanding local nationals was another vital dimension of global integration. Sending lawyers from the United States to take key positions in Germany or Russia or India or China was a clear second best. Finding great bicultural, bilingual lawyers with bi-educational experience (both inside and outside their nation) is a first priority for companies with significant international operations. One method is to take lawyers on secondment from local law firms, and then hire them permanently if the fit is good. Another initiative is to recruit heavily at masters in law (LLM) programs in the United States that are populated by outstanding international law students. This worked well at GE due to the initiatives of our first generation of American-born and -trained lawyers in Asia, lawyers who wanted to replace themselves with great Asian lawyers. I remember with fondness my last dinner with GE's

30 or so China lawyers on my final trip as GC. It was, of course, at an Asian-International restaurant on the Bund looking out on the sparkling lights of Shanghai and Pudong. The chief regional lawyer who worked directly for me was an old China hand, an American who had been in Asia for most of his career. But he had been instrumental in hiring the other 30 lawyers, who were all Chinese nationals, most with degrees from both Chinese and U.S./EU law schools. They were an incredible group. And future leaders of the regional legal team would be local nationals. In fact, the next head of the GE lawyers in Asia was a Chinese national with an undergraduate degree in China, law degrees in the United States, and prior experience with multinationals in China who had such stature that he was made an officer of GE.

It is hard to overstate the importance of the GC's direct, personal role in global integration—in setting out the vision of inside lawyering, of being a statesman and a partner-guardian, of a great performance with integrity global corporation. I tried to visit every major region at least twice a year. I tried to attend country or regional lawyers' meetings. I tried to speak at business division lawyers' meetings. Most importantly, I tried to meet the younger lawyers in our big organization, especially those from different cultures. Yes, I did video conferences, too. And periodic web-chats, where I took any and all questions for several hours, were valuable. But, nothing could replace the opportunity for me directly to ask questions and listen to younger, more junior members of the organization—to hear their concerns and to indicate, as best I could, that we really were one Legal organization, one partnership, despite the incredible geographical sweep and remarkable diversity. And, nothing was more valuable than delivering in person an essential message: They should never be afraid to speak out, and speak up (all the way up to me).

F. DUTIES TO INSIDE LAWYERS

General Counsels have a host of ethical responsibilities, but none is more important than the duty to inside lawyers. I have, of course, emphasized the GC's task in creating conditions where direct and indirect reports at all levels of the corporation can function as partners and guardians. But there are many other duties, in my view, that GCs owe to lawyers working inside the corporation.

1. HONEST EVALUATIONS/CAREER PATHS

All the way down into the organization, the GC must establish personnel systems that give lawyers honest, constructive, and *detailed* evaluations of their strengths and areas for improvement, both on a per matter and per year basis. HR systems are notorious for the failure of supervisors to take the time and make the effort to give helpful, individual evaluations to the people working for and with them. I certainly plead guilty to this charge, although we tried to improve this vital process over the years. These evaluations need to be the basis for explaining individual compensation decisions—or for letting people go if necessary. Differentiation among great, good, and challenged lawyers is thus important, but mechanistic HR systems (high pay for top 20 percent, solid pay for middle 70 percent, fire the bottom 10 percent) are contrary to the core HR principle of evaluating individuals fairly against their job spec and annual goals/objectives.

Careful evaluations also need to take place within the framework of career possibilities inside the corporation so that individual lawyers can have a realistic sense of how far they can advance. Again, I tried to express the career framework in a single chart—the "gameboard"—which was available to all supervisors and all lawyers. It showed lawyers' development opportunities in their current positions and then four different career paths with way stations from junior to senior along each path: specialists to specialty leader, generalists to General Counsels, practice group participation to practice group leader (e.g., M&A or IP), and lawyer to business positions—from participating on cross-company task forces to moving across to a business side job to becoming a business leader. The annual evaluation should include discussion with the lawyer about where they wanted to move on the career framework chart—and whether that was realistic—and what needed to be done, in what time frame, to get there.

But, I also spoke out frequently that individuals are responsible for their careers and must not wait passively for superiors to tell them what to do and where to go. Corporate Legal has a duty to be candid and to explain potential growth, but senior lawyers must encourage more junior lawyers to press hard, on their own initiative, for development opportunities on a wide variety of tasks. The senior lawyers should initiate personal development plans for their lawyers—but the junior lawyers must also assume personal responsibility because of the bureaucratic history that personnel development is not something normally done with the appropriate intensity by the leaders of the Legal organization who are, invariably, diverted by the press of other business.

Mentoring from a senior lawyer who is not a direct supervisor should also be available to all lawyers, including but not limited to women and minority lawyers. Two or three times a year, the General Counsel should send to the Legal organization a list of senior lawyers who will serve as mentors and urge people to seek out one of those people, if they wish. Supervisors, when doing personnel reviews, should also urge their lawyers to find an independent mentor to get independent advice and counsel outside the reporting relationship. And the General Counsel needs to ask the lawyers, with some frequency, to assess the strengths and weaknesses of the mentoring process.

2. CAREERS FOR INTERNATIONAL LAWYERS

How to promote local nationals outside of their country or region is an issue that bedevils all global legal organizations. The customary problem is whether the highly talented bicultural, bilingual Chinese national lawyer working in Shanghai in one of the corporation's global businesses can be promoted to a pan-Asian job or beyond that into a global job. A newer version of that problem is whether American-trained lawyers can have top-level overseas assignments (if they have the language) when the trend (appropriately so) is to hire local nationals. A truly global Legal department should allow highly talented, experienced, broad-minded lawyers to transcend their nationalities and move up and around the global organization. Good personnel policy balances the importance of learning a job thoroughly with the challenge of moving people outside their "comfort zone" so they can learn and grow. These cross-cultural moves are another key step in global integration. It speaks volumes about the organization being a meritocracy. But it is hard to do. One step is to send national lawyers to other countries on "bubble" assignments for three or six months. A related step is to engage in lawyer "swaps": A competition law lawyer in Europe would exchange places with a competition law lawyer in China for three months. These ideas are great for education, but they don't always comport with short-term legal effectiveness and may require leaders in different divisions to continue bearing the economic cost even if their lawyer is temporarily working in another unit. GCs and senior lawyers need real willpower and courage to take risks on these cross-cultural assignments and, ultimately, on cross-cultural promotions.

3. HIRING YOUNG LAWYERS

I represented the old school General Counsel view about hiring interns or lawyers just out of law school. Don't do it. Inside lawyers don't have enough time to provide the kind of care and training appropriate for young lawyers. It would be a disservice to them and a drain on inside lawyers. Let the law firms train. Then hire laterally after a minimum of four or five years. Whatever the merits of that view in the past, it clearly should be questioned now—and is. When corporations complain about the high cost of associates; are unwilling to allow them to engage in meaningful work for the company; yet want them have an enlivening, not deadening, early career experience—*then they need to reconsider their approach and discharge a duty to help young lawyers have meaningful and motivating early career experiences.* One way to do this is to find creative ways of partnering with law firms to enhance the experience of young associates, as I discuss in Chapter 11 on law firms (see pp. 428–438).

But, a new generation of General Counsel, in companies like Cisco, HP, IBM, and Pfizer, are pioneers in bringing young lawyers directly into the corporation in sharp contrast to my "old school paradigm." The rationale is to get young talent at less cost than imposed by firms and to provide broader, better direct training and experience for young lawyers. There are many questions about such programs: Are there real competency training and mentoring programs? Are young lawyers given meaningful work and real responsibility? Are lawyers who come in so early able to move up the ladder in the legal organization, or do they come in second to talented laterals? Can such corporate-trained lawyers have diverse careers by moving out to law firms or government after five or six years? However, this is a very promising development because young associates so often have such bad experiences at major law firms. Innovative General Counsels who develop such programs should make their methods and results available across the legal community. *I profoundly believe that corporations and law firms have a joint obligation to do a far better job of providing meaningful entry-level jobs to young lawyers—jobs that excite and motivate, not jobs that deaden the spirit and instill a dislike for a life in the law, as is so often the case in law firms due, importantly, to limitations imposed by companies.*[3]

4. THE LAW OF LAWYERING

The General Counsel owes it to the inside lawyers to have crystalline education and training—and clear monographs for reference—on the law that directly affects them. For example, the partner-guardian role will continually raise questions of when a lawyer is giving legal advice that is covered by the attorney–client privilege and when she is providing counseling that is not. It is vital for every inside lawyer to understand the privilege and work product rules (including warnings, exceptions, and waiver), the lead cases involving inside lawyers, the kind of record that should exist when the privilege does apply to a variety of non-attorney actors working for—or being interviewed by—lawyers on legal affairs, and the key areas of ambiguity. The GC simply must ensure that understanding exists for all. Similarly, in jurisdictions like the EU where there is no attorney–client privilege for inside lawyers, the General Counsel must make sure that company lawyers in the jurisdiction know how to protect confidential communications (involve an outside lawyer) and that company lawyers from outside the jurisdiction are aware of the problem if they are doing work inside it. Similarly, inside lawyers must understand thoroughly the reporting up and reporting out regulations under Sarbanes-Oxley and the Model Rules of Professional Conduct, although I advocate a much broader set of reporting up duties for inside lawyers (see pp. 71–74). Further, inside counsel also should know how all the Model Rules apply to them in the context of a corporation. And inside lawyers who are not expert in such matters need to have familiarity with the proper way to conduct internal investigations because they may be involved in such matters, even if they do not lead them. These are just salient examples of the "law of lawyers," which the GC must make sure all inside counsel fully understand.[4]

5. BUSINESS LITERACY

Inside lawyers need basic business literacy if they are to be effective inside the corporation as experts and, more importantly, if they are to be partner-guardians. General Counsels must deploy resources to make this happen. Inside counsel should, at a minimum, have understanding of the following: basic corporate financial analysis (including capital allocation, portfolio management, and competitive analysis), accounting, auditing, controllership, tax, and financial risk management. They should also understand how their corporation assesses actual transactions and investment from a financial perspective so that they learn the particular financial vocabulary their institution uses (including the proliferation of acronyms) and so they can, at a most basic level, understand the financial Management Discussion and Analysis (MD&A) in the Annual Report.

General Counsels have a wide range of options to fill in this knowledge gap for those lawyers who have not already had experience with business matters (or a joint JD-MBA). My effort was called the Advanced Business Course for Lawyers. It was given each year to about 25 high potential lawyers who attended a week-long course at GE's business school where they were taught by experts in corporate finance, including visiting professors from business schools. But this initiative didn't reach enough people, and I should have realized this mistake earlier than I did. I should have created an online course that could have covered some of the basics and been available to everyone. GE had the resources to create its own online education, but today there are many opportunities outside the corporation, including mini-MBA courses for inside lawyers offered by the Association of Corporate Counsel, "executive education" offered for lawyers at both law schools and business schools, as well as a variety of online offerings.

Although I focus here on business literacy, there are a number of subjects appropriate for the continuing education of inside lawyers covering such topics as leadership, organizational change, communicating to non-legal audiences, geopolitical risk, and scientific literacy. General Counsel and their senior lawyers will have to make choices, given resource priorities, but the explosion of good online courses should alleviate this problem. At a minimum, education and training in business literacy should be available.

6. DIVERSITY

General Counsels have a special duty to hire, retain, and promote qualified women, minorities, and lawyers from different cultures. This cliché is true: Corporations serve multicultural communities and need diversity in employees, including in the Legal organization. Although corporate legal departments may, on the whole, have a significant number of women lawyers and some representation of minority lawyers, the process of promoting them into leadership positions still has a great distance to go. For example, in 2014, only 106 Chief Legal Officers (CLOs) in the *Fortune* 500 were women, or 21 percent, progress from 15 percent a decade ago, but still far from the rough parity that should obtain. And, in that year, only 29 CLOs were men of color (6 percent). Moreover, women and minorities are not paid as well as their white male counterparts.[5]

Many of the tools for increasing diversity are well known: widely publicizing senior leadership openings across the organization, keeping good records on trends in diversity profiles in different units of the organization, hiring sensitive headhunters, inclusion of women and minorities on slates, giving stretch and cross-functional assignments, mentoring for those who wish to have it, providing for flex-time, and conducting exit interviews. Corporations should also visibly reward senior lawyers who are diversity leaders. Special preference should also be given to hiring back merit-worthy lawyers who have taken leave to raise a family (and paid leave should be available to both men and women after the birth of a child). The question is not the tools, but the will. On diversity, GCs must make a difference in their law departments and hold senior lawyers accountable for robust processes that should lead to real, meritocratic diversity results. Another test of leadership! (Corporate law departments also have an important role in improving diversity in law firms. See pp. 428–438.)

7. PRO BONO[6]

Corporate law departments have not historically been active in pro bono activities. In one 2013 survey, only 5 percent of GCs said their legal department had a pro bono program! Nonetheless, some GCs have in the past 20 years been leaders in creating special pro bono opportunities for inside counsel. Lawyers for corporations, no less than lawyers in law firms, have a basic professional duty—and often a basic desire—to represent the un- or underrepresented. For example, an umbrella effort, Corporate Pro Bono, is a partnership of Georgetown Law's Pro Bono Institute and the Association of Corporate Counsel. It has a number of programs, including a 2007 initiative challenging signatory companies to involve 50 percent or more of their lawyers in pro bono activities. In another example, GE joined with other corporations in the New York area in 1997 to create the Pro Bono Partnership, which pooled funds to hire an experienced staff to work with 501(c)(3) community organizations in Westchester and Fairfield Counties in defining their legal needs (e.g., employment, environmental, contract, or nonprofit corporation law). The staff then found lawyers inside member corporations to meet those needs. The Partnership grew dramatically over the years, with a budget of $2.3 million in 2014 that served 650 community organizations. It also worked with participating law firms. The model was then used in other communities across the United States. The Pro Bono Partnership is just one example of innovative programs that corporate law departments created, ranging from assistance in local communities to helping the underrepresented in the global economy.

But corporations—and law firms—must face a brute fact: There is a huge gap between the need for civil and criminal representation and resources provided. A next generation of pro bono activities could be more systematic—undertaking a needs assessment for particular communities (cities? states?) with law firms, public defenders, legal aid lawyers, public officials, academics, and community groups in order to define more systematically the need for legal assistance and then develop a plan, with real public/private resource commitments that could help close the scandalous gap between needs and lawyers. For example, 90 percent of people in civil cases in New York State (2.3 million!) needed lawyers according to a 2009 study. In recognition of this problem, GE and United Technologies have started a program, called LawyersCorp Connecticut, to pay a few young lawyers (not inside the corporation) to work with legal aid groups. But, this is just a symbol of the need for a far greater effort from both public programs and private providers. It hardly meets the significant needs.

8. HAVING A LIFE

One of the fallacious arguments for becoming an inside counsel is that the workload is easier than in a law firm. While it is true that billing pressures are not there, a multinational corporation has an infinite number of issues and infinite ways to improve. It is a huge beast swimming in a vast economic and political sea—with huge shoals to navigate and raging hurricanes to survive. Demands from business leaders, from legal leaders, and from lawyers' own sense of duty can easily lead to a 24/7 mentality among inside counsel. Of course, there are huge projects and tight deadlines, and, in a large global company, there is usually a crisis a day of some shape or size. But, in my view, General Counsels need to establish an ethos of keeping work under control—and mean it—so that lawyers may have time for family, pro bono, community, religion, or other activities outside the workplace. GCs should want inside lawyers to be broad citizens, not just expert lawyers, because that is a good in itself but because it also helps them be wise counselors and leaders in their own right. General Counsels and other law department leaders can work hard to increase law department productivity, effect efficiencies, and distinguish between real emergencies and the normal press of business. They have a duty to make sure that they pay close attention to lawyers' workloads so that their colleagues can have a life.

G. INNOVATION, MANAGEMENT, AND COST

Let me note three other critical dimensions of the GC's leadership of the legal organization.

1. INNOVATION

Every year, I tried to work with the company's senior lawyers, at our final quarterly meeting, to establish an "innovation" agenda for the legal organization. I believe that this is a best practice for most corporate law departments. I recognized that every lawyer was working incredibly hard and already had a full plate. But I felt that we all continually needed to make time to change and improve GE Legal. If we didn't confront this issue directly, and establish initiatives explicitly, change would never occur. In some cases, I was seeking ways to define and implement initiatives set by the CEO: Six Sigma/quality, productivity, simplification, continuous improvement, work-out. But, in other instances, the senior lawyers all contributed ideas about company-wide initiatives, and together we would set priorities for the coming year. These included such issues as diversity; early warning systems; creating new technology platforms for businesses, practice groups, or regions; the advanced business course for lawyers; developing new technology compliance tools; improving knowledge sharing; upgrading the technology for reviewing bills and allowing/disallowing cost; and outsourcing functions performed by firms to other vendors—from paralegals to contract legal work to invoice review. The list could go on and on.

I had two favorites. One was outsourcing document analysis, research, and contract work to India, which began in the late 1990s and was unheard of at the time. We did it, in part, to scare developed world law firms—after ensuring quality was good for less cost. But it turned out that the quality of work was excellent, and a real improvement in and of itself for certain types of tasks, because the Indian colleagues were so talented and productive—so we expanded it. A second initiative was the "Manhattan Project." We tried to move outside legal work away from New York firms—"blow them up"—because they were markedly more expensive than outstanding firms in other cities that were comparable in quality. This effort prompted many interesting discussions with firms in New York City that were at risk of losing business and firms outside the city that were eyeing potential matters.

This kind of law department innovation would never have occurred without the remarkable effort from senior lawyers. Because of their commitment to the "partnership" as a whole, these lawyers were willing to take on added responsibility for company-wide initiatives in addition to their taxing specialty or business roles. Of course, innovation can also occur when a particular specialty or business developed a best practice—such as record retention or e-mail training for businesspeople—that other legal groups in the company could adopt/adapt. This cross-fertilization and knowledge sharing can occur in any company of moderate size, but it is a special imperative—and opportunity—in mega-companies with many disparate units and different legal specialties spread across the world.

2. ADMINISTRATIVE LEADER/COO

I never had a Deputy General Counsel. I never had a single special assistant. I never had a chief of staff. I did not want anyone to come between me and the senior lawyers in the company. I did not want anyone else making substantive requests on legal or policy matters that would take up the time of my direct (or strong dotted line) reports. In trying to hire the best, I was, as noted, prepared to delegate. Every GC and every legal organization will have its own style and culture, but I felt that, to the extent the senior lawyers had loyalty to me (they will speak for themselves!), it was because, importantly, I left them alone (most of the time).

In a legal organization of any size (from 12 lawyers to 1,200), the GC still needs certain key types of support, however. In a large company like GE, specialists from the HR function handled personnel issues with lead lawyers both at corporate and in the business divisions. The same was true for members of the finance function who assisted with the Legal organization's financial and budgetary issues. In smaller companies, the GC must work with the CFO and HR head to get properly tailored personnel and finance assistance for the Legal organization.

In my view, GCs also need a Senior Counsel–Legal Operations (the name I used) or Chief Operating Officer/COO (the title widely used today). This leader for operations is now becoming more and more common in legal organizations of moderate size (20 to 50 lawyers) and *de rigueur* in mega-corporations (more than $10 billion in annual revenue). This person will often have a law degree but may also have an MBA and/or managerial experience. *In essence, the job of the COO is to manage inside and outside resources and to drive innovation in order to continuously improve the law department's efficiency and effectiveness.* This person undertakes visible initiatives with real impact. She will work with the legal leaders to drive innovation ideas across the legal organization, whether they are reducing cost, increasing productivity, implementing uniform standards, being on the forefront of technology, or increasing the effectiveness of the legal intranet. Alternatively, she will lead innovative initiatives herself, especially ones that mirror broader corporate efforts like productivity or quality. The fundamental mission of improving legal operations through innovation is now a critical job in law departments, not only because of inevitable cost pressures, but because the pace of technological change is so rapid. Continuous improvement covers better management in such key areas as information, intellectual property, litigation, contracts, transactions, and day-to-day administration. It can provide tools to create virtual deal rooms, digitized environmental compliance, practice group document troves, and early case assessments.

Of all the possible tasks, there is little doubt that the legal organization's head of operations must have changing technology—and its numerous applications—as a primary focus. Increasingly, technology touches, and can improve, almost every aspect of law department operations. It is, of course, based increasingly on the capacity to digitize core functions and to utilize computerized databases. It increasingly uses third-party vendors, not law firms (a broad trend often called "Legal Process Outsourcing"). The Legal Operations Leader/ COO can bring to the legal organization's annual process of setting innovative priorities a cutting-edge set of alternatives for changing everything from organizational needs assessment and strategy, to intra-organizational best practices sharing, to global integration, to using big data for important decisions (including fixed fees with firms), to moving work from law firms to more technology-savvy vendors, to tracking law department initiatives, to step function improvements in the management of budgets, projects, documents, and cases. A second closely related core task is working with the finance staff to develop sophisticated and disaggregated metrics for measuring costs, effectiveness, and efficiency. She will then work with the whole organization to embed those metrics in legal operations in quest of the business holy grail: true productivity improvements. This will usually mean a central role in patrolling the contested frontier over economics between law departments, law firms, and third-party vendors, a subject I cover in Chapter 11.[7]

3. COST

The importance of sophisticated metrics is illustrated by the inadequacy of the traditional measures of law department expenditures.

A key historic metric for legal organizations is total annual legal spend: the cost of inside lawyers plus the amount spent on outside law firms and other vendors serving the Legal function (but excluding the costs of verdicts or settlements). A crude measure of legal organization efficiency is total legal spend as a percentage of total corporate revenues compared to peer companies. On this metric during my tenure, GE was at the bottom of the second lowest quartile of large companies (defined at the time as having more than $5 billion in revenue) as surveyed by third-party accountants or consultants. But there were all sorts of problems with this number. To be at all meaningful, the number had to be viewed over time. In one year, there could be an unusually large amount of transaction work—which might be good but would raise legal costs as a result of business, not legal, decisions. In another year or sequence of years, there could be sharp increases in suits or enforcement actions brought against the company and in the legal spend to respond—which would be bad but could be the result of bad business practices, not legal decisions (unless the lawyers had failed in their compliance duties). Another key methodology question, of course, is the definition of "peer" companies. The diversity of companies with revenues greater than $5 billion was huge. More appropriate comparisons would be between large companies *in like industries* because the baseline legal needs of different industries will be different: oil and gas not the same as technology not the same as capital goods not the same as financial services not the same as communications. But the surveys did not make those distinctions.

Another common number is inside legal spend as a percentage of total legal spend: 40 percent, 50 percent, 60 percent? An increase in inside legal spend can mean lower total legal spend if highly talented and productive lawyers are working closely with business leaders and doing the corporation's legal work rather than using their contact lists to call law firms. In my time at GE, we changed the inside/outside ratio from about 40–60 percent to 60–40 percent. The inside spend would have been higher but for GE Capital, which did about $20 billion a year in transactions with outside lawyers serving as the "deal factory." There is a clear trend for corporate law departments to bring more and more *high-value work inside to reduce cost, increase efficiency, and generally improve service to businesspeople.* But, the ratio by itself may be misleading. For example, increasing inside cost can be harmful in the longer run if that head count, with attendant accumulating benefit cost, is being directed to increasingly commoditized work that could be being provided even more cost-effectively by non-law firm outside vendors.

In the new, more sophisticated world of law department management and finance, *determining appropriate cost would ideally be "reality based," turning on the opportunities and risks associated with different corporate activities.* The cost analysis should involve developing and implementing not just metrics for the legal organization as a whole, but, importantly, for specific legal areas—Tax, Trade, Antirust, M&A, etc.—as applied to specific businesses within the corporation and to different geographies. Where can there be fewer resources? Where should there be more? What is the mix between inside/outside legal and non-lawyer resources? As I emphasize in Chapter 11 on law firms, within that disaggregated matrix, law departments *must prioritize and segment the work* from routine with low risk to recurrent with moderate risk to repeating cases with high risk to one-off consequential cases to one-off potentially catastrophic or transformative matters. This type of segmentation is a fundamental first step in deciding whether work is done most effectively and efficiently with inside counsel or outside law firms or other vendors or software programs, leaving enough flexibility to alter the mix as technology and other fast-emerging methods affect cost structures. There are now legions of consultants and experts willing to assist legal departments with these fine-grained, context-specific issues. There are also public materials—including those available from the Association of Corporate Counsel—that systematically array the linked sets of issues relevant to Legal organization cost (covering such topics as evaluation methods, performance metrics, staffing options, budgeting, process management, technology, knowledge management, and value-based fee structures with law firms).[8]

There are two problems with what I suggest as the ideal—a risk-and-opportunity-based approach that looks at discrete areas across prioritized, segmented activities in different business units and geographies. One problem is that the legal department may lack the financial sophistication to produce such an analysis. Another is that the corporate budget process for staff functions is usually too blunt and too truncated to accommodate sophisticated detail. Critical as staff functions are, they are a tiny fraction of the budgetary and resource allocation decisions the CEO makes. So, after grinding through days of long meetings on big divisions during budget season, business leaders may want it "short and simple" on staff functions. Legal can work with Finance prior to the CEO meeting, but that meeting may still be relatively brief. Although they reserve the right to make final budget decisions, business leaders may not want to spend too much time or listen too carefully. GCs and other legal leaders, therefore, may want to present their budgets according to the following business themes *and always in the context of total inside/outside legal spend to avoid* **stupid** *inside head count reductions that actually increase outside spend and total legal costs.* Here are some possible thematic areas explaining the gives and takes in the legal organization budget:

- Areas where there can be *increased productivity and reduced cost*—by doing the classic "more with less" or, if possible, simply eliminating work. For example, lawyers in GE's litigation function developed an "Early Dispute Resolution" process to mediate private suits or other controversies immediately (during the initial months of the matter). This literally cut the litigation budget of the company in such private disputes by almost 50 percent because many cases were resolved without lengthy discovery or trial. Demonstrating productivity enhancements or simple cost reductions, especially with new technology, creates a precious commodity for General Counsel: budgetary credibility.

- Areas where an increased investment in legal resources can *add actual direct financial value to the corporation*: for example, tax (to increase lawful tax efficiency and book income), trade (to make markets more open), intellectual property (to secure license income), litigation (if there are circumstances where the company can be plaintiff), M&A (if there is a high level of deal flow and skilled inside lawyers are better business partners and cheaper than outside law firms), and improving the quality and simplicity of fully compliant environmental protection (to improve manufacturing productivity).

- Areas where continuation at current levels (assuming, again, demonstrated productivity and efficiency with existing resources) or an increase in legal resources is necessary *to avoid important risks*: for example, meeting an actual pattern of increased government enforcement/private litigation or preventing a serious or catastrophic risk from occurring that would occasion significant reputational and financial costs far beyond the increase in budgetary resources. For example, although it was a hard sell and I failed more often than I succeeded, I believed that we needed to "over-resource" emerging markets because the integrity risks were so high.

- Address existing one-off high-risk or high-value areas that are nonrecurring and that constitute a spike in the budget. This can include defensive matters, like response to a catastrophic event such as BP's rig explosion in the Gulf, or offensive ones, like a huge global transaction that will require both extensive due diligence and negotiations as well as substantive clearances in many jurisdictions. It may be desirable to break these out of the regular budget and display them as the special, one-off items they are. This special budgetary treatment accords with the special treatment given to the issue as a whole by the CEO, who is doubtless preoccupied with matters of such large magnitude.

The General Counsel, with the aid of the senior lawyers and finance experts, must make a solid, impactful case either for expenditures to achieve productivity/cost reductions or for investments that will create financial value. GCs and their teams must explain their systematic assessment of the effectiveness and efficiency of using inside v. outside resources (as discussed in Chapters 11 and 12). These demonstrations then give her credibility also to secure the resources necessary for prevention and risk mitigation even though, as discussed, proving the "benefit" of avoided cost is a challenging financial assignment.

Without question, the future health of the inside counsel revolution will turn on the ability of General Counsel, senior counsel–legal operations, and other senior legal leaders to take their game up significantly in financial analysis and budget discussions regarding evaluation, performance metrics, productivity, and cost savings. Only then will the GC be able to secure additional resources, as necessary, both to create concrete financial value and to address the broad array of risks now facing global corporations, resources that may be deployed for inside lawyers, outside law firms, or third-party non-law firm vendors.

H. EXPLAINING THE LEGAL ORGANIZATION TO BUSINESS LEADERS

GCs need to find a forum apart from the Procrustean, truncated budget process in which to present to the CEO and other business leaders a vision of the legal organization that would encompass many of the ideas not just in this chapter but in this book as a whole. When I was GC, I failed in this explicit task. But word of mouth saved me—as business leaders all across the company saw the constructive contribution a new breed of inside lawyers could make to the corporation. Nonetheless, developing an hour-long briefing on such basic topics as mission, performance with integrity, partner-guardian, culture, adding direct economic value, compliance, ethics, risk, corporate governance, citizenship, and legal organization finance and structure (centralized v. decentralized, inside v. outside) could have many uses. The GC could present it alone to the CEO; present it to a quarterly meeting of top business leaders; present to division CEOs; and, of course, present it to the board of directors. The presentation could demonstrate the alignment between the priority tasks of the Legal organization and the core business tasks of commercial strategy, innovation, productivity, risk management, emerging markets, and talent upgrades. It could advance metrics beyond legal budget, head count, and number of cases against the company to measurements more robustly capturing the value creation of the legal function. This pitch would make explicit for senior executives the nature and benefits of the inside counsel revolution so that fundamentals like partner-guardian become a cornerstone of corporate culture. Because it would provide a framework for budget discussions outside the budget process, it could help provide critical context for subsequent CEO decisions about legal cost. It could have the added benefit of being the foundation of the training for lawyers new to the organization—both during and after initial orientation—that, as suggested earlier, could explore the complexities of being inside counsel in a more nuanced and sophisticated fashion.

11

LAW FIRMS—
AND ALTERNATIVES

The inside counsel revolution has changed the legal profession. There has been a dramatic shift in power from outside law firms to inside legal departments as General Counsel and senior lawyers assert their leadership over outside suppliers. Inside lawyers have forged new forms of authority and new forms of cooperation on *matters* and fostered new competition, new control, and new partnerships on *money*. On matters, inside counsel—who increasingly have knowledge, skills, and experience at least comparable to their peers in outside firms—now often set strategy and provide day-to-day oversight in major law department–law firm engagements affecting the corporation. On money, inside lawyers—driven by the endless corporate drive to do more with less—increasingly exercise control, often seeking to restrain and focus the law firm spend in quest of high value at a fair price *or to replace law firms altogether.*

This chapter explores key issues for the General Counsel and senior inside lawyers in managing the vital but fraught relationship with law firms in an era of significant economic transformation of the legal profession. But it makes a larger point. General Counsel and senior lawyers need to look at all types of resources when determining the appropriate mix for different types of matters or problems: inside lawyers, law firm lawyers, other types of lawyer organizations, and non-lawyer vendors of law-related services, especially technology. The mix will, in turn, depend on the segmentation of the corporation's legal work—from simple to complex, from low risk to high risk, from low stakes to catastrophic impact.

Since the beginning of the inside counsel revolution, legal department relationships with law firms have been driven by two fundamental General Counsel and inside counsel attitudes. Corporate law departments respect the talents of outstanding practitioners, who can be great partners in providing both superior technical expertise and wise counseling on issues of performance, integrity, and risk. *But legal departments dislike, often intensely, a law firm economic model that inexorably is seeking to increase revenues, often without regard to value, at the same time that corporations are inexorably striving to reduce costs and enhance value.*

A. PROBLEMS: A BRIEF BILL OF PARTICULARS

As described in Chapter 1, the inside counsel movement began in the late 1970s due, in part, to problems law firms presented. In that era, the emerging bill of particulars against law firms would have included the following charges. Despite numerous law firms, most major companies dealt with an oligopolistic structure of relatively few outside firms, which reduced competition. This structure was due to docile inside lawyers at the time who gave business to their favorite firms or to the favorite firms of their business leaders. This oligopolistic structure spawned other problems. Invoices were opaque with a line item—"for services rendered"—followed by a large number. That number was not predictable. Other billing practices were abusive as law firms marked up routine support services such as copying or travel or typing to gain additional margin. Legal costs were on the rise as complexities of the regulatory state and burgeoning globalization affected business. The outside lawyers were arrogant, viewing the inside lawyers as failed, second-class citizens who had not become law firm partners. Those outside lawyers, with their alleged superior knowledge and skill, took control of matters inside counsel had thrown to them over the transom. The imbalance in information and skill made inside counsel reluctant to switch law firms. This schema of the problems is overdrawn, but perhaps not by much. Certainly, the pioneers of the inside counsel movement, who began to take back power, had concerns like these.

The inside counsel revolution introduced more competition into the law firm market. But, as a result, inside counsel also had to address a new, significant set of issues that emerged as major law firms, responding to competitive forces, began the transformation from an association of professionals to more disciplined business organizations. This process began more than a generation ago, and I lived through its rise. Although the issues are today well known and much discussed, I mention them briefly because they remain problematic. They are still the frequent backdrop as law departments seek to structure law firm relationships.

First, partner loyalty to law firms broke down with the growth of "free agency." At first shockingly, and then routinely, partners with large books of business left their firms for a more remunerative package (including annual guarantees) at other firms. Following the publication of law firm revenues and compensation in *The American Lawyer* in 1987, the key metric for many law firms became profits per partner (PPP). The spontaneous combustion of free agency and the cult of PPP further eroded loyalty to firms as associations of professionals. Law firms competed more openly and intensely for clients. But a second important market developed: the competition among law firms for top business getters who could grow the top line. This competition, in turn, led law firms to ever-more-intense efforts to increase revenues, expand margins, and boost PPP to keep their business getters in the fold and to stop other valued lawyers from defecting. When partners with business and without loyalty deserted firms in droves, the law firm could go into a death spiral (e.g., Brobeck, Coudert, Heller, Howrey, Dewey).

Second, in order to feed the PPP mouths, law firms and corporations began to have increasing conflicts over money, which has been—in my long-standing view and the view of many others—nothing less than a cancer in inside lawyer/outside lawyer relations for more than a generation. As part of companies that are on an endless quest for lower costs, corporate law departments continuously had to demonstrate to their business leaders that they could meet the traditional definition of productivity: Do more with less. As they evolved toward a more rigorous business model, law firms defined "productivity" in exactly the opposite way: They measured success by increasing the number of lawyers and the number of billable hours—and the rates of increase in fees charged. Put a different way, they measured "inputs" for the firm (hours, lawyers per matter) rather than "outputs" for the client. The symbol of this backward view of productivity was "leverage," the ratio of lawyers to equity partners. For many firms (although not all), a high leverage ratio became an important measure of financial success based on the simple equation that more lawyers per equity partner equals more money. But this created short-term pressures to reduce the number of equity partners and to find work for all those non-equity lawyers (regular associates, permanent associates, and the increasing number of "non-equity partners"). This short-term pressure, in turn, inhibited firms from spending "margin dollars" on innovation for clients, associate competency training, using leaner teams, or providing elderly partners a graceful exit. The emerging "business model" law firms generally did not sail by the north star of client-oriented performance measures such as value in results, client satisfaction, and percentage of clients who are repeat customers. Rather than seeking to reduce costs and prices to retain profit margin as businesses do in normal competition, law firms sought to increase revenues and price to maintain or expand margin—and profits per partner. The economic approaches of the legal department and the law firm, as I have presented them here in outline, were sharply in conflict. There was a true "productivity disconnect," a "primal and fundamental tension," or, in my terms, a recurring cancer.[1]

Third, additional problems from an inside counsel perspective stemmed from two related trends: the emergence of mega-firms though acquisitions of other firms or practice groups and the planting of the mega-firm flag around the world as multi-office global institutions. The theory of the mega-firms, in simplest terms, was that they could provide one-stop shopping for all legal problems of their globalizing corporations. They could provide high value through true collaboration among their different practice groups and different offices. They could return to the days when they had a dominant oligopolistic or even monopolistic position with clients. Thus, we saw the emergence of far-flung firms with lawyers numbering more than 2,000: Jones Day; Clifford Chance; Linklaters, Allen & Overy; Latham & Watkins; and Freshfields. By 2013, there were 24 American firms with more than 1,000 lawyers, most with international outposts.[2]

But, I have always been highly skeptical about the capacity of mega-firms—especially those that are global empire builders (Clifford Chance is in 26 countries)—to offer true, high-level service across diverse subject matter areas and across diverse geographies. The general problem is this: They try to cross-sell specialties and geographic presence that vary widely in quality and culture. Here, in brief, are some of the more particular inside counsel concerns: (1) Mega-firms may not achieve cost synergies when buying other domestic and international firms, often using debt financing. Instead personnel, infrastructure, space, and debt service costs can increase, which leads to pressure for higher prices and greater revenue. Megas may have to bill for two-thirds of a year to meet a very large cost "nut" before they make any profit. The anxiety of this annual money chase to cover a big cost number can lead to revenue targets per lawyer—and to overstaffing, excess billing, and lack of quality control. (2) Thus, the megas are *especially prone* to adopting the Orwellian definition of productivity: "less with more." (3) As firm locations expand and both professional and nonprofessional employees multiply, the risk of a "mediocre middle" in these megas raises significant problems. With size and dispersion, it is very hard to sustain excellence and create and maintain a unified culture of quality and service. This may be especially so when there are culture clashes between the different offices in different nations. This is a problem for global corporations, and it is surely one for global law firms. (4) If there is no strong, uniform culture of excellence, then one of the main claims for the mega-firm—the cross-selling of specialties—is a very questionable proposition. Why should a great deal lawyer in a London Magic Circle firm be able to sell a global corporation an environmental lawyer in the UK? Why wouldn't the environmental specialists in the corporation determine which outside counsel is best for a tough environmental problem in Britain? (5) Similarly, the geographic cross-sell is also a questionable proposition. Why should that great deal lawyer in the London Magic Circle firm be able to sell the global corporation the firm's environmental lawyer in India, when the inside environmental specialists and the corporation's Indian counsel should make that determination on the merits in a very complex jurisdiction? (6) The mega-firm is a maze of conflicts of interest. When there is a conflict about a new matter between existing clients, which one does the firm jettison—assuming the conflict is picked up at all?[3]

As law firms began to focus more and more on being business organizations, they professionalized key staff, with bigger firms having business school graduates serving as COOs, CFOs, directors of Pricing, and HR directors. But this business orientation tended only to drive the firms more "professionally" in their quest for revenue often without regard to productivity from a client perspective.

B. SOLUTIONS: A BRIEF HISTORY

Just as the problems law firms presented changed over time, so did the solutions General Counsel and inside counsel adopted to address them. It is important to summarize the phases of this response because the future of law department–law firm relations also builds on different elements of these past efforts. I describe five different phases. But they were not that clearly distinct. Elements of earlier phases remained in later phases. And corporate legal departments did not uniformly march from one phase to the next. As one would expect, there was— and is—great variation in how corporations have tried to manage their law firm relations. Thus, what follows is obviously just a sketch, but one I hope highlights the essential changes that have occurred and that will shape the future.

In Phase One, which began in the 1980s after the start of the inside counsel movement in the late 1970s, the fundamental goal was to break up the oligopolies and to end the dominant position over different pieces of a corporation's legal business held by a relatively few major law firms. The mantra, which is now a cliché (but clichés are true!), was vibrant then: *"We hire lawyers, not law firms."* As General Counsels began to hire outstanding inside counsel, especially outstanding specialists, these inside lawyers would make their own ad hoc decisions on who would handle the wide variety of corporate matters in a wide variety of legal domains. Initially, the approach was not systematic. The inside lawyers, who had often come from law firm practice, began to place or compete business based on their knowledge of excellent practitioners. They were not bound to the corporation's old war horses. They also began to do much more of the high-quality work themselves. A signal was sent. The new breed of inside counsel were going to challenge the long-standing relationships between client and the old firm. Competition among outside firms, and moving work inside, would begin.

In Phase Two, which followed soon thereafter and continues to this day, General Counsel and inside lawyers sought to *make competition much more systematic* and to attack costs much more directly. Legal departments issued detailed "outside counsel guidelines" for law firms. These guidelines, among other things, disallowed double billing on air travel or mark-ups on a host of routine activities like word processing, photocopying, faxing, or telephone use. More importantly, corporate lawyers began to formally bid out work through real competitive procedures. These ranged from the informal (letting several major firms know that they could make a proposal to take on a major deal or case) to the more formal (putting out a Request for Proposal that required formal bids) to the extreme (electronic real-time, online bidding contests). These competitive bidding processes often sought a "blended rate" and discounts off "list price" hourly rates. At least in the early days, they generally did not attempt to negotiate a fixed fee. But, *law departments did use tasked budgeting and billing in an attempt to control costs at the front end.* This initiative was so important that it led to "task codes" for different types of matters developed with the assistance of the Association of General Counsel and the ABA. And cost control also involved a variety of techniques at the back end. Detailed invoices replaced one-line bills. E-billing systems emerged with "search" capacity that could spotlight items that were outside the counsel guidelines or that could highlight other questionable charges.

Formal audits were sometimes imposed on a spot or systematic basis. Law departments began to negotiate for bill reduction or simply to disallow billed amounts.

In Phase Three, which began to take hold in the mid-1990s, General Counsel sought to simplify the competitive landscape that was changing outside counsel interactions from the "relational" (days of yore) to "transactional" ("lawyers, not law firms"). Law departments started to develop lists of *preferred providers* for different areas of the law. Even before this formal "preferred provider policy," the upgraded inside counsel often had special relationships with new law firm lawyers with whom they worked frequently, counsel who were implicitly preferred providers. The cliché of moving law department–law firm interactions from "relational" to "transactional" was never entirely accurate. The "lawyers, not law firms" dictum never led to universal, atomistic "spot contracting" on most matters as some have claimed. Even the early competition introduced by legal departments had strong elements of preference in limiting competitors and strong modes of continuing cooperation and relationships with outside lawyers.[4] The relationships were just more on the merits, and the players were changing.

In establishing formal preferred provider programs, inside lawyers often relied on personal relationships with the key senior lawyers in competing law firms. Preferred providers qualified on a number of criteria: quality of work; ethic of service; knowledge of the company; results; and, in some programs, their efforts on diversity and pro bono. The law department committed to limit consideration of representation from the list of preferred providers—or to give that provider a minimum amount of business each year. In return, the preferred provider committed to having certain high-quality lawyers ready to work on the particular type of matter and often to give a discount on rates. I always viewed discounting with skepticism because legal departments often could not cut through the fog to understand how the fee had been set or could not stop firms from increasing the number of hours and thereby trumping discounts by generating even more revenue. A 10 percent discount off a rate that was too high to begin with and that was attached to too many hours was obviously not much of a deal. In response to this problem, some preferred provider relationships began to rest on negotiated fixed fees, rather than on hourly rates, a new development that would become increasingly important. Often, preferred providers were simply a small law practice inside a big law firm. The inside counsel had a relationship of trust and dealt directly with the key partner leading that group in that firm.

In Phase Four, some General Counsel and inside lawyers took the concept of preferred providers a step further to develop *strategic alliances* with far fewer law firms, as summarized in a leading article by Professor Wilkins. Pioneers like DuPont and Pfizer dramatically reduced the number of firms serving the corporation.[5] They struck a deal to give the law firm much or all of the company's work in a particular area. In exchange, the firm would take a flat annual fee for that effort. Law firm lawyers could work inside the company and learn it more thoroughly. The company would pay the total cost in regular increments, reducing cash flow problems for the firm. The company could budget predictably and sharply reduce (but not totally avoid) the back-end effort of parsing bills. But these arrangements were negotiated, unlike the old oligopolistic days of favored relationships, and they were time limited (several years). They were also subject to equitable adjustments, depending on the experience during the year. Unlike the first three phases, which were widely followed by many corporations, these broad strategic alliances covering large blocks of work for a year or more were not for everyone. Indeed, under a new General Counsel, Pfizer itself has begun to question the quality of services and the inflexibility of its model. But a less dramatic variation on the "strategic alliances" theme was to give a law firm a narrower book of business, which looked a lot like a preferred provider arrangement except the law firm was paid on a fixed-fee basis.

Finally, in an emerging Phase Five, some corporate legal departments are seeking to *integrate more completely with law firms and make them strategic advisors*. Intel is an example of this development, which Bill Lee, former managing partner of WilmerHale, described in an essay on future roles and responsibilities of lawyers, co-authored with David Wilkins and me. Intel identifies three groups of attorneys at its preferred law firms: (1) leaders, who are the senior advisors with whom Intel entrusts its major cases; (2) the next generation of partner-leaders, identified by Intel and its firms, who will handle the major matters of the future; and (3) promising and talented non-partner attorneys and staff working on Intel matters. The law firm and Intel team leaders set goals and objectives at the outset of every major matter, which are reviewed quarterly. For each major matter, there are joint Intel and law firm teams that include lawyers from all three firm categories. The firm and Intel team leaders together determine matter-appropriate fee arrangements from fixed to incentive to hourly. And at the conclusion of every case or matter, Intel and the law firm conduct a "lessons learned" session in which they discuss what went well—and not so well.

But Intel's commitment to its firms extends beyond specific cases or books of business. For example, Intel brings its outside and inside lawyers together each year to meet with business executives at Intel to give the law firm attorneys the opportunity to understand Intel's business plan and see how Intel's legal work fits into that business plan. To instill loyalty, Intel also commits to give "next-generation" attorneys mid-size cases to handle. It provides a steady stream of work to both the next-generation attorneys and to the identified non-partner attorneys so they can gain institutional knowledge about Intel. Intel also hosts periodic "fireside chats" with selected, younger outside lawyers—during which the identified attorney presents and discusses with the leaders of Intel's legal department a long-term business or legal issue Intel may confront. Each quarter, Intel inside lawyers sit down with the leaders of its law firms to discuss and review each attorney working on Intel cases and provide individual feedback to the inside lawyers on those attorneys. Likewise, Intel seeks and receives feedback on its inside lawyers from the law firms in order to understand how the relationship is viewed from the law firms' perspective. All of these "integration" commitments ensure that Intel can help the firm identify and train a group of lawyers that will deliver the best services possible over the short and long term.[6]

Beginning in Phase Two (more competition/cost controls), corporate law departments also began to look for alternatives to law firms altogether—in other lawyer providers and other non-lawyer vendors. For example, in addition to outsourcing legal work to India in the mid-1990s, GE started to seek stand-alone paralegal firms that charged far less than the firm's paralegal services. Many other legal departments experimented as well. As the different phases of law department–law firm relationships evolved, the search for alternatives to law firms grew with increasing velocity

C. THE PRIMACY OF SEGMENTATION

In thinking about what resources to use on a corporation's legal matters, a first and fundamental step is to segment the type of work according to degree of expertise and judgment required and degree of complexity and risk/opportunity presented. This segmentation analysis—which has its roots in the beginning days of the inside counsel revolution—has at least two dimensions. First, what is the *type* of work? And second, what are the component *tasks* of that type of work? Decisions about what mix of resources is appropriate and how to manage them stems from sophisticated segmentation. Here, for example, are five different *types* of legal matters facing a corporation:

- A single project involving expertise and judgment, but presenting limited complexity and risk, such as writing a handbook, creating form contracts, developing a compliance education and training program, or monitoring developments in evolving areas of law.
- A repeating, routine book of business, which involves expertise and judgment and moderate risk and complexity, such as filing a certain type of patent or trademark application, monitoring compliance with environmental permits, handling routine labor matters in arbitration (as opposed to court), or negotiating contracts with franchisees.
- A repeating, but more complex book of business that involves a higher level of judgment, expertise, and risk, such as annual securities reporting, a line of product liability cases, a series of venture capital financings, or more complex multiparty contracts for capital equipment sales.
- A one-off, highly complex, high-risk matter that requires a great degree of expertise and judgment. Some one-off matters may

have historical antecedents: the expensive class-action litigation for the drug company; the antitrust investigation in multiple jurisdictions; the transaction to double the company's size with a target in similar lines of business; the patent infringement case against a major competitor. Other high-risk matters may arise on new frontiers: a patent-defense action in China; a novel set of product liability suits with major potential liability; the huge acquisition of a company in a different line of business operating in different jurisdictions.

• The high-impact, potentially catastrophic or potentially transformative matter that is in the somewhat hyperbolic "bet-the-company" category. Due to outsized impact, this is the extreme variant of the previous type—the one-off, highly complex, high-risk matter. Examples are the Siemens bribery scandal; the BP *Deepwater Horizon* explosion; the concerted enforcement actions against financial services firms; or the mega-merger that will completely reshape the company, like Comcast and Time Warner (which failed).

As noted, after determining types of matters, there is a second aspect of segmentation that breaks the matter into different *tasks*. To take a common example, in litigation, there are a wide variety of discrete tasks just relating to documents alone: document production, document discovery, document analysis, document authentication, document management, and document organization for trial. Each of these tasks may require a different kind of legal process resource or combination of resources. It is simply not possible to manage a corporation's legal business sensibly without segmentation into types of matters and different tasks within those types.

D. RETHINKING RESOURCE ALLOCATION

The legal marketplace is in a period of transformation with long-term secular trends in transparency, competition, globalization, and technology (especially digitized information technology). These fundamental factors are today having impact in the shadow of the Great

Recession. The economic downturn may have, itself, altered the shape of the legal market in enduring ways by forcing corporations to be ever-more cost conscious and by thus reducing the demand for legal services. Business spending on legal services provided by law firms dropped 25 percent in real terms from 2004 to 2014, from $159 billion to $118 billion. And the General Counsel of the top 200 companies control about 50 percent of that spend (some estimate as high as 80 percent of it). These developments—occurring in the framework of the law firm problems and the law department solutions described earlier—mean that the General Counsel and senior inside lawyers will constantly be rethinking and resetting the inside/outside relationship. Just as importantly, General Counsel must constantly reevaluate *other resources beyond inside lawyers and outside lawyers.* Some core thoughts follow on this inevitable and inexorable process of resetting and reevaluation.[7]

1. MANAGEMENT BY INSIDE COUNSEL

A pillar of the inside counsel revolution is the shift in control over matters from outside law firms to the General Counsel and the inside lawyers. The right-sized role in controlling matters—what it means and when it is important—is the place to start when considering and constantly reevaluating resource allocation. Obviously, control over matters occurs when the work is done by the inside legal team itself, and a fundamental question after segmentation is how much of the work in a particular segment should be handled solely (or primarily) by inside counsel. But control over matters also applies when law firms have an important role. In a substantive sense, control means that the inside lawyers are the decision makers, short of business leaders, on the goals, objectives, and strategy on a range of matters from the routine to the "bet-the-company." They seek advice from outside lawyers and other experts. *They forge strong, respectful partnership relationships with those outside lawyers and experts in handling particular matters. But the inside lawyers make the basic calls on the first-order issues of strategy.* Depending on the size of the Legal department, the number of inside lawyers, and the complexity and risk of the matter, the corporation's lawyers may also have final review on the substance of the essential tasks. They review discovery plans, due diligence outlines, briefs, and transaction documents—and "have the pen," the control over the final written product, unless they wish to delegate piece parts. Inside counsel also need to conduct postmortems on major matters to evaluate strengths and weaknesses of law firm performance (and to listen to law firm perspectives on performance of the Legal department.) But, at the end of the day, the accountability of the General Counsel and senior lawyers to the CEO, senior executives, and the board of directors includes having direct responsibility and control for the important, outside legal work of the corporation, especially at the most difficult (and visible) end of the segmentation spectrum. They must take the blame for poor results—and not blame the law firms. (Success, of course, has the proverbial thousand parents.)

The inside lawyers also have control over *money and resources.* Following segmentation analysis on substance, they need to decide how to deploy a variety of inside and outside resources on particular matters or books of business. Of course, *how the Legal department manages the money flows from how it manages the matter.* But to integrate substantive leadership with fiscal disciplines is an increasingly complicated task. Effective inside counsel management of matters and money now requires skills in project management—budgeting, timetables, milestones, performance evaluations, mid-course corrections, legal team coordination, cross-functional coordination, etc. The senior counsel for legal operations and experts in other company disciplines can help devise management methodologies for different types of matters. For example, law departments have begun to make alliances with the corporation's sourcing function. Other than lower cost, sourcing at first didn't understand legal services and the professional aspects of the relationship. But over time, legal departments and corporate sourcing have begun to speak the same language and work effectively together. *In sum, a systematic approach to the merger of substance and resources, matters, and money, through a disciplined project management approach, is now a much-discussed hallmark of an effective legal department.*

But there should be no mistake. Once there is an agreement on the substance—on the type of matter, on the tasks, and on the strategic and tactical approach in different phases—then the process of managing outside providers' billing is a difficult and often uninspiring task, especially as the investigations, litigations, and transactions become ever-more complex and time-consuming. These issues of money are almost always a struggle not just because of complexity, but because the inside/outside interests are often not aligned. But there is a deeper cultural problem. The demands of corporate executives on a good law department are significant, and inside lawyers, for whom limited time is a great constraint, will always favor responding to business leaders over managing outside legal costs. Indeed, while inside counsel may put substantive management of the matter with a law firm high on their list, they often put cost management low on their "actual" list of priorities even though, paradoxically, their credibility in the company often depends on cost control. The head of Legal operations or the sourcing function can bring important discipline to this large issue, but it is still the substantive inside lawyers who understand the legal work and need to stay close to money management. The General Counsel must impress on senior lawyers that the creativity of managing the substance of the matter with outside firms must be matched with the disciplines of managing the money, as I will reiterate later.

2. BRINGING MORE WORK INSIDE?

Despite budgetary pressures, many surveys of General Counsel indicate that they are bringing work inside the corporation—hiring more inside counsel—in order to serve the business better and to reduce outside legal costs. But adding inside lawyers should only occur *when there is steady and appropriate high-value-added work to justify putting additional lawyers on corporate headcount and incurring the cost of future increases in compensation and benefits.* Will there be a continuous additional stream of litigation or transactions or IP work or compliance in new geographies that can be more efficiently and effectively handled by inside experts over a reasonable time line compared to temporary retention of law firms or other vendors? If so, the intangible benefits of inside lawyers of working closely on complex problems with business teams and other corporate experts can be substantial, as I have emphasized. A hard economic case can be made *if the need for continuing high-value work is there.* A simple (and simplified) example: If a company is paying $600,000 per year over a number of years for important work of one outside associate ($300 per hour × 2,000 hours), then it should surely consider whether that amount might be used toward hiring a more senior and productive inside lawyer. As discussed in Chapter 10 on the global legal organization, the General Counsel and senior lawyers need to develop sophisticated tools of financial analysis to make this case to business leaders. The value of "in-sourcing" is described well by the General Counsel of Bombardier:

> [W]e have insourced the expertise of selling trains and plains and negotiating with customers from all over the world. We excel at the procurement of our supply chain. We provide risk-based advice, well tailored to the nature of the business we serve. This advice is integrated within the risk management of the overall corporation. I believe there is no law firm that can match our law department's expertise and experience in selling trains and planes.[8]

But, GCs should only add resources when they are very confident that the law department can meet the "Bombardier" test: that it is sound economically and culturally over a reasonably long time horizon and cannot more effectively be addressed by alternatives.

3. OTHER ALTERNATIVES

General Counsels and their senior lawyers should, as I have emphasized, seek to reduce law firm costs—or perhaps slow the pace of additional inside hiring—by using the rapidly expanding armament of alternatives to law firm or legal department lawyers: for example, use contract lawyers to meet "peaking" needs; use contract administrators to handle systematic implementation of agreements; outsource to lawyers in contract firms or in non-U.S. jurisdictions to do basic legal research and drafting (such as in common or civil or sharia law jurisdictions); use alternative dispute resolution experts to mediate or arbitrate matters; hire legal process outsourcing firms to organize a wide array of tasks (such as e-billing, document production, litigation support); use outside paralegal firms to avoid law firm markups; or, as necessary, hire the dreaded outside legal audit team for wood-shedding persistently dubious law firm bills. Twenty years ago, GE started a "preferred vendor" movement to match preferred providers in law firms. It bid out to third-party vendors such functions as paralegals, court reporting, word processing, and e-discovery. Law firms had to use these preferred vendors in their GE work—but the vendors billed GE directly, with no law firm markup. The options for this type of arrangement have, of course, exploded.

The increasingly broad array of technology, usually in some IT/ digitized form, is an obvious source of alternatives. Technology can not only organize documents and help search law firm bills, but can also track actuals v. budgets, do legal research, draft documents, or embed environmental regulations in a plant's operating systems. In *Tomorrow's Lawyers*, Richard Susskind, a persistent critic of the legal status quo, makes a passionate case for widespread use of these new methods, especially technology and especially at the lower, commoditized end of the segmentation ladder.[9] As discussed, the law department's senior counsel for legal operations must be a conduit of best practices for inside lawyers on alternatives to law firms and to more permanent inside lawyers. The General Counsel and his senior lawyers must consistently be reevaluating how to deploy different mixes of resources to manage different types of matters and different types of tasks.

E. RESETTING THE RELATIONSHIP

If General Counsels can properly segment their legal activity, then all the "solutions" corporate legal departments developed in the five phases past to address "problems" posed by law firms may be useful in structuring current relationships: from straight competition to preferred providers to strategic alliances to inside/outside integration. These strategies—or some combination of them—all involve the fundamental inside counsel leadership on substance and cost of the matter or matters. It is not possible to generalize about which approach is the best because so much depends on (1) the size and business lines of the corporation—from small/one product to large/diverse products, (2) the mix of the different types of matters revealed by segmentation analytics, and (3) the size and specialization of the inside legal staff—from a few generalists to many generalists/specialists. Indeed, it is entirely possible that some combination of all the approaches developed in all of the phases may be appropriate.

1. VALUE RELATIONSHIPS

But regardless of approach, the elusive lodestone in law department–law firm relationships is value. In my view, value has four ideal elements. First, law firms need to have "character": integrity, a strong ethic of service, knowledge of the business, responsiveness, creativity, courtesy—and ultimately a strong desire to help the company perform with integrity. The character of the firm should be reciprocated by the character of the inside lawyers in its relations with the law firm. Second, law firms need to demonstrate excellent quality in their work on the type of matter and the tasks that comprise it. Excellence, excellence, excellence. The substantive quality of the work is elemental. No excuses for the shoddy or the mediocre. Third, firms and vendors, of course, need to achieve results with integrity. Winning—the right way—is essential to legal department and corporate success. But, General Counsel know that it is not possible on contentious matters with outside decision makers to bat 100 percent. The GC should recognize that inside and outside lawyers can do an outstanding job and still not achieve the desired result due, among other things, to bias of the decision maker or irrational intransigence of a counterparty. Law department fairness in evaluating effort is important in having a reciprocal value relationship with outside firms. Finally, the matter should be provided at "the lowest reasonable" cost. Other than with a pure commodity product, the "lowest reasonable" cost is not the absolute lowest possible cost. In this day and age, cost is obviously very important. But firms' and vendors' "character" and "quality" and "history of results" all need to be factored into a retention, into establishing a value relationship. This "value relationship" should be at the core of law firm engagements.

2. HOME TRUTHS

With ultimate control over matters and money and with the value relationship as a foundation, corporate law departments should follow certain basic precepts as they continually reset their law firm relationships, whatever the approach along the essential segmentation spectrum.

All engagements—including preferred providers, strategic alliances, and more complete integration—should be achieved through competition. The General Counsel should insist that there be some comparisons between firms on the value relationship—character, quality, past results, and cost—before entering into preferred provider or strategic alliances/integration. Indeed, complex types of legal matters may be a combination of competitively-arrived-at partnerships, with different firms or alternative service providers all having a role. The ultimate arrangement may be reached through negotiation, but, at root, the inside counsel should not enter into that arrangement without direct or indirect competition/comparisons. The commentators who maintain that these partnerships may reduce competition are, in my view, simply wrong. They are—or should be—the results of competition, albeit in a different form than matter-by-matter beauty contests.

Whatever the form of the partnership relationship, it should be time limited, subject to reevaluation, and open to termination or continuation. Firms that make commitments should have time to demonstrate their worth. Reciprocal loyalty from the law department matters. But, from the perspective of the General Counsel, there are no permanent partnerships. There are hungry firms out there and disruptive change in the legal industry. Supplier relationships should be periodically analyzed in light of performance *and* emerging competitors/alternatives. The world is changing—continually. General Counsel have an enormous source of power: They control the purse.

Control over the substance of matters (which inside lawyers like) must be integrated with control over money (which inside lawyers must do but generally don't like) as emphasized earlier. The substantive strategy for a matter or book of matters—the details about phases and tasks and other providers—must be integrated with the strategy for money. In this new era of resource constraint, this is just reality and, as I discuss in a moment, alternative fee arrangements can be important but don't resolve the problems.

Inside/outside partnerships are still built on "lawyers, not firms." From an inside counsel perspective, the personal relationship with the head of the firm's practice group or the head of an elite team within the firm is the building block for these different types of arrangements. No matter what form the inside/outside partnership takes, the General Counsel and the senior inside lawyers must have a strong, direct personal connection with the lead lawyers in the firm who actually do the work—and who should be sensitive to staffing, responsiveness, and money. Especially when the outside law firm is taking on blocks of important business with complexity and risk to the corporation, this "relational" rather than "transactional" inside/outside connection is still vital. Law firm partners can be colleagues, but they must be held to account (rather than run off on marketing efforts or working for other clients if they have made commitments to you).

If the corporation is large enough and has an established inside legal presence around the globe, the General Counsel should require that the mega-firms compete in each market and in each subject matter area. There should be no automatic one-stop shop, although there are clear benefits in using one firm on a global matter *if* lawyers in its foreign offices are competitive with other lawyers in the jurisdiction. Obviously, if a corporate law department is small and not globalized, it may not have the expertise or the lawyers to integrate the right firms/vendors in a complex global matter. The choice of the mega-firm may be one realistic alternative. But another alternative is to use an elite firm that has informal associations with elite firms in other nations and a track record of working together on the type of matter at issue. That informal "string of pearls" may provide better service than the supposedly integrated, too often mediocre, mega-firm. But large, talented law departments in major global companies should be able to construct the best possible team when moving up the segmentation scale to one-off high-complexity, high-risk matters. To avoid reliance on the mediocrity of mega-firms on important geographical pieces of a complex transnational problem, it is very important for a multinational corporation to have a preferred strong provider or even more structured relationship with outstanding law firms in foreign nations comprised primarily of local lawyers. In my tenure, we were fortunate to have retainers—and very strong experience built up over time—with fine local firms across Austra-Asia (e.g., Australia, India, Japan, Korea) and Europe. The powerful global legal department can have its own "string of pearls" (i.e., different, elite cooperating firms) on significant cross-border matters.

Much has been made about "convergence" and "consolidation"—the reduction of the number of outside firms serving the corporation and the consolidation of law firms generally. Virtually every corporation in the past 20 years has reduced the number of firms that represent them in the name of simplification, cost savings, and stronger relationships. But, given the variation in companies, product lines, geographies, mix of matters, and size and the specialization of the inside legal staff, there is no magic number. For some companies, five firms may be right, but so may 50 or even 100 for a decentralized, diversified, global company. The virtues of fewer firms and less administrative complexity can be outweighed by the need to retain customized law firms that more closely fit the needs of different business units in different geographies that have salient, industry-specific issues. In addition, reliance on too few firms exposes the law department to demonstrable risks that can undermine its stability and continuity. The needs of the company, rather than a numbers game, is obviously what is important. Convergence is worth pursuing with common sense; it is not the be-all–end-all. Again, it depends greatly on an overall segmentation analysis of the legal department's work across different business units. As to law firm consolidation, given my doubts about mega-firms, I think inside law departments should look at firm mergers with a very jaundiced eye because both cost and quality may suffer. I admit to a bias: Rarely is bigger better.

A sharp distinction should be made between firms that have a high "value add" on complex matters and firms that provide commoditized or routine services. The focus of the inside lawyers—especially the General Counsel—should be on identifying and utilizing the "value add" lawyers for the complex, high-risk, high-impact matters.

These are the special lawyers in firms that can make a difference. For many other lower-complexity, lower-risk matters—whether alone or repeating—there are any number of firms that can handle that type of assignment well. It is the unusual or even unique firm/lawyers for the segmented matters at the upper end of the complexity/risk/impact scale that really matter to the reputation of the company—and the reputation of the General Counsel and the inside legal team.

It should hardly need mentioning, but inside lawyers must continue to be ever vigilant about law firms marking up routine non-legal services—a problem that goes all the way back to the beginning of the inside counsel movement but that can now be more readily addressed through information technology. In their outside counsel guidelines, law departments should be as explicit as possible about items they will not reimburse (travel, copying, certain types of research). Moreover, other routine non-legal services should be provided at cost, if they are provided at all (rather than by a third-party vendor). And, in this age of a buyers' market, legal departments can arrange for law firms to provide important services for free or for a nominal cost that deepen the relationship: for example, secondment of associates to the corporation for a year, education and training of inside lawyers by law firm super-specialists, access to the firm library of briefs and memoranda, and sample documents/templates/forms.

Legal departments must beware of arrogance, however. They must treat outside lawyers with great respect and forge genuine cooperative and constructive relationships on the handling of specific matters. Moreover, even if, in the wake of the Great Recession, the profession is in transition to less demand for law firms due to weakened demand, the growth of inside law departments, and the emergence of alternative vendors, the reality is that there will always be huge trends and developments that will be profitable for the most expert firms. Outside firms will always benefit from a burst of global deal making or a spate of mega-bankruptcies or major regulatory change or new aggressive enforcement strategies or corporate misdeeds that require a huge global investigation (viz Siemens or Volkswagen). Inside counsel must treat all outside lawyers with the deep respect due to outstanding professionals all along the segmentation spectrum. This should be so as a matter of their "character" in the reciprocal value relationship. But inside counsel must also be mindful that their market power has constraints. The limited number of truly "super-high-value" firms/lawyers—which may be at the top of the field in certain areas like capital markets or M&A or sovereign debt or bankruptcy or high-stakes litigation—may have more business than they can handle. In addition, new clients are emerging in this era of globalization. The head of a large firm recently told me that clients from China were a growing source of business in the United States—either from "private" or state-owned industries. They had significant legal issues and, due to lack of knowledge about the U.S. legal market, wanted to give most of their business to a single firm. These foreign clients, at this point, really did want one-stop shopping.

3. FIXED/ALTERNATIVE FEE ARRANGEMENTS

A critical dimension in any law department–law firm partnership is aligning incentives and risks—getting rid of the malignant "productivity disconnect" that stems from conflicting economic objectives. An oft-discussed answer to this problem is reducing reliance on the endlessly (and justly) criticized hourly rate, reducing law firm's "fee for service" revenue generation, and moving to fixed-fee or alternative-fee arrangements. In 2009, I co-authored an article with Bill Lee, then WilmerHale co-managing partner, arguing that the time had come for both inside counsel and law firms to move toward such arrangements. The rationale was straightforward. We wrote:

> For in-house counsel facing tremendous budgetary pressures, the fixed fee addresses problems caused by the hourly rate, such as unpredictability, high costs divorced from value and, most importantly, the maddening law firm definition of "productivity"—defined as more hours and more lawyers per matter. For law firms, facing reduced demand and cash flow problems (if not crises), the fixed fee addresses the issues of increasing overhead devoted to the billing process, clients flyspecking bills and demanding after the fact discounts, and delays in payments and falling realization rates [percent of list price actually collected].

We were joining many other voices calling for this change to reduce inefficiency and increase productivity.[10]

The trend toward alternative fee arrangements has, in fact, occurred. How deeply the practices have penetrated the law department–law firm relationship is subject to debate, but most legal departments are searching for alternatives to the billable hour and will continue to do so. This may occur with greater frequency in larger companies that have both economic leverage and the expertise needed to effect alternative fee arrangements. The fixed or alternative fee is not just about cost. Ideally, it takes into account all elements of the value relationship as I have defined it in setting "price": character, quality, and past results as well as lowest reasonable cost. The methodology for setting such fees is not simple, however, and I now note some of the most prominent variations and problems.

Strategy and segmentation are critical to fixing fees. A repeating set of matters with low risk and limited complexity is, of course, a much different (and easier) subject for setting a fixed fee than a higher risk, higher complexity matter or books of businesses. On the latter, difficult types of legal business, it may be necessary to break the matter into phases and set the fixed fee for each phase: for example, the different stages of a transaction—evaluation, initial deal documentation, due diligence, closing documents, and post-close. The inside lawyers must also assess the discrete tasks within each phase of different types of segmented matters. Obviously, defining the scope of work with as much precision as possible—for the whole matter or for the "phase"—is necessary for the success of any approach.

Whether simple or complex, whether a single matter or a repeating set of matters, the fixed fee can be set through a formal competitive bidding process or through a negotiation with several competing firms or through negotiation with a single firm (*but* with other firms in the background). Fixed fees, in other words, should be arrived at only in the shadow of competition.

Historical data can provide the starting point for negotiating the fixed fee, especially for books of recurring business/cases. Both firms and corporations have detailed information on the past costs of a variety of matters, especially if task-based billing codes have been used in good faith over a number of years. This is an instance where new technology can really be important. Big data and data-mining techniques can determine reasonable ranges of cost for the different types of matters. While this may be a good way to start, a history of the costs of matters may be an imperfect guide because it is the sum of hourly rates plus out-of-pocket costs and may reflect precisely the type of inefficiency and overbilling that the fixed fee seeks to eliminate. Developing big data screens to deal with this issue is vital.

But how then should the rate be set? In simplest business terms, the legal department and the law firm should agree on the estimated cost of the matter and the appropriate profit margin, which will vary depending on complexity, risk, and importance. But both cost and margin are highly problematic. Law firms have had historic difficulty in controlling noncompensation costs—which are built into hourly rates. Moreover, big firms have become accustomed to over-staffing matters and overpaying the entry-level associates from top law schools. Shadow hourly rates for shadow lawyers are used by firms to build up a fixed-fee price, which includes margin. But this just repeats the problems of the fee-for-service system. In addition, deciding what is an appropriate margin (or range of margins) on different types of segmented business is, of course, a tricky exercise. Corporations should want firms to make a profit—but how much? Reaching an understanding on the right actual (not hourly rate) cost of the right number of lawyers and an appropriate margin for the law firm is thus an extremely difficult task. That is why it may be necessary to let the market, rather than a negotiation, set the fixed rate if the matter is on the less complex/less risky rung of the segmentation ladder and if it can thus be bid out more readily.

Whatever the "starting number" for a fixed arrangement, law departments and law firms can allocate the risk that the prospective fixed fee does not reflect the actual cost of the type of matter. A number of well-known alternatives have emerged. Among the most common are the following. A flat fixed fee gives the law firm both the upside (if the matter is completed for less than the fee) and the downside (if the matter costs more than the fee). A fixed fee with a collar (120 percent/80 percent of the fee) can be used to share both upside and downside between Legal department and law firm—that is, each equally bear the cost of overruns or receive the benefits of performance under budget. Outside the collar, the law firm takes the risk/gets the reward. Another alternative is a hold-back/performance bonus approach: The corporation pays 80 percent of the fixed fee on a monthly basis; if there is a poor result, that is all the firm receives; if there is a satisfactory result, the firm receives 100 percent (the withheld 20 percent); for an excellent result, the firm can receive 120 percent of the original fixed fee. Defining the concepts of *poor, satisfactory,* and *excellent* are, like defining the scope of the matter, important at the outset. Obviously, there are many variations of these basic, fixed-fee alternatives.

Implementing a fixed-fee agreement is not a walk in the park. Most importantly, inside counsel, as they would with any matter, must ensure the quality of the legal services the law firm is providing. The good news about fixed fees is that they may drive firms to leaner, more productive staffing. The bad news is that, even though they need to produce a good result, firms may cut resources too far and impair quality in order to get a bonus for coming in under the fixed fee. Or, despite the sales pitch up front, the key partner may spend less time on the matter than promised (or warranted). That is why inside counsel must either consistently—or on a sampling basis—review the quality of the "tasks" that comprise the "type" of work. So, too, if the corporation is on the hook for absorbing part of an overrun, it will want to track costs the firm is actually incurring. This may result in review of "shadow hours billed" or other law firm "cost" categories—if not on a monthly basis, then perhaps on a quarterly or half-year basis. Technology and project management in both corporations and law firms can make this tracking more transparent, effective, and, perhaps, timely. Technology also may have an important role in helping inside counsel manage the matter when multiple outside parties may have tasks to perform. And, among the host of other implementation details, there should be a provision for systematically assessing the need for mid-course corrections as fixed-fee assumptions about the matter—or about the world—change.

Alternative fee arrangements do not remove the burden of inside counsel management—both of matters and of money—that began this discussion. They are not a magic bullet. They are not easy to implement. They may not entirely do away with the hourly rate as the unit "price" of service. But, if not nirvana, fixed fees can help both Legal departments and law firms create incentives for efficiency and productivity, can create rewards for success and penalties for failure, and can more clearly align interests. They can be an important building block in creating the various types of "partnerships," *in the shadow of competition*, that have emerged. *They are, in fact, just a more sophisticated, comprehensive, and value-oriented version of task-based budgeting and billing that inside counsel started to use 30 years ago to manage uncontrolled law firm costs, which were one of the causes of the inside counsel revolution.*

4. SPECIAL HIGH-IMPACT, ONE-OFF MATTERS

When faced with one-off, highly complex, high-risk, and high-impact matters, the General Counsel will, necessarily, focus on reducing the problems for the corporation. "Partnerships" and "fixed fees" are likely to take a back seat as General Counsels—and the corporations—try to get their bearings. This is as it should be. If the rig blows up in the gulf of Mexico, if a bribery scandal cuts a broad swath across the top of the company, if the government is imposing emergency measures when the financial system is about to tank, then General Counsels know that they have to get the very best assistance as fast as possible. They know that the consequences for the company are so huge that legal fees are the least of their problems. Price is literally no object in a limited number of supremely important matters. Preferred providers and strategic partners are nice—and they can handle highly complex, high-risk matters if the case is in their sweet spot and if they are at the top of the league tables. High-rolling IP litigation may be just a variant of other IP work that a firm handles in a strategic relationship. But the last category of my segmentation types—the one-off matter with potentially catastrophic consequences—will usually require a uniquely crafted response and a unique combination of resources. Almost by definition, it has surprised the company and is threatening to run out of control—and the General Counsel has to throw resources until it is under control (which can be a matter of years). Despite responsibility for myriad other legal matters, it is the type of matter, I must emphasize, that can define the General Counsel's tenure both inside the company and out.

I mention this problem to note the irony that, with all the important changes in inside/outside convergence, "strategic" partnerships, and fixed fees, this type of matter—the most important the corporation will face—has financial elements of "back to the future." On strategy and coordination of multiple actors in a many-front war, the General Counsel will exert ultimate control over substance per the inside counsel revolution. It is hard to overstate the importance of the new breed of General Counsel in preventing and then responding to such issues. But, once such an event has occurred, the GC will be racing to get the right firms—and other experts and consultants—involved whatever the cost. When the situation stabilizes, and the discrete dimensions of the matter can be more carefully defined, then the various cost control techniques can help "domesticate" the crisis from a financial point of view. But, in such situations, the importance of the "matter" far exceeds the need to control the "money." To me, the symbol of this occurred during the 2008–2009 financial crisis, when financial services firms were reaching out to the very best lawyers. One attorney was so superior and so much in demand that he sent his clients one-line bills: "for services rendered." The companies didn't ask for an itemized invoice. Sound like 1970? When the world is turned upside down—back to the future.

F. COOPERATION ON ETHICS

The General Counsel and senior inside lawyers must not only seek a partnership with their law firms on matters and money, but also on the four ethical duties I have identified: to their own organization, to clients/stakeholders, to law and the administration of justice, and to society. Indeed, I argue here (as Lee, Wilkins, and I argued in our essay on lawyer roles and responsibilities) that many of those problems will require new cooperative approaches on both sides of the inside/outside divide. Just as on legal work, the General Counsel and lead inside law-yers must *seek cooperative, constructive, and respectful approaches with law firm counterparts to core problems lawyers face as professionals and as citizens*. It is time for enhanced joint law department–law firm partnerships on "service" not just on "business." Innovation and coop-eration on these issues can alleviate the discontent felt among clients, partners, and associates for which inside counsel surely bear their fair measure of responsibility.

1. REQUESTING FIRM VIEWS ON "WHAT IS RIGHT"

Critics say the shift of power to law firms, the advent of hyper-specialization, and the pressure to increase profitability have impaired the broad, independent judgment of law firms. It is said that too many outside lawyers don't see the client's interests as a whole and too many lawyers are too willing to provide the client's desired answer. They're afraid to ask hard questions or provide a broader perspective on an apparently narrow issue for fear of losing a billable client. So, too, the critics say that, with their increasing power, law departments force law firms to forego independence and wise counseling and just give the corporation the answer that it wants. This tension between addressing the client's immediate, narrow matter and counseling on the corpo-ration's broader interests—between opining on what is "legal" rather than probing on what is "right"—parallels the partner-guardian ten-sion that inside lawyers face.[11] On complex and controversial matters, the General Counsel and lead inside lawyers should structure outside relationships to encourage (or rehabilitate) the important "guardian" role for outside counsel—to the extent that it has been damaged by the changes in law departments and law firms. A request for both astute lawyering and raising issues of broader "counseling" should be an explicit part of the retention, included, for example, in the scope of many fixed-fee arrangements. The legal department should explicitly ask for law firms' views on what is right. And, inside counsel should be prepared to task the outside lawyers with exploring such issues as necessary.

General Counsel and lead inside counsel must underscore this point to the whole cadre of inside lawyers—who may, especially in the middle of the company, beat up firms to meet budgets and oversee outside lawyers who, anxious to keep business, hew strictly to a narrow assignment rather than offering a broader view. So, too, leaders of law firms—like CEOs and General Counsel—must create a law firm culture that balances economic needs with professional aspirations. Partnership meetings that pay lip service to professionalism, don't discuss the counseling role, and then spend most of the time on growing profits per partner and increasing leverage don't help. Are firm leaders continually seeking best practices for achieving the right balance between business imperatives and professional ideals, between narrow lawyering and wise counseling, between respecting client wishes and calling out questionable client actions? Just as law departments should seek wise counseling so, too, should law firms provide such counseling—or at least raise important issues—without trying to recover every nickel for their time. The excuse that firms don't see the whole company is lame. There is a vast amount of public information about corporations if outside lawyers are willing to collect it and read it (without billing the time). Start with the Internet and with analysts' reports (which, in important part, reflect company briefings). Outside lawyers can also do something that is supposed to be a core skill: Ask questions. Inside counsel say that, too often, outside lawyers are good talkers but poor listeners. And law departments can arrange for law firm lawyers to get briefings and make connections at the corporation itself, per the Intel integration model. That is one of the best ways to connect law departments and select law firms. There are, of course, many distinguished outside counsel who perform the wise counselor/guardian role very well. General Counsel should encourage more law firms to instill in their lawyers the ethic of at least raising broader questions "outside their lane" for the company to consider.

2. YOUNG LAWYERS

The problems facing many young associates in major firms are legion, and the solution requires joint law department–law firm effort. The litany of issues is discouraging: high hourly rates that corporate clients are unwilling to pay; pressure to bill 2,200+ hours per year, which leaves young lawyers no time for family, community service, religion, or other important dimensions of individual life; lack of personal mentoring by senior lawyers; absence of a competency model that systematically trains young lawyers in skills and techniques of a broad-gauged practice; being buried in huge teams with limited understanding of the theory of the case and limited to no partner supervision or evaluation; pressure to specialize unleavened by generalist experience through department rotation; large doses of donkey work—hour upon hour of e-mail reviews for document production—that are demoralizing to a young professional; a concomitant lack of responsibility; decisions to leave the firm, on their own motion, after three to four years when they have paid off much of their heavy debt; and, ultimately, an unpleasant experience in their first job after law school that, rather than inspiring young lawyers about a career in the law, may sour them on the profession.[12]

Some of these problems are created by pressure from corporations: don't want to pay high rates, don't want to let young lawyers have responsibility on company matters, indifference to mentoring and competency training, and demands for super-specialists. Most broadly, corporations often appear to take no responsibility for the development of young lawyers, even though they want experienced senior associates or junior partners to work on their matters—or to hire them in their legal departments after firms have trained them. There are important steps major corporations can take—and should take—to address the shared responsibility with law firms for development of young lawyers.

Inside law departments could reverse their general practice and begin hiring students right out of law school, as discussed earlier. In doing so, they could have cooperative arrangements with firms in which those young inside lawyers can also work some of the time at the law firm on the corporation's matters and receive training from partners. The flip side of this is that law departments and law firms could agree on a developmental program for young associates in the law firm: mentoring, competency training, blending specialization and generalist skills, and phased responsibility on client matters. Major corporations could agree to use the associates on their matters as they go through these early developmental phases. Legal departments might agree, through a flat fee, to pay full or partial cost with no or little margin for the firm in the early phases. The margin corporations pay would increase as associates gain more experience. For example, if a first-year associate salary/bonus is $200,000 and that person works 1,900 real, billable hours, then the hourly cost to the law firm is about $105 (plus an incremental amount for overhead). For a highly intelligent, high-energy person, companies might be willing to pay that reduced amount or to share the cost with the firm, which would be making an investment in a promising person. As part of this arrangement, law departments and law firms could agree that young lawyers can attend meetings or depositions or court appearances or negotiations or hearings to learn—but not to charge—in the early years. This could also mean that scut work is not done by junior associates at absurd rates but outsourced to venders or handled by non-lawyers at more appropriate prices.

As associates gained experience, they could be "seconded" to corporations in their third or fourth years. They stay on the payroll of the firm but have an office at the company and work with the inside lawyers, with a mix of specialist and more generalist work, which all corporations have. Again, the law department might pay the law firm the cost and negotiated margin of such an associate. But it is in the firm's interest for the young lawyer to be in the belly of the beast and to learn corporate problems in general and the client in particular, including the many ethical and judgment calls inside lawyers must make. Evaluations of the young lawyer for partnership can continue, with input from both firm and inside lawyers. This would also give young lawyers and corporations an opportunity to really know each other, with a possible in-house hire to follow, which then, in turn, can create a client relationship for the law firm. Legal departments can also use these secondments for diverse lawyers so they can have a cadre of talented potential diversity hires. A hybrid where a junior lawyer is hired jointly by a law department and a law firm could combine the two approaches described.

The specialization v. generalist tension must be addressed. Major corporations should have a significant interest not just in specialists, but also in lawyers with broad perspectives and skills. It is thus critically important that leaders of law departments should work with law firms (and heads of firm practice groups) to support rotation of young lawyers during the early years of their career (where their expertise is not that great in any event) in order to create a foundation for young lawyers to become either generalists (in a broad area of the law like litigation or M&A) or specialists (in more technical areas like tax or IP). A generalist background—an appreciation of the broader set of considerations that define the "real" problems lawyers are trying to solve—can be very, very important even for those lawyers who become specialists. It is in the interest of corporations to support this type of breadth in young lawyers, but, in an era of constrained resources, making this aspiration reality has costs that corporations and law firms should bear as part of their ethical responsibilities.

Major corporations could also clearly state that a factor in selecting firms will be a firm policy and practice of setting the expected average annual associate billable hours at some "non–death dealing amount"— for example, 1,900 hours. This can apply in fixed-fee settings where hours are counted even if not directly billed. More billable hours per years for young lawyers reduces productivity and effectiveness (and often causes bill-padding) as well as leading to significant distortions in personal life, including narrowness and burn-out. Restraining the number of hours for young lawyers is an important step in a return to sanity in how inside and outside counsel treat recent graduates. Interestingly, some firms are experimenting with compensating associates on client- and society-based values in addition to receipts from the associates' work, looking at such factors as efficiency, client service, responsiveness, team effectiveness, and pro bono commitment.

3. PROMOTING DIVERSITY IN LAW FIRMS

Both as a simple question of morality and as a business benefit in an era of globalization, the importance of having diversity in law firms as well as in legal departments is beyond argument from my perspective. Women, minorities, and lawyers from other cultures should be given an equal chance to be hired and promoted—and should be given "stretch" assignments just as frequently as all other lawyers so they are able to show how far they can advance. In making decisions about whether to retain firms, General Counsel and inside lawyers can, at a minimum, ask the outside counsel firm for the diversity profile of the firm (associates, partners, leaders) and the trends in that profile. Law departments can also ask for the diversity profile on the corporation's matters in general and on particular matters or a particular block's business. They can also ask for data on pay differentials and for firm policies and implementation practices relating to diversity. They can ask further about how diverse candidates fare in promotion to partnership and firm leadership. Just asking for this information to see if the law firm keeps it in a systemic way can have some benefit. This is information they should be keeping, and it should not be viewed as burdensome "paperwork." Beyond simply making the inquiry, corporate law departments can state as a guideline that this information will be relevant to a decision to hire the firm and can be decisive, "all other things being equal" (more or less). It may be neither feasible nor desirable for major corporations to set goals for major law firms on this range of diversity issues, but asking for information, *and being serious about the relevance of that information to hiring decisions, can be a powerful tool nonetheless. **But** if this information is accumulated but ignored in the Legal department's retention decisions, then it sends a terrible message to the law firms and to diverse lawyers for which the General Counsel and his senior lawyers are responsible.* Legal departments could also issue an Annual Report praising those firms with strong efforts in diversity that the firms could use in their marketing efforts. Obviously, this kind of inquiry, and its use in decisions, is even more credible when the legal department itself has strong policies, creative implementation practices, and a good record. (See pp. 382–390.)

Law departments should consider going beyond these steps—given the paramount importance in hiring and promoting diverse lawyers—and having them advance to leadership positions. For example, under highly regarded GC Brad Smith, Microsoft pays its law firms an annual bonus (2 to 3 percent) on their total fees if they meet one of several different predefined diversity goals both in the firm generally and in firm leadership positions. Microsoft and other leading corporations helped found the Leadership Council on Legal Diversity (LCLD), which brings together the managing partners and General Counsels of about 220 major institutions across the country. It focuses on professional development of diverse lawyers, starting with internships for diverse law students, assisting entry-level hiring, and extending to lawyers in the mid-career stage.[13]

4. PRO BONO AND IMPROVING THE JUSTICE SYSTEM

So, too, General Counsel can ask that firms provide information about the scope and trends of their pro bono programs, especially how they are giving young lawyers experience, responsibility, and accountability that might not occur until later in their careers on paying firm matters. As with diversity, law departments can choose to use this information in deciding whether to retain firms. They can use the tremendous example of some firms with discrete pro bono departments and partner-level pro bono leaders—who do magnificent work on hard cases or problems—to ratchet up the effort of other firms. The Association of General Counsel (GCs of major corporations) can seek to work with the Association of Pro Bono Counsel, which is an umbrella organization for pro bono activities in major law firms. Moreover, there are numerous opportunities for law departments and law firms to work together in jointly providing pro bono services. The Pro Bono Partnership, which GE and other corporations founded in 1997 for corporate lawyers to work on pro bono matters, now also draws on lawyers from firms in serving community organizations. It has become a joint law department–law firm entity. The Intel example of law department–law firm integration described earlier includes joint planning and cooperation on pro bono services. Also, as previously noted, major law firms and large corporations, working with local bar associations and local public defender and legal aid groups, should consider a systematic legal needs assessment for their local communities followed by a more comprehensive action plan—with real resource allocation—to close the gap. Although precise numbers are hard to come by, the total annual resources used by law departments and law firms on pro bono services as a percentage of total inside and outside annual spend is likely to be but a fraction of 1 percent. This number should be a source of embarrassment, not pride, for law departments and law firms.[14]

More broadly, General Counsel could consider alliances with other companies and with law firms to address broader issues in the administration of justice in various venues at the international, federal, state, and local levels. In the United States, important issues are limitless: closing the yawning gap between need and current funding for legal aid/public defender services; improving state judicial selection processes; seeking increases in judicial salaries; helping design and implement "diversion" programs to keep young offenders out of the prison system; or working on steps to reduce the many dimensions of racial discrimination, which observers believe still blights the legal system. Similarly, promoting "rule of law" in emerging markets is important. But law is power—and changing structures of power is as much or more a matter of politics as rational "law reform." And neither corporate law departments nor law firms can or should be too entangled in the politics of less developed countries because of corruption, lack of expertise about history and culture, and the looming risks to reputation of being involved in local politics. Developing a vehicle for providing technical assistance—*if asked*—may be the best that can be done. An emerging issue for possible joint law department–law firm cooperation is liberalizing strict professional rules that limit access to justice. An important—if controversial—subject is helping develop materials that laypeople can use to handle rudimentary legal problems. A related controversy is authorizing creation of a cadre of the legal equivalents of nurse practitioners ("limited license legal technicians") who can assist people with basic legal issues if general lawyers are not available or are too expensive. Such legal technicians would be immune from engaging in the "unauthorized practice" of law if those rules were less restrictive. More broadly, leading companies and leading firms can join the movement to de-mystify, "liberalize," and "deregulate" the law so that it works better in people's daily lives.

Although pro bono efforts are heavily "financed" with the "sweat equity" of lawyers, they can also be financed by company and law firm philanthropic efforts. General Counsel, as members of corporate foundation boards, must press to have these "justice" issues be part of a company's charitable giving in support of "corporate citizenship." Law firms, too, should consider broader initiatives on improving the justice system as part of a "law firm citizenship," a concept law firms need to consider seriously, if they are not already doing so.

5. BROADER SUPPLIER/OUTSIDE COUNSEL GUIDELINES

Given the importance of these ethical issues, and assuming that the corporation has discharged its own ethical duties, General Counsels could consider explicitly including in their outside counsel guidelines discussion about firms' activities in discharging the four ethical duties. Corporations could ask law firms to connect the dots and provide specific information, if they wish to do so, on the overall approach to the duties to employees, to clients/stakeholders, to the rule of law, and to the broader society, with specifics on treatment of associates, diversity, pro bono, administration of justice, and other law firm citizenship initiatives. As noted, this approach can let corporations leverage up from the notable efforts of lead law firms that are outstanding at the business of law but also at discharging duties as professionals and as citizens.

Thus, corporate legal departments could take four steps. First, they could formulate this broader set of outside law firm guidelines that covers topics relating to roles and responsibilities and seek information from the firms on these subjects. Second, legal departments could— unlike third-party global supply chain information that is used in a "hard" sense to qualify third parties—use this information in a "soft" sense when deciding whether to hire the firm, especially for various types of repeating books of business where there is robust competition and much similarity between firms. Third, they could train law department lawyers on the importance and proper use of these guidelines, driving home to them that this is not just a paper exercise, but also one that should be guided by flexibility and sensitivity. Finally, in forging "partnerships" of the "strategic" or "integrative" types, General Counsels and heads of law firms could also reach agreements on some of the suggested joint ethical responsibilities described earlier as an explicit part of these arrangements, building off the information provided pursuant to the outside counsel/supplier guidelines.

G. A PERSONAL NOTE

In a large company, with excellent inside lawyers, the General Counsel may not spend much direct personal time on law firm relations. I didn't. My relationships with the board, the CEO, business leaders, my direct reports, and a host of stakeholders/influencers outside the company were far more important. Because of the strong specialist/generalist lawyers at GE, I generally wanted all the corporation's subject-matter experts and division General Counsel to manage their outside counsel relationships. On the huge matters of concern to the CEO or the board of directors, I would be involved in selection and oversight of outside counsel. But this didn't happen often. I generally relied on my senior lawyers. I viewed my basic role as providing cross-company leadership on initiatives to improve law firm efficiency and effectiveness, with the assistance of the Senior Counsel–Legal Operations. In essence, this meant *working with the inside partnership in setting the overall goals, objectives, value relationships, and strategy relating to the crucial, changing relationships with outside law firms.* But, within that framework, the General Counsel should then defer to the top inside lawyers to develop the specifics of the very hard tasks of segmentation, consideration of alternatives, forging partnerships, and setting alternative fees—of managing outside suppliers. This builds up the stature of the inside lead lawyers within the profession and preserves precious GC time. Moreover, with respect to some "leading law firms," the GC and senior inside lawyers should work with the firm leader on rethinking and restructuring the overall relationship to create innovative inside/outside models the senior lawyers would then implement and evaluate.

Finally, despite all the changes in the past 25 years, there is little question, in my view, that on any matter of signal complexity and consequence—the ones high up on the segmentation ladder and on which the GC will be judged—it is still the "lawyer not the firm." The "free agency" of talented lawyers and the churn as firms poach each other's top partners—with corporations following the lawyer—demonstrates the continuing power of the "lawyers not law firms" rubric. Top inside lawyers must spend time identifying the neurosurgeons—and having a relationship with them—as an important insurance policy for the deeply important "predictable surprises" that will invariably occur and will require the absolute best talent. And, based on innumerable interviews with inside counsel, a long-time observer of the legal profession recently told a conference of law firm leaders that General Counsel were looking, above all, at a direct, trusting close personal relationship with their key outside lawyers.

In addition, I also have a presumption against big firms if there are outstanding lawyers in small-firm alternatives. I worked with many wonderful outside lawyers. I am deeply grateful for their outstanding work. I have many dear friends who are—or were—senior partners in major law firms. But, looking back, I was far too often disappointed in major firms—both in the work and the bills when I had occasion to be deeply involved in evaluating briefs or memoranda or presentations or in reviewing overall charges on major matters. The huge staffing structures—which we tried to break up—too often produced mediocre work and excessive invoices. This view was shared by my inside lawyer colleagues (most of us law firm alums), who often shook their heads at less-than-sterling law firm performance. As the General Counsel of a global company said recently, "We found that the firms that were performing the poorest were the multinational large firms, so we started gravitating towards regional and smaller firms."[15]

On the trickiest, riskiest matters, my preference was thus for small, elite firms whenever possible—or for elite groups within larger firms. I have always believed that both law departments and law firms are better off with a much smaller number of highly skilled associates and partners on a matter—with lower-level work outsourced. This elite, smaller group can bill at a higher rate but, because they are so talented and know the case or matter so well, they are far more productive than the customary big-firm, three-ring circus. The overall quality of the work would be higher and the overall bill would be lower with these smaller, elite groups. This can occur by retaining smaller specialty firms. (I have a soft spot in my heart for them due to my 1970s stint at Williams & Connolly when it had 40 lawyers in total and when two or three of those lawyers would litigate against New York–based teams of 15+ lawyers.) Indeed, there is an emerging trend toward legal boutiques (also occurring in investment banking).[16] The small firm ethos can occur, in effect, by creating such a "firm within a firm"—working out such arrangements with a powerful, talented partner who may have to resist firm injunctions about leverage and total lawyers/hours per matter. Perhaps, I have had a "hardening of the categories" in my advancing years, but I would still put my money on a small group of elite lawyers, not a law firm with a big name, in handling the more difficult problems—the "bespoke" matters that really matter—as legal departments go up the segmentation ladder in their search for outside counsel. And even in huge matters of monumental import that require an army of lawyers, I would want an elite group to "ride side car" with the inside team to see the matter as a whole and provide overview counsel. In addition, even strategic alliances or strategic integration models that involve legal problems of significant, if not surpassing, complexity and risk are going to be built on named lawyers, not firms with fancy names. Some things don't change.

12

THE FUTURE: PROBLEMS AND POSSIBILITIES

The inside counsel revolution has transformed business and law as the General Counsel has assumed a significant role on the core leadership team of the corporation and shifted power over matters and money from outside law firms to inside legal departments. As technical expert, wise counselor, and accountable leader, the position of General Counsel is now characterized by capacious scope—by broad substantive and organizational responsibilities in such key areas as business, law, compliance, ethics, risk, governance, public policy, and citizenship. As a lawyer-statesman, the General Counsel must provide lead guidance on the issue of "is it legal" but, on both legal and non-legal matters, must also relentlessly raise the "is it right" question about corporate decisions and corporate actions as seen through the lenses of performance, integrity, and risk. As a partner and a guardian working directly for the CEO, the General Counsel has core responsibility in fusing high performance with high integrity and sound risk management in order to carry out the basic mission of the global corporation. In so doing, the General Counsel plays a vital role in devising and implementing major strategies and operational objectives that create value and competitive advantage and help the corporation secure the fundamental trust among stakeholders and other affected parties upon which durable enterprise success is based. This, at least, is the practical ideal I have tried to set out in this book.

A. EXTENDING THE GC'S REACH

The scope of the General Counsel's responsibilities is daunting because it extends far beyond opining on what is law and far beyond leading the legal organization. One can fairly ask whether it is possible for a single person to handle all the issues that I have termed "fundamental" or "foundational" or "core" or "essential" throughout this book. The short answer is: "no." I certainly couldn't do it. There are not enough hours in the day or weeks in the year to be deeply involved as expert, counselor, and leader in ascertaining the law in myriad domains in more than 100 nations; in helping establish compliance systems and a performance with integrity culture; in helping to establish ethical standards relating to the company, the stakeholders, the legal system, and society; in assessing and mitigating the vast array of economic and noneconomic risks facing the corporation; and in addressing the multi-faceted subjects of governance and citizenship—all while being responsive to daily crises; dealing with requests of the CEO, the board, and top business leadership; and leading not just the legal organization, but other units within the company.

But the answer can't be "no" because every one of the issues I discuss truly are "fundamental" or "foundational" to the corporation and require the involvement—the initiative, drive, *and vision*—of the General Counsel, directly or indirectly. So the answer is that the General Counsel needs to do what every leader must do in large, complex organizations. Across all her domains, the GC must prioritize those central issues she will learn and manage herself. And she must prioritize the others and delegate—relying on outstanding people for the creative but detailed work required to resolve them. By "hiring the best," either as corporate specialists or as General Counsel of the Business Divisions, the GC will create a powerful set of partners who can extend the reach and influence of the legal organization in immeasurable ways. I must underscore that any success of the GE Legal organization during my tenure was due to world-class senior lawyers both at corporate head-quarters and in the businesses.

The General Counsel must also make strong alliances with the other key staff leaders—in Finance, HR, Compliance, Risk, and IT—because (allow me to emphasize this, too, one more time) *cross-functional integration is necessary on virtually all complex performance, integrity, and risk issues facing the company.* The GC must be prepared to work with, *and for,* these other staff corporate leaders as a member of teams, with the nature of the alliance varying across the wide range of corporate needs. For example, the senior inside SEC lawyer will be closely tied into the Finance function on a host of disclosure, audit, and controller-ship issues; the head of Corporate Taxes will report both to the GC and the CFO; the senior Labor and Employment lawyer will be a virtual member of the HR organization. Finally, the GC must find a select set of individual partners outside the corporation—in law firms or in alternative providers or in academia or in think tanks or in consulting firms—who can take responsibility for the systemic issues described here, not just discrete problems, that cannot be led and managed by people inside the corporation. If the corporation does not have the resources or the volume of work to hire outstanding inside lawyers, the General Counsel must have a very direct, very personal substantive relationship with these outside experts/leaders whom the legal depart-ment must rely on to extend its reach and impact on priority matters. Without this structure of inside and outside delegation and alliances, the practical ideals of the General Counsel as lawyer-statesman and partner-guardian—with a set of responsibilities as broad as the cor-poration—cannot be realized.

Another personal obstacle for the General Counsel is whether she has the vision and the skills to conceptualize and then execute on the broad role outlined here. To some extent, such vision and skills are a product of innate breadth of mind and actual breadth of experience. But there is also a need for education and training to build a broad and strong foundation for those who would assume the General Counsel position. I believe that we must start by dramatically changing law school education. It must emphasize the roles of expert, counselor, and leader. It must underscore the ethical responsibilities of lawyers, as professionals and as citizens, to their own institution and its people, to their clients/stakeholders, to the rule of law and the administration of justice, and to the broader society. It must inculcate an understanding of complementary competencies needed beyond the core competencies of law: a broader set of capabilities that are so necessary to solving the broad problems law graduates will face because the accurate definition of those problems—and their solution—depends on many other factors and disciplines beyond law itself. Such a revised education would include courses and cases that look at a broad range of legal, business, and policy subjects and a broad range of societal problems from the perspective, not just of the appellate judge, but from a broad range of actors in the public, private, and nonprofit sectors. It would mean far closer connections between the world of ideas and the world of action. Small steps in this direction are being taken in an increasing number of courses on the role of the General Counsel that are now being offered at some law schools.[1] In addition, General Counsels themselves also have an obligation to the members of their legal organization to provide education and training on the vision for inside counsel—including real case studies exploring dilemmas, options, and trade-offs—and on "complementary competencies" both at initial orientation but, more importantly, throughout their careers in the corporation (see pp. 41–46).

B. ATTITUDES: BOARDS OF DIRECTORS, CEOS, AND BUSINESS LEADERS

CEOs and boards of directors must genuinely believe in the fundamental goal of fusing high performance with high integrity and sound risk management as a means of creating the corporate trust so necessary to sustainability. Similarly, company leaders must believe in the value of broad-gauged lawyers who have skills beyond law, from ethics to country risk to corporate citizenship. And, ultimately, the CEO and the board of directors must understand the partner-guardian role of the key staff leaders, including the General Counsel. The CEO and the board must make clear to the corporation's business leaders that they need wholeheartedly to support the efforts of these staff leaders—business leaders must also genuinely believe in the role of the GC in helping attain the corporation's high performance and providing an independent point of view as guardians of the corporation's integrity and risk management. Everyone who has held the position of General Counsel knows that the attitudes and behavior of the CEO are key to the realization of the prescriptions advanced here. Yes, a strong partner-guardian ethic in the legal organization can help. Yes, an alliance among the GC, CFO, HR head, and other staff leaders is vital. Yes, the board of directors can take a number of steps to promote a partner-guardian relationship, including oversight of hiring, regular meetings with the GC, inclusion of the GC in the board culture, and direct involvement in setting and structuring GC compensation (see pp. 75–81). But, for all the governance mechanisms and for all the variety in styles of leadership, the corporation is still a much more hierarchical entity than other large public or nonprofit organizations where power and authority is more diffuse. The broad role I urge for General Counsel will be possible *only if the CEO wills it*. In carrying out the multiplicity of tasks necessary in a modern corporation, it is without question that the GC must navigate complex internal relationships (with business leaders, the board of directors, peer senior officers, the corporate bureaucracy, the legal organization) and challenging external ones (with diverse stakeholders, governments, NGOs, and media in nations and regions across the globe). *This is only possible with the support of the CEO. That support must constantly be earned but, if earned, constantly given.*

So, yes, the ability of the General Counsel to be an exemplar of the practical ideal of lawyer-statesman *within a corporation* is contingent on many factors, with none more important than the vision and attitude of the CEO, supported by the vision and attitude of the board of directors. *Due to the external pressures on corporations that have been a major cause of the inside counsel revolution and that are only going to increase, I believe the revolution will continue to gain board and CEO adherents in many, many companies.* High performance with high integrity is not goo-goo idealism, but is the bedrock goal now for many global corporations exposed increasingly to complex commercial challenges and to a broad variety of "business in society" risks and opportunities. Sophisticated CEOs and boards know that successful performance depends importantly on navigating effectively and fairly the myriad laws and regulations that limit business. They know that the legal function itself can create significant value: in tax, trade, environment, IP, M&A, commercial law, and public policy. They know that the company must deal in a systematic and rigorous way with the core issues of compliance, ethics, risk, governance, and citizenship. They also know that highly talented, broadly experienced, analytically rigorous, and consistently innovative General Counsel—and an outstanding law department—are essential to discharging those basic corporate responsibilities and to enhancing discussion and debate on key corporate decisions. I have tried to make the case that CEOs and boards "should know" all these things. But, of course, there will be companies where such attitudes simply may not exist. Nor can anyone "prescribe" the creation of good chemistry between the CEO and the GC—on that we are back to the ineffable importance of serendipity and contingency.

As with General Counsels, so too with CEOs there is the potential obstacle that, at least when they assume the top spot, CEOs simply do not have the breadth of vision about the appropriate mission of the corporation—and about the appropriate role of the General Counsel. One answer is that business schools, like law schools, need to reorient their basic education to deal with broad business in society issues that are so important in leading global enterprises in this era and to focus on the imperative of the partner-guardian role in the key Finance, Legal, HR, Compliance, Risk, and IT leaders. In addition to a new emphasis on entrepreneurship, some business schools are also seeking to give new emphasis to business in society issues.[2] More importantly, this issue must be addressed by boards of directors in the first three of the six essential tasks of leadership I discuss in Chapter 8 on governance: redefining the mission of the corporation; changing programs for leadership development to address the range of performance, integrity, and risk issues; and ensuring that the CEO succession/selection process focuses on candidates who, in fact, have the necessary experience, vision, and commitment. If the board fails in this task and the CEO has to develop these traits on the job, then the General Counsel may have an even more important role in aiding that process or may find herself in "GC Hell" with a tone-deaf and narrow-minded boss.

C. MAKING THE CASE THAT COST CREATES VALUE

In a highly competitive global corporation, the cost of the legal function—and of the larger issues of compliance, ethics, risk, and citizenship—are always an issue for the CEO. The General Counsel must pay intense, personal attention to questions of cost and productivity as the foundation in a relationship of trust with the CEO, the board, and other senior executives. In other words: *The GC must make the case that cost creates value.* To do this, the GC must develop financial methodologies that are as sophisticated as possible for the different issues she confronts. Yet, many of the decisions about resource allocation are issues of judgment, and the General Counsel will need to make cogent and persuasive nonfinancial arguments as well. The question of cost is a potential obstacle to all the functions of the General Counsel, but it is also an opportunity to have very sophisticated, realistic, and hard-headed discussions and debates with the board, the CEO, and the senior business leaders about what is in the corporation's best interest and what the corporation stands for.

Whether the subject is the cost of compliance, of ethics, of risk, of governance, of citizenship, or of inside/outside legal spend, five different approaches to cost should be distinguished in making the case to the CEO and other business leaders that "cost creates value" and that existing or additional expenditures are warranted and will generally be used with efficiency and effectiveness.

First, the expenditure can lead to *increased productivity and net reductions in direct cost.* Investment in preventive legal initiatives to meet either legal/financial requirements or to comply with corporate ethical decisions can lead to clear cost savings—for example, reduction in customer complaints or lawsuits; resolving commercial disputes through mediation, not litigation; or simplifying and improving the manufacturing process as part of complying with environmental laws or reducing workplace injuries and lost time. These and many other initiatives can lead, in a relatively short time-frame, to hard net cost savings.

Second, the expenditure can lead to *net added direct financial value.* Many investments in the legal function can create hard, measurable net value creation in such areas as tax (increase in book income and cash flow), IP (license income), trade (opening markets and increasing revenue and profits), and M&A (good due diligence disciplines, including integrity issues, so deal pro formas don't blow up down the road and may even exceed projections). Other investments have the potential of creating hard, ascertainable value such as the broad array of public policy initiatives discussed earlier (see pp. 335–353).

Third, the expenditure can lead to *less tangible but still real future value that turns as much on judgment as on hard financials.* The value of voluntary actions taken under the rubric of "ethics" or the closely related and more expansive heading of "citizenship" may be hard to estimate in a hard financial sense. But companies still engage in ethical sourcing. They still seek to reduce the harmful externalities from making products that impose costs on society. They seek still to build facilities to world, not local, environmental standards. All these steps require careful analysis and judgment, even if they do not lend themselves to precise financial expression, because *not only may they avoid reputational harm, but they may benefit the company internally, in the marketplace, and in broader society.* Having a regular, systematic process for identifying, analyzing, and deciding issues that require voluntary action by the corporation is important in order to have a meaningful debate about whether the direct costs are worth it to create real benefit, which may have a directional, but not precise, financial expression.

Fourth, the expenditure can *avoid costs, financial and nonfinancial, arising from the risks of noncompliance with mandatory legal and financial rules or from other economic and noneconomic risks.* Decisions about nature of the compliance must be risk based. Corporations need to make explicit decisions about which compliance and legal risk issues are serious enough to warrant a platinum compliance regime and which issues are of lesser concern (while still important) and can be addressed with a silver or bronze regime. Amid the welter of laws and regulations affecting a global corporation, risk-assessing obligations to comply with formal, mandated rules is one of the most challenging tasks for the General Counsel, in important part because of the difficulty in predicting the cost of events that have not yet happened. Similarly, funds for the legal department may help mitigate a wide variety of other risks (e.g., in understanding specific issues of country or geopolitical risk in areas where the corporation is considering significant investments).

Fifth, the expenditure can flow from a special process *to identify and address the potentially catastrophic events* where the resulting costs would be vastly greater than the outlays to prevent and detect. In a fast-changing world, corporations are faced with an increasing number of potentially catastrophic risks from natural acts; terrorism; cyber crime; geopolitical shifts; and failures in their own systems, processes, and products (see pp. 244–249). Identifying the high-impact/low-probability occurrences worthy of high-level attention, and resourcing systems of prevention and response, is a supreme act of corporate leadership that demands General Counsel statesmanship.

There is no rote script for determining whether those costs occur solely in the province of the General Counsel or jointly in the province of the General Counsel and other senior staff and business leaders in the corporation. But General Counsels must generally work with other staff and business leaders to distinguish between these types of expenditures and to then make the case for them. In concert with her peers, she must know when a hard financial expression works and when, on the other hand, a complexity of factors are implicated and judgment more than numeracy is required. General Counsel must have this set of skills to demonstrate that "cost creates value"—or must develop them—if they are effectively to address the financial constraints that demand the CEO's constant attention and pose a constant obstacle to doing what is "right" for the corporation.

The issues of cost—and the attainability of the goals in this book—are of great moment for small and medium-sized companies. They, too, must strive for high performance with high integrity and sound risk management. They, too, must address the core issues of compliance, ethics, risk, governance, and citizenship. They, too, must grapple with many of the difficult choices facing large corporations. But, of course, they must scale their efforts to fit their size, not ignoring these core concerns but focusing on what is essential for them in terms of impact on their stakeholders and risk to their sustainability. They must comply with law, but their program may be bronze, not gold. They may adopt some ethical standards, but not a full complement. They have to mitigate the most salient risks but may not have the capacity to address others. The resource allocation decisions for these small and medium-sized companies are even more difficult than those made by global behemoths. Doing more with less is a vital watchword in these companies—and even more of an imperative for the CEO, business leaders, General Counsel, and other staff as they try to grow their companies while managing, with unyielding good faith, core integrity, risk, and citizenship issues. *I deeply believe that the framework advanced here applies to small and medium-sized enterprises. The question is not applicability. It is scalability.*

D. GOING GLOBAL?[3]

The inside counsel movement is going global. In the UK and, increasingly, in Western Europe, the General Counsel has an emerging, important role as partner-guardian in company leadership and in asserting control over outside law firms on both matters and money. This is occurring in major multinationals and, to a more limited extent, in important national companies. Similar trends are beginning to take hold in the rest of the world, especially in developing economies with rule of law like India and Brazil. Even in societies with weak rule of law and undue influence of the ruling political party, like China and Russia, the role and importance of inside counsel is changing in global companies headquartered there, whether private or state owned.

At this stage in the global transformation of the legal profession, trends are suggestive, but not definitively established. Moreover, the specific roles and characteristics of lawyering inside corporations will vary with the history and culture of particular nations, including differences in legal systems, and with the size and reach of corpora-tions. This is the tentative conclusion of the project on Globalization, Lawyers, and Emerging Economies (GLEE) at Harvard Law School's Center on the Legal Profession, a leader in academic research on the legal profession around the world. GLEE is studying the role of inside counsel in jurisdictions outside the United States according to six cri-teria drawn from U.S. experience: the size of in-house departments; the credentials and demographics of the lawyers working inside these departments; the relationship to, and degree of control over, outside counsel; the internal standing, jurisdiction, and authority of in-house lawyers within their organizations; the professional standing of inter-nal counsel in the profession as a whole; and the participation and influence of general counsel in larger public policy debates, both nationally and internationally. Although the research is in its early stages, the data on some of the six criteria indicate growth of Gen-eral Counsel and Legal department importance in Europe and the BRIC countries (Brazil, Russia, India, and China). One symbol of this growth is the globalization of corporate counsel associations—includ-ing the Association of Corporate Counsel, which dropped "American" from its name in 2003 and now has members in more than 75 nations. It is also reflected in the emergence of inside counsel associations and inside counsel "trade press" outside the United States.[4]

These trends are driven, in important part, by multinational cor-porations in the developed world as they seek to address the myriad issues of compliance, ethics, risk, governance, and citizenship in their activities all across the globe. But multinationals in the developing world, faced with the challenges of navigating complex legal and ethical issues both inside and outside their home nations, are hiring sophisticated international lawyers to assume broad expert, counsel-ing, and leadership roles. Multinationals of all stripes, in turn, provide models for major in-country or regional corporations that, faced with international competition and growing regulation, may choose to have stronger inside Legal departments to provide wise counseling to busi-ness leaders and to limit or replace outside counsel.

To be sure, even as current trends begin to gather momentum, the inside counsel movement—much less an inside counsel revolution—is hardly universal outside the United States (or even inside it). For example, even in Europe, inside lawyers may not be members of bar associations and, in an infamous, wrong-headed—indeed, laughable— decision, the European Court of Justice ruled that lawyers employed by corporations could not invoke the protections of the attorney–client privilege because they were not as "independent" as outside counsel (who, of course, are totally dependent on clients for their livelihood). In some non-U.S. companies, General Counsel may not report to the CEO. Moreover, compensation for the General Counsel outside the United States may be much less than for lawyers in law firms, in contrast to leading American General Counsel, who receive comparable or even higher compensation (if counting deferred equity) than most successful law firm partners. Moreover, in nations like China or Russia where rule of law as we know it is weak (at best), the role of inside counsel will, of course, be quite different from the role of General Counsel of American multinationals. But, even in those nations, a person with expertise in the law, policy, and politics may have an important function because the state is so involved in the economy and because there is thus a huge body of formal and informal rules that is unclear in meaning and enforcement and because the line between politics/power and those rules is so blurry.

Here is a recent summary about Europe from Harvard's David Wilkins, a renowned expert on the legal profession and leader of the GLEE program:

> But even in Europe where the formal status of in-house lawyers remains largely unchanged, there is evidence of the growing power and influence of general counsel, particularly in large companies. Given the European Union's complex legal landscape of centralized directives which are implemented by decentralized laws enacted by member states many European companies have begun to develop increasingly large and sophisticated internal legal departments to help them understand and navigate these differing—and often competing—standards. In recent years, this trend has been reinforced by corporate scandals such as Enron, WorldCom, and Parmalat, and the new

regulatory requirements that have followed in their wake, which have further convinced many European companies of the value of a robust in-house legal department that can anticipate and help to avoid these regulatory pitfalls. [Footnotes omitted][5]

And here is an anecdotal view from an Indian General Counsel about his country:

I think the major shift happened post-1995 when the liberalization actually took off with telecom, power and information technology sectors opening up. With a lot of American joint ventures and business houses being established in India, the concept of an "in-house" counsel gained credence. Today, it is an integral and inevitable part of any organization—big or small—with some large business houses boasting of large in-house teams.[6]

Wilkins offers the following general observation about inside lawyering in the emerging economies of Brazil, Russia, India, China, and South Africa: "[T]he trend appears to point clearly in the direction of the growing sophistication and importance of in-house counsel working within BRICS-based companies."

A recent *Financial Times* survey of legal departments in Asia—both in global multinationals and Asia-Pacific companies—supports Wilkins's view: "In-house lawyers in Asia-Pacific companies are taking on new roles to help business expand and invest overseas, while those at global companies are developing solutions to navigate the unique challenges of managing legal functions across the region . . . With essential technical expertise and international experience, in-house lawyers have been propelled from the back-office to the frontline of strategic decision-making and complex deals." The *Financial Times* report notes that "the international experience of lawyers working in growing Asian companies makes them best equipped to bridge traditional management and business culture. Lawyers have become pivotal communicators and translators between their companies and overseas investors, regulators and partners."[7] Increasingly, lawyers from many nations are educated, trained, and initially employed in sophisticated law firms or law departments—and then change positions to work for both multinational and local corporations in the developing world.

In sum, despite diversity in the shape and momentum of trends in particular countries, the inside counsel movement will continue to grow in *global companies* because both global or in-country business is increasingly complex; because broad business and society issues of law, ethics, risk, and governance are increasingly front of mind for boards and business leaders; and because highly talented inside lawyers are increasingly seen as adding significant value to corporations. So, too, the role of General Counsel will increase in importance—though perhaps not to the same extent—in *major local and regional companies* that face competitive threats from global companies; increasingly complex commercial issues; and business in society challenges from in-country government, NGOs, and the media. Although the developing role of General Counsel and inside lawyers will vary within companies and countries, there is likely to be one important constant. The positions of General Counsel and top inside lawyers will only attract the best talent if the GC and senior corporate lawyers have a strong, direct relationship with the CEO and other business leaders and if the compensation packages CEOs and boards set are competitive with private law firms.

E. PARTNER AND GUARDIAN

For the General Counsel to play a critical role in helping corporations achieve their foundational goal of fusing high performance with high integrity and sound risk management, she must resolve two fundamental tensions.

First, there is the tension between the GC as lawyer-statesman and as a subordinate of the CEO. As expert, counselor, and leader, the General Counsel must perform the fundamental task of the lawyer-statesman: Consistently and insistently ask not just what is "legal" but what is "right" in terms of performance, integrity, and risk both inside the corporation and in the corporation's many interactions with society. This "what is right" question occurs because the General Counsel plays *a vital role in contributing to major decisions and in implementing strategies and operational objectives that create value and that infuse the corporation with high integrity and sound risk management.* I have used the "lawyer-statesman" phrase to connote the practical idealism of the worldly, broad-gauged lawyer who focuses on the purposes of corporate decisions, on the consequences of corporate actions, and on both the prudential and moral dimensions of what the corporation does. But the General Counsel works for a board of directors and CEO and has peers on the senior corporate staff and in business operations. She is part of a complex institution where power, under the CEO, is shared and where her voice is often collegial not authoritative. She can seek to advance the lawyer-statesman's vision and ideals, but she can, in most instances, only do that when able to persuade her colleagues and her CEO about the soundness of her position. She may be the final decision maker on some issues, but on most matters of corporate consequence, she is one voice—a senior, important, and proactive voice to be sure—but only one voice who advances superb analysis and then articulates a vision of what course of action is in the enlightened self-interest of the corporation. Only rarely on firm-wide issues is it a voice that commands. But, paradoxically, it can still be a voice of statesmanship inside a corporation.

Second, to carry out this lawyer-statesman role as expert, counselor, and leader, the General Counsel must resolve the second tension of being both partner to the CEO and guardian of the company. Virtually every critique of the concept of the General Counsel I advance here is a variation on the same theme: lack of independence. In Chapter 3 on partner-guardian realities, I describe a variety of factors that can erode or impair the General Counsel's exercise of broad independent judgment. Yet, as with the tension of a lawyer-statesman operating in a structure of shared power, so the tension of being partner to the CEO and guardian of the company can be resolved and the force of the critique substantially reduced. To be a trusted guardian, a General Counsel must be a trusted partner. CEOs must want to have as their chief inside lawyer a person who has broad range and judgment as expert, counselor, and leader and who is not a reflexive "naysayer" nor a reflexive "yea-sayer." Instead, the CEO must want a General Counsel who will be a great contributor to performance goals and a powerful and independent voice on integrity and risk. The inside counsel revolution has been built on General Counsels and other senior inside lawyers who are both partners and guardians in a fast-changing world where their experience, skills, and vision are necessary for companies facing great global commercial complexity and pressing business and society issues. I believe that the revolution will grow apace because both senior executives and General Counsel will continue to understand that the vitality of enduring trust between business leader and business lawyer—in the service of a high performance with high integrity global corporation operating in complex global society—is based on deep respect for both the partner and guardian roles.

NOTES

Chapter 1

1. Schumpeter, "A Guardian and a Guide: Chief Legal Officers Have More Power Than Ever Before," *The Economist* (April 7, 2012); Michael H. Trotter, *Declining Prospects: How Extraordinary Competition and Compensation are Changing America's Major Law Firms* (Atlanta: Trotter, 2012) at 130–31; David B. Wilkins, "Is the In-House Counsel Movement Going Global? A Preliminary Assessment of the Role of Internal Counsel in Emerging Economies," 2012 *Wisconsin L. Rev.* 251, 252–53 (2012); Prashant Dubey and Eva Kripalani, *The Generalist Counsel: How Leading General Counsel Are Shaping Tomorrow's Companies* (Oxford: Oxford Univ. Press, 2013) at 163.

2. See, e.g., these oft-cited articles: Abram Chayes and Antonia H. Chayes, "Corporate Counsel and the Elite Law Firm," 37 *Stanford L. Rev.* 277 (January 1985); Robert Eli Rosen, "The Inside Counsel Movement, Professional Judgment and Organizational Representation," 64 *Ind. L. J.* 479, 508–09 (1989); Ronald J. Gilson, "The Devolution of the Legal Profession: a Demand Side Perspective," 49 *Maryland L. Rev.* 869, 902–03, 915 (1990) (general counsel "creating" a "revolution").

3. Anthony Borden, "Ben Heineman's In-House Revolution," *American Lawyer* (September 1989); Ben W. Heineman, Jr., "In the Beginning," *Corporate Counsel* (April 2006). My initial colleagues are listed in a special sidebar in the *Corporate Counsel* article with their positions as of the publication date. Other important GE inside lawyers during my tenure include Nancy Barton, Ted Boehm, Barbara Daniele, Ugo Draetta, Scott Gilbert, Ralph Gonzalez, Suzanne Hawkins, Scott Gilbert, Bob Healing, Bruce Hunter, Rick Jackson, Art Joyce, Burt Kloster, Phil Lacovara, Elizabeth Lee, Steve Maloy, Mike McAlevey, Liam McCollum, Paul McElhiney, Keith Morgan, Mark Nordstrom, Leon Roday, Bob Sloan, Peter Solmssen, and Nick Spaeth.

4. See, generally, Constance E. Bagley and Mark D. Roellig, "The Transformation of General Counsel: Setting the Strategic Legal Agenda," in Charles Wild and Stuart Weinstein, eds., *Legal Risk Management, Governance and Compliance: A Guide to Best Practice from Leading Experts* (London: Globe Law and Business, 2013) at 45–66; Carl D. Liggio, Sr., "A Look at the Role of Corporate Counsel: Back to the Future—Or Is It the Past?" 44 *Ariz. L. Rev.* 621 (2002); Sarah Helene Duggin, "The Pivotal Role of the General Counsel in Promoting Corporate Integrity and Professional Responsibility," 51 *St. Louis Univ. L. J.* 989, 990–1001 & n.43 (2007); Prashant Dubey and Eva Kripalani, *The Generalist Counsel: How Leading General Counsel Are Shaping Tomorrow's Companies* (Oxford: Oxford Univ. Press, 2013) at 46–47. Liggio, then GC of Ernst & Young, Robert Banks, GC of Xerox, and Jack Brigham III, GC of Hewlett-Packard, were principal founders of the American Association of Corporate Counsel (now the Association of Corporate Counsel) in 1982.

Chapter 2

1. Sue Reisinger, "Balancing Legality and Ethics In-House," *Corporate Counsel* (November 10, 2014) (discussing views of Stuart Levey, general counsel of HSBC: "Levey's 'aha' moment came when he read the work of Ben Heineman, Jr., the former general counsel of General Electric Co . . . who urged GCs to be lawyers/statesmen, to consider not just what is legal but also what is right, and to advise not only about current problems but about potential future ones as well."); Constance E. Bagley, *Winning Legally: How to Use Law to Create Value, Marshall Resources and Manage Risk* (Cambridge, MA: Harvard Business School Press, 2005) at 227 (quoting Indira Nooyi, when Pepsi's President and CFO, urging lawyers to bring both legal and business judgment to bear: "We can't afford this separation of church and state."); Kenneth C. Frazier, "Remarks," *American Law Institute 90th Annual Meeting* (May 21, 2013) (as a CEO urging his lawyers to provide broad counseling, citing Rule 2.l of the Model Rules of Professional Conduct: "In representing a client, a lawyer shall exercise independent professional judgment and render candid advice. In rendering advice, a lawyer may refer not only to law but to other considerations such as moral, economic, social and political factors that may be relevant to the client's situation.").

2. Alexis de Tocqueville, *Democracy in America*, trans. Harvey Mansfield and Delba Winthrop (Chicago: University of Chicago Press, 2000); Joseph J. Ellis, *Founding Brothers: The Revolutionary Generation* (New York: Alfred

A. Knopf, 2000); Ben W. Heineman, Jr., "The Origins of Today's Bitter Partisanship: The Founding Fathers," *The Atlantic* (September 9, 2011).

Modern discussions of the lawyer-statesman ideal usually begin with a book decrying its decline: Anthony Kronman, *The Lost Lawyer: Failing Ideals of the Legal Profession* (Cambridge, MA: Harvard Univ. Press, 1995). See also, William H. Rehnquist, "The Lawyer-Statesman in American History," 9 *Harv. J. L. & Pub. Pol'y* 537 (1986); James M. Altmant, "Modern Litigators and Lawyer-Statesmen," 103 *Yale L. J. 1031* (1994) (book review of Kronman); David B. Wilkins, "Practical Wisdom for Practicing Lawyers: Separating Ideals from Ideology in Legal Ethics," 108 *Harv. L. Rev.* 458 (1994) (book review of Kronman). It is far beyond the scope or intent of this book to present an intellectual history of the lawyer-statesman ideal, but I have elsewhere offered a critique of Kronman's unduly dire account of modern lawyering. See Ben W. Heineman, Jr., "Law and Leadership," 56 *J. Legal Education* 596 (2006). As emphasized in the text, the phrase, as used here, connotes the practical act of asking the question in very concrete corporate settings of whether an action is "right" from a broad array of perspectives, including commercial, prudential, legal, ethical, risk, and citizenship. For my purposes, the concept of lawyer-statesman at core involves a *general commitment to the insistent act of "asking what is right," with attention to purpose and consequences and against the screens of performance, integrity, and risk and associated concepts like ethics and citizenship.*

3. Louis D. Brandeis, "The Opportunity in the Law" (1905), http://www .minnesotalegalhistoryproject.org/assets/Brandeis%20-%20%20(1905). pdf. See also, Melvin I. Urofsky, *Louis D. Brandeis: A Life* (New York: Schocken Books, 2009), 202–06.

4. Robert W. Gordon, "A New Role for Lawyers: The Corporate Counselor after Enron," 35 *Connecticut L. Rev.* 1185, 1208–09 (2002).

5. *Id.* at 1209–10. Professor Gordon has written extensively on the need for lawyers serving corporations to maintain an independent perspective. See, e.g., Robert W. Gordon, "The Independence of Lawyers," 68 *Boston Univ. L. Rev.* 1 (1988); Robert W. Gordon, "Money! Power! Ambition Gone Awry!: A Frank History of the Big-Time American Lawyer," *Legal Affairs* (March–April 2006).

6. Anthony Kronman, *The Lost Lawyer: Failing Ideals of the Legal Profession* (Cambridge, MA: Harvard Univ. Press, 1995) at 308–09, 379.

7. See, e.g., E. Norman Veasey and Christine T. Di Guglielmo, *Indispensable Counsel: The Chief Legal Officer in the New Reality* (Oxford: Oxford Univ.

Press, 2012), 35–46; Association of Corporate Counsel, "Anticipating the Challenges and Meeting the Demands in Today's Corporate Practice," *Docket* (October 2004).

8. Ben W. Heineman, Jr., William F. Lee, and David B. Wilkins, "Lawyers as Professionals and as Citizens: Key Roles and Responsibilities in the 21st Century," *Harvard Law School Center on the Legal Profession* (2014).

9. Geoffrey C. Hazard, Jr., "Ethical Dilemmas of Corporate Counsel," 46 *Emory L. J.* 1011 (1997).

10. Prashant Dubey and Eva Kripalani, *The Generalist Counsel: How Leading General Counsel Are Shaping Tomorrow's Companies* (Oxford: Oxford Univ. Press, 2013), 118–36; Leigh Dance, "CEOs Higher Expectations of General Counsel," *Corporate Counsel* (June 3, 2015) (describing business roles of Accenture GC Julie Sweet before being promoted to CEO for North America); David Hechler, "Brad Smith Talks About Getting Kicked Upstairs," *Corporate Counsel* (September 17, 2015) (discusses his business role as chief legal officer, both before and after being promoted to *both* president and CLO of Microsoft).

11. I initially enumerated these complementary competencies in a lecture on lawyers as leaders at Yale Law School in 2006: Ben W. Heineman, Jr., "Law and Leadership," 56 *J. Legal Education* 596 (2006). They were refined and restated in a subsequent co-authored essay: Ben W. Heineman, Jr., William F. Lee, and David B. Wilkins, "Lawyers as Professionals and as Citizens: Key Roles and Responsibilities in the 21st Century," *supra*, note 8, at 13–17, 51–52.

12. Association of Corporate Counsel, "ACC Chief Legal Officers 2015 Survey" (2015) at 10, http://webcasts.acc.com/handouts/ACC_273_77C5_610_ACC-Chief-Legal-Officer-CLO-2015-Survey-Executive-Summary.pdf; Association of Corporate Counsel, "Skills for the 21st Century General Counsel," 2013, http://www.acc.com/legalresources/upload/GCSkills EbookRevised.pdf. These surveys are directional. They point to a broader array of non-legal skills General Counsels need, although they do not track precisely the detailed list of "complementary competencies" presented here.

13. Steven Levy, *In the Plex: How Google Thinks, Works, and Shapes Our Lives* (New York: Simon & Schuster, 2011) at 272–314; David Drummond, "A New Approach to China: An Update," *Google Official Blog* (March 22, 2010), http://googleblog.blogspot.com/2010/03/new-approach-to-china-update.html; Michael Wines, "Google to Alert Users to Chinese Censorship," *The New York Times* (June 1, 2012).

14. Neal Batson, *Final Report of Court Appointed Examiner in Enron Bankruptcy Case* (November 4, 2003), at 6–13, 48–55, http://www.concerned-shareholders.com/CCS_ENRON_Report.pdf. See also, *Appendix C* (Role of Enron's Attorneys in Watkins Inquiry), 159–78, http://www.acc.com/vl/public/Article/loader.cfm?csModule=security/getfile&pageid=16097; Gordon, "A New Role for Lawyers? The Corporate Counselor After Enron." 35 *Connecticut L. Rev.* 1185, 1208–09 (2002).

15. Ben W. Heineman, Jr., "General Counsel Are *One* Conscience of the Company: A Response to IBM's Robert Weber," *Corporate Counsel* (January 24, 2013).

Chapter 3

1. Sue Reisinger, "Did Ann Baskins See No Evil at HP?" *Corporate Counsel* (2006); see, e.g., In the Matter of Google, Inc. and David C. Drummond, Admin. Proc. Rel. No. 33-8523, http://www.sec.gov/litigation/admin/33-8523.htm; January 13, 2005; Securities and Exchange Commission v. Nancy R. Heinen, Case No. C-07-2214 (JF) (N.D. Cal.), http://www.sec.gov/litigation/litreleases/2008/lr20683.htm, August 14, 2008; Sung Hui Kim, "Gatekeepers Inside Out," 21 *Georgetown J. Legal Ethics* 411, 413 (2008) (resignations of general counsel due to back-dating issues).

2. See, generally, John K. Villa, *Corporate Counsel Guidelines* (St. Paul, MN: Thomson Reuters, 2014), Section 6:18; E. Norman Veasey and Christine T. Di Guglielmo, *Indispensable Counsel: The Chief Legal Officer in the New Reality* (Oxford: Oxford Univ. Press, 2012); Jonathan C. Dickey and Jeffrey E. Minnery, "Trends in Claims Against Lawyers," *Securities Litigation Report* (February 2007, volume 4, no. 2); Association of Corporate Counsel, "In-House Counsel in the Liability Cross-Hairs" (September 2007), www.acc.com/vl/public/Article/upload/ACCReportsInHouse CounselintheLiabilityCrosshairs.pdf.

　　See also, Sue Reisinger, "In-House Lawyers, Compliance Officers Cited in BNP Deal," *Corporate Counsel* (July 2, 2014) ("Yet another corporate investigation . . . cites lax in-house lawyers and compliance officers for allowing the company to commit criminal acts."); Marjorie J. Peerce, Charles Stillman, and Elizabeth J. Lee, "Criminal Prosecution of In-House Counsel and Compliance," *Corporate Counsel* (March 3, 2015).

3. See, e.g., John C. Coffee, Jr., *Gatekeepers: The Professions and Corporate Governance* (Oxford: Oxford Univ. Press, 2006) at 195; Deborah A. DeMott, "The Discreet Roles of General Counsel," 74 *Fordham L. Rev.*

955, 967 (2005–2006); Sarah Kellogg, "Financial Crisis 2008: Where Were the Lawyers?" *Washington Lawyer* (January 2010).

4. Ben W. Heineman, Jr., "How GCs Can Avoid Being Caught in the Middle," *Corporate Counsel* (March 2007). The Association of the Bar of the City of New York, "Report of the Task Force on the Lawyer's Role in Corporate Governance," *New York City Bar* (2006); Veasey, *supra*, note 2 at 4, 53, 116; Sarah Helene Duggin, "The Pivotal Role of the General Counsel in Promoting Corporate Integrity and Professional Responsibility," 51 *St. Louis Univ. L. J.* 989 (2007); Omari Scott Simmons and James D. Dinnage, "Inkeepers: A Unifying Theory of the Inside Counsel Role," 41 *Seton Hall Law Rev.* 77 (2011); Sung Hui Kim, "Gatekeepers Inside Out," 21 *Georgetown J. Legal Ethics* 411 (2008); Lawrence A. Hamermesh, "Who Let You into the House?" 2012 *Wisconsin Law Rev.* 359 (2011); Christine Bader, "Corporate Lawyers Can Be More Than Naysayers-in-Chief," *The Atlantic* (May 8, 2015).

5. Constance E. Bagley, *Winning Legally: How to Use the Law to Create Value, Marshall Resources and Manage Risk* (Boston: Harvard Business School Press, 2005) at 8–10, 223–45; Charles H. Veigel, "The Chief Opportunity Counsel—How to Increase Your Value Through Participation in Strategic Business Conversations," *ACC Docket* (July–August 2014) at 30 ("Confirmed by a recent survey of general counsel and boards of directors, strategic input is an area of increasing value for the 21st century general counsel . . .").

6. Mary C. Daly, "The Cultural, Ethical, and Legal Challenges in Lawyering for a Global Organization: The Role of the General Counsel," 46 *Emory L. J.* 1057 (1997).

7. For discussion of desirable traits in legal leaders, see Anthony Kronman, *The Lost Lawyer: Failing Ideals of the Legal Profession* (Cambridge, MA: Harvard Univ. Press, 1995); Deborah L. Rhode and Amanda K. Packel, *Leadership: Law, Policy and Management* (New York: Wolters Kluwer, 2011); Ben W. Heineman, "Law and Leadership," 56 *J. Legal Education* 596 (2006).

8. 17 CFR 205; ABA Model Rules of Professional Conduct, Rule 1.13. Understanding and interpreting the technicalities of these rules—what lawyers are covered; what kinds of offenses; what triggering standards require reporting up; and what are the varying responsibilities of the reporting lawyer, the General Counsel, and the board—is complex. Inside lawyers, and GCs, must take great care in trying to follow these rules, the interpretation of which are not within the purpose or scope of this book. See,

e.g., The Association of the Bar of the City of New York, "Report of the Task Force on the Lawyer's Role in Corporate Governance," *New York City Bar Association* (2006) at 70–94; Veasey, *supra*, note 2 at 105–17, 200–04; Lawrence J. Fox and Susan R. Martyn, *The Ethics of Representing Organizations; Legal Fictions for Clients* (Oxford: Oxford Univ. Press, 2009); Sarah Helene Duggin, "The Pivotal Role of the General Counsel in Promoting Corporate Integrity and Professional Responsibility," 51 *St. Louis Univ. L. J.* 989, 1023–31 (2006–2007).

9. See, e.g., American Bar Association, "Report of the American Bar Association Task Force on Corporate Responsibility," 59 *Bus. L.* 145, 161 (November 2003); Duggin, *supra*, note 6, at 1039ff; Veasey, *supra*, note 2, at 68–86.

10. Sue Reisinger, "How HP General Counsel Michael Holston Handled CEO's Sex Harassment Nightmare," *Corporate Counsel* (August 10, 2010); Peter Lattman, "H-P Mess Casts Harsh Spotlight on Ann Baskins," *The Wall Street Journal* (September 12, 2006); James B. Stewart, "The Kona Files: How an Obsession with Leaks Brought Scandal to Hewlett-Packard," *The New Yorker* (February 19, 2007); Neal Batson, *Final Report of Court Appointed Examiner in Enron Bankruptcy Case* at 6–13, 48–55, http://www.concernedshareholders.com/CCS_ENRON_Report.pdf. See also, *Appendix C* (Role of Enron's Attorneys in Watkins Inquiry) at 159–78, http://www.acc.com/vl/public/Article/loader.cfm?csModule=security/getfile&pageid=16097.

11. Ben W. Heineman, Jr., "Before You Sign Up: Prospective GCs Need to Do Some Due Diligence on the CEO Before They Say Yes," *Corporate Counsel* (October 2008).

12. 17 CFR 205.3(d)(2); ABA Model Rules of Professional Responsibility, Rule 1.13 and Rule 1.6. Again, these rules require care in interpretation because they are far from self-executing. See note 8, *supra*. For example, Model Rule 1.6 requires that the lawyer's services have been used when there is wrong-doing, but Rule 1.13 does not. But Rule 1.13 is triggered only if there is the threat of substantial injury to the company, while Rule 1.16 encompasses a broad range of actual or threatened illegalities. These reporting up and out requirements for lawyers must be read in conjunction with various government whistleblower statutes, which provide bounties for reporting wrong-doing without any "exhaustion" or "reporting-up" requirement.

13. Sue Reisinger, "2 GCs Battled Their Companies, Got 2 Different Results," *Corporate Counsel* (August 10, 2015).

Chapter 4

1. Leslie Gaines-Ross, *Corporate Reputation: 12 Steps to Safeguarding and Recovering Reputation* (Hoboken, NJ: John Wiley & Sons, 2008) at 98–99.

2. John P. Kotter and James L. Heskett, *Corporate Culture and Performance* (New York: Free Press, 1992).

3. Anton R. Valukas, *Report to Board of Directors of General Motors Company Regarding Ignition Switch Recall* (May 29, 2014) at 1–12, 102–13, 139–44, 194–224, 226–58, 364–66, 275–77, https://assets.documentcloud. org/documents/1183508/g-m-internal-investigation-report.pdf; *GM CEO Mary Barra Remarks on Valukas Report Findings* (June 5, 2014), http:// media.gm.com/media/us/en/gm/news.detail.html/content/Pages/news /us/en/2014/Jun/060514-mary-remarks.html; *General Motors Executives Who Were Fired in Wake of Valukas Report Named*, June 6, 2014, http:// gmauthority.com/blog/2014/06/general-motors-executives-who-were -fired-in-wake-of-valukas-report-named/; Ben W. Heineman, Jr., "GC and CEO Responsibility for GM's Dysfunctional Culture," *Corporate Counsel* (June 6, 2014); John D. Stoll and Joseph B. White, "GM's General Counsel to Retire," *The Wall Street Journal* (October 17, 2014); Chris Woodyard, "GM Ignition Switch Deaths Hit 124," *USA Today* (July 13, 2015); Department of Justice, Office of Public Affairs, "Manhattan U.S. Attorney Announces Criminal Charges Against General Motors and Deferred Prosecution Agreement with $900 Million Forfeiture" (September 17, 2015); Danielle Ivory and Bill Vlasic, "G.M. Settles Ignition Switch Flaw Cases," *The New York Times* (September 18, 2015).

  The organizational delay at Ford and Bridgestone in addressing tread separation on Ford Explorers prior to a major tire recall in 2000 resembles GM's ignition switch failures and must have been well known to GM personnel. Lynn Sharp Paine, *Value Shift: Why Companies Must Merge Social and Financial Imperatives to Achieve Superior Performance* (New York: McGraw-Hill, 2003) at 89–90, 178–81. So, too, GM would have been well aware of the much more recent criminal investigation of Toyota for not disclosing issues relating to accelerator problems. A four-year government inquiry into Toyota had received extensive publicity during a critical period when GM took no action despite problems. Charles Levinson, Jeff Bennett, and Devlin Barrett, "Toyota to Pay $1.2 Billion to Settle U.S. Probe," *The Wall Street Journal* (March 19, 2014).

4. Arnold & Porter, "Siemens Pays Record $800 Million to Settle Systemic and Widespread FCPA Violations," *Client Advisory* (March 2009); Siemens Plea Agreement with Department of Justice, http://www.justice

.gov/opa/documents/siemens.pdf; Department of Justice's Sentencing Memorandum, United States v. Siemens Aktiengesellschaft et al., Criminal No. (December 12, 2008), http://www.justice.gov/sites/default /files/opa/legacy/2008/12/19/siemens-sentencing-memo.pdf; U.S. Justice Department, Office of Public Affairs, "Former Chief Financial Officer of Siemens Argentina Pleads Guilty To Role in Multi-Million Dollar Foreign Bribery Scheme" (September 30, 2015).

5. Richard Acello, "Enron Lawyers in the Hot Seat," *ABA Journal* (June 1, 2004); Special Investigative Committee of the Board of Directors of Enron Corp., *Report of Investigation* (February 1, 2002), http://news.find law.com/wsj/docs/enron/sicreport/; Ellen Joan Pollock, "Enron's Lawyers Faulted Deals But Failed to Blow the Whistle," *The Wall Street Journal* (May 22, 2002); Neal Batson, *Final Report of Court Appointed Examiner in Enron Bankruptcy Case,* http://www.concernedshareholders.com /CCS_ENRON_Report.pdf.

6. Ben W. Heineman, Jr., "Why Are Some Sectors (Ahem, Finance) So Scandal-Plagued?" *Harvard Business Review* (January 10, 2013); Sue Reisinger, "Big Bank Update: Fined, But It's Business As Usual," *Corporate Counsel* (September 1, 2015); Ben W. Heineman, Jr., "The JP Morgan 'Whale' Report and the Ghosts of the Financial Crisis," *Harvard Business Review* (January 24, 2013); Ben W. Heineman, Jr., "Too Big to Manage: JP Morgan and the Mega Banks," *Harvard Business Review* (October 3, 2013). For summary of JPM fines, see Jared Cummans, "JP Morgan's Fines to Date: A Brief History," *Dividend.com,* http://www.dividend.com/dividend-education/a-brief-history-of-jp-morgans-massive-fines-jpm/; "Tracking the JP Morgan Investigations," *The New York Times* (October 23, 2013), http://www.nytimes.com/interactive/2013/10/22/business/dealbook /jpmorgan-settlements-updates.html.

7. Jamie Dimon, "2013 Annual Letter to Shareholders" (April 10, 2013). See also, JP Morgan Chase, *How We Do Business—The Report* (December 2014) (on mistakes, culture and governance).

8. John Plender, "No End in Sight to a Rotten Culture," *Financial Times* (November 12, 2014); Richard Lambert, "The Blight at the Core of Banking Goes Beyond a Few Bad Apples," *Financial Times* (October 30, 2014); Victoria McGrane, "Yellen Says Supervision of Big Banks One of Fed's Top Priorities: Fed Chief Says Big Banks Have Too Often Flouted Law, Ethics in Recent Years," *The Wall Street Journal* (March 3, 2015); Lewis B. Kaden, "The Unfinished Work of Reform in the Global Financial System," *Mossabar-Rahmani Center for Business and Government Harvard*

Kennedy School (May 2015) (essay adapted from remarks given by the author at Cambridge University on February 27, 2015), http://www.hks. harvard.edu/centers/mrcbg/publications/awp/awp40; Gina Chon, Caroline Binham, and Laura Noonan, "Six Banks Fined Total of $5.6bn Over Rigging of Foreign Exchange Markets," *The Financial Times* (May 20, 2015); John Kay, *Other People's Money: The Real Business of Finance* (New York: Public Affairs, 2015) at 255–61 (private ordering and change in culture key to reform of financial services industry).

9. Ben W. Heineman, Jr., "'News of the World' Shuts Down: Who Should Take the Blame?," *The Atlantic* (July 10, 2011); Ben W. Heineman, Jr., "Is Murdoch to Blame for 'This Whole Fiasco'?" *The Atlantic* (July 21, 2011); Ben W. Heineman, Jr., "News Corp, Wal-Mart and CEO Failure to Investigate Wrong-Doing," *Harvard Business Review* (May 4, 2012). See generally, Brian Leveson, *An Inquiry Into the Culture, Practices and Ethics of the Press* (volume 1) (November 2012), https://www.gov.uk/government/uploads/system/uploads/attachment_data/file/270939/0780_i.pdf; Nick Davies, *Hack Attack: How the Truth Caught Up with Rupert Murdoch* (New York: Faber and Faber, 2014). See also Sarah Lyall, "Murdoch's British Tabloids Clean Up Their Acts," *The New York Times* (November 29, 2015) (major culture change in Murdoch UK tabloids in aftermath of scandal: papers "set out new rules for its reporters on topics like bribing public officials (do not), paying for stories (only sometimes), using private investigators (only with approval) and collecting private information electronically (do not do that, either)").

10. Andy Sharman, Gina Chon, and Chris Bryant, "Volkswagen Shares Tumble as Inquiries Are Launched Worldwide," *The Financial Times* (September 22, 2015); Jack Ewing and Bill Vlasic, "Germans Are Investigating Former Chief of Volkswagen in Diesel Scandal," *The New York Times* (September 29, 2015).

11. Erik Holm and Anupreeta Das, "Buffett Reminds His Top Managers: Reputation Is Everything," *The Wall Street Journal* (December 19, 2014).

12. 15 U.S. Code 78j-1(m)(4); 17 CFR 240.10A-39(b)(3). Sarbanes-Oxley Section 301 states that an audit committee must establish procedures for receiving and treating complaints about accounting and auditing matters, including complaints from those who wish to remain anonymous.

13. Vincent & Elkins, *Report on Sherron Watkins Concerns* (October 2001), http://online.wsj.com/article/0,,SB1011142769622726480,00.html; Special Investigative Committee of Enron Board of Directors, *Report of Investigation* (February 1, 2002), http://news.findlaw.com/wsj/docs/enron/

sicreport/; Robert W. Gordon, "A New Role for Lawyers? The Corporate Counselor After Enron," 35 *Connecticut L. Rev.* 1185, 1187-88 (2002).

14. Lynn S. Paine, Rohit Deshpande, and Joshua D. Margolis, "A Global Leader's Guide to Managing Business Conduct," *Harvard Business Review* (September 2011).

15. See, e.g., Latham & Watkins, "Dealing with the SEC's Focus on Protecting Whistleblowers from Retaliation," *Client Alert* (February 19, 2013).

16. Emily Glazer and Christina Rexrode, "What Banks Are Doing to Improve Their Culture," *The Wall Street Journal* (February 2, 2015).

Chapter 5

1. Two books by a person who has taught at Harvard and Yale schools of business are excellent primers on law for non-lawyers which inside counsel can use in creating education modules for business leaders inside the corporation. Constance E. Bagley and Diane W. Savage, *Managers and the Legal Environment: Strategies for the 21st Century* (Mason, OH: Thomson-West, 2006); Constance E. Bagley, *Winning Legally: How to Use Law to Create Value, Marshall Resources and Manage Risk* (Boston: Harvard Business School Press, 2005).

2. Peter Kurer, *Legal and Compliance Risk: A Strategic Response to a Rising Threat for Global Business* (Oxford: Oxford Univ. Press, 2015) at 32.

3. Kurer, *supra*, note 2 at 45–49. Kurer's book provides an excellent account of the complexity and changing nature of global legal frameworks affecting multinational corporations and the resulting legal risk.

4. For discussion of global complexity and trends, see, e.g., Brandon L. Garrett, *Too Big to Jail: How Prosecutors Compromise with Corporations* (Cambridge, MA: Harvard Univ. Press, 2014); Kurer, *supra*, note 2; Stephen Breyer, *The Court and the World: American Law and the New Global Realities* (New York: Alfred E. Knopf, 2015); E. Norman Veasey and Christine T. Di Guglielmo, *Indispensable Counsel: The Chief Legal Officer in the New Reality* (Oxford: Oxford Univ. Press, 2012); *The Economist*, "Briefing: Criminalizing the American Company" (August 30, 2014); Wayne M. Carlin, "White Collar and Regulatory Enforcement: Emerging Trends," *Harvard Law School Forum on Corporate Governance and Financial Regulation* (January 13, 2013); Deloitte & Touche and Compliance Week, "In Focus: Compliance Trends Survey 2014" (May 2014); Ben McLannahan, "Banks Post-Crisis Legal Costs Hit $300bn," *The Financial Times* (June 8, 2015); Conduct Costs Project Research Foundation, "Press Release" (June 8, 2015) (detail on cost to top banks of legal problems);

Caroline Binham, "Price-Fixing Fines Hit $5bn Record High," *The Financial Times* (January 7, 2015); Zhiwu Chen, "Foreign Companies Are Easy Targets in China," *The Financial Times* (July 17, 2014); Conor Dougherty and Mark Scott, "Google Antitrust Inquiries Spread Over Globe, With India the Latest Problem," *The New York Times* (September 1, 2015); Remarks of Deputy Attorney General Sally Quillian Yates, "New Policy on Individual Liability in Matters of Corporate Wrongdoing," *U.S. Justice Department* (September 10, 2015); De Matt Apuzzo and Ben Protess, "Justice Department Sets Its Sights on Executives," *The New York Times* (September 9, 2015); Marjorie J. Peerce, Charles Stillman, and Elizabeth J. Lee, "Criminal Prosecution of In-House Counsel and Compliance," *Corporate Counsel* (March 3, 2015); Rebekah Mintzer, "Is SEC Being Too Tough on Compliance Officers?" *Corporate Counsel* (August 11, 2015); The Securities and Exchange Commission, *2015 Report to the Congress on the Dodd-Frank Whistleblower Program* (November 16, 2015) (number of people reporting to SEC steadily increasing).

5. DOJ Criminal Division and SEC Enforcement Division, *A Resource Guide to the U.S. Foreign Corrupt Practices Act* (November 2012) at 58 (government acknowledgment of importance of risk-based compliance systems). These guidelines are a thoughtful account of how DOJ and the SEC approach FCPA cases, discussing the types of steps corporations can take to implement compliance programs credited by the government in prosecution decisions (as opposed to sentencing guidelines following a conviction). Of course, DOJ and the SEC retain authority in this document to weigh all factors in exercising prosecutorial discretion.

6. Rebekah Mintzer, "Companies Making Anticorruption Compliance a Priority," *Corporate Counsel* (May 7, 2015) ("companies have kicked their anti-corruption programs into gear by identifying and declining to enter into relationships with partners that might be corrupt").

7. Transparency International-USA, "Verification of Anticorruption Compliance Programs" (2014); LRN, "The 2014 Ethics and Compliance Program Effectiveness Report" (2015), http://www.corporatecompliance-insights.com/wp-content/uploads/2014/05/LRNEffectSurveyReport.pdf.

8. Remarks of Deputy Assistant Attorney General Deborah P. Majoras, "GE-Honeywell: The U.S. Decision," *U.S. Justice Department* (November 29, 2001), http://www.justice.gov/atr/speech/ge-honeywell-us-decision; Remarks of Deputy Assistant Attorney General William J. Kolasky, "Conglomerate Mergers and Range Effects: It's a Long Way from Chicago to Brussels," *U.S. Justice Department* (November 9, 2001), http://www

.justice.gov/atr/speech/conglomerate-mergers-and-range-effects-its -long-way-chicago-brussels. *See also*, William J. Kolasky, "GE/Honeywell: Narrowing, But Not Closing, The Gap," 20 *Antitrust* 69 (Spring 2006).

9. Ben Protess and Michael J. De La Merced, "Inquiry into Foreign Bribes at Biomet Hangs Over \$13 Billion Merger," *The New York Times* (December 23, 2014). The GE-Alstom deal was approved by U.S. and EU antitrust authorities in September 2015.

10. Amy Conway-Hatcher, "The Big Three FCPA Lessons from the Morgan Stanley Case," *Corporate Counsel* (June 14, 2012); Lucinda A. Low, Owen Bonheimer, and Tom Best, "Avoiding FCPA Prosecution for Employee Conduct," *Law 360* (May 25, 2012); DOJ Criminal Division and SEC Enforcement Division, *supra*, note 5 at 61 (description of Morgan-Stanley declination without naming company).

11. Report of the Ethics Resource Center's Independent Advisory Group on the 20th Anniversary of FSGO, "The Federal Sentencing Guidelines for Organizations at Twenty Years: A Call to Action for More Effective Promotion and Recognition of Effective Compliance and Ethics Programs," *Ethics Resource Center* (2012); Ben W. Heineman, Jr., "Give Credit Where Credit Is Due," *Corporate Counsel* (June 1, 2012).

12. Department of Justice's Sentencing Memorandum, *United States v. Siemens Aktiengesellschaft et al.*, Criminal No. (2008) at 2-3, http://www. justice.gov/opa/documents/siemens-sentencing-memo.pdf.

13. Ben W. Heineman, Jr., "Wal-Mart Bribery Case Raises Fundamental Governance Issues," *Harvard Law School Forum on Corporate Governance and Financial Regulation* (2012). Wal-Mart, "Global Compliance Program Report on Fiscal Year 2014," (2014); Ben W. Heineman, Jr., "Who's Responsible for the Wal-Mart Mexico Scandal?" *Harvard Business Review* (May 15, 2014).

14. U.S. Sentencing Commission, "2014 Guidelines Manual: Chapter 8—Sentencing of Organizations," Section §8B2.1(b)(2)[emphasis supplied]:

(A) The organization's governing authority shall be knowledgeable about the content and operation of the compliance and ethics program and shall exercise reasonable oversight with respect to the implementation and effectiveness of the compliance and ethics program.

(B) High-level personnel of the organization shall ensure that the organization has an effective compliance and ethics program, as described in this guideline. *Specific individual(s) within high-level personnel shall be assigned overall responsibility for the compliance and ethics program.*

(C) *Specific individual(s) within the organization shall be delegated day-to-day operational responsibility* for the compliance and ethics program. Individual(s) with operational responsibility shall report periodically to high-level personnel and, as appropriate, to the governing authority, or an appropriate subgroup of the governing authority, on the effectiveness of the compliance and ethics program. To carry out such operational responsibility, such individual(s) shall be given adequate resources, appropriate authority, and direct access to the governing authority or an appropriate subgroup of the governing authority.

See, Ryan McConnell, "Ask a CCO: Simon Lorne of Millennium Management," *Corporate Counsel* (June 18, 2015) (arguing for CCO reporting to broad-gauged GC); Rebekah Mintzer, "How C-Suite Superstars Help Improve Corporate Compliance" (June 19, 2015) (GC's effectiveness in leading compliance due to continual access to CEO on broad range of matters).

15. Nitin Nohria, "Global Consequences of Corruption," *Livemint* (January 14, 2015); Rawi E. Abdelal, Rafael M. Di Tella, and Prabakar Kothandaraman, "Infosys in India: Building a Software Giant in a Corrupt Environment," *Harvard Business School Case No. 707-030* (December 2006).

Chapter 6

1. *See* views of the former Chief Justice of the Delaware Supreme Court: E. Norman Veasey and Christine T. Di Guglielmo, *Indispensable Counsel: The Chief Legal Officer in the New Reality* (Oxford: Oxford Univ. Press, 2012) at 120 & nn.87,88 (citing Delaware cases and American Law Institute, *Principles of Corporate Governance*). See also, Lynn Sharp Paine, *Value Shift: Why Companies Must Merge Social and Financial Imperatives to Achieve Superior Performance* (New York: McGraw-Hill, 2004) at 81–105. Business Round Table, *Principles of Corporate Governance* (2002) at 30 (value to corporation and shareholders of reputation for "civic responsibility").

2. Sandra J. Sucher and Nien-he Hsieh, "A Framework for Ethical Reasoning," *Harvard Business School Background Note 610-050* (2010, revised December 2011) (good teaching tool for business leaders as well as employees and business students). See also, Max H. Bazerman and Ann E. Tenbrunsel, *Blind Spots: Why We Fail to Do What's Right and What to Do About It* (Princeton, NJ: Princeton University Press, 2011); Kirk O. Hanson, "The Ethical Challenges Facing Entrepreneurs," *The Wall Street Journal* (November 23, 2015).

3. Lynn Paine, Rohit Deshpandé, Joshua D. Margolis, and Kim E. Bettcher, "Up to Code: Does Your Company's Conduct Meet World-Class Standards?" *Harvard Business Review* (December 2005); Joshua D. Margolis, Lynn S. Paine, and Rohit Deshpande, "A Global Leader's Guide to Managing Business Conduct," *Harvard Business Review* (September 2011); OECD, *Guidelines for Multinational Businesses: Responsible Business Conduct Matters* (2011).

4. Andrew Crane and Dirk Matten, *Business Ethics: Managing Corporate Citizenship and Sustainability in the Age of Globalization* (Oxford: Oxford Univ. Press, 2007) at 515.

5. Paine, *supra*, note 1 at 141, 203–08, 223–24 (resolution of moral and financial conflicts draws on practical considerations and on different strands of thought from different schools of philosophy).

6. Thomas Donaldson, "Shared Values That Are Lost in Translation," *The Financial Times* (April 23, 2014). See also, Thomas Donaldson, Patricia H. Werhane, and Margaret Cording, *Ethical Issues in Business: A Philosophical Approach* (Upper Saddle River, NJ: Prentice Hall, 2002, 7th ed.).

7. International Labor Organization, "Minimum Age Convention" (1973); United Nations, "Convention on the Rights of the Child" (1989); International Labor Organization, "Worst Forms of Child Labour Convention" (1999); U.S. Department of Labor, *Apparel Industry Partnership's Agreement* (April 1997); IKEA, "The IKEA Group, Approach to Sustainability: How We Manage Sustainability in Our Business," (2011) at 12–17 (suppliers); IKEA, "IKEA Group Sustainability Report FY14" (2014) at 5, 73–96; Fair Labor Association, "FLA Workplace Code of Conduct and Compliance Benchmarks" (October 2011).

8. See, e.g., Fair Labor Association, "Foxconn Verification Status Report" (August 21, 2012); Ben W. Heineman, Jr., "Apple Is About to Discover the Price of Fair Labor," *The Atlantic* (March 30, 2012); Charles Duhigg and Steven Greenhouse, "Electronic Giant Vowing Reforms in China Plants," *The New York Times* (March 29, 2012); Apple, "Supplier Responsibility 2014 Progress Report," https://www.apple.com/anzsea/supplier-responsibility/pdf/Apple_SR_2014_Progress_Report.pdf.

9. Dominic Gates, "Boeing 787's Problems Blamed on Outsourcing, Lack of Oversight," *The Seattle Times* (February 2, 2013); Mark Venables, "Dreamliner Becomes Boeing Nightmare as Fleet Grounded," 8 *Engineering & Technology* 2 (February 2013).

10. Jim Yardley, "Horrific Fire Revealed a Gap in Safety for Global Brands," *The New York Times* (December 6, 2012); Steven Greenhouse, "U.S.

Retailers See Big Risk in Safety Plan for Factories in Bangladesh," *The New York Times* (May 22, 2013); Steven Greenhouse, "Bangladesh Inspections Find Gaps in Safety," *The New York Times* (March 11, 2014); Ben W. Heineman, Jr., "The Cost of Saving Lives in Bangladesh," *The Atlantic* (May 10, 2013); Sarah Labowitz and Dorothee Baumann-Pauly, "Business as Usual Is Not an Option: Supply Chains and Sourcing After Rana Plaza," *NYU Stern Center for Business and Human Rights* (April 2014).

11. U.S. Department of Labor Factsheet, *What Is Trade Adjustment Assistance?* http://www.doleta.gov/tradeact/ (includes description of 2015 reauthorization of TAAA); Jonathan Weisman, "House Approves Trade Bill's Expansion of Workers' Aid," *The New York Times* (June 25, 2015).

12. See, e.g., Neil Forbes, *Doing Business with the Nazis: Britain's Economic and Financial Relations with Germany 1931–1939* (London: Frank Cass Publishers, 2000); Edwin Black, *IBM and the Holocaust: The Strategic Alliance between Nazi Germany and America's Most Powerful Corporation* (New York: Crown Publishing, 2001); Gordon A. Craig, "Keeping Germany Fat," *The New York Review of Books* (September 20, 2001).

13. Gay W. Seidman, "Monitoring Multinationals: Lessons from the Anti-Apartheid Era," *Politics and Society* (March 2003); Bill Keller, "U.S. Companies Quietly Returning to South Africa," *The New York Times* (March 19, 1993).

14. Steven Levy, *In the Plex: How Google Thinks, Works, and Shapes Our Lives* (New York: Simon & Schuster, 2011) at 272–314; David Drummond, "A New Approach to China: An Update," *Google Official Blog* (March 22, 2010), http://googleblog.blogspot.com/2010/03/new-approach-to-china-update.html; Michael Wines, "Google to Alert Users to Chinese Censorship," *The New York Times* (June 1, 2012); Amir Efrati and Loretta Chao, "Google Softens Tone on China," *The Wall Street Journal* (January 12, 2012); Charles Clover, "China's Month-Long Google Clampdown Hits Businesses," *The Financial Times* (July 1, 2014).

15. Paul Mozur and Vindu Goel, "To Reach China, LinkedIn Plays by Local Rules," *The New York Times* (October 5, 2014); Alistair Barr, "Google Pursuing a Return to China," *The Wall Street Journal* (September 4, 2015). See, generally, Harvard Berkman Center for Internet & Society, *Global Network Initiative* (2008); Larry Downes, "Why No One Will Join the Global Network Initiative," *Forbes* (March 30, 2011); Patricia M. Figliola, Kennon H. Nakamura, Casey L. Addis, and Thomas Lum, "U.S. Initiatives to Promote Global Internet Freedom: Issues, Policy, and Technology," *Congressional Research Service* (2010); Margaret Sullivan, "The

Thorny Challenge of Covering China," *The New York Times* (December 7, 2013); Vindu Goel, "Facebook Clarifies Rules on What It Bans and Why," *The New York Times* (March 16, 2015) (describing Facebook's self-censorship as well as acquiescence in some government censorship).

The pervasive tension between private company standards and national policy relating to material on the Internet is reflected in the opposition of private technology companies, in the wake of the Edward Snowden document disclosures, to subpoenas from the U.S. government seeking encrypted information as part of national security inquiries. Matt Apuzzo, David E. Sanger, and Michael S. Schmidt, "Tech Companies Tangle With U.S. Over Data Access," *The New York Times* (September 7, 2015).

Chapter 7

1. See, e.g., Max H. Bazerman and Michael D. Watkins, *Predictable Surprises: The Disasters You Should Have Seen Coming, and How to Prevent Them* (Boston: Harvard Business Press, 2008); Francis Fukuyama, ed., *Blindside: How to Anticipate Forcing Events and Wild Cards in Global Politics* (Baltimore, MD: Brookings Institution Press, 2007); Cass R. Sunstein, *Worst-Case Scenarios* (Cambridge, MA: Harvard Univ. Press, 2007); Arnold M. Howitt and Herman B. Leonard, eds., *Managing Crises: Responses to Large-Scale Emergencies* (Washington, DC: CQ Press, 2009); Peter Kurer, *Legal and Compliance Risk: A Strategic Response to a Rising Threat for Global Business* (Oxford: Oxford Univ. Press, 2015); Richard E. Nisbett, *Mindware: Tools for Smart Thinking* (New York: Farrar, Straus and Giroux, 2015); Donald C. Langevoort, "Chasing the Greased Pig Down Wall Street: A Gatekeeper's Guide to the Psychology, Culture and Ethics of Financial Risk Taking," 96 *Cornell L.R.* 1209 (2011) (complexity for lawyers of assessing risk prior to financial crisis of 2008–2009). There is a voluminous literature of official and unofficial reports on catastrophic events, some of which will be cited in the Notes that follow and all of which are easily accessible on the Internet. Increasingly, companies are also required to report on different explicit dimensions of risk, inter alia, to regulators, credit rating agencies, and institutional investors.

2. Fukuyama, *supra*, note 1, at 1; Bazerman and Watkins, *supra*, note 1 at 69-152 (cognitive, organizational, and political causes of failure to anticipate risk). See also, British Petroleum U.S. Refineries Independent Safety Review Panel, "The Report" (January 2007) ("Baker Report), http://news.bbc.co.uk/2/shared/bsp/hi/pdfs/16_01_07_bp_baker_report.

pdf; National Commission on the BP Deepwater Horizon Oil Spill and Offshore Drilling, "Report to the President: Deep Water—The Gulf Oil Disaster and the Future of Offshore Drilling" (January 2011); National Commission on the Causes of the Financial and Economic Crisis in the United States, "The Financial Crisis Inquiry Report" (January 2011).

3. The Fukushima Nuclear Accident Independent Investigation Commission, "Official Report" *The National Diet of Japan* (2012); Yukiya Amano, "Report of the Director General: The Fukushima Daiichi Incident," *International Atomic Energy Agency* (August 2015) at 4 (original design considerations did not provide safety margins for extreme flooding from tsunami and no systematic and comprehensive reevaluation of external risks since 1970s); George Johnson, "When Radiation Isn't the Real Risk," *The New York Times* (September 21, 2015) (studies estimate 1,600 died from stress of evacuation); Frances F. Townsend, Assistant to the President for Homeland Security and Counterterrorism, "The Federal Response to Hurricane Katrina: Lessons Learned," *The White House* (February 2006); The Senate Committee on Homeland Security and Governmental Affairs, "Hurricane Katrina: A Nation Still Unprepared" (May 2006). For discussion of Executive Branch "Red Team Blue Team" debate on the bin Laden special forces operation, see Michael Morell, *The Great War of Our Time: The CIA's Fight Against Terrorism—From al Qa'ida to ISIS* (New York: Hachette Book Group, 2015) at 162–65. See also Micah Zenko, *Red Team: How to Succeed by Thinking Like the Enemy* (New York: Basic Books 2015).

4. Baker Report, *supra*, note 1; U.S. Chemical Safety and Hazard Investigation Board, "Investigation Report, Refinery Explosion and Fire: BP, Texas City, Texas" (March 2007); Presidential Commission Report on Deepwater Horizon, *supra*, note 1; National Academy of Engineering and National Research Council of the National Academies, "Macondo Well-Deepwater Horizon Blowout: Lessons for Improving Offshore Drilling Safety" (2012); British Petroleum, "*Deepwater Horizon* Accident Investigation Report" (September 8, 2010); Ben W. Heineman, Jr., "BP's Accident Report: Look at the Recommendations for the Future," *The Atlantic* (September 10, 2010); Ben W. Heineman, Jr., "How the BP Commission Dropped the Ball," *Harvard Business Review* (January 17, 2011); United States v. BP Exploration & Production, Inc., *Guilty Plea Agreement* (November 15, 2012), http://www.justice.gov/iso/opa/resour ces/43320121115143613990027.pdf. The federal district court approved the agreement in January 29, 2013.

See also, Michael Watkins, "How BP Could Have Avoided Disaster," *Harvard Business Review* (June 7, 2010); Andrew Winston, "Five Lessons from the BP Oil Spill," *Harvard Business Review* (June 3, 2010); Rosabeth Moss Kanter, "BP's Tony Hayward and the Failure of Leadership Accountability," *Harvard Business Review* (June 7, 2010); Ed Crooks, "Issues at the Heart of Deepwater Horizon, *The Financial Times* (April 25, 2013); Ed Crooks, "Spill Settlement Papers Leave BP in a Bind," *The Financial Times* (July 13, 2013); Ed Crooks, "BP Faces Resumption of Deepwater Horizon Compensation Payments," *The Financial Times* (May 28, 2014); Susan Beck, "How BP Decided to Fight the Deepwater Settlement," *The American Lawyer* (March 5, 2015); Ben W. Heineman, Jr., "A Cautionary Tale for Regulated Industries," *Harvard Business Review* (September 14, 2012).

On 2015 comprehensive BP settlement, see, e.g., Campbell Robertson, John Schwartz, and Richard Perez-Pena, "BP to Pay $18.7 Billion for Deepwater Horizon Oil Spill," *The New York Times* (July 2, 2015); Gina Chon, "BP Finalizes $20.8bn Deepwater Horizon Settlement," *The Financial Times* (October 5, 2015); Christopher Adams and Ed Crooks, "BP: Into Uncharted Waters. After Oil Group Settles Last Big Penalty for Deepwater Horizon, Is It More Nimble—Or Vulnerable?" *The Financial Times* (July 9, 2015); Ed Crooks, "BP Braced for Billions More in Deepwater Payments," *The Financial Times* (July 12, 2015).

5. A good primer on country risk, referencing other sources, is Mina Toksoz, *Guide to Country Risk: How to Identify, Manage and Mitigate the Risks of Doing Business Across Borders* (London: The Economist, Profile Books Ltd., and Public Affairs, 2014). See also, Robert S. Kaplan and Anette Mikes, "Managing Risk: A New Framework," *Harvard Business Review* (June 2012); James Kynge, "Redefining EM: Choosing the Best Matrix," *The Financial Times* (August 18, 2015) (arguing that phrase "emerging markets" is too crude to describe risk and describing different, more fine-grained ways experts assess risk in less developed nations).

6. See, e.g., Lloyd's, *Under Attack? Global Business and the Threat of Political Violence* (April 2007); Elsa Lee, *Homeland Security and Private Sector Business: Corporation's Role in Critical Infrastructure Protection* (Boca Raton, FL: CRC Press, 2009); General Electric Co., *The Spirit and the Letter* (2014) at 15.

7. CIA Director John Brennan made these remarks in a public presentation at Harvard's Kennedy School of Government on April 7, 2015. See, e.g., Joseph S. Nye, Jr., "The Regime Complex for Managing Global Cyber

Activities," *The Global Commission on Internet Governance* (May 20, 2014); ABA Cybersecurity Legal Task Force, *Report and Resolution* 109 (August 2014); David Clark, Thomas Berson, and Herbert Lin, eds., *At the Nexus of Cybersecurity and Public Policy: Some Basic Concepts and Issues* (Washington, DC: The National Academies Press, 2014); SEC's Division of Investment Management, "Guidance Update No. 2015-02" (April 2015) (listing cyber issues companies should address to "prevent, detect, and respond to cyber-attacks"); Randy Milch and Zachary Goldman, "From the War Room to the Board Room: Effectively Managing Cyber Threats Without Joining the Front Lines," *NYU Law School Center on Law and Security* (June 2015).

8. Anton R. Valukas, " Report to Board of Directors of General Motors Company Regarding Ignition Switch Recalls" (May 29, 2014) at 266-72 (recommendations for changes in GM legal organization).

9. U.S. Department of Justice, Office of Public Affairs, "GlaxoSmithKline to Plead Guilty and Pay $3 Billion to Resolve Fraud Allegations and Failure to Report Safety Data" (July 2, 2012).

10. National Commission on the Causes of the Financial and Economic Crisis in the United States, "The Financial Crisis Inquiry Report" (January 2011). One of the best of the many books on the financial crisis is Alan S. Blinder, *After the Music Stopped: The Financial Crisis, The Response, and the Work Ahead* (New York: Penguin Books, 2013). See also, Langevoort, *supra*, note 1.

Chapter 8

1. Adolf A. Berle and Gardiner C. Means, *The Modern Corporation and Private Property* (New York: The Macmillan Company, 1932); Stephen M. Bainbridge, *The New Corporate Governance in Theory and Practice* (New York: Oxford Univ. Press, 2008); Roger L. Martin, *Fixing the Game: Bubbles, Crashes, and What Capitalism Can Learn From the NFL* (Boston: Harvard Business School Press, 2011); Lynn Stout, *The Shareholder Value Myth: How Putting Shareholders First Harms Investors, Corporations and the Public* (San Francisco: Barrett-Koehler Publishers, 2012). See also, John Kay, "Put the Good Corporation at the Heart of the Economy," *The Financial Times* (May 13, 2015) ("The purpose of the corporation is to produce goods and services to meet economic and social needs, to create satisfying and rewarding employment, to earn returns for its shareholders and other investors and to make a positive contribution to the social and physical environment in which it operates."); Steven Pearlstein,

"Social Capital, Corporate Purpose and the Revival of American Capitalism," *Brookings Institution* (January 10, 2014).

2. GE, "Governance Principles," http://www.ge.com/investor-relations/ governance/principles. Regarding ballot access, see "General Electric Current Report on Form 8-K" (February 6, 2015), www.ge.com /investor-relations/shareholder-services/personal-investing/sec-filing /general-electric-company.

3. E. Norman Veasey and Christine T. Di Guglielmo, *Indispensable Counsel: The Chief Legal Officer in the New Reality* (Oxford: Oxford Univ. Press, 2012) at 14–22, 131–57, 200–10.

4. Remarks by Lloyd Blankfein to the Council of Institutional Investors, "Goldman Sachs" (April 2009), http://www.goldmansachs.com/our -thinking/archive/lcb-speech-to-cii.html; Ben W. Heineman, Jr., "FCIC: The Private Sector Failed," *The Atlantic* (January 31, 2011) (quoting Dimon).

5. See, e.g., Stout, *supra*, note 1; Peter F. Drucker, *The Practice of Management* (New York: Harper Business, 1954).

6. Roger L. Martin, *supra*, note 1. Apple's relentless focus on customers is mirrored in the business principles of Amazon, the most highly valued retail company in the world as of this writing. Jodi Kantor and David Streitfeld, "Inside Amazon: Wrestling Big Ideas in a Bruising Marketplace," *The New York Times* (August 15, 2015).

7. Michael C. Jensen, "Value Maximization, Shareholder Theory, and the Corporate Objective Function," 14 *J. Applied Corp. Fin.* 8,16 (2001). See also, Francesco Guerrera, "Welch Condemns Share Price Focus," *The Financial Times* (March 12, 2009) (quoting Jack Welch, viewed by many as a follower of the early Jensen and as a proponent of shareholder value when CEO, from 1981–2001, on problems with focusing on shareholder value today: "On the face of it, shareholder value is the dumbest idea in the world. Shareholder value is a result, not a strategy . . . Your main constituencies are your employees, your customers and your products.").

8. Srikant M. Datar, David A. Garvin, and Patrick G. Cullen, *Rethinking the MBA: Business Education at a Crossroads* (Boston: Harvard Business Review Press, 2011); Rakesh Khurana, *From Higher Aims to Hired Hands: The Social Transformation of American Business Schools and the Unfulfilled Promise of Management as a Profession* (Princeton: Princeton Univ. Press, 2007). See also Ben W. Heineman, Jr., "Management as a Profession: A Business Lawyer's Critique," *Harvard Business Review* (November 2, 2010).

9. Michael Skapinker, "CEO Pay: It Is Time for One Brave Leader to Ask for Less," *The Financial Times* (May 20, 2015); James Shotter and Laura Noonan, "Bonuses Don't Make Bankers Work Harder, Says Deutsche's John Cryan," *The Financial Times* (November 18, 2015); Peter Eavis, "SEC Approves Rule on C.E.O. Pay Ratio," *The New York Times* (August 5, 2015); Kathryn Dill, "Report: CEOs Earn 331 Times as Much as Average Workers, 774 Times as Much as Minimum Wage Earners," *Forbes* (April 15, 2014). In response to concerns that excessive pay is causing undue risk-taking, the EU has recently proposed capping bonuses for bankers at no more than 200 percent of annual salary, a limitation that is scheduled to take effect at the end of 2016. Jim Brundsen, "Banks Seek to Clarify New Bonus Rules With Brussels," *The Financial Times* (August 25, 2015).

10. Peter Rudegeair, "Pay Gap Between Wall Street CEOs and Employees Narrows," *The Wall Street Journal* (April 5, 2015).

11. Section 954 of the Dodd-Frank Wall Street Reform and Consumer Protection Act of 2010 added Section 10D to the Securities Exchange Act of 1934 (17 CFR 240.10D). Jason Brenkert and Kimberley R. Anderson, "SEC Issues Proposed Rule for Clawback Policies and Related Disclosure," *Dorsey & Whitney* (July 1, 2015), http://www.dorsey.com /eu-sec-proposed-clawback-policies-disclosure/.

12. Ben W. Heineman, Jr., "The JP Morgan 'Whale' Report and the Ghosts of the Financial Crisis," *Harvard Business Review* (January 24, 2013); Ben W. Heineman, Jr., "Can JP Morgan Transparently Police Itself?" *Harvard Business Review* (May 31, 2012); Ben W. Heineman, Jr., "Two Cheers for JP Morgan's 'Clawbacks,'" *Harvard Business Review* (July 13, 2012). See also, JPMorgan Chase, *How We Do Business—The Report* (December 19, 2014) at 23 (stating the total amount canceled or withheld in the "Whale" incident and noting that company claw-back provisions "hold executives accountable, when appropriate, for significant actions or items that negatively affect business performance in current or future years").

13. Ben W. Heineman, Jr., and Stephen Davis, "Are Institutional Investors Part of the Problem or Part of the Solution," *Committee for Economic Development and Millstein Center for Corporate Governance and Performance at Yale School of Management* (October 2011); Simon C. Y. Wong, "Why Stewardship Is Proving Elusive for Institutional Investors," *Butterworths Journal of International Banking and Financial Law* (July/August 2010).

14. The Ira M. Milstein Center for Global Markets and Corporate Ownership at Columbia Law School was formed in order to undertake pioneering research and analysis on institutional investors and to explore issues

about their positive and negative impacts on publicly held corporations, http://web.law.columbia.edu/millsteincenter/programs.

15. Roger W. Ferguson, Jr., "Riding Herd on Company Management: Institutional Investors Have the Power—And They Should Use It," *The Wall Street Journal* (April 27, 2010). See, Ben W. Heineman, Jr., "A 'Stewardship Code' for Institutional Investors," *Harvard Business Review* (January 18, 2010).

16. Weil, Gotshal, & Manges, "Shareholder Activism, Engagement, Proxy Access and Other Governance Challenges in 2015," *Weil Alert* (April 30, 2015); Michael D. Goldhaber, "Marty Lipton's War on Hedge Fund Activists," *The American Lawyer* (March 30, 2015) (quoting Ira Milstein: "As far as Marty's concerned, I disagree because he's damning the whole movement . . . I know activist hedge funds that are in the business of promoting long-term growth. I know other activists who are only interested in jerking the stock a little bit. I think there are plenty of both.")

Chapter 9

1. See views of the former Chief Justice of the Delaware Supreme Court: Norman Veasey and Christine T. Di Guglielmo, *Indispensable Counsel: The Chief Legal Officer in the New Reality* (Oxford: Oxford Univ. Press, 2012) at 120 & nn.87, 88 (citing Delaware cases and American Law Institute, *Principles of Corporate Governance*). Business Round Table, *Principles of Corporate Governance* (2002) at 30 (reputation for "civil responsibility" provides value to corporation and shareholders).

2. Committee Encouraging Corporate Philanthropy, in association with The Conference Board, *Giving in Numbers, 2014 Edition*, http://cecp.co /pdfs/giving_in_numbers/GIN2014_Web_Final.pdf]. "Corporate Philanthropy," http://www.referenceforbusiness.com/encyclopedia /Con-Cos/Corporate-Philanthropy.html. (1986 estimate).

3. These examples (and many more) can be found in online "Citizenship" or "Corporate Social Responsibility" reports for the named companies for recent years. See, e.g., Wal-Mart, "2015 Global Responsibility Report," http://corporate.walmart.com/global-responsibility/environment -sustainability/global-responsibility-report; JPMorgan Chase, "Corporate Social Responsibility," http://www.jpmorganchase.com/corporate/ Corporate-Responsibility/corporate-responsibility.htm; GE, "GE Sustainability," http://www.gesustainability.com/. See, generally, V. Kasturi Rangan, Lisa Chase, and Sohel Karim, "The Truth About CSR," *The Harvard Business Review* (January–February 2015); Matteo Tonello, "The

Business Case for Corporate Social Responsibility," *Harvard Law School Forum on Corporate Governance and Financial Regulation* (June 26, 2011).

4. *See,* Committee Encouraging Corporate Philanthropy, *supra,* note 2; "Corporate Philanthropy," http://www.referenceforbusiness.com/ency clopedia/Con-Cos/Corporate-Philanthropy.html (1986 estimate).

5. See, e.g., Mark R. Kramer and Michael E. Porter, "Strategy and Society: The Link Between Competitive Advantage and Corporate Social Responsibility," *Harvard Business Review* (December 2006); Rosabeth Moss Kanter, "How Great Companies Think Differently," *Harvard Business Review* (November 2011).

6. Hiroko Tabuchi, "How CVS Quit Smoking and Grew Into a Health Care Giant," *The New York Times* (July 12, 2015); IBM, "Smarter Cities," http:// www.ibm.com/smarterplanet/us/en/smarter_cities/overview/; GE, "Ecomagination." http://www.ge.com/about-us/ecomagination.

7. See, e.g., JPMorgan Chase, "Honoring the Military, Veterans and Their Families," http://www.jpmorganchase.com/corporate/Corporate -Responsibility/military-veterans.htm; Claire Cain Miller, "From Microsoft, a Novel Way to Mandate Sick Leave," *The New York Times* (March 26, 2015); Rachel Feintzeig and Lauren Weber, "Netflix's Unlimited Parental Leave Is a Surprising Gift for Workers," *The Wall Street Journal* (August 5, 2015); Pilita Clark, "Ikea Pledges E1bn for Cleaner Energy," *Financial Times* (June 4, 2014).

8. There is a vast literature on corruption. See, e.g., Daron Acemoglu and James Robinson, *Why Nations Fail: The Origins of Power, Prosperity and Poverty* (New York: Crown Publishing, 2012); Sarah Chayes, *Thieves of State: Why Corruption Threatens Global Security* (New York: W.W. Norton, 2015); Susan Rose-Ackerman and Paul D. Carrington, *Anti-Corruption Policy: Can International Actors Play a Constructive Role* (Durham, NC: Carolina Academic Press, 2013); The World Bank Group Integrity Vice Presidency, "Annual Update Fiscal Year 2015: Toward a Global Anti-Corruption Movement," *World Bank Group* (2015); Daniel Kaufman, "Aid Effectiveness and Governance," *Brookings Research Opinion* (March 17, 2009). See also, Transparency International website, https://www.transparency.org/; Transparency International, "Exporting Corruption, Progress Report 2015: Assessing Enforcement of the OCED Convention on Combatting Foreign Bribery" (2015); Robert Appleton, "Despite Prosecutions, Corruption Levels Stay the Course," *Corporate Counsel* (September 1, 2015); Ben W. Heineman, Jr., "Stop Bribery Everywhere," *Corporate Counsel* (June 2009); Ben W. Heineman, Jr., "In China,

Corruption and Unrest Threaten Autocratic Rule," *The Atlantic* (June 29, 2011); Ben W. Heineman, Jr., "The Afghan Black Hole: Governance and Corruption," *The Atlantic* (October 24, 2010).

9. Joseph L. Bower, Herman B. Leonard, and Lynn S. Paine, *Capitalism at Risk: Rethinking the Role of Business* (Boston: Harvard Business Review Press, 2011) (arguing that corporate leaders must devote substantial time to the public dimensions of "disrupters" of capitalism, including the financial system, state capitalism, inequality and populism, environmental degradation, aging and migration, terrorism, institutional failure, and public health/education). As discussed in the text, these huge issues, which may have an *indirect* impact on corporate performance, are hard for CEOs and top business leaders to address because of pressure to deal with a host of *direct* strategic and operational issues (including public policy issues that more directly affect the company) and because of the inordinate amount of time, complexity, and political conflict associated with serious involvement in these mega-issues. When these issues are, instead, addressed by business associations (U.S. Chamber of Commerce, National Association of Manufacturers, PHARMA, the Business Roundtable), the result is often one-sided generalities without much policy balance or punch. Yet, hard as these issues are to formulate and implement, corporations need to recognize the value of addressing serious problems through legislation or regulation to level the playing field. This point is illustrated in Christopher Jenson, "Fifty Years Ago, 'Unsafe at Any Speed' Shook the Auto World," *The New York* (November 27, 2015) (famous auto executive Robert Lutz stating today that, while he didn't like author Ralph Nader, "the book had a seminal effect." Lutz said safety regulations leveled the playing field among automakers: "It sets ground rules where everybody has to do something and nobody has to worry" about being at a competitive disadvantage, [Lutz] said.).

10. For a summary of rules governing campaign finance, lobbying, and gifts, see Dickstein Shapiro, "Influencing Government: The Rules of the Game (US Campaign Finance, Lobbying Disclosure, and Gift Laws)," *The Association of Corporate Counsel* (September 2015). There are, of course, many who believe *Citizens United* was rightly decided and who recommend deregulation of rules relating to campaign finance and lobbying, epitomized by the U.S. Chamber of Commerce. See, e.g, U.S. Chamber of Commerce, "Free Speech," https://www.uschamber.com/free-speech. But, there are many critics of money in politics as well. See, e.g., Robert G. Kaiser, *Act of Congress: How America's Essential Institution Works, and*

How It Doesn't (New York: Vintage Books, 2013); Thomas E. Mann and Norman J. Ornstein, *It's Even Worse Than It Looks: How the American Constitutional System Collided with the New Politics of Extremism* (New York: Basic Books, 2012); Lawrence Lessig, *Republic Lost: How Money Corrupts Congress—and a Plan to Stop It* (New York: Hatchette, 2012). See also, Nicholas Confessore, Sarah Cohen, and Karen Yourish, "Small Pool of Rich Donors Dominates Election Giving," *The New York Times* (August 1, 2015). See also, *Money, Politics and Transparency* website, http://moneypoliticstransparency.org/, and website of Center for Public Accountability, http://www.politicalaccountability.net/ (arguing for more voluntary disclosure by corporations of political giving). In April 2011, a group of law professors petitioned the SEC to adopt a rule requiring corporations to disclose political spending, http://www.sec.gov/rules/petitions/2011/petn4-637.pdf, but, as of this writing, the petition is not listed on the Commission's regulatory agenda.

For a learned set of essays on the tension between the First Amendment and campaign finance reform, see Robert C. Post, *Citizens Divided: Campaign Finance Reform and the Constitution* (Cambridge: Harvard Univ. Press, 2014). For broad, magisterial historical analysis of how the conditions for a stable democracy are eroding in the United States in part because of money in politics, see Francis Fukuyama, *Political Order and Political Decay: From the Industrial Revolution to the Globalization of Democracy* (New York: Farrar, Straus & Giroux, 2014) (fundamental conditions of liberal democracy are strong state, rule of law, and political accountability, and rich elites and powerful interest groups have eroded public accountability and undermined the ability of the state to represent the people and act in the broad public interest). The scope of the Petrobras scandal is described at Simon Romero, "An Anticorruption Drive Throws Brazil's Leadership into Disarray," *The New York Times* (August 13, 2015).

11. Global Reporting Initiative, "Standards and Reporting," https://www.globalreporting.org/standards/Pages/default.aspx. Major companies report their adherence to GRI standards: see, e.g., JPMorgan Chase, Global Reporting Initiative: 2014 Index and Appendices, http://www.jpmorganchase.com/corporate/Corporate-Responsibility/document/jpmc-cr-gri-2014.pdf; Sustainable Accounting Standards Board website, http://www.sasb.org/; Sustainable Accounting Standards Board, "Fundamentals of Sustainability Accounting" (October 2015), http://fsa.sasb.org/credential/. Robert Eccles of Harvard Business School is a leading

contemporary export on integrated business and sustainability reporting. See Robert G. Eccles and Michael P. Krzus, *One Report: Integrated Reporting for a Sustainable Strategy* (Hoboken, NJ: John Wiley and Sons, 2010); Robert G. Eccles and George Serafeim, "Corporate and Integrated Reporting: A Functional Perspective," Harvard Business School Working Paper 14-094 (May 5, 2014), http://www.hbs.edu/faculty/Publication%20 Files/14-094_30b9b0a2-4acb-47ec-bddc-8c1d810e3cde.pdf.

Chapter 10

1. This chapter is based, in part, on my GE experience but also on my research, speaking, teaching, and reflecting after leaving GE. In 2015, GE announced that it was going to divest itself of substantial parts of GE Capital that, in 2014, accounted for $43 billion of GE's $153 billion in revenue. When this process is completed, GE will still be a huge global company focusing on high-technology infrastructure in such segments as Aviation, Oil and Gas, Health Care, Power and Water, Energy Management, and Transportation. The number of inside lawyers in the "new" GE is not yet determined as of this writing, but it is likely to be just under 1,000.

2. Ben W. Heineman, Jr., "In the Beginning," *Corporate Counsel* (April 2006) (describing diverse career paths of senior GE lawyers at the time).

3. David Hechler, "From 3L to in-House," *Corporate Counsel* (February 13, 2015); David Hechler, "How IBM, Google and Microsoft Hire In-House Lawyers," *Corporate Counsel* (April 24, 2014); Prashant Dubey and Eva Kripalani, *The Generalist Counsel: How Leading General Counsel Are Shaping Tomorrow's Companies* (Oxford: Oxford Univ. Press, 2013) at 95–96; Ben W. Heineman, Jr., William F. Lee, and David B. Wilkins, "Lawyers as Professionals and as Citizens: Key Roles and Responsibilities in the 21st Century," *Harvard Law School Center on the Legal Profession* (2014) at 28–29, 42–44.

4. John K. Villa, *Corporate Counsel Guidelines* (St. Paul, MN: Thomson West, 2014); Michael A. Epstein and Dennis J. Block, *Corporate Counsellor's Desk Book*, 5th ed. (New York: Wolters Kluer, 2015); E. Norman Veasey and Christine T. Di Guglielmo, *Indispensable Counsel: The Chief Legal Officer in the New Reality* (Oxford: Oxford Univ. Press, 2012) at 14–24, 66–67, 105–17, 200–14; Andrew Kratenstein and Audrey Lu, "7 Best Practices for Preserving In-House Counsel Privilege," *Corporate Counsel* (June 2, 2015); Ben W. Heineman, Jr., "European Rejection of Attorney-Client Privilege for Inside Lawyers," *Harvard Law School*

Forum on Corporate Governance and Financial Regulation (October 2, 2010).

5. Marlisse Silver Sweeney, "Survey Backs Up Our Numbers on Big Biz Female GCs," *Corporate Counsel* (April 28, 2014); Sue Reisinger, "ACC Survey Finds Pay Disparity for Men and Women CLOs," *Corporate Counsel* (January 30, 2015); Minority Corporate Counsel Association, *16th Annual General Counsel Survey (*November–December 2015).

6. Brad Smith and Laura Stein, "Meeting the Challenge of In-House Pro Bono," *Corporate Counsel* (April 25, 2014); Susan Beck, "The Justice Gap: How Big Law Is Failing Legal Aid," *The American Lawyer* (June 29, 2015); Sue Reisinger, "GCs From UTC and GE Enlist in LawyerCorps," *Corporate Counsel* (February 18, 2015). See, generally, website of the Pro Bono Institute, http://www.probonoinst.org/, and website of Corporate Pro Bono, a partnership between the Association of Corporate Counsel and the Pro Bono Institute, http://www.cpbo.org/; Corporate Pro Bono, "2014 Benchmarking Report: An Overview of In-House Pro Bono" (March 2015).

7. Mike Haysley, "The Business Case for the Law Department COO," *Corporate Counsel* (May 28, 2015). A typical pitch from third-party vendors for Legal department management is George Dunn and Wendy L. Hufford, "A 3-Step Process Improvement Plan for Legal Departments," *Corporate Counsel* (February 24,2015). See also, Rebeka Mintzer, "Law Departments Taking a Mature Approach to Legal Spend," *Corporate Counsel* (December 3, 2104).

8. See, e.g., Association of Corporate Counsel, "ACC Value Challenge," an online resource that has materials relating to Legal department management issues such as budgeting, project management, technology, data management, and performance metrics, https://www.acc.com/valuechallenge/.

Chapter 11

1. Richard E. Susskind, *Tomorrow's Lawyers: An Introduction to Your Future* (Oxford: Oxford Univ. Press, 2013) at 68; Ben W. Heineman, Jr., William F. Lee, and David B. Wilkins, "Lawyers as Professionals and as Citizens: Key Roles and Responsibilities in the 21st Century," *Harvard Law School Center on the Legal Profession* (2014) at 37–39 (section on law firm problems primarily authored by Bill Lee, former managing partner of Wilmer Hale). See also, Chris Johnson, "The Am Law 100: Introducing Our New Profits Metric," *The American Lawyer* (April 27, 2015) (quoting a law

firm leader that PPP "dehumanized and corporatized" law firms) (equity
partners at top firms dropped from 36 percent in 1985 to 22 percent in
2015) (range of draw among highest/lowest equity partners often 10:1);
Larry E. Ribstein, "The Death of Big Law," 2010 *Wisconsin L. Rev* 749
(2010).

2. Chris Johnson, "The Global 100: A Smooth Ride," *The American Lawyer*
(October 2015); Aric Press, "Special Report: Big Law's Reality Check," *The
American Lawyer* (November 2014); Jeff Hodge, "Cause and Effect: How
Law Department Demand Is Disrupting the Legal Profession," *Corporate
Counsel* (October 13, 2015) ("Law departments are now in control of their
destinies and the benefactors of innovation and disruption will be general
counsel and law department operations teams").

3. Ben W. Heineman, Jr., "Bigger Isn't Better," *American Lawyer* (November
2008). *But cf,* Heidi Gardner, "Why It Pays to Collaborate with Your Colleagues," *The American Lawyer* (March 9, 2015) (arguing for methods
of meaningful collaboration in international law firms to address client
concerns about vacuity of "cross-selling"). Many of the problems with
integrated "mega-firms"—mediocrity, questions about cross-selling, difficulty in collaborating—also apply to the so-called mega-vereins, the
humongous agglomerations of disparate firms or offices under a single
name (like Baker & McKenzie or DLA Piper) that do not pool profits but
share marketing and branding.

4. David B. Wilkins, "Team of Rivals? Toward a New Model of the Corporate Attorney-Client Relationship," 78 *Fordham L. Rev.* 2067, 2081–82
(2010). Wilkins equates the "hire the lawyer, not the firm" mantra with
"spot contracting" on a per matter basis. But this oversimplifies. As corporate law departments introduced competition and broke up the old
oligopolies serving the corporation, that competition evolved relatively
quickly to the concept of competition between preferred providers, which
would handle books of business. This was far different than atomistic
spot contracting. The key to choice of outside resources is segmentation
by degree of difficulty. Hiring firms, not lawyers, occurs most easily at
the commoditized end of the spectrum of legal problems when any number of firms can handle a relatively straightforward book of business.
Hiring lawyers, not firms, occurs at the more complex, higher-risk end
of the segmentation spectrum on matters of highest visibility and highest
importance to the corporation (and to the GC's reputation inside and
outside the company). Even at the commoditized end of the spectrum,
the inside lawyers invariably have a strong relationship ("lawyers not law

firms") with the key, senior lawyer in the firm or with managing the commoditized book of business.

5. Wilkins, *supra*, note 4; Sue Reisinger, "Pfizer Law Dept. Shake-Up Hits Outside Counsel Program," *Corporate Counsel* (February 26, 2014).

6. See Heineman, Lee, and Wilkins, note 1, *supra,* at 44–46. For an earlier, general approach to better Legal department–law firm integration, see Association of Corporate Counsel, "ACC Value Challenge: Covenant with Counsel" (2009), https://www.acc.com/advocacy/valuechallenge/toolkit/upload/Covenant-for-Counsel.pdf.

7. Press, *supra*, note 2. For background information on legal market, see Georgetown Law School Center for the Study of the Legal Profession and Thomson Reuters, "2015 Report on the State of the Legal Market" (January 2015), http://www.law.georgetown.edu/academics/centers-institutes/legal-profession/upload/FINAL-Report-1-7-15.pdf (and earlier reports); Altman Weil, "2014 Chief Legal Officer Survey," http://www.altmanweil.com/CLO2014/ (annual reports available online).

8. Daniel Desjardins, "An Open Letter to GCs and Law Firms," *ACC Docket* (June 2014). Georgetown Law Report, *supra*, note 7.

9. Richard E. Susskind, *The End of Lawyers? Rethinking the Nature of Legal Services* (Oxford: Oxford Univ. Press, 2010); Susskind, *Tomorrow's Lawyers, supra,* note 1; Peter Kurer, *Legal and Compliance Risk: A Strategic Response to a Rising Threat for Global Business* (Oxford: Oxford Univ. Press, 2015) at 201–225.

10. Ben W. Heineman, Jr., and William F. Lee, "Getting Your Fix: Two Veteran Lawyers Say That Now Is the Time for Fixed Fees," *Corporate Counsel* (September 1, 2009); Association of Corporate Counsel, "ACC Value Based Fee Primer" (July 2010); http://www.acc.com/advocacy/valuechallenge/toolkit/upload/acc-value-based-fee-primer.pdf; Association of Corporate Counsel and Crowell & Moring, "Handbook for Value-Based Billing Engagements" (2012); Veta T. Richardson, "Law Dept. COOs: Contributing To, Not Just Measuring, Success," *Corporate Counsel* (December 15, 2014) (states that Bank of America "moved 80 percent of its litigation to fixed fees" and that United Technologies' "march toward value-based (non-hourly) fees reached 70 percent in 2013"); Chris Johnson, "Your Clients Want Alternative Fees: Is Your Firm Ready?" *The American Lawyer* (August 24, 2015) (GlaxoSmithKline says AFAs cover 85 percent of law firm relations; Microsoft says AFAs cover 90 percent).

11. Robert W. Gordon, "Money! Power! Ambition Gone Awry!: A Frank History of the Big-Time American Lawyer," *Legal Affairs* (March–April 2006);

Ben W. Heineman, Jr., "How GCs Can Avoid Being Caught in the Middle," *Corporate Counsel* (March 29, 2007) (partner-guardian problems facing *outside* counsel in light of changes in changes in legal marketplace).

12. Ben W. Heineman, Jr., and David B. Wilkins, "The Lost Generation: Demoralized and Dispirited, Big-Firm Associates Are Defecting in Droves. Here's What Firms, and Their Clients, Can Do About It," *The American Lawyer* (March 1, 2008).

13. Sue Reisinger, "Microsoft GC Ups Bonus for More Diverse Outside Counsel," *Corporate Counsel* (August 4, 2015); Brad Smith, "Letter to Participants in Law Firm Diversity Program," *Microsoft Legal Resources* (July 31, 2015), https://www.microsoft.com/en-us/legal/lcadiversity/lawfirmdiversityprogram.aspx. See also, website of Leadership Council on Legal Diversity, http://www.lcldnet.org/; Minority Corporate Counsel Association, "DuPont, General Mills, Verizon and Walmart Launch 'Engage Excellence' Minority Lawyer Inclusion Incentive Program" (July 29, 2014); MP McQueen, "Minority Ranks at Large Firms Show Little Growth, *The American Lawyer* (May 28, 2015); Laura Stiller Rikleen, "Women Lawyers Continue to Lag Behind Male Colleagues," *National Association of Women Lawyers Ninth Annual National Survey* (October 2015); Heineman, Lee, and Wilkins, *supra*, note 1 (bibliography includes select articles on diversity in legal profession).

14. Susan Beck, "The Justice Gap: How Big Law Is Failing Legal Aid," *The American Lawyer* (June 29, 2015); Rebecca Davis-O'Brien, "Backing Grows for Indigent Civil Counsel," *The Wall Street Journal* (April 6, 2015); Kim Kelman, "Big Law and Legal Aid," *The American Lawyer* (June 29, 2015) ("legal aid giving amounts to just 0.1 percent of revenues for even the most generous Am Law 200 firms"). The business sector spends approximately $437 billion on legal services annually ($160 billion, or about 37 percent of that amount, in the legal spend on inside lawyers). Press, *supra*, note 2; Legal Executive Institute, "Law Firm Leaders Forum: A Call to Professionalism," *Thomson Reuters* (October 8, 2015). Although there are no hard numbers, the total spend on pro bono services from law departments and law firms is likely to be but a fraction of 1 percent of that total corporate legal spend—i.e., *substantially* less than $4.37 billion. See, generally, website of the Pro Bono Institute, http://www.probonoinst.org/, and website of Corporate Pro Bono, a partnership between the Association of Corporate Counsel and the Pro Bono Institute, http://www.cpbo .org/; Corporate Pro Bono, "2014 Benchmarking Report: An Overview of In-House Pro Bono" (March 2015).

Some individual firms do have well-organized pro bono committees, special pro bono counsel, and significant numbers of attorneys and paralegals who spend more than 50 hours per year on pro bono activities. See, e.g., Weil, Gotshal & Manges, "Our Finest Hours: Pro Bono 2015" (August 2015). Notable efforts to advance rule of law in other societies include United Nations Global Compact, "Business for the Rule of Law Framework" (2015), https://www.unglobalcompact.org/library/1341; American Bar Association, "Rule of Law Initiative," http://www.american bar.org/advocacy/rule_of_law.html.

15. Rebeka Mintzer, "General Counsel Recalculate the Bottom Line," *Corporate Counsel* (June 27, 2014) (quoting Mark Smolik, GC at DHL/Exel Inc.). See also, Anthony Paonita, "Hello, I'm Talkin' to You," *Corporate Counsel* (September 17, 2014) ("biggest lesson of all" in assessing inside/ outside relationships: "Despite all the fashionable buzzwords of the past decade . . . the practice of law . . . remains an intensely personal one built on relationships of trust.").

16. Jacob Fischler, "10 Boutiques Giving Big Law a Run for Its Money," *Law360* (July 8, 2015) ("top boutiques continue to encroach on big firms' territory by blending the same high level of skill and expertise with a lower rate structure and greater client accessibility"). *Cf.* David Gelles, "Big Banks Miss Out: Boutiques Seal Deal," *The New York Times* (March 25, 2015) (Heinz-Kraft merger shows trend of using small independent investment banks). See also, Kurer, *supra*, note 9, at 182–84 (typology of firms, including boutiques, that might be used after segmentation analysis).

Chapter 12

1. Ben W. Heineman, Jr., William F. Lee, and David B. Wilkins, "Lawyers as Professionals and as Citizens: Key Roles and Responsibilities in the 21st Century," *Harvard Law School Center on the Legal Profession* (2014) at 49–64 (proposals for law school change). On courses about inside lawyering, see, e.g., Sue Reisinger and Catherine Dunn, "Training for Trouble: Law Schools Are Finally Preparing Students for In-House Careers," *Corporate Counsel* (November 2012) (mentioning Harvard, Stanford, Catholic University, Northeastern); Yale Law Report, "Lawyer-Statesman 101" (Summer 2012) (Yale); James Dinnage, "So You Want to Be an In-House Lawyer?" *Corporate Counsel* (May 5, 2014) (first of five articles on inside counsel course Dinnage teaches at Widener University School of Law); Steve Yeager, "Inside a Law School's In-House Training Program,"

Corporate Counsel (July 9, 2014) (Southern Methodist University's Dedman School of Law); Ryan McConnel and Michelle Jee, "Compliance in the Classroom: 3 Lessons Learned," *Corporate Counsel* (May 13, 2014) (University of Houston Law Center). Former and current General Counsels teach law school courses on inside lawyering (e.g., Dan Cooperman/Oracle and Stasia Kelly/AIG at Stanford; Bruce Kuhlik/Merck, Michael Holston/HP & Merck, and Helen Pudlin/PNC Financial Services at Penn; Michael Solender/E&Y and Ben Heineman/GE at Harvard and Yale [with HLS professor David Wilkins]), while many other current and former GCs are guest lecturers in courses on the General Counsel, inside lawyering, and business law/problems.

2. Srikant M. Datar, David A. Garvin, and Patrick G. Cullen, *Rethinking the MBA: Business Education at a Crossroads* (Boston: Harvard Business Review Press, 2011); Rakesh Khurana, *From Higher Aims to Hired Hands: The Social Transformation of American Business Schools and the Unfulfilled Promise of Management as a Profession* (Princeton, NJ: Princeton Univ. Press, 2007).

3. David B. Wilkins, "Is the In-House Counsel Movement Going Global? A Preliminary Assessment of the Role of Internal Counsel in Emerging Economies," *Wisconsin Law Rev.* 251 (2012); David B. Wilkins and Mihaela Papa, "The Rise of the Corporate Legal Elite in the BRICS: Implications for Global Governance," 54 *B.C. Law Rev.* 1149 (2013); website of Harvard Law School Center on the Legal Profession, "Globalization, Lawyers and Emerging Economies," https://clp.law.harvard.edu/clp-research/globalization/ (research agenda); Peter Kurer, *Legal and Compliance Risk: A Strategic Response to a Rising Threat for Global Business* (Oxford: Oxford Univ. Press, 2015) at 131–32, 177–78 (importance of law departments in multinational companies across the world).

4. Wilkins "Going Global," *supra*, note 3 at 277–78, 299–300.

5. Wilkins "Going Global," *supra*, note 3 at 263.

6. Wilkins "Going Global," *supra*, note 3 at 273.

7. Yasmin Lambert, "Global Reach Calls for Wide Skills Set," *The Financial Times* (June 10, 2015) (article on in-house lawyering in the Asia-Pacific region as part of a *Financial Times* Special Report on "Asia Pacific Innovative Lawyers").

ACKNOWLEDGMENTS

I am especially grateful to Michael Solender and David Wilkins who have co-taught our course on "The Challenges of the General Counsel" at Yale and Harvard Law Schools—and to the terrific students who taught the teachers at least as much as we taught them. Michael and David also gave me important comments on the book itself.

I am very grateful for perceptive insights from the following people who read drafts of the manuscript or discussed its ideas with me: Lauren Anstey, Ralph Baxter, Olivier Chaduteau, Pam Daley, Michele DeStefano, Alex Dimitrief, Ivan Fong, Heidi Gardner, Howard Gardner, Paul Gewirtz, Scott Gilbert, Suzanne Hawkins, Fritz Heimann, Lew Kaden, Sung Hui Kim, Randy Milch, Ira Millstein, Helen Pudlin, Steve Ramsey, Deborah Rhode, John Samuels, Peter Solmssen, and Ron Stern. My debt to my former business and legal colleagues at GE from great CEOs to young lawyers in China—some of whom are noted immediately above—is simply incalculable. And I have learned so much from so many others in my long career in law, government, business, and academia; they are far too numerous to name but have enriched beyond measure not just my professional life, but my view of the world.

Many thanks to Jim Levine for connecting me with Ankerwycke and Jonathan Malysiak—and to Jonathan for his unflagging support and acute comments. And, I want to thank Pallav Shukla for his tireless and helpful research assistance.

Of course, this book would not have been possible without the support of my wife, Cristine Russell, a brilliant writer and teacher as well as a wonderfully warm and caring person. No words can convey my profound reliance on her wisdom—and her love.

ABOUT THE AUTHOR

Ben W. Heineman, Jr., was GE's Senior Vice President–General Counsel from 1987–2003 and then Senior Vice President for Law and Public Affairs from 2004 until his retirement at the end of 2005. He is currently Senior Fellow at Harvard Law School's Program on the Legal Profession and its Program on Corporate Governance, Senior Fellow at the Belfer Center for Science and International Affairs at Harvard's Kennedy School of Government, and Lecturer in Law at Yale Law School. A Rhodes Scholar, editor-in-chief of the *Yale Law Journal*, and law clerk to Supreme Court Justice Potter Stewart, Mr. Heineman was assistant secretary for planning and evaluation at the U.S. Department of Health, Education, and Welfare and practiced public interest law and constitutional law prior to his service at GE. His book, *High Performance with High Integrity*, was published in June 2008 by the Harvard Business Press. He writes and lectures frequently on business, law, public policy, and international affairs. He is also the author of books on British race relations and the American presidency.

He is a member of the American Philosophical Society; a fellow of the American Academy of Arts and Sciences; a member of the Presidents' Circle of the National Academies of Sciences, Engineering, and Medicine; and a former member of the National Academy of Science's Committee on Science, Technology, and Law. He is recipient of *The American Lawyer* magazine's Lifetime Achievement Award, the Lifetime Achievement Award of *Corporate Counsel* magazine, and the Lifetime Achievement Award of *Board Member* magazine. He was named one of the Top 50 Innovators in Law in the Past 50 Years by *The American Lawyer*, one of America's 100 most influential lawyers by the *National Law Journal*, one of the 100 most influential individuals on business ethics by *Ethisphere* magazine, and one of the 100 most influential people in corporate governance by the National Association of Corporate Directors. He serves on the boards of Memorial Sloan Kettering Cancer Center, the Center for Strategic and International Studies, Central European University, and Transparency International–USA. He is a graduate of Harvard College (BA–History), Oxford University (B.Litt—Political Sociology), and Yale Law School (JD).

INDEX